The
ANGELICAL LANGUAGE

About the Author

Aaron Leitch has been a scholar and spiritual seeker for over two decades. He is a member of the Hermetic Order of the Golden Dawn, the Ordo Stella Matutina, and the Societas Magica. His writings (both in print and online) cover such varied fields as ancient Middle Eastern religion and mythology, Solomonic mysticism, shamanism, Neoplatonism, Hermeticism and Alchemy, Traditional Wicca and Neopaganism, the Hermetic Order of the Golden Dawn, Thelema, Angelology, Qabalah, Enochiana, African Diaspora religions, Hexcraft and Hoodoo folk traditions, psychology and consciousness expansion, cyberspace and virtual reality, and modern social commentary. He is the author of the book *Secrets of the Magickal Grimoires*, as well as many essays on various aspects of magick and the Angelical language.

Please visit his website at http://kheph777.tripod.com/.

The *ANGELICAL LANGUAGE*

VOLUME II

An Encyclopedic Lexicon of the Tongue of Angels

BASED ON THE JOURNALS OF
DR. JOHN DEE AND EDWARD KELLEY

AARON LEITCH

Llewellyn Publications
Woodbury, Minnesota

First Edition
First Printing, 2010

Cover design by Kevin R. Brown
Cover illustration © from Albrecht Dürer / SuperStock
Editing by Brett Fechheimer
Llewellyn is a registered trademark of Llewellyn Worldwide, Ltd.

Library of Congress Cataloging-in-Publication Data
Leitch, Aaron, 1974–
The angelical language, volume II : an encyclopedic lexicon of the tongue of angels / Aaron Leitch. — 1st ed.
p. cm.
Includes bibliographical references (p.).
ISBN 978-0-7387-1491-2
1. Enochian magic. I. Dee, John, 1527–1608. II. Title.
BF1623.E55L45 2010
130.92—dc22
2009046120

Llewellyn Publications
A Division of Llewellyn Worldwide, Ltd.
2143 Wooddale Drive
Woodbury, Minnesota 55125-2989, U.S.A.
www.llewellyn.com

Printed in the United States of America

Other books by this author

The Angelical Language, Volume I

Both Sides of Heaven (contributing author)

Diabolical (contributing author)

Secrets of the Magickal Grimoires

Contents

Introduction to Volume II

The work you hold in your hands is the second volume of a massive study of the Angelical language as recorded by Dr. John Dee and Edward Kelley—two magicians who lived during the Elizabethan era in England. In the introduction to the first volume, I explained who these men were, so I will not go into such detail here. Suffice it to say they were two extremely important figures in Western mysticism and occultism, and their recorded journals have had a profound impact on nearly every Western esoteric tradition that has followed them.

What concerns us most in this work are the records of their encounters with various Angels. Dee was a meticulous journalist, and he recorded his Angelic séances in every detail, along with the details of his daily life with Kelley during the years they were most active in speaking with the Angels. Not only did these celestial beings relate hundreds of sermons on religious and mystical philosophy, but they transmitted an entire system of Angel magick along with details about their own native language.

This book is not about that system of magick (although some obscure details about it can be found in volume I of this work). Instead, this volume focuses entirely upon the Angelical language itself. As I described in the previous volume, this is the aspect of Dee's work that fascinated me the most as I delved ever deeper in my own studies of so-called "Enochian" magick. That is, as a mystic, I was excited by the prospect of being able to pray to and evoke the Angels via their own native tongue.

To this end, I gathered Dee's original journals—published as *Five Books of Mystery, A True and Faithful Relation of What Passed for Many Years Between Dr. John Dee . . . and Some Spirits*, and Dee's own personal grimoire including the *48 Claves Angelicae*—a collection of the forty-eight Angelical invocations Dee was supposed to use to open the Gates of Heaven and call out the Angels therefrom. I also gathered the best texts available about Dee's magickal system—such as Donald Laycock's *Complete Enochian Dictionary*, Geoffery James' *The Enochian Magick of Dr. John Dee*, and Donald Tyson's *Enochian Magic for Beginners*.

However, when I was fortunate enough to become involved with a group of accomplished Enochian scholars, I soon learned that all of the texts *about* Dee's system left much to be desired when it came to understanding the Angelical language. Most of them had been written by authors who had not studied Dee's original journals page by page, and thus did not entirely understand the context surrounding the language.

For example, both James and Laycock focused upon the Keys outlined in Dee's *48 Claves Angelicae*, with limited reference to Causabon's *A True and Faithful Relation*. However, neither author had studied *A True and Faithful Relation* exhaustively, and were thus unaware of several corrections to the Keys made by the Angels later in Dee's records. (And the *48 Claves* does not always preserve these corrections.)

Another shortcoming is found in the breakdown of the Angelical words themselves. Both Laycock (who happened to be a linguist) and James attempted to analyze the words based upon their understanding of modern linguistics—which led to some conflicts with Dee's journals. Most of these conflicts arose from their sometimes unsuccessful attempts to recognize compound words and separate them into their base elements. Laycock, for instance, has broken the word *Cnoqod* (unto his servants) into *C Noqod*. In his dictionary section, one can find an entry for *Noqod*, but none for the actual Angelical word *Cnoqod*. Meanwhile, there is no indication in Dee's records that *Cnoqod* is a compound at all.

Once these words were broken down in such a fashion, the next step made by both Laycock and James was to correct the base words. For an example, we might look at James' work on Key Four. Toward the end of this Key—in the original diaries—we find the word *Zirenaiad* (I am the Lord God). James has this listed as three distinct words: *Zir* (I am), *Enay* (the Lord), and *Iad* (God). While the base words are correct, you will notice that breaking them apart caused James to add a letter *y* to complete the word *Enay*. Neither James nor Laycock had yet discovered that letters are dropped in Angelical compounds when two base words end and begin with the same letter. Thus, the phrase *Zir Enay Iad* is combined by dropping the *y*[1] and forming the compound *Zirenaiad*. Such compound words must be preserved if we want to understand how Angelical works.

There are even several cases in which the authors have added words into the Keys where they seemed necessary. This mostly involved parts of speech or grammatical elements such as articles, adjectives, and pronouns—all of which are rare or absent from Angelical. Thus, the language tends to work like ancient tongues (such as Egyptian or biblical Hebrew), which played no part in James' and Laycock's studies of Angelical.

Most of the shortcomings of previous Angelical scholarship related to pronunciation. The Hermetic Order of the Golden Dawn made up their own system based loosely on modern Hebrew pronunciation—and Aleister Crowley followed suit. (Some today consider this "Golden Dawn Liturgical" Angelical.) Geoffrey James left the subject alone entirely, and simply included Dee's phonetic cues as they appear in the *48 Claves Angelicae*. (However, without a key to those notations, they are of little help to most students.)

Laycock went so far as to offer a guide to pronunciation. However, I found it less than useful because it gives "probable" pronunciations for the *letters of the alphabet* rather than for the phonetic elements that actually make up the words when spoken—such as letter combinations, digraphs, diphthongs, and syllables. Not only this, but the given pronunciations were based upon modern English, with some inclusions from modern Italian and other languages. Laycock does not appear to have drawn from Early Modern (or "Shakespearean") English and Middle

English—both of which have much more to do with Dee's Angelical pronunciation than modern languages.

The available work on Angelical has also ignored Dee's pronunciation notes in *A True and Faithful Relation*. I will explain these notes later in this work—however, at the time James and Laycock were writing, Dee's notes were still an enigma. No one had cracked the phonetic system Dee was using in those notes, and thus they were simply ignored.[2] This has led to the modern misconception that "correct pronunciations" do not exist for Angelical at all—yet Dee's notes make it fairly clear that they do, in fact, exist.

Finally, I could find no source for the comprehensive information necessary to learn the language in a practical sense. I needed every word along with its meaning, all of its spelling variations, its use of root words, the sentence from the Keys in which it is found, its numbered location in the Keys, and commentary about the mystical meanings behind the word. Therefore, I had no choice but to begin work on my own Angelical Lexicon.

Some may object to granting such attention to what might be a constructed language. From a non-mystical point of view, it is just as possible that Angelical is a cypher of some sort (akin to Trithemius' famous *Steganographia*), or even a complete hoax generated to cover politically sensitive information. Personally, I feel it is immaterial if the language is "real" or constructed. If it is real, then it is nothing short of miraculous that we have access to it. If it is not real, then its creation is a work of genius comparable to—or even surpassing—Tolkien's creation of Elvish. We might study Angelical as we would Orwell's Newspeak or Heinlein's Martian—although we are fortunate to have a much larger sample of Angelical than we do of these latter sources.

In fact, from both a mystical *and* an historical point of view, I believe that Dee's Angelical language is the true mystery language of the West. An Angel named Nalvage informed Dee that Angelical was preferred before Hebrew, which had long been considered the mystery language of the West. Then, Dee's grimoire—containing the *48 Claves Angelicae* (said to be invocations composed of the native tongue of the Angels)—became foundational to the Western Hermetic and esoteric traditions.

It influenced the Golden Dawn and all who followed. From the rediscovery of Dee's documents to today, the deeper mysteries of the language have been slowly opening to the light of day.

Many students have encountered "Enochian" magick (in some form) previously, only to find pages full of invocations and names in an alien language. Rumors of its power (or even danger) surround the subject matter, but straightforward explanations of *what it is* and *how it works* are lacking. The student may ultimately put the material away and simply leave others to specialize in the subject. However, the willing seeker no longer has to feel intimidated. The understanding of the Angelic material has expanded greatly, and new resources are now being made available for all students who might take an interest. This work is one of those resources.

Since beginning my in-depth study of the Angelical language, I have found it extremely useful in practical areas. Reciting the Keys with full comprehension of every word is a wonderful and powerful experience. Not to mention the fact that it makes the actual voicing of the Keys more precise, and much less labored or forced. When working with spirits and the art of summoning, it is amazing what can be accomplished when one issues commands in Angelical. Even more impressive are the results of addressing an Angel in his or her own language!

I believe it is important to discover the real nature of the language, exactly as first received by Dr. John Dee and Sir Edward Kelley. We should not try to force the language into preconceived molds before attempting to observe it upon its own terms. Therefore, the words in this Lexicon are presented as they are recorded in Dee's journals—with all later corrections, and no omissions, additions, or (most importantly) alterations based on modern languages.

I have always felt that a grassroots study of Dee's Angelical (rather than later half-understood recensions) would lead to further expansions of the language. This is why I have taken the time to illustrate each word with all of its variations, to break down the elements of compounds, and discover the root words at their hearts. From these, along with a better understanding of Angelical grammar, we might go far in expanding the Lexicon.

With that in mind, know that this work is *not* offered as definitive of the Angelical language, but merely as a study aid for further research. This leaves a great amount of work and experience to be achieved by every individual student. I have presented the material as the Celestial Language of power that I have found it to be. The student of Angelic magick will find a comprehension of the language to be invaluable—and the deeper that comprehension, the more powerful the utterance of the Keys.

In order to create this Lexicon, it was first necessary to return to Dee's journals and generate a "corrected version" of the forty-eight Angelical Keys. Thankfully, I was not alone in this undertaking. As a member of the *Enochian-l* mailing list, I communicated with folks who had also done work toward analyzing and correcting the Keys.[3] Their results do not always agree with my own, as there are several places in the text that are obscure or incomplete in *A True and Faithful Relation*, and we (and even Dee himself) came to various opinions on what should be the correct wording.[4]

Once I had the corrected version of the Keys, I used that to create the *Angelical Keys Cross-Reference*—which adopts the numbering style used by Geoffrey James in his work. (You will find that my numbers do not match his, due to the fact that my corrected Keys have a different wording.) With that in hand, I was finally able to compile my *Encyclopedic Lexicon of the Tongue of Angels*. From there, I was able to analyze the language's grammar and linguistics. All of these together, plus an exhaustive study of Dee's journals, form the basis of the work you are now reading.

This second volume of my work is an exhaustive analysis of the Celestial Speech as recorded by Dee. This is where I have preserved all of the linguistic information concerning the language. I outline its basic principles, root words, affixes, parts of speech, and phonology. This is also where I explore the subjects of Middle English and Early Modern English, and the influence these stages of the language had on Dee's conception of Angelical.

This volume culminates in the Angelical Lexicon itself. This new work is not just another "Enochian dictionary." The Lexicon includes every word from the forty-eight Keys, all defined or related words from the *Book of Loagaeth*, and every random Angelical word or phrase found throughout Dee's lengthy journals. All of the words have been analyzed and cross-referenced to discover hidden word elements and root words. Every entry in the Lexicon includes:

- The Angelical word in English and Angelical characters.
- Its "English sense" (definition).
- Its location (cross-reference numbers for words from the Keys, page-references to Dee's published journals for all other words).
- Comparisons to every related Angelical word.
- Notes about the word's definition, history, or usage—both Dee's original marginal notations and new commentary.
- Dee also left phonetic notations for most of the words he recorded. For centuries these notes have been a source of confusion for scholars. In this new work, Dee's notations are deciphered at last! All of his pronunciation notes are included and fully explained. (A new pronunciation key has been invented to make reading the words much easier for the modern reader.)

As added features, this volume includes the Angelical Keys cross-reference (containing a fully corrected version of the forty-eight Keys, cross-referenced by number), and a lengthy English-to-Angelical section (including tips for translating English texts into proper Angelical).

Methodology

You will likely notice that my Lexicon does not resemble existing "Enochian dictionaries." Such dictionaries do not often illustrate the compounds, roots, affixes, and other linguistic intricacies of the Angelical words. Nor do they demonstrate how each word is used in the Keys, for *every* occurrence and version of the word (conjugations, compounds, etc). Nor do they provide commentary about the words, their origins, or the way they were used in Dee's journals and the Keys.

Thus, in order to unlock these mysteries, I set out to perform a deep analysis of the words of the Keys. I began my project with the first word of Key One (or word 1.1), and compared it with *each and every* individual word in the Keys. That way, I could discover if word 1.1 appeared again with alternate spellings, as part of compound words, or even if similar words shared a common root.

Then, I moved to the second word of Key One (or word 1.2) and repeated the procedure. I continued this tedious process through all the Keys until the very last word of the Key of the Aethyrs (word 30.157) had been compared and cross-referenced with *every* word in the forty-eight Keys (including both the spelling of the words *and* their English definitions). This arduous word-by-word comparison revealed several fascinating aspects of Angelical grammar—most of which I had never seen published. (Until now, of course!)

Besides the words of the forty-eight Keys, I have also included all words from the *Book of Loagaeth* for which Dee recorded definitions, or which appear similar to other defined words. I have also exhaustively scoured both Dee's *Five Books of Mystery* and his *A True and Faithful Relation* for each and every instance where the Angels spoke to Dee (or one another) in their native tongue. These words are all included in the Lexicon in this volume, even if they have no definitions.

This Lexicon does not include any Enochian material developed by those who followed Dee—such as the Golden Dawn and Aleister Crowley. I do not mean to negate their work or suggest that it has no merit—however, I again stress the importance of learning the language as Dee received it before moving on to these sources. Some of their material may be of little use, and some of it may be worthwhile.

The material in both volumes of *The Angelical Language* is based strictly upon Dee's journals and personal grimoire. All references to Dee's *Five Books of Mystery* ("Five Books") are drawn from Joseph Peterson's outstanding work *John Dee's Five Books of Mystery*. All references to *A True and Faithful Relation* ("TFR") are drawn from *The Magickal Review*'s edition of Meric Casaubaon's *A True and Faithful Relation of What Passed for Many Years Between Dr. John Dee . . . and Some Spirits*. Finally, any reference to Dee's personal grimoire (Sloane MS 3191) will point to Geoffery James' *The Enochian Magick of Dr. John Dee*. See the bibliography in this volume for further information on sources and manuscripts.

I sincerely hope that you will find this text to be an invaluable resource. I encourage you to use this book as a study tool, so that you can experience the mysteries behind the Angelical tongue.

Zorge,
Aaron Leitch
March 2009

Endnotes

1. Both *i* and *y* are the same letter in Angelical.
2. I even saw it suggested that these were not phonetic notes at all, but alternate spellings of the words!
3. As of this date (2010), some of this work can be found on Callisto Radiant's *Enochian Linguistics* website, at http://www.madimi.com/enochmnu.htm.
4. I used the *48 Claves Angelicae* as my secondary reference in these cases.

Chapter 1

Angelical Linguistics

There are two primary sources available for the Celestial Speech: The Holy *Book of Loagaeth* and the forty-eight Angelical Keys. The First ("hidden") Table of *Loagaeth* (sides A and B) contains approximately 4802 words compiled into ninety-eight lines of text. It is a wonderful sample of the language, which could be used to analyze the letters of the remaining forty-eight Tables.

Unfortunately, no translation of the Holy Book was ever recorded in Dee's surviving journals. We know only what the Angels claimed is in the text, and a few precious words translated here and there. In many ways, modern scholars have to approach the *Book of Loagaeth* as archaeologists once approached Egyptian hieroglyphics. We can examine the words and make a lot of educated guesses about linguistic patterns, but without an "Angelical Rosetta Stone," we are ultimately flying blind.

Perhaps this Rosetta Stone already exists in the forty-eight Angelical Keys. The Keys represent a much smaller sample of the language—totaling only 1070 words, and much fewer if we exclude words that repeat. However, unlike the Holy Book, the text of the Angelical Keys came with English translations. This grants us a wonderful opportunity to analyze the Angelical words closely—looking for syntax and grammar, root words, compounds, affixes, and so forth. (Then, with any luck, we can apply what we learn to the text of *Loagaeth*—beginning with the first Table.)[1]

When comparing the Holy Book with the forty-eight Keys, it can be easy to assume one is reading two different languages.[2] However, my own analysis of the text of *Loagaeth* leads me to believe that its language is one and the same with that of the Keys. I have found several words from the Keys within *Loagaeth* as well—some of them intact and some of them in modified forms. I have also found the names of several Angelical letters in the text, and a couple of direct references to *Heptarchic* Angels.[3] While the words of the forty-nine Tables do seem alien to those familiar with the Keys, I think this is merely because *Loagaeth* represents a much larger sample of the language.

Having said that, I will also concede that the language used in the Keys does seem to have a slightly different "feel" and flow than the text in the Holy Book. (Donald Laycock illustrates this adequately in the introduction to his *Complete Enochian Dictionary*.) Remember chapter 2 of volume I, where I quoted Raphael, who said of the forty-nine parts of *Loagaeth*:

> Every Element hath 49 manner of understandings. Therein is comprehended so many languages. They are all spoken at once, and severally, by themselves, by distinction may be spoken. [*Five Books of Mystery*, p. 297]

I assume that the "elements" of *Loagaeth* are the forty-nine individual Tables—forty-eight of which may be opened by human effort via the Keys. If each of these Tables contain forty-nine interpretations and languages (or, perhaps, *dialects* of Angelical), it makes for a total of 2401 interpretations/dialects. It is probable that the language of the forty-eight Keys represents a sample of one of these Angelical dialects.

Angelical "English Senses" and Fluid Definitions

Throughout Dee's journals, the Angels, when translating Angelical words, referred to the English equivalents as "senses" or "significations" rather than definitions or translations. This was because the given English elaborations are filled with glosses, poetic license, and implied adjectives. The Angelical words merely "signify a concept," and we are somewhat free to apply any English words that properly (and poetically) illustrate the concept. (If you refer to the third and fourth columns of the Angelical cross-reference, you will see how the "essential concepts" of the Angelical words differ from the English elaborations given by Nalvage.)

As an example, we can look at the various interpretations of the word *Malpurg* (Fiery Darts):

Malpurg (Fiery Darts)
Malprg (Through-thrusting Fire)
Malpirgi (Fires of Life and Increase)

An even better example of fluid definition is found in the word *Cocasb* (Time):

Acocasb (Time)
"Cacocasb" (Another While)
Cocasb (Time)
Cocasg (Times)
Qcocasb (Contents of Time)

Furthermore, *Cocasb* likely shares a root with:

Cacacom (Flourish)
Cacrg (Until)
Casasam (Abiding)
Capimali (Successively)
"Capimao" (While)
Capimaon (Number of Time)
Capmiali (Successively)

Angelical shares this trait of "fluid definitions" with ancient human languages such as Sumerian, Egyptian, and Hebrew. Modern English tends to possess more specific definitions, which are necessary in order to create and utilize our sophisticated technology. However, in previous ages it was possible to use a single word to represent any number of related concepts. (For instance, consider the ancient Egyptian word *Khepher*—which might indicate creation, formation, transformation, mutation, and so on.) The precise meaning intended by the author was indicated by context.

Root Words

Several Angelical words with dissimilar spellings turn out to have similar definitions—revealing many previously unknown root words. Compare the following words:

Londoh (Kingdom)
Adohi (Kingdom)

Both of these words translate as "Kingdom"—but they would not have appeared near one another in a simple alphabetical listing. We can see, however, that they share the letters *doh*—and this is likely an Angelical root word.

Conversely, I found that many words with similar spellings had *dissimilar* definitions. This often highlighted relationships between concepts within the language that were not apparent at first glance. For instance, compare the spelling similarities between these words:

Ors (Darkness)
Orsba (Drunken)
Orscor (Dryness)
Orscatbl (Buildings)

All of these seem to share a common linguistic root (*Or* or *Ors*), but they have definitions that are considered unrelated in English. By contemplating how these concepts might relate to one another, it can tell us something about how Angels "think."

These root words also support the idea that Angelical works similarly to ancient languages such as Hebrew. Such early tongues are based upon a series of simple root words—usually of two or three letters, each of which may or may not stand on its own as a proper word. Affixes can then be added to the roots to alter inflection or tense.

For example, consider the Angelical word *I* (Is)—which is the likely root of the word *Ip* (Not). By adding affixes, we obtain:

Ipam (Is Not)

Ipamis (Can Not Be)

An even more important root is *Ia*, which does not stand as a word on its own in the Keys.[4] However, it is possibly the root of several existing words—just a few of which are listed here as an example:

Iad (God)

Iaiadix (Honor)

Iaida (The Highest)

Iaidon (All Powerful)

Further, the first word in the above list, *Iad* (God), appears to be the root element of several additional words:

Geiad (Lord and Master)

Iadnah (Knowledge)

Iadpil (To Him)

Ioiad (Him the Liveth Forever)

Laiad (Secrets of Truth)

At the front of the Lexicon, I have included a list of all of the root words (or letter combinations) that I have discovered to date. (The list includes mostly those root words that do not already stand as words on their own.)

Compounds

Also akin to early (and, of course, many modern) languages, Angelical roots/words may be compounded in order to convey more sophisticated concepts. For instance, the three words *Zir* (Am), *Enay* (Lord), and *Iad* (God) are combined to form *Zirenaiad* (I am the Lord Your God).

I have found that, most often, compounds are made between nouns or verbs and the words that modify or indicate them. The following examples are an extremely small sample of such modifier-compounds found throughout the forty-eight Keys. (Note that I have placed the modifiers within each word in bold.) There are possessive adjective (*his, her*) compounds:

*Busdir**tilb*** (Glory [of] Her)

*Elzap**tilb*** (Her Course)

*Lonshi**tox*** (His Power)

Here are some demonstrative pronoun (*this, those*) and relative pronoun (*which/that*) compounds:

***Ar**coazior* (That Increase) ***Ar**tabas* (That Govern) ***Unal**chis* (These Are) ***Oi**salman* (This House)

***Ds**abramg* (Which Prepared) ***Ds**chis* (Which Are) ***Ds**i* (Which Is) ***Ds**om* (That Understand)

Conjunction (*and, or, but, as*) compounds are very common:

*Cors**ta*** (Such As) ***Crp**l* (But One) ***Ta**blior* (As Comforters) ***Ta**viv* (As the Second)

***Od**chis* (And Are) ***Od**miam* (And Continuance) ***Od**zamran* (And Appear) ***Q**mospleh* (Or the Horns)

Compounds are regularly created from forms of the verb *to be* (*is, are, were*, and—apparently—*is not*):

Chis**holq* (Are Measured) *Unal**chis (These Are) ***I**noas* (Are Become) ***I**dlugam* (Is Given)

*Page**ip*** (Rest Not) *Od**ipuran*** (And Shall Not See) ***Zir**enaiad* (I Am the Lord God) *Gchis**ge*** (Are Not)

There are fewer (although no less significant) examples of nouns compounded with adjectives or verbs other than *to be*.

I have also found that compounding Angelical words often results in changes to their spelling. For example, the word *Dsonf* (Which Reign) is a combination of *Ds* (Which) and *Sonf* (Reign). However, notice that there is only one *s* found in *Dsonf*. That is because Angelical combines duplicate letters when forming compounds. Therefore, the final *s* of *Ds* and the first *S* of *Sonf* combine into one *s* in *Dsonf*.

Another example is the word *Gmicalzoma* (Power of Understanding). This is a combination of *Gmicalzo* (Power) and *Oma* (Understanding). However, we can see that the final *o* of *Gmicalzo* and the first *O* of *Oma* have been combined into a single letter in the compound.

There are also several examples of completely inexplicable spelling changes when compounds are formed. For instance, the word for *Day* in Angelical is *Basgim*, while the compound word for "Midday the First" is *Bazemlo* (*Bazem* + "*Lo*"). The change of the *s* to a *z* is not surprising, because these letters represent a similar sound. However, note how the *gi* of *Basgim* has disappeared entirely from the compound *Bazemlo*. We can therefore guess that *Bas*/*Baz* is an Angelical root indicating "daytime." However, we cannot guess what rules apply to the spelling change between *Basgim* and the *Bazem* element in *Bazemlo*.

It might be helpful to provide another example, so we will look at the word *Soba* (Whose). In the compound *Sobhaath* (Whose Works), the spelling has altered to *Sobha*. In the compound *Sobolzar* (Whose Courses), the spelling becomes *Sobo*. Even more inexplicable, in the compound *Solamian* (Whose Continuence), the spelling is altered to *Sola*.

Conjugation

Further spelling changes may come from conjugation instead of compounding. These changes appear so random, even professional linguists can find no rhyme or reason behind them.[5] Several examples follow:

Goho (Sayeth)	*Naoln* (May Be)	*Zir* or *Zirdo* (Am)
Gohia (We Say)	*Noan* (To Become)	*Zirom* (Were)
Gohol (Saying)	*Noar* (Has Become)	*Zirop* (Was)
Gohon (Have Spoken)	*Noas* (Have Become)	
Gohus (I Say)	*Noasmi* (Let Become)	
Gohulim (Is Said)		

Unfortunately, I cannot report that I have discovered anything useful in this regard. Given the apparently haphazard manner in which the spellings are altered, I can't even state with surety that conjugations, as we would recognize them, even exist in Angelical. Many Angelical words (verbs and nouns) alter their spelling even when they do not conjugate or compound with other words. Just a few examples are:

Aai, Aao (Amongst)

Acocasb, Cocasb (Time)

Butmon, Butmona (Mouth)

Efafafe, Ofafafe (Vials)

Netaab, Netaaib (Government)

Affixes

Having learned somewhat about Angelical roots and compounds, I was able to isolate what *appear* to be several Angelical affixes. For example, there are some instances where the addition of *-o* to a word seems to add the connotation of *of*:

Caosg (Earth)	-	*Caosgo* (Of the Earth)
Vonph (Wrath)	-	*Vonpho* (Of Wrath)
Iad (God)	-	*Oiad* (Of God)

However, this does not appear to be a set rule. First, an equivalent to the word *of* is *extremely* rare in Angelical. (Usually, it is simply implied by context.) Second, some words appear with additional *-o* affixes without gaining an *of* connotation. Examples are:

Zol (Hands)	-	*Ozol* (Hands)
Zien (Hands)	-	*Ozien* ([My Own] Hand)
Micalz (Mighty)	-	*Micalzo* (Mighty / Power)

Another likely affix is *-ax*, which may be an indicator of action similar to our own suffix *-ing*, which can turn verbs into active participles (e.g., "The running water is very deep") or present progressives (e.g., "He is running very fast."):

Blior (Comfort)	-	*Bliorax* (To Comfort)
Om (Know)	-	*Omax* (Knowest)

There are other verbs that end with the *-ax* suffix, but we have no examples of the same words without the affix: *Camliax* (Spake), *Tastax* (Going Before). We might possibly add *Gizyax* (Earthquakes) and *Coraxo* (Thunders of Judgment and Wrath) to this list—they may be nouns by English standards, but they still indicate violently active forces. Meanwhile, there are some "*-ing* clause" verbs in the Keys that do not appear with the *-ax* suffix—such as *Dluga* (Giving unto) or *Panpir* (Raining Down).

Rarities: Pronouns, Prepositions, Adjectives, Articles, Case

There are several aspects of grammar that are rare or even nonexistent in the Angelical tongue. For instance, personal pronouns are used very infrequently in the Keys—and it is difficult to say why they are used in the places we do find them. However, while these pronouns are used less frequently than is the case in modern English, they are used more frequently than the other rarities we will discuss in this section. The existing personal pronouns are:

Ol (I)
Tox (Him / His)
Nonca (You, plural)
"*T*" (It)
Tiobl (Her)
Yls (Thou, singular)
"*Pi*" (She)
"*Ip*" (Her)
Par (Them)

Relative pronouns like the following seem to be a bit more common, as they are not as easily implied by context:

Sobam (Whom)
Ds, Dst (That, Which)
Casarm, Casarma (Whom)
Soba, Sobca, Sobra (Whose)

Plus, we find these possessive adjectives:

Tilb (Her)
Tox (His / Him)
Aqlo (Thy)

However, they are used sparingly, and—as we saw previously—they are often found in compound with their nouns. In such cases, I note that they often follow the noun—such as in *Lonshitox* (His Power) and *Elzaptilb* (Her Course).

Non-possessive adjectives are even more uncommon in the Angelical text of the Keys. When they *are* used, they typically follow the rule of English—falling immediately before the noun they indicate, and not usually compounded with it. Some examples are *Vohim Gizyax* (Mighty Earthquakes) and *Adphaht Damploz* (Unspeakable Variety).

On the other hand, most of the poetic adjectives we see in the English translations are not implied in the essential definitions of the Angelical words—such as *Orri* (Barren Stone), *Grosb* (Bitter Sting), or *Sapah* (Mighty Sounds), all of which are nouns that show no linguistic indication of their adjectives. It would appear that adjectives in such cases are left entirely up to the author, or reader, of the text.

Another rarity in Angelical is the use of prepositions (*at*, *on*, *in*, *for*). We already know that there *may* be an affix to indicate "of" (*-o*). There is also one instance of the word *De* (of) that stands alone in the Keys. Plus the following prepositions are found here and there throughout the Keys:

Aai, Aaf, Aaiom, Aao (Amongst)
Aspt (Before)
"Azia" (Like unto)
Oq (Except/But)
Bagle (For)[6]
De (Of)
Pugo (As Unto)
Vors, Vorsg (Over)
Mirc (Upon)
Nothoa (Amidst)
Oroch (Under)
Pambt (Unto)
Tia (Unto)
Zomdux (Amidst)
Zylna (Within)

All of this indicates that prepositions exist to some extent in Angelical, but they are not often used unless context makes them unavoidable.

Meanwhile, I have discovered that articles (*a*, *an*, *the*) are not used in Angelical at all. Articles are implied entirely by the context of the sentence. This trait is also common to many historical languages, such as Latin.

I have also found that grammatical case does not often apply to Angelical. In modern English, the case of a noun or pronoun can be subjective (*he*), objective (*him*), or possessive (*his*). In Angelical, much as with conjugation, there do *appear* to be some examples of spelling changes from one case to another. (See the list of pronouns at the beginning of this section.) However, there is no indication these changes have anything at all to do with case.

Meanwhile, there are several examples of *vocative* case in the Angelical tongue. A noun takes the vocative case when it indicates someone being *addressed*. For example, in the phrase "Open the door, John," the word *John* is vocative. The sentence does not need the addition of *John* in order to be complete, but we include it to specify that John is being addressed. Of course, there is no vocative *case* in English—so we do not see any spelling change to the word *John* when used vocatively.

However, some older languages such as Latin do utilize a vocative case. The most famous example comes from Shakespeare's play *Julius Caesar*, during the scene in which Caesar's best friend Brutus stabs him in the back. After the assault, Caesar turns to Brutus and says, "*Et tu, Brute*?"[7] *Brute* is the vocative case of the name *Brutus*.

The first example of the vocative case in Angelical is found within the First Table of *Loagaeth*, where we find the word *Befas*.[8] It would appear this word aroused the curiosity of Dee and/or Kelley, because it is similar to the name of a Heptarchic Angel the men had already met: *Befafes*—the Angelic Prince of Tuesday. In the margin, Dee makes the following notation:

> Befes the vocative case of Befafes. [*Five Books of Mystery*, p. 310]

Therefore, we know that someone in the text of the First Table of *Loagaeth* (presumably the Creator) is directly addressing Befafes for some reason—and the vocative case alters *Befafes* to *Befes*.

The second example of vocative case appears in *A True and Faithful Relation*, while Dee and Kelley are having a conversation with the Heptarchic Angel Madimi. The Angel suddenly halts the discussion to say:

> *Carma geta, Barman.* [*A True and Faithful Relation*, p. 32]

When Dee asked Madimi what this phrase meant, she translated it as "Come out of there, Barma." *Barma* turned out to be the name of a spirit inhabiting Kelley, which Madimi proceeded to exorcise. The form *Barman*, then, is a vocative case of *Barma*.

Finally, there *may* be a third example of vocative case—also found in the First Table of *Loagaeth*—in the word *Bobogelzod*. This word certainly appears to have some relationship with the Heptarchic King of Sunday *Bobogel*—and could very well represent a vocative case of his name.

Thus, we know that Angelical makes use of the vocative case. We do not know, however, what rules govern the spelling changes.

Phonetic Glosses

> **Note:** Throughout the remainder of this chapter, I will illustrate some pronunciations according to a key found on page 95 of this volume as well as with the Angelical Psalter in volume I. You can also find a chart illustrating the Angelical characters on page 106 of this volume.

It is vital to remember that Dee was *not* recording the words in Angelical characters. Kelley spoke the language fluently while in his trance state, and Dee merely wrote down in English letters what he heard. I have no doubt that many of the words recorded by Dee are exact in their Angelical spelling—meaning we could take the English letters and transliterate them directly into Angelical. However, there are many examples of words that have "phonetic glosses." This is what I call spelling "peculiarities" that appear in different instances of the same word—which are apparently intended to give us pronunciation cues.

Take, for example, the word *Crip* (But), which appears without the *i* in the compound *Crpl* (But One). Therefore, the *i* likely does not represent an Angelical character in this word—leaving only *Crp* (But). The shortest and most radical[9] version of the word should be the "correct" spelling. What we have in *Crip* is a phonetic gloss—letting us know that *Crp* is pronounced "krip" rather than "kurp."

There is also the element *Purg* (Flames), which appears in such words as *Ialpurg* (Burning Flames) and *Malpurg* (Fiery Darts). Yet these same words appear elsewhere as *Ialprg* (Burning Flame) and *Malprg* (Throughthrusting Fire). Therefore, *Prg* and *Purg* are likely the same word with the same Angelical spelling. The extra *u* is merely a phonetic gloss, telling us where to place the vowel sound. Elsewhere, we even see the word *Prge* (Fire)—yet another phonetic gloss, adding the *e* to tell us the *g* is a soft "juh" sound. All of these clues suggest the true pronunciation of the Angelical word *Prg* is identical to the English word *purge*. However, the word is probably spelled *Prg*.

Compounds are not the only places we can look for phonetic glosses. Several words that stand alone in the Keys appear more than once with different spellings. For example, consider the word *Abramig* (Prepared). This word appears only once in this form. Meanwhile, it appears in three other places in the Keys in the form of *Abramg*—twice standing alone and once in a compound. Therefore, we might suspect that *Abramg* is the radical spelling of this word. The extra *i* in *Abramig* merely tells us where to place the vowel sound ("ay-bray-mig" rather than "ay-bram-jee").

Another good example is the word *NA*—which appears in the *Five Books* and the *Book of Loagaeth* as a Name of God. We might assume this word is pronounced "nah" or "nay." However, in the Keys we can find the same word written phonetically as *Enay* (Lord). Thus, we know the proper pronunciation of *NA* is "en-ay," and it should be spelled with only two letters.

As further examples, we can compare the following words:

F (Visit)	-	*Ef* (Visit)
L (First)	-	*El* (First)
S (Fourth)	-	*"Es"* (Fourth)

The added *E* in each case is apparently a phonetic gloss—once again showing us where to place the vowel sound in the pronunciation of the words.

Further phonetic glosses seem to be associated with the Angelical digraphs—although the subject is fairly uncertain. In ancient languages (at least, those that possessed an alphabet), digraphs are usually indicated by a single character. For example, the Hebrew letter *Peh* represents the sounds of both "P" and "Ph." The letter *Tau* represents both "T" and "Th." Likewise, there are several examples of this in Angelical:

Cnoqod is pronounced "see-noh-kwod" (Q = Qu)
(Also see: *Cnoquod*)
Cormp is pronounced "kormf" (P = Ph)
(Also see: *Cormf*)
Lonsa is pronounced "lon-sha" (S = Sh)
(Also see: *Lansh*)
Noncp is pronounced "non-sef" (P = Ph)
(Also see: *Noncf*)
Sapa is pronounced "say-fa" (P = Ph)
Telocvovim is pronounced "tee-loch-voh-vee-im" (C = Ch)
(Also see: *Teloch*)
Vonpo is pronounced "von-foh" (P = Ph)
(Also see: *Vonpho*)

The above is fairly convincing evidence that Angelical digraphs are indeed represented by single letters. That would mean that the secondary letters in these digraphs (the *h* in *Ph* and *Ch*, the *u* in *Qu*, etc.) are merely phonetic glosses, and should not be included when the words are spelled in Angelical characters.

However, there also exist *counter*examples in Dee's journals. The very first word of the Holy *Book of Loagaeth* (Table One, side A) was originally recorded by Dee as *Zuresk*. Later, Raphael corrected this by telling Dee the word must contain seven letters—*Zuresch*. (The *ch* taking its hard sound, as in the English words *ache* or *chrome*.) Because of this correction, we know the *Ch* digraph is—in this case—actually written with two letters instead of just one.

If we continue to look through the first few lines of *Loagaeth* (which Raphael spelled out in Angelical character by character)[10], we find several further examples of two-character digraphs as well.

Another good counterexample is the word *Hoath* at the end of the first Angelical Key. I included the transmission of this word in volume I, chapter 3 (in the section "Dee Suspected of Cryptography?"), where Nalvage was still associating numbers with each letter of the words.

There we can see undeniably that Nalvage transmitted both a *t* and an *h* for *Hoath*, and gave a number to each letter. Therefore, once again we can see an Angelical digraph represented with two letters as in modern English.

Thus, we are left with several examples of one-character digraphs and several examples of two-character digraphs. That leaves us with a large number of two-character digraphs in Dee's records that give no clue to their proper Angelical-character spelling. Was Dee writing these words in transliteration (letter for letter) or phonetically? Where no such clues exist, I have recorded the digraphs in the Lexicon in Angelical characters just as Dee recorded them in English. Yet there remains some room for debate on the issue.

As a final entry in this section, I would like to mention a short phonetic note that Dee recorded in his journal for a word in the *Book of Loagaeth*. For Table One, side A, line 23, Dee recorded the word *Au*. In the margin, he noted "*au* sounds *af*." It might seem that Dee was indicating that the *u* could sound like an *f*. However, it is more likely that he was indicating a "v" sound for this word—so that *Au* is actually *Av*. In the written English of Dee's time, *u* and *v* were essentially the same letter. So Dee would have had to utilize the *f* as a kind of phonetic gloss, to approximate the phonetic sound of *v*.

Early Modern English and Angelical

Before we continue discussing the pronunciation of Angelical, we must first consider a few points about the English used by Dee to record the words. As mentioned previously, Kelley spoke the Angelical words aloud while Dee recorded them in English characters. (He also added marginal notes with phonetic pronunciation clues.) These words and notes are all recorded in—and represent sounds familiar to—Elizabethan English. A little study into this vernacular will make sense of many of Dee's seemingly inexplicable phonetic notes.

Dee lived from 1527 until 1608 CE, making him a contemporary of people such as William Shakespeare (1564–1616), Edmund Spenser

(1552–99), and Francis Bacon (1561–1626). These men all spoke "Elizabethan" English, albeit with different regional dialects. (Queen Elizabeth I reigned from 1558 until 1603.) As any Enochian scholar can tell you, reading Dee's journals is a challenge similar to reading Shakespeare's plays or King James' (1566–1625) authorized Bible. (Remember that the quotes you read throughout this book have had their spelling modernized.) Therefore, a study of Shakespeare's English is necessary if one wishes to estimate the sound of the Angelical language recorded by Dee.

Contrary to what some people may believe, the English spoken by Dee and Shakespeare was *not* Old English or Middle English. It was, in fact, a form of English called *Early Modern English*. This stage of the language existed roughly between the late 1400s and the late 1600s.[11] In other words, it was the standard version of the language during the Renaissance era in England. It was *not* spoken with the "Queen's English" accent we currently associate with the British upper class and royalty. Nor was it the Cockney dialect we associate with the working class in London's East End.[12] These accents did not originate (as we know them) until the eighteenth and nineteenth centuries.

Those who study Shakespearean phonetics commonly suggest that spoken Early Modern English sounded more like the "hillbilly" accent found in the Appalachian regions of the eastern United States. That is because the ancestors of so many of the people who live in Appalachia migrated from England when Early Modern English was prevalent, and then settled into isolated communities. Their language therefore remained unchanged for hundreds of years, and it currently contains the most similarities with Early Modern English. Of course I am not suggesting that we read the Angelical Keys in the voice of Jed Clampett. It is important, however, to place the phonetic sounds we are going to explore in their proper context.

Early Modern English is a transitional stage of the language between Middle English and what we speak today (present-day English). It retained some of the spelling conventions of Middle English, but had shifted to a pronunciation more familiar to the present day. That, in fact, is why Early Modern English so often confuses modern students. We can listen to plays by Shakespeare and—for the most part—understand what we are hearing. There may be puns or catchphrases we don't recognize, and there are a few words that have changed in meaning, but the words still sound basically like present-day English.

However, when we try to *read* the same material, there are some glaring departures from what we learned about English in school. These departures are partially thanks to the Middle English spelling conventions that had not yet passed out of the system by the time of Shakespeare and Dee.

Further departures and confusion arise from the fact that English had not been standardized during the Early Modern English phase.[13] The "educated" languages such as Latin had reached a standard, but English had not. Just as the definitions of the words were somewhat fluid, so were the spellings. Most words were spelled according to how they sounded to the author (a factor that could vary widely from region to region), or according to how the author believed they "should" be spelled. The rules were so fluid that the same word might be spelled in different ways within the *same text*. (Of course, we have already discovered this within Dee's record of the forty-eight Keys.)

Thankfully, there is a brighter side to Early Modern English as well. *Most* of the grammatical rules you learned in school—and take for granted to this very day—apply to Dee's English. (That is why the language sounds similar to our own when spoken.)

For the most part, the consonants in Early Modern English sounded pretty much the way we use them today. A *g* before an *e* or *i* generally had the soft "juh" sound (as in *general*, *budge*, and *giant*), but otherwise a *g* took the hard sound (as in *grand*, *glad*, and *haggard*). The letter *r* probably sounded longer and more drawn out than present-day English. For example, the name *Henry* has three syllables in Early Modern English. So does the word *angry*.[14] The letter *z*[15] was rare, but was used by Dee and Kelley as we use it today (as in *zest*, *zip*,and *sizzle*). The letter *x* took the sound of "ks" in the middle or at the end of a word (as in *excite*, *taxes*, and *fox*), but the sound of "zee" or "tz" at the beginning (as in *xylophone* and *xenophobe*).

Most of the digraphs are familiar: *Th* (as in *this*, *that*), *Sh* (as in *sheet*, *dish*), *Ph* (as in *phantasm*, *phone*), and so on. The digraph *Ch* also existed—sometimes representing the "tch" sound (as in *church*, *chain*), and other times a guttural "kh" sound (as in *ache*, *chrome*, and *chronicle*). *Kn* had finally developed the "nh" sound we know today (as in *knight*, *knife*). Early Modern English also recognized the rare *Gn* digraph as a throaty "nh" sound (as in *gnat*, *gnaw*, and *gnarl*).

Therefore, if you are a native English speaker, you can read the Angelical Keys pretty much as they appear. You can most often go with your gut reaction on how the letter combinations of the words should sound.

Most of the differences between Early Modern and present-day English appear where vowel sounds are concerned. Of course, most of the grammatical rules are still the same as we know them. For instance, an *e* following a consonant at the end of a word will become silent, and make the preceding vowel long (as in *bake*, *precede*, *pipe*, *hope*, and *duke*).

However, as we shall see, the written form of Early Modern English used many peculiar letter combinations to represent the vowel sounds—many of them left over from the more archaic spellings of Middle English. I would like to highlight a couple of points that most often result in confusion for students:

First, written Early Modern English used the letters *i*, *y*, and *j* interchangeably. The basic rule was that *i*/*y* represented the vowel sounds, while *j* (actually an elongated *i*) represented the consonant sound.

I/*y* could be used at the beginning or end of a word—making the sounds of "yuh" at the beginning (as in *yard*, *your*, and *yellow*) and "ee" at the end (as in *lady*, *windy*). Sometimes, an *i*/*y* at the end of a word could have the long "eye" sound (as in *sty*, *ply*, and *sky*). If it follows an *a*, it makes that vowel long (as in *day*, *stay*, and *dais*). In the middle of a word, *i* possessed its typical short sounds (as in *bit*, *sit*, and *whither*) or long sounds (as in *bite*, *kite*, *blight*, and *sight*).

Meanwhile, either the letter *i or* its elongated *j* version could appear in a word with the consonant "juh" sound.[16] It might appear at the start of a word (as in *justice, jump,* and *John*)[17] or in the middle (as in *adjust, object,* and *majestic*). Finally, as if to confuse matters further, the "juh" sound could also be represented by a *g* (as in *danger, sage,* and *range*).

The next common point of confusion, for modern students, is between the letters *u* and *v*. These letters were also interchangeable in Early Modern English, and might indicate either a vowel or a consonant sound.

If the letter was used at the beginning of a word, it was always written as *v*. It might take the consonant "vuh" sound if preceding a vowel (as in *very, visit,* and *vast*). Or, it might take the vowel sound if preceding a consonant: either the long "yew" sound (as in *vtopia, vtilize,* and *vseful*),[18] or the short "uh" sound (as in *vp, vtmost,* and *vsher*).[19]

The *u* form of the letter could be used anywhere else in the word. Whether it took the vowel or consonant sound was the same as for the letter *v*. It could take the consonant sound if it preceded a vowel (as in *sauage, saue,* and *Dauid*).[20] Or, it could take the vowel sound if it preceded a consonant (as in *mud, scrub,* and *button.*)[21]

I should also point out that the letter *w* was fairly rare. It was more often written like a literal double *u* (or *v*)—*uu* or *vv*.

On the following pages, you will find reference charts for Early Modern English phonetics, which can be applied to Angelical words, as well as the pronunciation notes Dee left in his records. It is not an ultimate guide to proper Angelical pronunciation (as we shall see later, there are also several Middle English influences upon Angelical), but it gives us a much clearer picture than systems based upon Hebrew or other phonologies.

When you encounter an Angelical word with an obscure spelling—*or* one of Dee's seemingly inexplicable phonetic notes—simply look for that word's letter combinations in the right-hand column of these charts. The left-hand column will indicate the sound likely made by those letters in Angelical (and Early Modern English):

Early Modern English Phonetics Chart[22]

(for Angelical Pronunciation)

Consonant Sounds	
Phonetic Sound (as in)	Letter Combinations in Early Modern English
B (*boat, clobber*)	b, bb
D (*dive, ladder*)	d, dd
F (*fan, rough, phone*)	f, ff, gh, ph
G (*guard, giggle*)	g, gg
H (*house, hover, who*)	h, wh
J (*budge, jump, adjust, magic*)	dg, dge, j, i, d, di, dj, g
K (*cake, back, chrome*)	k, kk, c, cc, ck, ch
L (*land, spill, will*)	l, ll
M (*metal, mammal*)	m, mm
N (*name, manner, knight, gnome*)	n, nn, kn, gn
P (*pine, speck, puppet*)	p, pp
R (*road, serrate, write*)	r, rr, wr
S (*save, bless, cereal*)	s, ss, c
T (*Table, little, lottery*)	t, tt
W (*water, work, what*)	uu, vv, w, wh
X (*except, flax, excite*)	x
Y (*yes, yellow, your*)	y, i
Z (*zoo, haze, blizzard, xylophone*)	s, z, zz, (very rarely: x)

Vowel Sounds	
Phonetic Sound (as in)	Letter Combinations in Early Modern English
A – long (*date, day, eight, whey*)	a, aa, ai, ay, ei, ey, (maybe: eh)
A – short (*bat, cat, apple*)	a, æ[23]
E – long (*beet, heat, believe, only*)	e, ee, ea, ie, y, æ[24]
E – short (*fed, bed, head, dead*)	e, ea
E – silent (*taste, hope, wage*)	e
I – long (*I, bite, blight, style, height*)	i, igh, ai, y, ei, ye
I – short (*bit, cliff, miss, pen*)	i, j, e
O – long (*oar, bone, although*)	o, oo, ou, ov, ow, oa, ough, ovgh
O – short (*hot, tall, father, auburn*)	o, a, au, av, aw, augh, avgh, ough, ovgh
U – long (*root, through, brute*)	o, u, v, ou, ov, oo, ough, ovgh, eu, ew
U – short (*cup, of*)	u, v, o

Digraphs	
Phonetic Sound (as in)	Letter Combinations in Early Modern English
"Kwuh" (*queen, quick*)	qu
"Ow" (*out, drought, house, town*)	ou, ov, ow, ough, ovgh
"Oy" (*oil, boy*)	oi, oy
"Shuh" (*shine, shower, wish*)	sh
"Tch" (*chase, church, witch*)	ch, t, c, cch, tch
"Thuh" (*that, whither, thorn*)	th, (very rarely: y)[25]

Take note that several of the above letter combinations appear more than once. For example, the combination *ough* appears under four different headings, because it might indicate any of the following sounds:

Long *o* (as in *although, dough*)

Short *o* (as in *thought, cough*)

Long *u* (as in *enough, rough, tough*)

digraph *ow* (as in *drought, bough*)

This means that—just as with Early Modern English itself—there will always be some ambiguity in the pronunciation of Angelical words. However, at the very least, this information will allow us to make educated guesses rather than engaging in blind speculation based upon present-day English, Hebrew, or other languages.

Middle English and Angelical

Having said the above about Early Modern English, I feel it is necessary to add a few words about Middle English and its influence on the Angelical language.

Dee may have been writing his notes in his own contemporary English; however, we must keep in mind that he was receiving a sacred magickal language from the Angels, which they claimed was an ancient proto-tongue. This is not uncommon for magickal languages, most of which are archaic in some form. For example, the priests of ancient Babylon made use of the older Sumerian language in their rites. In Dee's time, dead languages like Latin and Hebrew (the latter was solely a liturgical language in Dee's time) were the standard mystery languages. Therefore, it is no surprise that Angelical would have also had an archaic sound to the ears of Dee and Kelley. That is where Middle English comes into the picture.

Middle English was the language used by Chaucer to write his *Canterbury Tales*. One of the best-known traits of Middle English was the manner in which it tended to pronounce most of the letters in each word—so the vowels were clearly pronounced. As the English language drifted toward its Early Modern phase, the syllables began to blend together into the sounds we are familiar with today.

By taking Dee's phonetic clues into account, I have discovered a general "Middle English" trait throughout Angelical. This is especially applicable to vowels or groups of consonants. For example, all the vowels in the word *Aai* are sounded ("ay-ay-ii"). In the word *Balye*, the *a*, *y*, and *e* are all sounded distinctly ("bay-lii-ee"). The word *Momao* follows the same rule—with the *a* and both *o*'s sounded distinctly ("moh-may-oh").

For consonants, we can look at the final *m* in *Mapm*, which sounds alone ("map-em"). Or the initial *L* in *Lring*, which also makes its own sound ("el-ring"). Another example is the word *Zlida*, where the initial *Z* stands alone ("zohd-lida").

I could give dozens of examples of this convention, but I think these should suffice as an illustration. This in no way means that *every* letter in every Angelical word should be pronounced! However, the convention appears often enough to give the language a slightly "Middle English" flavor. In this way, the Angelical tongue would have sounded archaic to Dee and Kelley—thus fulfilling the "requirement" for a magickal language.

General Notes on Angelical Phonology

This section is where I have gathered all of my notes on the phonology of the Angelical language. They are taken from everything we have seen in this chapter so far, as well as Dee's own pronunciation notes. (See the Lexicon for more on Dee's notes.) What you see below can be applied directly to the Angelical words, as Dee recorded them, and which you will find in the Lexicon.

Vowels

Pronouncing the vowels in the Angelical tongue does not present much of a problem. As we shall see in the Lexicon, a vowel will usually take its short sound when it is followed by a consonant in its syllable. For some examples, see *Lap*, *Iad*, and *Zir*. However, when a vowel is attached to the *preceding* consonant (i.e., it stands at the end of its syllable), or when it stands alone in a syllable, it takes its long sound. For examples of this, see *Momao*, *Napeai*, and *Paradial*. Dee's phonetic notes—which we shall see in the Lexicon—usually divide the words by syllables, thus indicating to which consonant (if any) each vowel is attached.

Consonants

Of course, it is the consonants that cause most students (and adepts!) to stumble with Angelical pronunciation. While the consonants generally make the sounds we are familiar with, there are several words that contain peculiar groupings of consonants that make little or no phonetic sense to modern English-speaking readers. There are certain grammatical rules one must learn to make sense of it all:

When two consonants are placed together, they can:

1) Make a digraph as they would in present-day English (*Ph*, *Ch*, *Th*, *Qu*, etc.), as in *Dorpha*, *Ethamz*, *Chis*, *Teloch*, and *Norquasahi*. Or they can:

2) Make a new consonant sound as they would in present-day English (*Gr*, *Tr*, *Gn*, etc.), as in *Grosb*, *Trian*, *Gnay*, etc.

However, if neither of the above apply (as in *Nazpsad*, *Farzm*, *Zchis*), then:

3) The "peculiar" consonant letter is pronounced as a syllable unto itself, after the manner of Middle English. By "peculiar," I mean the consonant in the cluster that stands as the "odd man out." For instance, in the cluster *gsp*, we find that the letters *sp* naturally form a sound together (as in *spot* or *speak*). Meanwhile, the letters *gs* do not make a natural sound in English. Therefore, that *g* is the peculiar one in the group—and it is pronounced by itself, in its own syllable.

In Angelical, a letter standing alone in a syllable is not pronounced phonetically. To continue our *gsp* example, the *g* would take neither its hard sound ("guh"—as in *game* or *good*) nor its soft sound ("juh"—as in *giant* or *huge*). Instead, one would actually pronounce the letter's *name*—sounding like "gee."

Let's take a look at some examples in Angelical: the word *Nazpsad* is pronounced "nayz-pee-sad." The central *p* stands out in this case as the peculiar consonant, and is therefore pronounced as "pee." The word *Farzm* is pronounced "farz-em." The final *zm* does not combine naturally in English, and the *m* is pronounced by itself as "em." As a final example, the word *Zchis* is pronounced "zohd-kiis." The initial letters *Zch* do not combine, therefore the *Z* is pronounced as "zohd." In each case, the peculiar consonant stands alone as its own syllable.

I admit it seems odd that Angelical consonants should sound like the *names* of English letters. (After all, they have their own Angelical names!) However, notice that long vowels also sound like their English names (long *a* = "ay," long *e* = "ee," long *o* = "oh," etc.)—and any Angelical vowel that stands alone in a syllable takes the long sound. It would appear, then, that the same principle is applied to Angelical consonants when they stand alone. That is to say, Angelical recognizes "long consonants." Just as a long *Un* (A) sounds like "ay," so a long (or extended) *Tal* (M) sounds like "em."

While we are still on the subject of "long consonants," I should mention that the letter *Ceph* (Z) sometimes takes its long sound ("zohd") for no apparent reason. For example, when the Angel Nalvage transmitted the *Corpus Omnium* to Dee and Kelley, he informed them that the word *Moz* could be pronounced "moz" or "moz-ohd." The shorter pronunciation indicates "Joy," while the pronunciation with the extended Z ("zohd") indicates "Joy of God."

As we can see, there is no grammatical reason why the *z* in *Moz* should be extended. The same is true for the word *Zacar* (zay-kayr)—which appears in the forty-eight Keys several times with the extended Z (zohd-ay-kayr). My best guess is that this is not based upon a grammatical rule at all. Perhaps, instead, it is merely a poetic (or lyrical) gloss—after the manner in which a singer will elongate or add syllables to a word in a song to fill metre or emphasize emotion. This is suggested by the difference between "moz" as "Joy" and "moz-ohd" as "Joy of God."

Special Cases

Another quirk of the letter *Ceph* (Z) is that it is sometimes interchangeable with *Pal* (X). This is perhaps because *z* was somewhat rare in the Elizabethan era, and *x* more often served for the "z" sound (as in *xenophile* or *xylophone*). We see evidence of this in the *Book of Loagaeth*, where the Angelical letter-name *Drux* (N) is given the alternate spelling of *Druz* in the margin.[26]

The letter *Don* (R) is another Angelical character of interest. When the letter *r* becomes the peculiar consonant in a cluster, it is neither pronounced "ar" (the long consonant sound) nor given its own syllable. Instead, it is merely pronounced "ur" (as in the English words *turn* or *spur*)—so that it combines with the consonant before it. For example, see *Prdzar* ("purd-zar"), *Prge* ("purj"), and *Dialprt* ("dii-al-purt").

There is one final special case I want to record here. In his journals, Dee established that the word *Baltle* was pronounced "bal-tayl" (the first syllable rhyming with *ball* and the second with *tail*).[27] I found the pronunciation of the three-letter cluster in the second syllable—*tle*—very odd. I decided to investigate further by searching for other words ending in *le*, and found *Bagle* and *Cicle*. As you will see in the Lexicon, Dee's notes on these words are less than helpful. I find it likely that each of these words should end with the sound of "ayl" (as in the English words *bail* or *tail*). In fact, I suspect that any time we see *le* as the final two letters of a three-consonant cluster, they will have the "ayl" sound.

Endnotes

1. The Archangel Raphael says of the first Table: "Let this lesson instruct thee to read all that shall be gathered out of this book hereafter. [. . .] It shall be sufficient to instruct thee." [*Five Books of Mystery*, p. 291]
2. See the introduction to Laycock's *The Complete Enochian Dictionary*.
3. All of these are included in the Lexicon.
4. It does, however, appear in *Loagaeth*—although without definition. I note it is very similar to the Hebrew word *Iah* or *Yah* (God).
5. See the introduction to Laycock's *The Complete Enochian Dictionary*.
6. *Bagle* appears elsewhere as a form of *because*.
7. "And you, Brutus?"
8. Table One, side A, line 21.
9. *Radical*, used in this sense, means "root" or "smallest unit."
10. See *John Dee's Five Books of Mystery*, pp. 288–95.
11. After what linguists refer to as the "Great Vowel Shift." The main difference between Middle English and Modern English is the pronunciation of the vowels.
12. Think of Eliza Doolittle in the play *My Fair Lady*: "The rine in spine styes minely on th' pline!"
13. The first English dictionary was not published in London until 1604.
14. Based on Shakespearean phonetics.
15. Called *Zed*, *Ezod*, *Zod*, and sometimes *Izzard*.
16. Present-day English entirely dropped the use of *i* for the consonant sound.
17. Or: *iustice*, *iump*, *Iohann*.
18. Which we write today as *utopia*, *utilize*, *useful*.
19. That is, *up*, *utmost*, *usher*.
20. That is, *savage*, *save*, *David*.

21. In the Lexicon, I have sometimes modernized the usage of *u* and *v* in order to make the words more comprehensible to the modern eye. For instance, the word *Zomdux* (Amidst) appears in Dee's journals as *Zomdvx*.
22. Do not confuse this chart with my own phonetic Angelical pronunciation guide and notes found in the Lexicon and Angelical Psalter.
23. This character—which appears as a combination of *a* and *e* (or *Æ*)—is called an "ash." Sometimes it has the short "a" sound (as in *ash, apple, ask*), and sometimes it has a long "e" sound (*ether, eon*)
24. See the previous footnote.
25. In Old and Middle English, the letter *y* could often indicate the *Th* digraph. This is where we get words like *ye* that are pronounced "thee." This convention was formally dropped from Early Modern English, although some authors in Shakespeare's time still used it. I doubt, however, that it applies to any Angelical words, as Dee seems to have regularly used *y* to indicate the "yuh" sound.
26. See the *Five Books of Mystery*, p. 291, footnote 136, and *Loagaeth*, Table One, side A, line 1.
27. See the entry for *Baltle* in the Lexicon.

Chapter 2

The Forty-Eight Angelical Keys: A Cross-Reference

In order to create the Angelical Lexicon, it was first necessary to create this cross-reference, which contains the entire text of the forty-eight Keys—with the words arranged into columns and categorized by cross-reference numbers. The numbers are then used throughout the Lexicon to indicate in which Key, and where in the Key, any Angelical word can be found.

Dee left two manuscripts containing the forty-eight Keys: The first is his personal Angelical journal, where he recorded Nalvage's transmission of the Keys.[1] The other is a text called the *48 Claves Angelicae*—which is part of a grimoire Dee created separately from his journals, containing the major points of his Angelic magick.[2] The words of the Keys in the *48 Claves* have some differences from those in Dee's private records. I assume the differences are corrections Dee made between recording the words in his journal and recopying them into his grimoire.

Students might notice that the Keys in my cross-reference do not match the same Keys in *The Enochian Magick of Dr. John Dee* by Geoffrey James, in *The Complete Enochian Dictionary* by Donald Laycock, and in other sources. While these books are legendary, and were instrumental in my own study of the Angelical language, I ultimately discovered conflicts between their work and Dee's journals.[3]

Therefore, the text in my cross-reference represents my own analysis of the Keys and their grammatical structure—drawn first from *A True and Faithful Relation*, and secondarily from Dee's *48 Claves Angelicae*. I have striven to preserve the text as received by Dee and Kelley, rather than force it to match my own ideas of what it "should" look like. Where I have encountered ambiguities in Dee's journals or doubt in my own work, I have used the *48 Claves Angelicae* as Dee's final say on the matter.

The following presentation of the Angelical Keys is divided into four columns:

First Column: Cross-Reference Numbers

In *The Enochian Magic of Dr. John Dee*, Geoffrey James introduced a cross-reference numbering system for the Angelical Keys, which seems to have become somewhat traditional among "Enochian" scholars. Although my presentation of the Keys differs from James', I have chosen to retain the same style of cross-referencing. (Note: The Call of the Aethyrs is really the nineteenth in the series. However, again following tradition, I have used "30" for its reference number because the Call actually represents thirty Keys.)

Every word of the Keys has been assigned a number to designate its location. For instance, the fifth word of the twelfth Key is numbered 12.5. We can, then, easily reference the Keys in this cross-reference to see that word 12.5 is *Chis* (Are). These numbers are then used throughout the Lexicon to indicate the locations of the words in the Keys. Therefore, if we look up the word *Chis* in the Lexicon, we can easily discover the locations of *every* appearance (or version) of that word in the Keys.

Second Column: Angelical Words

These are the actual Angelical words as recorded by Dee in his journals, or in his *48 Claves Angelicae*.

Any corrections I have made to this text are indicated with footnotes. Also, you will note some instances of a hyphenated *z-* in this column. This indicates places where the Angels appear to have given the full "zohd" (or "zed") pronunciation of the letter *z*. For example, the word *Zchis* (They Are) is pronounced "zohd-kiis," and is written in column 2 as "Z-chis."

Third Column: "English Senses"

This column contains the poetic translations of the Angelical words from column 2. These are also found in Dee's journals or the *48 Claves Angelicae*.

Because the poetry of the Calls was written during the time of King James and Shakespeare, I have found it necessary to modernize the text in some places. (See my analysis of the poetry of the Keys in volume I, chapter 3.) Any additions I have included in the text are contained in parentheses. Footnotes will indicate other thoughts, changes, corrections, and so forth.

Fourth Column: Literal Translations

This column is entirely new to the study of the Angelical Keys. As we have seen in the last chapter, many aspects of grammar (such as pronouns and articles) are rare or absent from Angelical. In order to illustrate this, column 4 presents the forty-eight Keys in their *literal* translation. This will show us these missing aspects of grammar at a glance, and can teach us much about how Angelical actually works from a linguistic point of view.

Note that some words appear in this column within quotation marks. These are words that appear strikingly different from the "English senses," and are fully explained in the Lexicon.

Key One			
1.1	Ol	I	*I*
1.2	sonf	reign	*"to reign"*
1.3	vorsg	over you	*over (you)*
1.4	goho	sayeth	*"to say"*
1.5	Iad	the God of	*God*
1.6	Balt	Justice	*justice*
1.7	lansh	in power exalted above	*"exalted power"*
1.8	calz	the firmaments	*firmaments (heavens)*
1.9	vonpho	of wrath:	*of wrath*
1.10	sobra	in whose	*whose*
1.11	z-ol	hands	*hands*
1.12	ror	the Sun	*Sun*
1.13	i	is	*is*
1.14	ta	as	*as*
1.15	nazpsad	a sword	*sword*
1.16	graa	and the Moon	Moon
1.17	ta	as	*as*
1.18	malprg	a through-thrusting fire:	*"Fiery Arrow"*
1.19	ds	which	*which*
1.20	holq	measureth	*"to measure"*
1.21	qaa	your garments	*"created form"*
1.22	nothoa	in the midst of	*amidst*
1.23	zimz	my vestures	*vestures*
1.24	od	and	*and*
1.25	commah	trussed you together	*"to truss together"*
1.26	ta	as	*as*
1.27	nobloh	the palms of	*palms*
1.28	zien	my hands:	*hands*
1.29	soba	Whose	*whose*
1.30	thil	seats	*seats*

1.31	gnonp	I garnished with	*garnished*
1.32	prge	the fire of	*fire*
1.33	aldi	gathering	*gathering*
1.34	ds	and (which)	*which*
1.35	urbs	beautified	*"to beautify"*
1.36	oboleh	your garments	*garments*
1.37	grsam	with admiration,	*admiration*
1.38	casarm	to whom	*whom*
1.39	ohorela	I made a law	*"legislate"*
1.40	caba	to govern	*to govern*
1.41	pir	the holy ones,	*holy ones*
1.42	ds	and (which)	*which*
1.43	zonrensg	delivered you	*"to deliver"*
1.44	cab	a rod	*rod*
1.45	erm	(along with) the ark of	*ark*
1.46	iadnah	knowledge.	*knowledge*
1.47	pilah	Moreover,	*moreover*
1.48	farzm	you lifted up your voices	*"to speak up"*
1.49	znrza	and swore	*"to swear"*
1.50	adna	obedience	*obedience*
1.51	gono	and faith	*faith*
1.52	iadpil	to Him	*(unto) Him*
1.53	ds	that	*that*
1.54	hom	liveth	*"to live"*
1.55	toh	and triumpheth	*"to triumph"*
1.56	soba	whose	*whose*
1.57	ipam	beginning is not	*"is not"*[4]
1.58	ul	nor end	*end*
1.59	ipamis	cannot be,	*cannot be*
1.60	ds	which	*which*
1.61	loholo	shineth as	*"to shine"*
1.62	vep	a flame	*flame*

1.63	zomdux	in the midst of	*"amidst"*
1.64	poamal	your palace	*palace*
1.65	od	and	*and*
1.66	bogpa	reigneth	*"to reign"*
1.67	aai	amongst you	*amongst (you)*
1.68	ta	as	*as*
1.69	piap	the balance of	*balance*
1.70	baltle	righteousness	*righteousness*
1.71	od	and	*and*
1.72	vaoan/vooan	truth.	*truth*
1.73	zacar	Move,	*move*
1.74	ca	therefore,	*therefore*
1.75	od	and	*and*
1.76	zamran	show yourselves:	*"to appear"*
1.77	odo	open	*"to open"*
1.78	cicle	the mysteries of	*mysteries*
1.79	qaa	your creation:	*creation*
1.80	zorge	Be friendly unto me:	*be friendly unto me*
1.81	lap	For	*for*
1.82	zirdo	I am	*(I) am*
1.83	noco	a servant of	*servant*
1.84	mad	the same your God:	*god*
1.85	hoath	the true worshipper of	*true worshiper*
1.86	iaida	the Highest.	*The Highest*

Key Two			
2.1	Adgt	Can	*Can*
2.2	upaah	the wings of	*wings*
2.3	zong	the winds	*winds*
2.4	om	understand	*"to understand"*
2.5	faaip	your voices of	*"voicings" (songs)*
2.6	sald	wonder	*wonder*
2.7	viiv	o you the second of	*second*
2.8	L	the First,	*First*
2.9	sobam	whom	*whom*
2.10	ialpurg	the burning flames	*burning flames*
2.11	izazaz	have framed within	*"to frame"*
2.12	piadph	the depths of my jaws	*"my gut"*
2.13	casarma	whom	*whom*
2.14	abramg	I have prepared	*"to prepare"*
2.15	ta	as	*as*
2.16	talho	cups	*cups*
2.17	paracleda	for a wedding	*wedding*
2.18	qta	or as	*or as*
2.19	lorslq	the flowers	*flowers*
2.20	turbs	in their beauty	*(in) beauty*
2.21	ooge	for the chamber	*chamber*
2.22	baltoh	of righteousness.	*righteousness*
2.23	givi	Stronger	*stronger*
2.24	chis	are	*are*
2.25	lusd	your feet	*feet*
2.26	orri	than the barren stone:	*(barren) stone*
2.27	od	And	*and*
2.28	micalp	mightier	*mightier*
2.29	chis	are	*are*
2.30	bia	your voices	*voices*
2.31	ozongon	than the manifold winds.	*manifold winds*

2.32	lap	For	*for*
2.33	noan	you are become	*"have become"*
2.34	trof	a building	*a building*
2.35	cors	such	*such*
2.36	tage	as is not	*as (is) not*
2.37	oq	but	*but*
2.38	manin	in the mind of	*mind*
2.39	iaidon	the All Powerful.	*the All Powerful*
2.40	torzu	Arise	*arise*
2.41	gohel	sayeth the First.	*sayeth the First*
2.42	zacar	Move	*move*
2.43	ca	therefore	*therefore*
2.44	cnoqod	unto His servants.	*(unto) servants*
2.45	zamran	Show yourselves	*"to appear"*
2.46	micalzo	in power	*power*
2.47	od	and	*and*
2.48	ozazm	make (for) me	*make (me)*
2.49	urelp	a strong seething	*seething*
2.50	lap	for	*for*
2.51	zir	I am of	*am*
2.52	Ioiad	Him that liveth forever.	*Him That Liveth Forever*

Key Three			
3.1	Micma	Behold	*behold*
3.2	goho	sayeth	*"to say"*
3.3	piad	your God	*(your) God*
3.4	zir	I am	*(I) am*
3.5	comselh	a Circle	*circle*
3.6	azien	on whose hands	*hands*
3.7	biab	stand	*"to stand"*
3.8	oslondoh	12 Kingdoms.	*12 kingdoms*
3.9	norz	Six	*six*
3.10	chis	are	*are*
3.11	othil	the seats of	*seats of*
3.12	gigipah	living breath	*living breath*
3.13	undl	the rest	*the rest*
3.14	chis	are	*are*
3.15	tapuin	as sharp sickles:	*as (sharp) sickles*
3.16	qmospleh	or the horns of	*or the horns*
3.17	teloch	death	*death*
3.18	quiin	wherein	*wherein*
3.19	toltorg	the creatures of the earth	*creatures*
3.20	chis	are	*are*
3.21	ichisge	[and][5] are not	*are not*
3.22	m	except (by)	*except*
3.23	ozien	mine own hand,	*hand*
3.24	dst	which (also)	*which*
3.25	brgda	sleep	*"to sleep"*
3.26	od	and	*and*
3.27	torzul	shall rise.	*"arise"*
3.28	ili	In the first	*the first*
3.29	eol	I made you	*made*
3.30	balzarg	stewards	*stewards*

3.31	od	and	*and*
3.32	aala	placed you	*"to place"*
3.33	thilnos	in seats 12 of	*12 seats (of)*
3.34	netaab	government,	*government*
3.35	dluga	giving unto	*"to give"*
3.36	vomzarg	every one of you	*every one*
3.37	lonsa	power	*power*
3.38	capmiali	successively	*successively*
3.39	vors	over	*over*
3.40	cla	456,	*456*
3.41	homil	the true ages of	*(true) ages*
3.42	cocasb	time,	*time*
3.43	fafen	to the intent that	*intent*
3.44	izizop	from your highest vessels	*vessels*
3.45	od	and	*and*
3.46	miinoag	the corners	*corners*
3.47	de	of	*of*
3.48	gnetaab	your governments	*(your) governments*
3.49	vaun	you might work	*"to work"*
3.50	nanaeel	my power:	*(my) power*
3.51	panpir	pouring down	*"to pour down"*
3.52	malpirgi	the fires of life and increase	*fires of life and increase*
3.53	caosg	upon the earth	*earth*
3.54	pild	continually.	*continually*
3.55	noan	Thus, you are become	*"have become"*
3.56	unalah	the skirts of	*skirts*
3.57	balt	justice	*justice*
3.58	odvooan	and truth	*and truth*
3.59	dooiap	In the Name of	*(in the) name*
3.60	mad	the same your God,	*god*
3.61	goholor	lift up,	*lift up*

3.62	gohus	I say,	*(I) say*
3.63	amiran	yourselves.	*yourselves*
3.64	micma	Behold,	*behold*
3.65	iehusoz	His mercies	*(God's) mercies*
3.66	cacacom	flourish	*"to flourish"*
3.67	od	and	*and*
3.68	dooain	Name	*name*
3.69	noar	has become	*(has) become*
3.70	micaolz	mighty	*mighty*
3.71	aaiom	amongst us.	*amongst (us)*
3.72	casarmg	In whom	*in whom*
3.73	gohia	we say,	*(we) say*
3.74	z-acar	move	*move*
3.75	uniglag	descend	*"to descend"*
3.76	od	and	*and*
3.77	imuamar	apply yourselves unto us	*"to apply unto"*
3.78	pugo	as unto	*as unto*
3.79	plapli	partakers of	*partakers*
3.80	ananael	the secret wisdom of	*secret wisdom*
3.81	qaan	your creation.	*creation*

Key Four			
4.1	Othil	I have set	*"to set"*
4.2	lasdi	my feet	*feet*
4.3	babage	in the south	*south*
4.4	od	and	*and*
4.5	dorpha	have looked about me	*"to look about"*
4.6	gohol	saying	*"to say"*
4.7	gchisge	are not	*are not*
4.8	avavago	the Thunders of Increase	*Thunders of Increase*
4.9	cormp	numbered	*"to number"*
4.10	pd	33	*33*
4.11	dsonf	which reign in	*which reign*
4.12	viudiv	the second Angle	*second angle*
4.13	casarmi	under whom	*whom*
4.14	oali	I have placed	*"to place"*
4.15	mapm	9639	*9639*
4.16	sobam	whom	*whom*
4.17	ag	none	*none*
4.18	cormpo	hath yet numbered	*hath (yet) numbered*
4.19	crpl	but One,	*but one*
4.20	casarmg	in whom	*(in) whom*
4.21	croodzi	the second beginning of things	*beginning*[6]
4.22	chis	are	*are*
4.23	odugeg	and wax strong	*and wax strong*
4.24	dst	which also	*which (also)*
4.25	capimali	successively	*successively*
4.26	chis	are	*are*
4.27	capimaon	the number of time:	*number of time*
4.28	odlonshin	And their powers	*and powers*
4.29	chis	are	*are*
4.30	talo	as the first	*as the first*
4.31	cla	456:	*456*

4.32	torgu	Arise	*arise*
4.33	norqrasahi	you sons of pleasure	*sons of pleasure*
4.34	od	and	*and*
4.35	fcaosga	visit the earth,	*visit the earth*
4.36	bagle	for	*for*
4.37	zirenaiad	I am the Lord your God	*I am Lord God*
4.38	dsi	which is	*which is*
4.39	odapila	and liveth.	*and live*
4.40	dooaip	In the Name of	*(in the) Name*
4.41	qaal	the Creator,	*Creator*
4.42	z-acar	move	*move*
4.43	odzamran	and show yourselves	*and "appear"*
4.44	obelisong	as pleasant deliverers	*pleasant deliverers*
4.45	restil	that you may praise Him	*to praise (Him?)*
4.46	aaf	amongst	*amongst*
4.47	normolap	the sons of men.	*sons of men*

Key Five			
5.1	Sapah	The Mighty Sounds	*Mighty Sounds*
5.2	zimii	have entered into	*"to enter"*
5.3	duiv	the third angle	*third angle*
5.4	od	and	*and*
5.5	noas	are become	*(have) become*
5.6	taqanis	as olives	*as olives*
5.7	adroch	in the olive mount	*olive mount*
5.8	dorphal	looking with gladness upon	*"looking upon"*
5.9	caosg	the earth	*earth*
5.10	od	and	*and*
5.11	faonts	dwelling within	*dwelling*
5.12	piripsol	the brightness of the heavens	*heavens*
5.13	tablior	as continual comforters,	*as comforters*
5.14	casarm	unto whom	*whom*
5.15	amipzi	I have fastened	*"to fasten"*
5.16	nazarth	pillars of gladness	*pillars (of gladness)*
5.17	af	19	*19*
5.18	od	and	*and*
5.19	dlugar	gave them	*"to give"*
5.20	zizop	vessels	*vessels*
5.21	z-lida	to water	*"to water"*
5.22	caosgi	the earth	*earth*
5.23	toltorgi	with her creatures	*(with) creatures*
5.24	od	and	*and*
5.25	z-chis	they are	*they are*
5.26	esiasch	the brothers of	*brothers*
5.27	L	the First	*The First*
5.28	taviv	and second	*and second*
5.29	od	and	*and*
5.30	iaod	the beginning of	*beginning*
5.31	thild	their own seats	*seats*

5.32	ds	which	*which*
5.33	hubar	are garnished with[7] continually burning lamps	*lamps*
5.34	peral	69636	*69636*
5.35	soba	whose	*whose*
5.36	cormfa	numbers	*numbers*
5.37	chista	are as	*are as*
5.38	la	the first,	*the first*
5.39	uls	the ends,	*ends*
5.40	od	and	*and*
5.41	qcocasb	the contents of time.	*contents of time*
5.42	ca	Therefore,	*therefore*
5.43	niis	come you	*come*
5.44	od	and	*and*
5.45	darbs	obey	*obey*
5.46	qaas	your creation.	*creation*
5.47	fetharzi	Visit us in peace	*visit (in) peace*
5.48	od	and	*and*
5.49	bliora	comfort.	*comfort*
5.50	iaial	Conclude us as	*"to conclude"*
5.51	ednas	receivers of	*receivers*
5.52	cicles	your mysteries:	*mysteries*
5.53	bagle	For why?	*for*
5.54	geiad	Our Lord and Master	*Lord and Master*
5.55	il	is all one.	*is one*

Key Six			
6.1	Gah	The spirits of	*spirits*
6.2	sdiv	the fourth Angle	*fourth angle*
6.3	chis	are	*are*
6.4	em	nine,	*nine*
6.5	micalzo	mighty in	*mighty*
6.6	pilzin	the firmaments of waters	*firmaments of waters*
6.7	sobam	whom	*whom*
6.8	el	the First	*the First*
6.9	harg	hath planted	*"to plant"*
6.10	mir	a torment to	*torment*
6.11	babalon	the wicked	*wicked*
6.12	od	and	*and*
6.13	obloc	a garland to	*garland*
6.14	samvelg	the righteous:	*the righteous*
6.15	dlugar	giving unto them	*"to give"*
6.16	malpurg	fiery darts	*"Fiery Arrows"*
6.17	arcaosgi	to van the earth	*(to van?) the earth*
6.18	od	and	*and*
6.19	acam	7699	7699
6.20	canal	continual workmen	*workmen*
6.21	sobolzar	whose courses	*whose courses*
6.22	fbliard	visit with comfort	*visit (with) comfort*
6.23	caosgi	the earth	*earth*
6.24	odchis	and are	*and are*
6.25	anetab	in government	*(in) government*
6.26	od	and	*and*
6.27	miam	continuance	*continuance*
6.28	taviv	as the second	*as second*
6.29	od	and	*and*
6.30	d	the third.	*third*
6.31	darsar	Wherefore	*wherefore*

6.32	solpeth	harken unto	*hearken (unto)*
6.33	bien	my voice.	*(my) voice*
6.34	brita	I have talked of you	*"to speak of"*
6.35	od	and	*and*
6.36	zacam	I move you	*move*
6.37	gmicalzo	in power and presence	*in power*
6.38	sobhaath	whose works	*whose works*
6.39	trian	shall be	*shall be*
6.40	luiahe	a song of honour	*song of honor*
6.41	odecrin	and the praise of	*and praise*
6.42	mad	your God	*god*
6.43	qaaon	in your creation.	*creation*

Key Seven			
7.1	Raas	The east	*east*
7.2	isalman	is a house of	*is a house*
7.3	paradiz-	virgins	*virgins*
7.4	oecrimi	singing praises	*"to sing praises"*
7.5	aao	amongst	*amongst*
7.6	ialpirgah	the flames of the first glory	*flames of the first glory*
7.7	quiin	wherein	*wherein*
7.8	enay	the Lord	*the Lord*
7.9	butmon	hath opened His mouth	*mouth*
7.10	od	and	*and*
7.11	inoas	they are become	*(have) become*
7.12	ni	28	*28*
7.13	paradial	living dwellings	*living dwellings*
7.14	casarmg	in whom	*in whom*
7.15	ugear	the strength of men	*strength*
7.16	chirlan	rejoiceth	*"to rejoice"*
7.17	od	and	*and*
7.18	zonac	they are appareled with	*appareled*
7.19	luciftian	ornaments of brightness	*(ornaments of) brightness*
7.20	corsta	such as	*such as*
7.21	vaulzirn	work wonders	*work wonders*
7.22	tolhami	on all creatures.	*(upon) all creatures*
7.23	soba	Whose	*whose*
7.24	londoh	kingdoms	*kingdoms*
7.25	odmiam	and continuance	*and continuance*
7.26	chistad	are as the third	*are as the third*
7.27	odes	and fourth	*and fourth*
7.28	umadea	strong towers	*strong towers*
7.29	od	and	*and*
7.30	pibliar	places of comfort,	*places of comfort*
7.31	othilrit	the seats of mercy	*seats of mercy*

7.32	odmiam	and continuance.	*and continuance*
7.33	cnoquol	O you servents of	*servants*
7.34	rit	mercy,	*mercy*
7.35	z-acar	move,	*move*
7.36	zamran	appear,	*appear*
7.37	oecrimi	sing praises unto	*"to sing praises"*
7.38	qadah	the creator,	*Creator*
7.39	od	and	*and*
7.40	omicaolz-	be mighty	*(be) mighty*
7.41	aaiom	amongst us.	*amongst (us)*
7.42	bagle	For	*for*
7.43	papnor	to this remembrance	*remembrance*
7.44	idlugam	is given	*is given*
7.45	lonshi	power	*power*
7.46	od	and	*and*
7.47	umplif	our strength	*strength*
7.48	ugegi	waxeth strong	*"to wax strong"*
7.49	bigliad	in our Comforter.	*(in our) comforter*

Key Eight			
8.1	Bazemlo	The midday the first	*midday the first*
8.2	ita	is as	*is as*
8.3	piripson	the third heaven	*(third?) heaven*
8.4	oln	made of	*made (of)*
8.5	nazavabh	hyacinth pillars	*(hyacinth) pillars*
8.6	ox	26	*26*
8.7	casarmg	in whom	*in whom*
8.8	uran	the Elders	*elders*
8.9	chis	are	*are*
8.10	ugeg	become strong	*become strong*
8.11	dsabramg	which I have prepared for	*which prepared*
8.12	baltoha	my own righteousness,	*righteousness*
8.13	gohoiad	sayeth the Lord,	*sayeth God*
8.14	solamian	whose long continuance	*whose (long) continuance*
8.15	trian	shall be	*shall be*
8.16	talolcis	as bucklers to	*as bucklers*
8.17	abaivonin	the stooping dragons	*stooping dragons*
8.18	od	and	*and*
8.19	aziagiar	like unto the harvest of	*like unto the harvest*
8.20	rior	a widow.	*widow*
8.21	irgilchisda	How many are there	*how many are there*
8.22	dspaaox	which remain in	*which remain*
8.23	busd	the glory	*glory*
8.24	caosgo	of the earth	*of the earth*
8.25	dschis	which are	*which are*
8.26	odipuran	and shall not see	*and shall not see*
8.27	teloah	death	*death*
8.28	cacrg	until	*until*
8.29	oisalman	this house	*this house*
8.30	loncho	fall	*fall*
8.31	od	and	*and*

8.32	vovina	the dragon	*dragon*
8.33	carbaf	sink.	*sink (i.e., stoop)*
8.34	niiso	Come away,	*come away*
8.35	bagle	for	*for*
8.36	avavago	the Thunders	*Thunders*
8.37	gohon	have spoken.	*spoken*
8.38	niiso	Come away,	*come away*
8.39	bagle	for	*for*
8.40	momao	the crowns of	*crowns*
8.41	siaion	the temple	*temple*
8.42	od	and	*and*
8.43	mabza	the coat of	*coat*
8.44	iadoiasmomar	Him that is, was, and shall be crowned	*"God eternally crowned"*
8.45	poilp	are divided.	*"to divide"*
8.46	niis	Come,	*come*
8.47	zamran	appear	*appear*
8.48	ciaofi	to the terror	*terror*
8.49	caosgo	of the earth	*of earth*
8.50	od	and	*and*
8.51	bliors	to our comfort	*comfort*
8.52	od	and of	*and*
8.53	corsi	such	*such*
8.54	ta	as	*as*
8.55	abramig	are prepared.	*prepared*

Key Nine			
9.1	Micaoli	A mighty	*mighty*
9.2	bransg	guard of	*guard*
9.3	prgel	fire	*fire*
9.4	napta	with two edged swords	*swords*
9.5	ialpor	flaming	*flaming*
9.6	dsbrin	(which have	*which have*
9.7	efafafe	vials	*vials*
9.8	p	8	*8*
9.9	vonpho	of wrath	*(of) wrath*
9.10	olani	for two times	*twice*
9.11	od	and	*and*
9.12	obza	a half:	*half*
9.13	sobca	whose	*whose*
9.14	upaah	wings	*wings*
9.15	chis	are of	*are*
9.16	tatan	wormwood	*wormwood*
9.17	od	and of	*and*
9.18	tranan	the marrow of	*marrow*
9.19	balye	salt),[8]	*salt*
9.20	alar	have settled	*"to settle"*
9.21	lusda	their feet	*(their) feet*
9.22	soboln	in the west	*west*
9.23	od	and	*and*
9.24	chisholq	are measured	*are "to measure"*
9.25	cnoquodi	with their ministers	*(with) ministers*
9.26	cial	9996.	*9996*
9.27	unal	These	*these*
9.28	aldon	gather up	*"to gather"*
9.29	mom	the moss	*moss*
9.30	caosgo	of the earth	*of earth*
9.31	ta	as	*as*
9.32	lasollor	the rich man	*rich man*

9.33	gnay	doth	*doth*
9.34	limlal	his treasure:	*treasure*
9.35	amma	Cursed	*cursed*
9.36	chiis	are they	*are (they)*
9.37	sobca	whose	*whose*
9.38	madrid	iniquities	*iniquities*
9.39	z-chis	they are.	*(they) are*
9.40	ooanoan	In their eyes	*eyes*
9.41	chis	are	*are*
9.42	aviny	millstones	*millstones*
9.43	drilpi	greater than	*greater than*
9.44	caosgin	the earth	*earth*
9.45	od	and	*and*
9.46	butmoni	from their mouths	*mouths*
9.47	parm	run	*run*
9.48	zumvi	seas of	*seas*
9.49	cnila	blood:	*blood*
9.50	dazis	Their heads	*heads*
9.51	ethamz-	are covered with	*"to cover"*
9.52	achildao	diamond	*diamond*
9.53	od	and	*and*
9.54	mirc	upon	*upon*
9.55	ozol	their [hands][9]	*hands*
9.56	chis	are	*are*
9.57	pidiai	marble	*marble*
9.58	collal	sleeves.	*sleeves*
9.59	ulcinin	Happy is he	*happy*
9.60	asobam	on whom	*(on) whom*
9.61	ucim	they frown not.	*frown not (i.e., smile)*
9.62	bagle	For why?	*for*
9.63	iadbaltoh	The God of Righteousness	*God of Righteousness*
9.64	chirlan	rejoiceth	*"to rejoice"*

9.65	par	in them.	*(in) them*
9.66	niiso	Come away,	*come away*
9.67	od	and	*and*
9.68	ip	not	*not*
9.69	ofafafe	your vials.	*vials*
9.70	bagle	For	*for*
9.71	acocasb	the time	*time*
9.72	icorsca	is such as	*is such as*
9.73	unig	requireth	*"to require"*
9.74	blior	comfort.	*comfort*

Key Ten

There were many difficulties in the reception of Key Ten. The original reception of the Key on pages 130–33 of *A True and Faithful Relation* was flawed, and corrected somewhat on page 192 during the transmission of the English. However, Dee's final result in his *48 Claves Angelicae* does not match the English given in the journal. Both James and Laycock took stabs at fixing it, and Patricia Shaffer has worked on it from her unique standpoint.

The following is my own work on Key Ten. Readers who reference the *48 Claves Angelicae* will see that Dee had "Eors" listed as the word for "thousand."[10] However, this was corrected to *Matb* on page 192 of *A True and Faithful Relation* (10.45 below).

No word was originally given for "hundred," but this was also corrected on page 192 of *A True and Faithful Relation*, where the word for "hundred" was given as *Torb*. "Eors" itself does not seem to have a place in the Calls (see the Lexicon).

There is one final problem with Key Ten, and this is an odd placement of the word *Ol*. It appears in the *48 Claves Angelicae* between *Vohim gizyax*—"Mighty Earthquakes" (10.42–43 below[11]). Of course *Ol* is given as "I" in Key One, and is also given as "24" in Keys Ten and Fourteen. Neither of these translations fit within this part of Key Ten. What struck me as significant is that *Ol* as "24" is given only a few words before the "Mighty Earthquakes" portion of the Key. My current theory is that this recurrence of the word is merely a mistake (perhaps on the part of Kelley), and I have thus removed it from the Call below.

Key Ten			
10.1	Coraxo	The Thunders of Judgment and Wrath	*Thunders of Judgment and Wrath*
10.2	chis	are	*are*
10.3	cormp	numbered	*"to number"*
10.4	od	and	*and*
10.5	blans	are harboured	*"to harbor"*
10.6	lucal	in the north	*north*

10.7	aziazor	in the likeness of	*likeness of*
10.8	paeb	an oak	*oak*
10.9	soba	whose	*whose*
10.10	lilonon	branches	*branches*
10.11	chis	are	*are*
10.12	op	22	*22*
10.13	virq	nests of	*nests*
10.14	eophan	lamentation	*lamentation*
10.15	od	and	*and*
10.16	raclir	weeping	*weeping*
10.17	maasi	laid up	*stored*
10.18	bagle	for	*for*
10.19	caosgi	the earth	*earth*
10.20	ds	which	*which*
10.21	ialpon	burn	*burn*
10.22	dosig	night	*night*
10.23	od	and	*and*
10.24	basgim	day:	*day*
10.25	od	and	*and*
10.26	oxex	vomit out	*"to vomit"*
10.27	dazis	the heads of	*heads*
10.28	siatris	scorpions	*scorpions*
10.29	od	and	*and*
10.30	salbrox	live sulphur	*live sulfur*
10.31	cinxir	myngled with	*"to mingle"*
10.32	faboan	poison.	*poison*
10.33	unalchis	These be	*these are*
10.34	const	the thunders	*thunders*
10.35	ds	that	*that*
10.36	daox	5678	*5678*
10.37	cocasg	times	*times*
10.38	ol	in the 24th part of	*24th*
10.39	oanio	a moment	*moment*

10.40	yor	roar	*roar*
10.41	torb	with a hundred	*hundred*
10.42	vohim	mighty	*mighty*
10.43	gizyax	earthquakes	*earthquakes*
10.44	od	and	*and*
10.45	matb	a thousand	*thousand*
10.46	cocasg	times	*times*
10.47	plosi	as many	*as many*
10.48	molui	surges	*surges*
10.49	ds	which	*which*
10.50	pageip	rest not	*rest not*
10.51	larag	neither	*neither*
10.52	om	know	*know*
10.53	droln	any	*any*
10.54	matorb	(long)	*long*
10.55	cocasb	time	*time*
10.56	emna	here.	*here*
10.57	lpatralx	One rock	*one rock*
10.58	yolci	bringeth forth	*"to bring forth"*
10.59	matb	1000	*a thousand*
10.60	nomig	even as	*even (as)*
10.61	monons	the heart of	*heart*
10.62	olora	man	*man*
10.63	gnay	doth	*doth*
10.64	angelard	his thoughts.	*thoughts*
10.65	ohio	Woe	*woe*
10.66	ohio	woe	*woe*
10.67	ohio	woe	*woe*
10.68	ohio	woe	*woe*
10.69	ohio	woe	*woe*
10.70	ohio	woe	*woe*
10.71	noib	yea	*yes*
10.72	ohio	woe	*woe*

10.73	caosgon	be to the earth,	*unto the earth*
10.74	bagle	for	*for*
10.75	madrid	her iniquity	*iniquity*
10.76	i	is	*is*
10.77	zirop	was	*was*
10.78	chiso	and shall be	*shall be*
10.79	drilpa	great.	*great*
10.80	niiso	Come away,	*come away*
10.81	crip	but	*but*
10.82	ip	not	*not*
10.83	nidali	your noises.	*noises*

Key Eleven			
11.1	Oxiayal	The Mighty Seat	*The Mighty Seat*
11.2	holdo	groaned	*groaned*
11.3	od	and	*and*
11.4	zirom	they were	*(they) were*
11.5	o	5	*5*
11.6	coraxo	Thunders	*Thunders*
11.7	ds	which	*which*
11.8	zildar	flew into	*fly into*
11.9	raasy	the east	*east*
11.10	od	and	*and*
11.11	vabzir	the Eagle	*eagle*
11.12	camliax	spake	*spake*
11.13	od	and	*and*
11.14	bahal	cried with a loud voice,	*"to cry loudly"*
11.15	niiso	Come away!	*come away*
11.16	od	And	*and*
11.17	aldon	they gathered themselves together	*"to gather together"*
11.18	od	and	*and*
11.19	noas	became	*"to become"*
11.20	salman	the house of	*house*
11.21	teloch	death[12]	*death*
11.22	casarman	of whom	*whom*
11.23	holq	it is measured	*"to measure"*
11.24	od	and	*and*
11.25	ti	it is	*it is*
11.26	ta	as	*as*
11.27	z-chis	they are	*(they) are*
11.28	soba	whose	*whose*
11.29	cormf	number	*number*
11.30	iga	is 31.	*is 31*
11.31	niisa	Come away,	*come away*

11.32	bagle	for	*for*
11.33	abramg	I have prepared for	*"to prepare"*
11.34	noncp	you.	*you*
11.35	zacar	Move,	*move*
11.36	ca	therefore,	*therefore*
11.37	od	and	*and*
11.38	zamran	show yourselves:	*"to appear"*
11.39	odo	open	*"to open"*
11.40	cicle	the mysteries of	*mysteries*
11.41	qaa	your creation:	*creation*
11.42	zorge	Be friendly unto me:	*be friendly unto me*
11.43	lap	For	*for*
11.44	zirdo	I am	*(I) am*
11.45	noco	a servant of	*servant*
11.46	mad	the same your God:	*god*
11.47	hoath	the true worshipper of	*true worshiper*
11.48	iaida	the Highest.	*the Highest*

Key Twelve			
12.1	Nonci	O you	*you*
12.2	dsonf	that reign	*that reign*
12.3	babage	in the south	*south*
12.4	od	and	*and*
12.5	chis	are	*are*
12.6	ob	28	*28*
12.7	hubaio	the lanterns of	*lanterns*
12.8	tibibp	sorrow	*sorrow*
12.9	allar	bind up	*"to bind up"*
12.10	atraah	your girdles	*girdles*
12.11	od	and	*and*
12.12	ef	visit us.	*"to visit"*
12.13	drix	Bring down	*"to bring down"*
12.14	fafen	your train	*train*
12.15	mian	3663	*3663*
12.16	ar	that	*that*
12.17	enay	the Lord	*the Lord*
12.18	ovof	may be magnified	*"to magnify"*
12.19	soba	whose	*whose*
12.20	dooain	name	*name*
12.21	aai	amongst you	*amongst*
12.22	ivonph	is wrath.	*is wrath*
12.23	zacar	Move,	*move*
12.24	gohus	I say,[13]	*I say*
12.25	od	and	*and*
12.26	zamran	show yourselves:	*"to appear"*
12.27	odo	open	*"to open"*
12.28	cicle	the mysteries of	*mysteries*
12.29	qaa	your creation:	*creation*
12.30	zorge	Be friendly unto me:	*be friendly unto me*
12.31	lap	For	*for*
12.32	zirdo	I am	*(I) am*

12.33	noco	a servant of	*servant*
12.34	mad	the same your God:	*god*
12.35	hoath	the true worshipper of	*true worshiper*
12.36	iaida	the Highest.	*the Highest*

Key Thirteen			
13.1	Napeai	O you swords of	*swords*
13.2	babagen	the south	*south*
13.3	dsbrin	which have	*which have*
13.4	ux	42	*42*
13.5	ooaona	eyes	*eyes*
13.6	lring	to stir up	*to stir up*
13.7	vonph	wrath of	*wrath*
13.8	doalim	sin,	*sin*
13.9	eolis	making	*"to make"*
13.10	ollog	men	*men*
13.11	orsba	drunken	*drunken*
13.12	dschis	which are	*which are*
13.13	affa	empty:	*empty*
13.14	micma	Behold	*behold*
13.15	isro	the promise of	*promise of*
13.16	mad	God	*god*
13.17	od	and	*and*
13.18	lonshitox	His power	*his power*
13.19	ds	which	*which*
13.20	iumd	is called	*(is) called*
13.21	aai[14]	amongst you	*amongst*
13.22	grosb	a bitter sting.	*(bitter) sting*
13.23	zacar	Move	*move*
13.24	od	and	*and*
13.25	zamran	show yourselves:	*"to appear"*
13.26	odo	open	*"to open"*
13.27	cicle	the mysteries of	*mysteries*
13.28	qaa	your creation:	*creation*
13.29	zorge	Be friendly unto me:	*be friendly unto me*
13.30	lap	For	*for*
13.31	zirdo	I am	*(I) am*
13.32	noco	a servant of	*servant*

13.33	mad	the same your God:	*god*
13.34	hoath	the true worshipper of	*true worshiper*
13.35	iaida	the Highest.	*the Highest*

The transmission of Key Fourteen is missing from Dee's journals. We only have the English for this Key given later (see *TFR*, page 193), and the Angelical provided in Dee's *48 Claves Angelicae*.

Key Fourteen			
14.1	Noromi	O you sons	*sons*
14.2	bagie	of fury,	*fury*
14.3	pasbs	the daughters	*daughters*
14.4	oiad	of the just,	*of God*
14.5	ds	which	*which*
14.6	trint	sit	*"to sit"*
14.7	mirc	upon	*upon*
14.8	ol	24	*24*
14.9	thil	seats	*seats*
14.10	dods	vexing	*"to vex"*
14.11	tolham	all creatures	*all creatures*
14.12	caosgo	of the earth	*of earth*
14.13	homin	with age,	*age*
14.14	dsbrin	which have	*which have*
14.15	oroch	under you	*under*
14.16	quar	1636.	*1636*
14.17	micma	Behold	*behold*
14.18	bial	the voice	*voice*
14.19	oiad	of God	*of God*
14.20	aisro	promise of	*"to promise"*
14.21	tox	him	*him*
14.22	dsium	which is called	*which (is) called*
14.23	aai	amongst you	*amongst*
14.24	baltim	fury, or extreme justice.	*extreme justice (fury)*
14.25	zacar	Move	*move*
14.26	od	and	*and*
14.27	zamran	show yourselves:	*"to appear"*
14.28	odo	open	*"to open"*

14.29	cicle	the mysteries of	*mysteries*
14.30	qaa	your creation:	*creation*
14.31	zorge	Be friendly unto me:	*be friendly unto me*
14.32	lap	For	*for*
14.33	zirdo	I am	*(I) am*
14.34	noco	a servant of	*servant*
14.35	mad	the same your God:	*god*
14.36	hoath	the true worshipper of	*true worshiper*
14.37	iaida	the Highest.	*the Highest*

The transmission of Key Fifteen is missing from Dee's journals. We only have the English for this Key given later (see *TFR*, page 193), and the Angelical provided in Dee's *48 Claves Angelicae.*

Key Fifteen			
15.1	Yls	O thou	*thou*
15.2	tabaan	the governor of	*governor*
15.3	lialprt	the first flame	*first flame*
15.4	casarman	under whose	*(under) whose*
15.5	upaahi	wings	*wings*
15.6	chis	are	*are*
15.7	darg	6739	*6739*
15.8	dsoado	which weave	*which weave*
15.9	caosgi	the earth	*earth*
15.10	orscor	with dryness	*dryness*
15.11	ds	which	*which*
15.12	omax	knowest	*knowest*
15.13	monasci	the great name	*great name*
15.14	baeovib	righteousness	*righteousness*
15.15	od	and	*and*
15.16	emetgis	the seal of	*seal*
15.17	iaiadix	honour.	*honor*
15.18	zacar	Move,	*move*
15.19	od	and	*and*
15.20	zamran	show yourselves:	*"to appear"*
15.21	odo	open	*"to open"*
15.22	cicle	the mysteries of	*mysteries*
15.23	qaa	your creation:	*creation*
15.24	zorge	Be friendly unto me:	*be friendly unto me*
15.25	lap	For	*for*
15.26	zirdo	I am	*(I) am*
15.27	noco	a servant of	*servant*
15.28	mad	the same your God:	*god*
15.29	hoath	the true worshipper of	*true worshiper*
15.30	iaida	the Highest.	*the Highest*

Key Sixteen			
16.1	Yls[15]	O thou	*thou*
16.2	vivialprt	of the second flame[16]	*second flame*
16.3	salman	the house of	*house*
16.4	balt	justice	*justice*
16.5	ds	which	*which*
16.6	acroodzi	hast thy beginning	*beginning*
16.7	busd	in glory	*glory*
16.8	od	and	*and*
16.9	bliorax	shalt comfort	*"to comfort"*
16.10	balit	the just:	*the just*
16.11	dsinsi	which walkest upon	*which walk*
16.12	caosg	the earth	*earth*
16.13	lusdan	with feet	*feet*
16.14	emod	8763	*8763*
16.15	dsom	that understand	*that understand*
16.16	od	and	*and*
16.17	tliob	separate creatures:	*"to classify creatures"*
16.18	drilpa	Great	*great*
16.19	geh	art	*are*
16.20	yls	thou	*thou*
16.21	madzilodarp	in the God of stretch forth and conquer.	*God of conquest*
16.22	zacar	Move	*move*
16.23	od	and	*and*
16.24	zamran	show yourselves:	*"to appear"*
16.25	odo	open	*"to open"*
16.26	cicle	the mysteries of	*mysteries*
16.27	qaa	your creation:	*creation*
16.28	zorge	Be friendly unto me:	*be friendly unto me*
16.29	lap	For	*for*
16.30	zirdo	I am	*(I) am*
16.31	noco	a servant of	*servant*

16.32	mad	the same your God:	*god*
16.33	hoath	the true worshipper of	*true worshiper*
16.34	iaida	the Highest.	*the Highest*

Key Seventeen			
17.1	Yls	O thou	*thou*
17.2	dialprt	third flame	*third flame*
17.3	soba	whose	*whose*
17.4	upaah	wings	*wings*
17.5	chis	are	*are*
17.6	nanba	thorns	*thorns*
17.7	zixlay	to stir up	*to stir up*
17.8	dodsih	vexation	*vexation*
17.9	odbrint	and hast	*and has*
17.10	taxs	*7336*	*7336*
17.11	hubaro	lamps living	*(burning) lamps*
17.12	tastax	going before	*"to precede"*
17.13	ylsi	thee.	*thee*
17.14	sobaiad	Whose God	*whose God*
17.15	ivonpovnph	is wrath in anger.	*is "wrath of wrath"*
17.16	aldon	Gird up	*"to gather"*
17.17	daxil	thy loins	*your loins*
17.18	od	and	*and*
17.19	toatar	harken.	*"to listen"*
17.20	zacar	Move,	*move*
17.21	od	and	*and*
17.22	zamran	show yourselves:	*"to appear"*
17.23	odo	open	*"to open"*
17.24	cicle	the mysteries of	*mysteries*
17.25	qaa	your creation:	*creation*
17.26	zorge	Be friendly unto me:	*be friendly unto me*
17.27	lap	For	*for*
17.28	zirdo	I am	*(I) am*
17.29	noco	a servant of	*servant*
17.30	mad	the same your God:	*god*
17.31	hoath	the true worshipper of	*true worshiper*
17.32	iaida	the Highest.	*the Highest*

Key Eighteen			
18.1	Yls	O thou	*thou*
18.2	micalzo	mighty	*mighty*
18.3	ialpirt	light and	*light*
18.4	ialprg	burning flame of	*burning flame*
18.5	bliors	comfort	*comfort*
18.6	ds	which	*which*
18.7	odo	openest	*"to open"*
18.8	busdir	the glory	*glory*
18.9	oiad	of God	*of God*
18.10	ovoars	to the center	*center*
18.11	caosgo	of the earth.	*of the earth*
18.12	casarmg	In whom	*in whom*
18.13	laiad	the secrets of truth	*secrets of truth*
18.14	eran	6332	*6332*
18.15	brints	have	*have*
18.16	casasam	their abiding	*abiding*
18.17	ds	which	*which*
18.18	iumd	is called	*(is) called*
18.19	aqlo	in thy	*thy*
18.20	adohi	kingdom	*kingdom*
18.21	moz	joy,	*joy*
18.22	od	and	*and*
18.23	maoffas	not to be measured.	*"measureless"*
18.24	bolp	Be thou	*(be) thou*
18.25	comobliort	a window of comfort	*window of comfort*
18.26	pambt	unto me.	*unto (me)*
18.27	zacar	Move	*move*
18.28	od	and	*and*
18.29	zamran	show yourselves:	*"to appear"*
18.30	odo	open	*"to open"*
18.31	cicle	the mysteries of	*mysteries*
18.32	qaa	your creation:	*creation*

18.33	zorge	Be friendly unto me:	*be friendly unto me*
18.34	lap	For	*for*
18.35	zirdo	I am	*(I) am*
18.36	noco	a servant of	*servant*
18.37	mad	the same your God:	*god*
18.38	hoath	the true worshipper of	*true worshiper*
18.39	iaida	the Highest.	*the Highest*

The Key of the Aethyrs			
30.1	Madriiax	O you heavens	*heavens*
30.2	dspraf	which dwell in	*which dwell*
30.3	[Lil]	[the First Aethyr]	*[the First Aethyr]*
30.4	chismicaolz	are mighty in	*are mighty*
30.5	saanir	the parts	*parts*
30.6	caosgo	of the earth,	*of the earth*
30.7	od	and	*and*
30.8	fisis	execute	*"to execute"*
30.9	balzizras	the judgment of	*judgment*
30.10	iaida	the Highest.	*the Highest*
30.11	nonca	To you	*(to) you*
30.12	gohulim	it is said,	*(it is) said*
30.13	micma	Behold	*behold*
30.14	adoian	the face of	*face*
30.15	mad	your God,	*god*
30.16	iaod	the beginning of	*beginning*
30.17	bliorb	comfort:	*comfort*
30.18	sabaooaona	whose eyes	*whose eyes*
30.19	chis	are	*are*
30.20	luciftias	the brightness of	*brightness*
30.21	piripsol	the heavens:	*heavens*
30.22	ds	which	*which*
30.23	abraassa	provided	*"to provide"*
30.24	noncf	you	*you*
30.25	netaaib	for the government of	*government*
30.26	caosgi	the earth,	*earth*
30.27	od	and	*and*
30.28	tilb	her	*her*
30.29	adphaht	unspeakable	*unspeakable*
30.30	damploz	variety	*variety*
30.31	tooat	furnishing	*"to furnish"*

30.32	noncf	you	*you*
30.33	gmicalzoma	with a power (of) understanding	*power of understanding*
30.34	lrasd	to dispose	*to dispose*
30.35	tofglo	all things	*all (things)*
30.36	marb	according to	*according to*
30.37	yarry	the providence of	*providence*
30.38	Idoigo	Him that sitteth upon the Holy Throne	*Him who sits upon the Holy Throne*
30.39	od	and	*and*
30.40	torzulp	rose up	*"to rise"*
30.41	iaodaf	in the beginning	*(in the) beginning*
30.42	gohol	saying,	*"to say"*
30.43	caosga	The earth	*earth*
30.44	tabaord	let her be governed by	*be governed*
30.45	saanir	her parts	*parts*
30.46	od	and	*and*
30.47	christeos	let there be	*let there be*
30.48	yrpoil	division	*division*
30.49	tiobl	in her,	*(within) her*
30.50	busdirtilb	that the glory of her	*glory (of) her*
30.51	noaln	may be	*may be*
30.52	paid	always	*always*
30.53	orsba	drunken	*drunken*
30.54	od	and	*and*
30.55	dodrmni	vexed	*vexed*
30.56	zilna	in itself:	*(within) itself*
30.57	elzaptilb	Her course	*her course*
30.58	parmgi	let it run with	*(let) run*
30.59	piripsax	the heavens	*heavens*
30.60	od	and	*and*

30.61	ta	as	*as*
30.62	qurlst	a handmaid	*handmaid*
30.63	booapis	let her serve them:	*"to serve"*
30.64	lnibm	One season	*one season*
30.65	oucho	let it confound	*"to confound"*
30.66	symp	another:	*another*
30.67	od	and	*and*
30.68	christeos	let there be	*let there be*
30.69	agtoltorn	no creature	*no creature*
30.70	mirc	upon	*upon*
30.71	q	or	*or*
30.72	tiobl	within her	*(within) her*
30.73	lel	the same:	*same*
30.74	ton	All	*all*
30.75	paombd	her members	*members*
30.76	dilzmo	let them differ in	*"to differ"*
30.77	aspian	their qualities:	*qualties*
30.78	od	And	*and*
30.79	christeos	let there be	*let there be*
30.80	agltoltorn	no one creature	*no one creature*
30.81	parach	equal with	*equal*
30.82	asymp	another.	*another*
30.83	cordziz	The reasonable creatures of earth, or men	*"mankind"*
30.84	dodpal	let them vex	*"to vex"*
30.85	od	and	*and*
30.86	fifalz	weed out	*weed out*
30.87	lsmnad	one another:	*one another*
30.88	od	And	*and*
30.89	fargt	the dwelling places,	*dwelling places*
30.90	bams	let them forget	*"to forget"*
30.91	omaoas	their names.	*names*

30.92	conisbra	The work of man	*work of man*
30.93	od	and	*and*
30.94	avavox	his pomp,	*his pomp*
30.95	tonug	let them be defaced:	*"to deface"*
30.96	orscatbl	His buildings,	*buildings*
30.97	noasmi	let them become	*(let) become*
30.98	tabges	caves for	*caves*
30.99	levithmong	the beasts of the field:	*beasts of the field*
30.100	unchi	Confound	*"to confound"*
30.101	omptilb	her understanding with	*her understanding*
30.102	ors	darkness	*darkness*
30.103	bagle	For why?	*for*
30.104	moooah	It repenteth me	*"to repent"*
30.105	olcordziz	I made man.	*made mankind*
30.106	lcapimao	One while	*one while*
30.107	ixomaxip	let her be known,	*let her be known*
30.108	odcacocasb	and another while	*and another while*
30.109	gosaa	a stranger:	*stranger*
30.110	baglen	Because	*because*
30.111	pii	she is	*she is*
30.112	tianta	the bed of	*bed*
30.113	ababalond	an harlot,	*harlot*
30.114	odfaorgt	and the dwelling place of	*and the dwelling place*
30.115	telocvovim	him that is fallen:	*"death dragon"*
30.116	madriiax	O you heavens	*heavens*
30.117	torzu	arise,	*arise*
30.118	oadriax	the lower heavens	*lower heavens*
30.119	orocha	beneath you,	*beneath*
30.120	aboapri	let them serve you:	*"to serve"*
30.121	tabaori	govern	*"to govern"*

30.122	priaz	those	*those*
30.123	artabas	that govern:	*that govern*
30.124	adrpan	Cast down	*cast down*
30.125	corsta	such as	*such as*
30.126	dobix	fall.	*"to fall"*
30.127	yolcam	Bring forth with	*"to bring forth"*
30.128	priazi	those	*those*
30.129	arcoazior	that increase:	*that increase*
30.130	odquasb	And destroy	*and destroy*
30.131	qting	the rotten:	*rotten*
30.132	ripir	No place	*no place*
30.133	paaoxt	let it remain	*"to remain"*
30.134	sagacor	in one number:	*in one number*
30.135	uml	Add	*"to add"*
30.136	od	and	*and*
30.137	prdzar	diminish	*"to diminish"*
30.138	cacrg	until	*until*
30.139	aoiveae	the stars	*stars*
30.140	cormpt	be numbered:	*(are) numbered*
30.141	torzu	Arise,	*arise*
30.142	zacar	move,	*move*
30.143	odzamran	and appear	*"to appear"*
30.144	aspt	before	*before*
30.145	sibsi	the covenant of	*covenant*
30.146	butmona	his mouth	*mouth*
30.147	ds	which	*which*
30.148	surzas	he hath sworn	*"to swear"*
30.149	tia	unto us	*unto (us)*
30.150	baltan	in his justice:	*justice*
30.151	odo	Open	*"to open"*
30.152	cicle	the mysteries of	*mysteries*
30.153	qaa	your creation:	*creation*
30.154	od	and	*and*

30.155	ozazma	make us	*"to make"*
30.156	plapli	partakers of	*partakers*
30.157	iadnamad	undefiled knowl-edge.	*pure knowledge*

Endnotes

1. *A True and Faithful Relation*, p. 79ff.
2. See Sloane MS 3191. James' *Enochian Magick of Dr. John Dee* is derived from this same grimoire.
3. See the Introduction to volume I of this work.
4. There is no indication of the word *beginning* in the Angelical here.
5. Dee had the word *to* in this place. However, the word *and* makes more sense. Remember, however, that neither *to* nor *and* (*Od*) are indicated in the Angelical. They are implied only by context.
6. There is no indication of the word *second* in this Angelical.
7. The word *garnish* (*Gnonp*) does not appear in this place.
8. Parentheses are Dee's.
9. Dee had *heads* in this place. However, the Angelical indicates *hands* instead, and that makes more sense in the Call.
10. *The Enochian Magic of Dr. John Dee*, by Geoffrey James, p. 85.
11. And James p. 85.
12. The English for words 11.16–18 is found in *A True and Faithful Relation*, p. 193. Dee noted that no Angelical had been given in the Key for (all of) those words, so he went back and added words 11.16 and 18 (*Od*) and 11.19 (*Noas*).
13. Note this departure from the Repetitive Formula Pattern (see the Lexicon). This addition of *Gohus* ("I Say!") is found in *A True and Faithful Relation*, p. 136.
14. Words 13.21–22 are missing from *TFR*. We have only the English given for them later (see *TFR*, p. 193), and we find the Angelical in Dee's *48 Claves*.
15. The first twelve words of this Key are missing from *TFR*. We have only the English given for them later (see *TFR*, p. 193), and we find the Angelical in Dee's *48 Claves*.
16. The Angel Illemese gives this English in *A True and Faithful Relation*, p. 200, adding *of the*.

Chapter Three

An Encyclopedic Lexicon of the Tongue of Angels

How to Use This Lexicon

I will illustrate here how to use this Lexicon with a few examples. First, a standard entry looks like this:

Busdir (buz-der) *n.* Glory

18.8 . . . openest *the glory* of God.

As we can see, the main entry appears in bold type. Immediately following that, in parentheses, is the word's pronunciation—given in a special key included in this chapter.

Following that is the grammatical function or part of speech (noun, verb, conjunction, and so on). Note that these designations are somewhat loose in Angelical. There are cases where a word might appear as different parts of speech depending on how it is used—such as the English word *promise*, which could be a noun (as in *a promise*) or a verb (*to promise*), although the Angelical does not indicate the difference by anything more than the context of the sentence. In such cases, I have generally applied the part of speech that matches its usage in the sentence in question. In several cases, I have suggested more than one part of speech for a given word.

Next is the definition—or "English sense"—of the word. See the "Angelical Linguistics" chapter for discussion about English senses and fluid definitions.

Then, to the extreme right of the page, we see the word spelled in Angelical characters (running right to left). Note that these characters will not always match the English letters given for the same word. This is due to what I call "phonetic glosses" utilized by Dee as he recorded the words. (Also see the "Angelical Linguistics" chapter for a full discussion of Dee's phonetic glosses.)

Finally, we have the cross-reference number indicating in which Key the word appears and the position of that word within the Key, followed by a sample of the sentence in which the word is used. (The English words indicated by the Angelical are in italics.) This allows one to see at a glance exactly how the word is used in the Keys, which is how we know its proper part of speech.

Following is an example of a compound word entry:

Busdirtilb (buz-der-tilb) [*Busdir* + *Tilb*] *comp.* Glory (of) Her

30.50 . . . that *the glory of her* may be . . .

This entry is the same as a standard entry, with one addition: the word elements that make up the compound are included in brackets directly after the pronunciation. These word elements will each have their own entries in the Lexicon, pointing back to the compound word itself.

There are three further types of entries to cover here. First, the main entry may appear in italics:

Iusmach (jus-mak) *v.* To Beget

The italics indicate that the word comes from a source other than the forty-eight Angelical Keys—such as words from *Loagaeth*, words from the *Corpus Omnium* (see chapter 3 in volume I), the names of the Angelical letters, words from the Alchemical Cipher the Angels gave to Dee, random words spoken by the Angels, and so on. These entries will always include a reference note explaining where the word comes from. (Also see the "Sources for All Words Found in This Lexicon" section of this chapter for a list of sources used to compile this Lexicon.)

Second, the main entry may appear in ALL CAPS:

PERAL (pee-AR-al) *69636*

30.50 . . . lamps *6936* whose numbers are. . .

These entries indicate an apparent word in the forty-eight Angelical Keys that, in translation, is defined as a grouping of numbers. Because of this ambiguity, I have indicated these words with ALL CAPS.

Third, the main entry may appear in quotation marks:

"Azia" (ay-ZII-ay) *prep.* Like (unto)

Compounds:

Aziagiar (ay-zii-AY-jii-er)
[*"Azia" + "Giar"*] Like unto the Harvest

This indicates a "word element." Most often, this is an element of a compound word, and the entry will point back to the compound itself. Such entries are in quotation marks because compounding often changes the spelling of the words (see the "Angelical Linguistics" chapter). Therefore, when they stand alone, both the spelling and the pronunciation of such word elements are suspect.

Searching out these "word elements" from the mass of known Angelical words represents a significant expansion of our previous understanding of the language. Although we can't be sure of their spelling and forms of proper usage, it offers us a solid foundation from which to explore the language deeper. At the very least, it definitely expands the available data in hunting for the root forms of the words.

Of course, sometimes compounds are made from words that appear elsewhere in the Keys on their own. In such cases, we know how such words are spelled and pronounced, so their entries do not appear in quotation marks. Their entries will, however, point to the compound as well.

Finally, here are the explanations of the various sections you will find within each main entry:

Pronunciation Notes

The pronunciation notes are perhaps the most unique and useful aspect of this Lexicon. While Dee included small phonetic notes with most of the words he recorded, modern students have found them less than useful. (Remember John Dee was writing in Early Modern English, which often confuses modern students.) Because of this, most existing "Enochian dictionaries" pay little attention to Dee's notations, and the authors have provided pronunciations based loosely upon their own understanding of present-day English.

On the other hand, I have spent some time deciphering Dee's notes on their own terms. His notations seem to be rather haphazard for the first two Keys, but he settles into a fairly standard format by the end of Key Two. My analysis of this format has led me to the following assumptions:

1) Dee generally divided his phonetic notes by placing spaces between the syllables.
2) A letter that stands alone in a syllable takes its long sound. For instance, an *a* standing alone will sound like "ay," an *l* standing alone will sound like "el," etc. Otherwise:
3) Vowels take their long or short sounds depending on their position within a syllable. If a vowel appears at the end of the syllable, it usually takes the long sound. If it appears in the middle of a syllable (i.e., it is directly followed by a consonant within the same syllable), it will most often take the short sound. Finally:
4) The general rules of Early Modern English apply overall, although there are some Middle English inclusions as well. (Again, see the "Angelical Linguistics" chapter for more information.)

I have arrived at the above assumptions primarily with the aid of marginal notations left by Dee along with his phonetic notes—which often gave examples of other words that rhymed with a given Angelical word or syllable. He also used several useful phonetic notations in the *48 Claves Angelicae* that further backed up my research.

In this Lexicon, I have included *all* of Dee's phonetic notes from his journals. If he left such a note (or notes) for a word, I have indicated it by adding an asterisk (*) to the word's pronunciation. Then, within the "Pronunciation Notes" section of the entry, I have recorded Dee's note (*in italics*) and followed it with my own explanation.

The bulk of these notes are found in *A True and Faithful Relation*, recorded as Dee received the forty-eight Angelical Keys. (Much thanks goes to Patricia Shaffer, who tirelessly gathered all of Dee's *TFR* notes into one document, entitled *DeesPronunciationNotes.RTF.*) Therefore, I do not include references with these notes, as the word is already cross-referenced by Key.

However, Dee also left pronunciation notes in the *Five Books of Mystery* and the *48 Claves Angelicae*. If such secondary notes exist, I have also included them and referenced their sources.

If Dee did not include any notes for a word, I have given a pronunciation based upon my overall study of the language. If I include a pronunciation note in such an entry, it is only to explain my own work, and there will be no asterisk or reference to Dee's journals.

"Also" and Shared Root

Angelical words are formed primarily of small root words that undergo (often inexplicable) metamorphosis when used in different ways. Therefore, most of the entries in the Lexicon include notes that compare the main word with other words from Dee's journals. This helps us discover the Angelical roots at the hearts of the words.

First and foremost is the "Also" section found in most entries, which points out all of the differing "versions" of the same word in the Lexicon.

Some entries also have a "Shared root" section, to indicate differing words that may share a linguistic root. (This is based upon both similar spellings and similar definitions.) In these cases, I will likely include a notation highlighting the probable root.

Other Notes

Sometimes Dee also left notes about the definition of a word. If so, the definition in this Lexicon will include an asterisk (*), and the word's entry will include a "Note" section with Dee's comment (*in italics*). I then include my own comments directly thereafter.

In many cases, I have comments to make on a word where Dee was silent. At such times, there will be no asterisk or italics, but my own notes will appear in the "Note" section. There may be more than one "Note" section for any given entry.

Compare from *Loagaeth*

Finally, some entires include a "Compare from *Loagaeth*" section. This is drawn from my work on the first Table of the Holy Book—which is the only Table containing entire words in each cell, rather than single letters. I believe this was intended primarily to help us decipher the words in the remaining forty-eight Tables.

My work on this first Table was similar to my earlier work on the Angelical Keys. I simply began with the first word on the first side of the Table (which happens to be *Zuresch*), and compared it with every other word in the Table. (Remember there are nearly 4802 words in total! See the chapter on the *Book of Loagaeth* in volume I.) I then moved to the second word in the Table and repeated the same process, and so on.

In fact, my work on the first Table is still ongoing, and I will present my results at a future date. Meanwhile, I have discovered several words in *Loagaeth* that also appear in the Keys, as well as many words that appear linguistically related to words from the Keys. I have also found the names of several Angelical letters and one or two known "Enochian" Angels. These *Loagaeth* words that are recognizably similar or identical to those in this *Lexicon* are included in the "Compare from *Loagaeth*" section. (This helps to illustrate that the language of the Holy Book is not separate from the language of the forty-eight Keys.)

Abbreviations Used in This Lexicon

1 Enoch	= The Ethiopic Book of Enoch
Five Books	= *John Dee's Five Books of Mystery*
48 Claves	= *48 Claves Angelicae* (from Sloane 3191)

RFP	= Repetitive Formula Pattern (*See note)
TFR	= *A True and Faithful Relation . . .*
adj.	= adjective
adv.	= adverb
comp.	= compound
conj.	= conjunction
n.	= noun
pl.	= plural
prep.	= preposition
pron.	= pronoun
prop. n.	= proper noun
sing.	= singular
v.	= verb

*Note on *RFP*: From Keys Eleven to Eighteen, Dee was instructed to append the last fourteen words of Key One—*Zacar, ca, od zamran. Odo cicle qaa. Zorge, lap zirdo noco mad, hoath Iaida.* This was dubbed the "Repetitive Formula Pattern" by Patricia Shaffer. In the Lexicon, each word that appears in the Repetitive Formula Pattern is simply marked *RFP*, instead of listing out all references for the word in Keys One and Eleven to Eighteen. *RFP* words will always be found within the last fourteen words of each of these nine Keys.

Note, however, that the final words of these Keys do differ in some minor details in Dee's *48 Claves Angelicae*. (For example, see the *RFP* at the end of Key Twelve.) When this occurs, I have stuck with the *48 Claves* as Dee's final say.

Sources for All Words Found in This Lexicon

The Angelical Keys are found in *TFR* on pages 79–138, 190–194, and 199–208. They are also found in Dee's *48 Claves Angelicae*, part of Sloane MS 3191. The words from the *48 Claves* are shown in the third column of Geoffrey James' section on the Keys in *The Enochian Magick of Dr. John Dee*, p. 65ff.

The names of the thirty Aethyrs are all found on page 209 of *TFR*. The names of the ninety-one Parts of the Earth are found on pages 140–152 of *TFR*. However, they are also found in Dee's Angelical grimoire (which he compiled from his raw journals), known as Sloane MS 3191 (specifically, part II: *The Book of Earthly Knowledge, Aid, and Victory*). Dee did some corrective editing of the Parts' names as he transferred them from his journals to the grimoire. I have opted to stick with his corrected versions. (See James' *The Enochian Magick of Dr. John Dee*, pages 103–116.)

The words of the *Corpus Omnium* are all found on pages 74–76 of *TFR*.

The names of the twenty-one Angelical letters are found on pages 269–271 of the *Five Books*. Their perfected forms are found in Kelley's handwriting at the end of *Loagaeth* (Sloane 3189)—see the *Five Books*, page 405.

The words of the Alchemical Cipher are found on pages 387–389 of *TFR*.

Words from the first ("hidden") leaf of *Loagaeth* are found on pages 288–343 of the *Five Books*. Those from the final leaf are found on page 19 of *TFR*. I have only taken words from the first and final Tables, the only two that contain entire words in each cell.

Exclusions from This Lexicon

I have been selective with the proper nouns I have included in the Lexicon. There are, by necessity, entries for names of God and Angels that appear in the forty-eight Angelical Keys. I have also included any names that appear in *Loagaeth*, as well as those Angels who are found only in Dee's journals (such as *Galvah*, *Murifri*, *Nalvage*, *Vasedg*, and so on).

However, you will not find entries for most of the proper names—of God, Angels, and spirits—found in the magickal squares Dee received in his advanced Angelic magick (namely, The *Heptarchia*, Parts of the Earth, and Great Table of the Earth—or Watchtower systems). I have used the Lexicon to analyze these proper names, and I have included references where I find similarities. (For example, see the entry for *Laiad*, which seems to be the root for the name of the Elder *Laidrom* from the Southern Watchtower.)

The ninety-one Parts of the Earth are not given their own entries, but you can find them included within the entries of their associated

Aethyrs. (The Aethyrs are included because they are named successively in the last thirty Keys.)

Finally, I have also excluded the thousands of undefined words in the Tables of *Loagaeth*. However, I have included the few words that were given definitions, that are identical to words already found in the Keys, or that appear linguistically similar to words from the Keys. (See the "Compare from *Loagaeth*" section above.) As stated previously, I will present my work with the undefined words of *Loagaeth* in a later work.

Pronunciation Key (Fully Explained)

Based on my studies of Dee's records (see the "Pronunciation Notes" section), I have offered pronunciations for almost every word in the Lexicon. You may notice that this key is very different from the pronunciation guides we normally see for the "Enochian" language. Most often, such guides are alphabetical—meaning that they present the Angelical (or English-equivalent) letters, and then suggest what sounds these letters might make *individually*. While it is good to know what sound each letter makes, it tells us little about what sounds are made when the letters are combined into actual syllables and words.

My pronunciation guide, on the other hand, is entirely phonetic. It begins with the sounds that make up the *syllables*. Then, it presents the phonetic notations I have created to represent those sounds. These notations are intended to be simple and intuitive to the modern reader.

Vowels

Short vowels are mostly represented by single letters, while I have extended the long vowels to two letters:

Phonetic Sound	-	*Notation*
a –long (*cake, day*)	-	ay
a –short (*bat, cat*)	-	a
e –long (*beet, seat*)	-	ee
e –short (*bed, wed*)	-	e
i –long (*bite, kite*)	-	ii
i –short (*bit, sit*)	-	i
o –long (*boat, slope*)	-	oh

o –short (*bot, stop, father*)	-	o, ah
u –long (*boot, blue*)	-	oo
u –short (*but, cup*)	-	u

Note: There are some cases where an *a* falls at the end of a word. I feel this likely indicates something between a long and short *a*—or a *schwa*. In such cases, I have simply left a single *a* in my pronunciation. It can be treated as a short *a*, but it is more akin to a schwa sound. (I assume Dee, had he intended the long "a" sound, would have ended the words with *ay* or *eh*.) For example, the word *Amma* (Cursed) likely ends with a sound somewhere in between the long and short *a* (schwa)—"am-a."

Consonants

If consonants are written together (as in *br, cr, gr, st, th*, and *tr*), simply pronounce the combined sound as you would in present-day English (*break, crate, grab, start*, and so forth). Otherwise, standard consonant sounds are indicated by the following:

Phonetic Sound	-	*Notation*
b (*branch, blurb*)	-	b
d (*dog, during*)	-	d
f (*far, fork*)	-	f
g (*gap, gourd*)	-	g
h (*half, heavy*)	-	h
j (*jump, giant, bludgeon*)	-	j
k (*kind, can*)	-	k
l (*large, loud*)	-	l
m (*many, move*)	-	m
n (*north, never*)	-	n
p (*pace, pardon*)	-	p
r (*rain, banner*)	-	r, er
s (*serve, circle*)	-	s
t (*test, tax*)	-	t
w (*water, wind*)	-	w
x (*exit, except*)	-	ks
y (*yellow, your*)	-	y
z (*zoom, zebra*)	-	z

"Long Consonants"

There are many cases where Dee indicated a consonant standing alone in a syllable. At these times, the letter does not make its usual consonant sound. Instead, the syllable is pronounced the same as the English name of the consonant. I have dubbed these "long consonants" (see the "General Notes on Angelical Phonology" section of the "Angelical Linguistics" chapter), and I represent their sounds as follows:

Phonetic Sound	-	*Notation*
d	-	dee
f	-	ef
g	-	jee
j	-	jay
l	-	el
m	-	em
n	-	en
p	-	pee
q	-	kwah
r	-	ur
s	-	es
t	-	tee
y	-	wii
z	-	zohd, zed

Digraphs and Diphthongs

The digraphs and diphthongs are fairly standard in modern English:

Phonetic Sound	-	*Notation*
ch (church, witch)	-	ch
ch (ache, chrome)	-	kh
ou, ow (out, town)	-	ow
oi, oy (oil, boy)	-	oy
qu (queen, quick)	-	kw
sh (shine, wish)	-	sh
ph (phone, philosophy)	-	f
th (that, whither, thorn)	-	th

Also Note

There are a few instances when the letters *sg* occur in Angelical words—such as *Caosg* or *Vorsg*. In these cases, Dee does not indicate that the "g" sound should stand alone as its own syllable. Thus, I find it likely it is intended to combine with the *s* to make a kind of "zh" (or hard "sh") sound—as we hear in English words like *measure*, *pleasure*, and *treasure*. I have indicated this sound in the Psalter and Lexicon with the digraph *zh*.

Accented Syllables

Dee included accent marks throughout the *48 Claves Angelicae* and *A True and Faithful Relation*. I have indicated these accents in my pronunciations by writing the related syllable in ALL CAPS. For instance, the word *Cacacom* (To Flourish) is recorded in the *48 Claves* as *ca-cá-com*. In the Lexicon, I have given the pronunciation of "kay-SAY-som"—showing an accent on the second syllable.

Dee did not record accents for all of the Angelical words. Yet many of the unaccented words are closely related to accented versions, so we can make educated guesses. For example, Dee left no accent marks for the word *Bliorax* (To Comfort). However, he did indicate—in both the *48 Claves* and *TFR*—that *Bliora* (Comfort) should be accented on the second syllable. Therefore, we can make an educated guess that *Bloriax* should also be accented on the second syllable.

I have included these speculative accents where I could, and noted my reasoning for each. In cases where no clues at all were left by Dee, I have avoided making uneducated guesses. Plus, only in rare cases have I adopted an accent from an uncompounded word into a compounded word, or vice versa. As discussed in the chapter on Angelical linguistics, compounding often drastically changes the pronunciation of the word —and Dee's notes indicate that this includes accented syllables as well.

Angelical Root Words

I have discussed the nature of Angelical root words in the chapter on Angelical linguistics. For the most part, these simple letter combinations are three to four letters in length, although there are some rare examples of one-letter or two-letter root words.

Below, I have included a list of root words I have found through analysis of the Lexicon. This list is not intended as concrete or exhaustive. Some of the entries are tentative at best, and I admit there could be any number of roots that I have missed or failed to recognize.

Moreover, I have included in this section mostly those roots that do not stand as words on their own. There are other Angelical words that appear to be in their root form (such as *Mal* or *Ror*) that do stand as words on their own. Such words have their own Lexicon entries, and do not appear in this brief list.

Thus, we can see the work on Angelical root words has only begun—the tip of the proverbial iceberg. However, I feel that learning these root concepts is essential to understanding, and eventually expanding, the Angelical tongue.

Aba: Stooping, Sinking
("Abai," Carbaf)

Abra: Prepair, Provide
(Abramig, Abramg, Abrassa)

Al: Gather, Bind, Settle, Place
(Aala, Alar, Allar, Aldi, Aldon, Oali)

Asb/Osb: Sting, Destroy
(Grosb, "Quasb")

Asch: [definition uncertain]
(Ascha, Masch)

Asp: Quality
(Asp, Aspiann Aspiaon)

Ava Avav: Thunder, Pomp
("Avav," Avavox, Avavago)

Azia: Alike, Likeness
("Azia," Aziazor)

Bab: Dominion, Wicked, Harlot
(Ababalond, Bab, Babalon, Babalel, Babage, Babagen, Bablibo, Bobogel)

Bag: Fury?
(Bag, Bagie, Bagenol, Bagnole)

Bal/Balt: Justice, Righteousness, Judgment
(Baligon, Balit, Balt, Baltan, Baltim, Baltle, Balzarg, Balzizras)

Bas/Baz: Day, Daytime
(Basgim, Basmelo, Basledf, Baspalo, Bazchim, "Bazem," Bazpama)

Bia/Bie: Voice
(Bahal, Bia, Bial, Bien)

Bli/Bil: Comfort
("Bigl," "Bliard," Blior, Bliora, Bliorax, Bliorb, Bliors, "Bliort," Pibliar)

Boap: Service
(Aboapri, Booapis)

Brin: Have, Has
("Brin," "Brint," Brints)

Chr: Let There Be, Be It (i.e., To Exist)
(Chr, Chramsa, Christeos)

Coa: Increase
("Coazior," Hecoa)

Coc/Cac/Cap: Time, Duration, Succession
(Acocasb, "Cacocasb," Cocasb, Cocasg, Qcocasb, Cacacom, Cacrg, Casasam, Capimali, "Capimao," Capimaon, Capmiali)

Com: Connect, Truss, Encircle
(Commah, Comselh)

Con/Cor: Man, Manmade and Number
(Conisbra, Cordziz)
(Cormf, Cormfa, Cormp, Cormpo, Cormpt, Sagacor, Coronzom)

Dod: Vexation
(Dodpal, Dodmni, Dods, Dodsih)

Doh: Kingdom
(Adohi, Londoh)

Ecr/Ecri: Praise
("Ecrin," Oecrimi)

Fa: Song, Singing
(Faaip, Farzem)

Fao/Far: Dwelling
(Faonts, Fargt, "Faorgt")

Gah: Pure Spirit
(Gah, Gahoachma, Gahire)

Goh: Speak, Say
(Goho, Gohia, Gohol, Gohon, Gohulim, Gohus)

Hom: Live, Age
(Hom, Homil, Homin)

Huba: Lamps, Lanterns
(Hubaio, Hubar, Hubaro)

I/Ip: The Verb *To Be*
(I, Ip, Ipam, Ipamis, Ripir)

Ia/Iad: God, The Highest, Divine
(Iad, Geiad, "Iadoias," Iadpil, Iadnah, Iaiadix, Laiad, Iaida, Iaidon, Iaisg, Ioiad, Oiad, Piad)

Ialp: Light, Fire
(Yalpamb, Ialpirt, Ialpon, "Ialpor," "Ialprt")

Isr: Promise
(Aisro, Isro, Isr)

L/Lo: One, First, You (sing.)
(Aqlo, Bolp, Yls, Ylsi, "Lo," El, L, La, Lu, Ol, Ili, Lil, Ul, Uls, "Yl")

Lans/Lons: Power
(Lansh, Lonsa, Lonshi, "Lonshin")

Lusd/Lasd: Feet, Base
(Lasdi, Lusd, Lusda, Lusdan)

Lza: Course
("Elzap," "Lzar")

Mad: Godly, Pure, Heavenly
(Mad, "Madriax," Madriiax, Madrid, Oadriax)

Mica/Mical: Might, Power
(Gmicalzo, Micalp, Micalzo, Micaoli, Micaolz, Miketh, Omicaolz)

Nan/Nana: Wisdom, Power
(Ananael, Nanaeel)

Nap: Sharpness
(Napeai, Napta, Nazpsad)

Naz: Straightness
(Nazpsad, Nazarth, Nazavabh)

Noa: Become
(Noaln, Noan, Noar, Noas, Noasmi)

Nonc: You (pl.)
(Nonca, Noncf, Nonci, Noncp)

Noqo: Servant
(Cnoqod, Cnoquodi, Cnoquol, Noco)

Nor: Son
("Nor," "Norm," Noromi)

Oan/Aon: Small Unit (as in Moment, Eye)
(Oanio, Ooanamb, Ooaona, Ooanoan, "Qanis")

Obl/Obo: Dressing, Garland, Garment
(Obloc, Oboleh)

Oia: Eternal/Forever
("Iadoias," Ioiad)

Ol: To Make
(Eol, Eolis, Oln)

Ola/Ala: Two, Twice
(Olani, Pala, Pola)

Olo/Ollo: Man, Men
("Olap," Ollog, "Ollor," Olora)

Om: Wisdom, Understanding
(Om, "Oma," Omax, "Omp")

Ooa/Oa: Name
(Dooain, Dooaip, Dooiap, Omaoas)

Or/Ors: Darkness, Dryness, Beneath, Barren, etc.
(Oroch, Orocha, Orri, Ors, Orsba, Orscatbl, Orscor)

Ox: masculine, active?
(Oxex, Oxiayal, Tox)

Paca/Pacad: ?
(Pacaduasam, Pacaph)

Pam: Not
(Ipam, Ipamis, "Pam," "Pamis")

Parac: Equate, Join, Wed
(Parach, Paracleda)

Pir/Pr: Holy, Celestial
(Pir, Piripsax, Piripsol, Piripson, "Pirgah," "Pirgi," "Prg," Prge, Prgel, "Purg")

Poil: Division
(Yrpoil, Poilp)

Qa/Qaa: Create
(Qaa, Qaal, Qaan, Qaaon, Qaas, Qadah)

Racl/Rocl: Weep?
(Raclir, Rocle)

Rza: To Swear
(Surzas, Znrza)

Sem/Sam: ?
(Samhampors, Sem, Semhaham)

Sm/Sym: Another
(Asymp, Symp, "Smnad")

Sob/Sol: Whose, Whom
(Asobam, Soba, Sobam, Sobca, "Sobha," "Sobo," Sobra, "Sola")

Tab/Cab: Govern
(Anetab, Gnetaab, Netaab, Netaaib, Tabaam, Tabaord, Tabaori, "Tabas," Tabitom, Cab, Caba)

Uch: Confuse, Confound
(Oucho, Unchi, Urch)

Von/Voh/Vov: Anger, Wrath, Might
(Vohim, "Vnph," "Vonin," Vonph, Vonpho, "Vonpo," "Vovim," Vovina)

Zie/Zo: Hands
(Azien, Ozien, Zien, Ozol, Zol)

Zil/Zyl: Go within, Fly into, Stretch forth
(Zildar, Zildron, "Zilodarp,", Zylna)

Zim: Enter, Territory
(Zim, Zimii, Zimz)

Zir: Am, Was, Were
(Zir, Zirdo, Zirom, Zirop, Zirzird)

Zli, Ilz: Water
(Pilzin, Zlida)

Zom: Amidst
(Zom, Zomdux)

Zong: Wind
(Zong, Ozongon)

Zur: Pray?
(Zuraah, Zurah, Zure)

The Angelical Alphabet

Graph	*Un*	*Or*	*Gal*	*Ged*	*Veh*	*Pa*
E	A	F	D	G/J	C/Ch/K	B

Drux	*Ger*	*Mals*	*Ur*	*Na*	*Gon*	*Tal*
N	Q/Qu	P/Ph	L	H	I/Y	M

Gisg	*Fam*	*Van*	*Ceph*	*Don*	*Med*	*Pal*
T	S	U/V	Z	R	O	X

An Angelical to English Dictionary

Un (A)

Aai (ay-AY-ii)* *prep.* Amongst (You)

1.67 . . . reigneth *amongst you* . . .

12.21 . . . whose name *amongst you* is wrath.

**13.21 . . . is called *amongst you* a bitter sting.

**14.23 . . . which is called *amongst you* fury.

Pronunciation notes:

(**Dee 1.67—AAI*)

(**Dee 12.21—A a i*) Three syllables. Each letter appears to stand alone.

(**Dee 1.67—aäl*) See the *48 Claves*. Here, Dee seems to have mistakenly written an *l* in place of the final *i*. However, he does include a dieresis over the second *a*, to indicate that it does not combine its sound with the preceding vowel.

I have adopted the accent from *Aaiom* (amongst).

Note:

**Words 13.21–22 are missing from Dee's journals. We are likewise missing the entirety of Key Fourteen. We have only the English given for these Keys on *TFR*, p. 193. However, this word does appear in these locations in Dee's *48 Claves*.

Also:

Aaf (ay-AF)	Amongst
Aaiom (ay-AY-om)	Amongst (Us?)
Aao (ay-ay-OH)	Amongst
Eai (ee-AY-ii)	Amongst
Oai (oh-AY-ii)	Amongst

Aaiom (ay-AY-om)* *prep.* Amongst (Us)

3.71 . . . is become mighty *amongst us*.

7.41 . . . be mighty *amongst us* . . .

Pronunciation notes:

(**Dee 3.71—A ai om*)

(**Dee 7.41—A AI om*) Three syllables. The first *a* stands alone in the first syllable. In the second syllable, the *ai* (or *ay*) makes essentially the same sound as the first syllable (as in the English words *dais* and *say*).

(**Dee 3.71—a-aí-om*) See the *48 Claves*. Note the accent on the second syllable.

(**Dee 7.41—aaîom*) See the *48 Claves*. I am unsure why Dee placed a circumflex over the *i* in this case.

Note:

This might appear to be a compound of *Aai* (amongst) and *Om* (understand). However, see below for *Aao*, another variant of this word that utilizes the letter *o* without the letter *m*.

Also:

Aaf (ay-AF) — Amongst
Aai (ay-AY-ii) — Amongst (You)
Aao (ay-ay-OH) — Amongst
Eai (ee-AY-ii) — Amongst
Oai (oh-AY-ii) — Amongst

Aaf (ay-AF)* *prep.* — Amongst

4.46 . . . praise him *amongst* the sons of man.

Pronunciation notes:

(**Dee—A af*) Two syllables, with the first *a* standing alone. I have adopted the syllable from other versions of this word.

Also:

Aai (ay-AY-ii) — Amongst (You)
Aaiom (ay-AY-om) — Amongst (Us?)
Aao (ay-ay-OH) — Amongst
Eai (ee-AY-ii) — Amongst
Oai (oh-AY-ii) — Amongst

Aala (AY-ay-la)* *v.* — To Place

3.32 . . . I made you stewards and *placed you* in seats . . .

Pronunciation notes:

(**Dee—A ala*) Dee originally wrote this word as *haala*. However, he excluded the *h* in his phonetic note. Three syllables, with the initial *a* standing alone.

(**Dee—áâla)* See the *48 Claves*. Here, Dee confirms that the *h* is unnecessary. He places the accent on the first syllable. He also placed a circumflex over the second *a*, indicating a long sound.

Also:

Oali (OH-ay-lii) To Place

Probable shared root:

Alar (AY-lar) To Settle / Place
Aldi (AL-dii) Gathering
Aldon (AL-don) Gird up
Allar (AL-lar) To Bind up

Aao (ay-ay-OH)* *prep.* Amongst

7.5 . . . singing praises *amongst* the flames . . .

Pronunciation notes:

(**Dee—A a ó*) Like the word *Aai*, this version is also divided into three syllables. (There is no *ao* letter combination in Early Modern English—these letters make two separate sounds, as in the English word *chaos*.) Dee places the accent on the last syllable.

Also:

Aaf (ay-AF) Amongst
Aai (ay-AY-ii) Amongst (You)
Aaiom (ay-AY-om) Amongst (Us?)
Eai (ee-AY-ii) Amongst
Oai (oh-AY-ii) Amongst

"Aath" (or "Ath") (ath) *n.* Works (or Deeds)

Compounds:

Sobhaath (sob-HAY-ath) [*Sobha* + *"Aath"*] — Whose Works

Note:

See also *Vaun* (to work)—which appears to be a verb, rather than the noun intended by "Aath."

Ababalond (ay-BAY-bay-lond)* *n.* — Harlot

30.113 . . . she is the bed of *an harlot* . . .

Pronunciation notes:

(**Dee—A bá ba lond*) Four syllables, with an accent on the second syllable. The initial *a* stands alone.

(**Dee—abábâlond*) See the *48 Claves*. Here, Dee again placed an accent over the second syllable. He also placed a circumflex over the third *a* to indicate its long sound.

Note:

The similarity between this word and the name of the ancient empire of Babylon. Beginning with *1 Enoch* (likely written during the Judaic captivity in Babylon), the kingdom of Babylon has been a biblical symbol of iniquity. See Revelation 17, where the iniquities of the world of man are symbolized by a woman whose forehead is inscribed with the words *Mystery, Babylon the Great, the Mother of Harlots and Abominations of the Earth*. Also see note at *Babalon* (Wicked).

Also:

Babalon (bay-BAY-lon) — Wicked

Possible shared root:

Bab (bab) — Dominion

Babage (bay-BAY-jee) — South

Babagen (bay-BAY-jen) — South

"Abai" (ay-bay-ii) *v.* — To Stoop

Compounds:

Abaivonin (ay-bay-II-voh-nin) [*"Abai"* + *Vonin*] Stooping Dragons

Note:

Stooping here means "diving," as in an eagle stooping after its prey. Note that *stooping* is a verb, but is used in the compound (*Abaivonin*) as an adjective.

Probable shared root:

Carbaf (kar-baf) Sink (or Stoop)

Abaivonin (ay-bay-II-voh-nin)* [*"Abai"* + *Vonin*] *comp.*

Stooping Dragons

8.17 . . . as bucklers to *the stooping dragons* . . .

Pronunciation notes:

(**Dee—A ba í uo nin*) Five syllables, with an accent on the third syllable. Dee originally wrote this word with a *u* in the fourth syllable. However, when *u*/*v* is written before a vowel, it should take the consonant sound of *v*.

(**Dee—Abaíuônin*) See the *48 Claves*. Dee again places the accent on the third syllable. He further places a circumflex over the *o* to indicate its long sound.

Aboapri (ay-BOH-ay-prii)* *v.* To Serve

30.120 . . . the lower heavens beneath you, *let them serve you*.

Pronunciation notes:

(**Dee—A bo a pri*) Appears to be four syllables. While Dee shows the second *a* standing alone, I have opted to give it the short sound in my pronunciation (as in the English word *boa*).

(**Dee—abóâpri*) See the *48 Claves*. Here, Dee placed an accent on the second syllable. He also placed a circumflex over the second *a* to indicate its long sound.

Also:

Booapis (boh-OH-ay-pis) To Serve

Note:
It would appear that *Boap/Booap* serves as the common root between these two words.

Abramig (ay-BRAY-mig)* *v.* To Prepare

8.55 . . . of such as *are prepared.*

Pronunciation notes:
(**Dee—A bra mig*) Three syllables. The initial *A* stands alone. The second *a* also appears to be long. See the pronunciation notes for *Abramg*—where we learn that the final *g* has a hard sound. Also, we can see from *Abramg* that the *i* in *Abramig* is likely a phonetic gloss.
(**Dee—a-brâmig*) See the *48 Claves*. Dee placed a circumflex over the second *a*, confirming the long sound.
I have adopted the accent from *Abraassa* (to provide).

Also:
Abramg (ay-BRAY-mig) To Prepare

Possible shared root:
Abraassa (ab-RAY-sa) To Provide

Compare from *Loagaeth*: *Abra, Abrimanadg*

Abramg (ay-BRAY-mig)* *v.* To Prepare

2.14 . . . whom *I have prepared* as cups for a wedding . . .
11.33 . . . *I have prepared* for you . . .

Pronunciation notes:
(**Dee 2.14—Abramg*)
(**Dee 11.33—Ab ramg. g not as dg*) Both *a*'s appear short in this note—however, the pronunciation notes for *Abramig* (to prepare) indicate both are long. In this note, Dee lets us know that the final *g* has a hard sound rather than the soft "dg" sound. Finally, Dee's note seems to indicate only two syllables. However, if the final *g* is hard, there should be a

vowel sound between the *m* and the *g*—making three syllables. Again see *Abramig* (to prepare), where this vowel sound is shown as a short *i*. I have adopted the accent from *Abraassa* (to provide).

Compounds:
Dsabramg (dee-say-bray-mig) [*Ds* + *Abramg*] Which Prepared

Also:
Abramig (ay-BRAY-mig) To Prepare

Possible shared root:
Abraassa (ab-RAY-sa) To Provide

Compare from *Loagaeth*:
Abra, *Abrimanadg*

Abraassa (ab-RAY-sa)* *v.* To Provide

30.23 . . . which *provided* you for the government . . .

Pronunciation note:
(**Dee—Abraássa*) Three syllables, with the accent likely on the second syllable. In Early Modern English, the double *a* makes a long "a" sound, and the double *s* makes a regular "s" sound.
(**Dee—abraássa*) See the *48 Claves*. This note essentially matches that from *TFR*.

Possible shared root:
Abramig (ay-BRAY-mig) To Prepare
Abramg (ay-BRAY-mig) To Prepare

ACAM (ay-KAM)* 7699

6.19 . . . and *7699* continual workmen . . .

Pronunciation notes:
(**Dee—A cám*) Two syllables, with the accent on the second syllable.
(**Dee—Acám*) See the *48 Claves*. Note the accent again on the second syllable.

Note:

This word was not originally given with Key Six. It was added later when Nalvage transmitted the English for the Key (see *TFR*, p. 190). This seems to have been the case with many of the numbers mentioned in the Keys.

Achildao (ay-KIL-day-oh)* *n.* — Diamond

9.52 Their heads are covered with *diamond* . . .

Pronunciation notes:

(**Dee—A chil da o kil*) Four syllables. Dee indicates that the *ch* should take the harder "k" (or "kh") sound. The first *a* stands alone. Both the second *a* and the final *o* should take their long sounds.

(**Dee—a-chíldao*) See the *48 Claves*. Dee again indicates the initial *A* stands alone. He also placed an accent over the *i* in the second syllable.

Acocasb (ay-KOH-kasb)* *n.* — Time

9.71 . . . for *the time* is such . . .

Pronunciation notes:

(**Dee—A co casb*) Three syllables. The initial *A* stands alone. The *o* of the second syllable should take a long sound.

(**Dee—acócasb*) See the *48 Claves*. Dee placed an accent over the second syllable.

Also:

"Cacocasb" (kay-KOH-kasb)	Another While
Cocasb (KOH-kasb)	Time
Cocasg (KOH-kazh)	Times
Qcocasb (kwah-KOH-kasb)	Contents of Time

Possible shared root:

Cacacom (kay-SAY-som)	Flourish
Cacrg (KAY-kurg)	Until
Casasam (kay-SAY-sam)	Abiding
Capimali (kay-pii-MAY-lii)	Successively

"Capimao" (kay-pii-MAY-oh) — While
Capimaon (kap-ii-MAY-on) — Number of Time
Capmiali (kap-mii-AY-lii) — Successively

Note:
Also see *Pild* (continually).

Acroodzi (ak-roh-OD-zii)* *n.* — Beginning

16.6 . . . which hast thy beginning in glory . . .

Note:
The transmission of the first twelve words of Key Sixteen is missing from Dee's journals. We only have the English given for it on *TFR*, p. 194. However, they do appear in Dee's *48 Claves*.

Pronunciation notes:
(**Dee—acroódzi*) See the *48 Claves*. Dee places an accent over the second *o*—which should be part of the third syllable. See pronunciation notes for *Croodzi* (beginning of things).

Also:
Croodzi (kroh-OD-zii) — Beginning (of things)

Note:
Also see *Iaod* (beginning), *Iaodaf* (in the beginning), *Amgedpha* (I will begin anew), and *Nostoah* (it was in the beginning).

Adgmach (aj-mak) *n.* — Glory (i.e., Adoration, Praise)*

Note:
(**Dee—Adgmach adgmach adgmach* [= much glory].) See the *Five Books* pp. 309–10. This seems to be a kind of *Trisagion* (like the "Holy Holy Holy . . . " songs sung by Angels in biblical literature.). The *Adgmach* phrase is spoken during a longer prayer offered by "many voices": "It is good, O God, for you are goodness itself. And great because of the size of greatness itself. *Adgmach, adgmach, adgmach*! I am, and this pace

is, holy. *Adgmach, adgmach, adgmach hucacha.*" *Adgmach* must therefore indicate "glory."

Also see:

Busd (glory), which seems to indicate "wondrous."

Prigah (glory), which relates to light and fire (possibly the light of the Sun).

Adgt (ajt)* *aux. v.* Can

2.1 *Can* the wings of the winds understand . . .

Pronunciation notes:

(**Dee—Adgt*) This appears to be only one syllable.

Adna (ad-nah) *n.* Obedience

1.50 . . . and swore *obedience* and faith to him . . .

Pronunciation notes:

Dee left no specific note, so this word likely sounds as it appears. I suggest two syllables, and both *a*'s should be short.

Compare from *Loagaeth*:

Adna, Adnay, Adney, Adnah, Adnih, Adnava, Adnab, Adnor

Adohi (ay-DOH-hii)* *n.* Kingdom

18.20 . . . which is called in thy *kingdom* Joy . . .

Pronunciation notes:

(**Dee—A do hi*) Three syllables. The initial *A* stands alone. The *o* likely takes the long sound, as does the final *i*.

(**Dee—adóhi*) See the *48 Claves*. Here, Dee placed an accent over the second syllable.

Also:

Londoh (lon-DOH) Kingdom

Note:
It would appear that "doh" is the root here.

Compare from *Loagaeth*:
Aldoh, Ardoh, Doh, Dohoh

Adoian (ay-doh-II-an)* *n.* Face

30.14 . . . behold *the face of* your God.

Pronunciation notes:
(*Dee—A do í an*) Four syllables, with an accent on the third syllable.
(*Dee—adoían*) See the *48 Claves*. Here, Dee again placed an accent over the *i* in the third syllable.

Adphaht (ad-fot)* *adj.* Unspeakable

30.29 . . . and her *unspeakable* variety . . .

Pronunciation notes:
(*Dee—Ad phaht*) Two syllables. The *ah* in the second syllable should indicate a short "o" sound ("ah")—as in the English word *father*.

Compare from *Loagaeth*:
Adepd, Adepoad, Adeph, Adaph, Adapagemoh, Adphamagel

Adroch (ad-roch)* *n.* Olive Mount

5.7 . . . and are become as olives *in the olive mount* . . .

Pronunciation notes:
(*Dee—Ad roch as otch*) Two syllables. The *ch* at the end of the word has the "tch" sound—as in the English words *church* and *churn*.

Note:
The "Mount of Olives"—to the east of Jerusalem—is an important location in biblical literature. (See 2 Samuel 15, Zechariah 14, Matthew 21, 24–26, 39.) It is supposed to be the place where God will begin to

redeem the dead in the End Times—and is thus a major burial site for Jewish people to this very day. It does *not* appear to be the mountain from Jesus' Sermon on the Mount.

Also see:
Qanis (olives).

Compare from *Loagaeth*:
Adroh, Adroth

Adrpan (ay-dir-pan)* *v.* To Cast Down

30.124 *Cast down* such as fall.

Pronunciation notes:
(*Dee—A dr pan dir*) Three syllables. Dee shows us that the second syllable is pronounced "dir." The initial *A* stands alone.

AF (af)* 19

5.17 . . . pillars of gladness *19* and gave them . . .

Pronunciation notes:
(*Dee—Af*) One syllable.

Affa (af-fa)* *adj.* Empty

13.13 . . . making men drunken which are *empty*.

Pronunciation notes:
(*Dee—Af fa*) Two syllables. When this word is spoken fluently, the two *f*s combine into one sound.

Note:
This word is a palindrome. It is spelled the same forward as it is spelled backward.

Ag (ag)* *adj.* or *pron.* — No/None (No One)

4.17 . . . whom *none* hath yet numbered . . .

Pronunciation notes:

(**Dee—Ag as agg in nag*) One syllable. Dee shows a double *g* in his phonetic note, which (in Early Modern English) indicates a hard sound instead of a soft sound (as in *stagger* or *bigger*). *Ag* sounds like the English words *nag* and *bag*.

Note:

The words *Ag* and "Agl" are pronouns ("none = no one"). However, the word *Ag* becomes an adjective in *Agtoltorn* (no creature).

Compounds:

"Agl" (ag-el) [Ag + L] — No One Creature
Agltoltorn (ag-el-tol-torn) [Ag + L + "Toltorn"] — No One Creature
Agtoltorn (ay-jee-tol-torn) [Ag + "Toltorn"] — No Creature

Note:

Also see *Ge* (Not), *Ip* (Not), and *Pam* (Not).

"Agl" (ag-el) [Ag + L] *comp., pron.* — No One

Compounds:

Agltoltorn (ag-el-tol-torn) [Ag + L + "Toltorn"] — No One Creature

Agltoltorn (ag-el-tol-torn)* [Ag + L + "Toltorn"] — No One Creature

30.80 . . . let there be *no one creature* equal with another . . .

Pronunciation notes:

(**Dee—Ag l ter torn*) Four syllables. The first *l* stands alone, leaving the *A* and *g* to combine together. Also note that Dee seems to have made a mistake in his phonetic note—giving the sound of "ter" for the letters *tol*.
(**Dee—ag L tortorn*) See the *48 Claves*. The *l* again stands alone. I also note that Dee once again indicates a "tor" sound where the letters *tol* should be. I have settled upon the *tol* version in my pronunciation.

Note:

The words *Ag* and *"Agl"* are pronouns (none = no one). However, the word *Ag* becomes an adjective in *Agtoltorn* (no creature).

Also:

"Agl" (ag-el) [Ag + L]	No One Creature
Agtoltorn (ay-jee-tol-torn) [Ag + "Toltorn"]	No Creature

Agtoltorn (ay-jee-tol-torn)* [Ag + "Toltorn"] *comp.* No Creature

30.69 . . . let there be *no creature* upon or within her . . .

Pronunciation notes:

(**Dee—A g tol torn*) Four syllables. The *g* does not combine with the *t*, and therefore must stand alone. Because of this, the *a* is also forced to stand alone.

Note:

The words *Ag* and "Agl" are pronouns (none = no one). However, the word *Ag* becomes an adjective in *Agtoltorn* (no creature).

Also:

"Agl" (ag-el) [Ag + L]	No One Creature
Agltoltorn (ag-el-tol-torn) [Ag + L + "Toltorn"]	No One Creature

Aisro (ay-ii-sroh)* *v.* To Promise

14.20 Behold the voice of God *promise of* him which is called . . .

Pronunciation notes:

(**Dee—aîsro*) See the *48 Claves*. Dee placed a circumflex over the *i* to indicate its long sound. This likely means the *A* must stand alone, so the word contains three syllables.

Note:

The transmission of Key Fourteen is missing from Dee's journals. We only have the English for this Key given later (see *TFR*, p. 193). Plus, the word *Aisro* appears in this location in Dee's *48 Claves*.

I believe this word is intended as a verb. "Promise of him which is called . . . " is likely an adjuration to make a promise *by* him who is called.

Also:

Isro (iz-roh) — Promise of

Note:

It is possible that the *-o* suffix (of) is in use here.

Also see:

Sibsi (covenant), Surzas (sworn), and Znrza (swore).

Alar (AY-lar)* *v.* — To Settle / To Place

9.20 . . . *have settled* their feet in the west . . .

Pronunciation notes:

(**Dee—A lar*) Two syllables. The *A* stands alone in the first syllable. I have adopted the accent from *Aala* (settle / place).

Also:

Allar (AL-lar) — To Bind Up

Probable shared root:

Aala (AY-ay-la) — To Place
Aldi (AL-dii) — Gathering
Aldon (AL-don) — Gird Up
Oali (OH-ay-lii) — To Place

Note:

See Note at *Allar*.

Alca (al-ka) *v.?* — To Signify(?)

Note:

See the *Five Books*, p. 354. Here, the Angel Illemese says of the *Book of Soyga*, "Soyga signifieth not Agyos. *Soyga alca miketh.*" (*Agyos* is Greek for "holiness," and is "Soyga" when spelled backward.) When Dee asked what these words meant, he was told, "The True Measure of the

Will of God in Judgment, Which Is by Wisdom." Based on context, I feel that the word *Alca* probably means "to signify"—while *Miketh* (related, perhaps by root, to *Micaolz*—mighty) is translated as the "True Measure of the Will of God . . . " etc.

Aldi (AL-dii) *v.* To Gather

1.33 . . . garnished with the fire of *gathering* . . .

Pronunciation note:
I have adopted the accent from *Aala* (settle / place).

Note:
This word should be a verb, but in Key 1.33, it is actually used in a prepositional phrase, indicating the noun *fire*. Taken all together, the words *fire of gathering* make a noun phrase.

Also:
Aldon (AL-don) Gird-up, Gather Together

Probable shared root:
Aala (AY-ay-la) To Place
Alar (AY-lar) To Settle / Place
Allar (AL-lar) To Bind Up
Oali (OH-ay-lii) To Place

Aldon (AL-don)* *v.* Gird Up, To Gather Together

9.28 These *gather up* the moss of the earth . . .
**11.17 And *they gathered themselves together in* the house of death . . .
17.16 *Gird up* thy loins and hearken.

Pronunciation notes:
(**Dee 9.28; 17.16—Al don*) Two syllables. Both vowels seem to take their short sounds. I have adopted the accent from *Aala* (settle / place).

Note:

**This word was not given during the transmission of Key Eleven. Nor does it appear in Dee's *48 Claves*. We have only the English for the Key given on *TFR*, p. 193. Patricia Shaffer suggests this word here, and I have to agree.

Also:

Aldi (AL-dii) Gathering

Probable shared root:

Aala (AY-ay-la) To Place
Alar (AY-lar) To Settle / Place
Allar (AL-lar) To Bind Up
Oali (OH-ay-lii) To Place

Compare from *Loagaeth*:

Aldex

Allar (AL-lar)* *v.* To Bind Up

12.9 . . . *bind up* your girdles and visit us.

Pronunciation notes:

(**Dee—Al lar*) Two syllables. Both *a*'s are likely short. When spoken, the double *l* should combine into one sound (as in Early Modern English). I have adopted the accent from *Aala* (settle / place).

Also:

Alar (AY-lar) Settled

Probable shared root:

Aala (AY-ay-la) To Place
Aldi (AL-dii) Gathering
Aldon (AL-don) Gird Up
Oali (OH-ay-lii) To Place

Note:
The concept of *Alar/Allar* seems to be of "setting" or "establishing." The phrase *gird up your loins* is an old one meaning to get ready or to set oneself firmly on a course, and this is likely the meaning of *bind up your girdles* in Key Twelve.

Compare from *Loagaeth*:
Alla

Amgedpha (am-JED-fa)* *v.* I Will Begin Anew

Pronunciation note:
(**Dee—Amgédpha*) See the *Five Books*, p. 324. Dee places an accent over the *e*.

From *Loagaeth*:
(***Dee—Amgedpha* = *I will begin anew.*) See the *Five Books*, p. 324.

Note:
Also see *Acroodzi* (beginning), *Croodzi* (beginning of things), *Iaod* (beginning), *Iaodaf* (in the beginning), and *Nostoah* (it was in the beginning).

Amipzi (ay-mip-zii)* *v.* To Fasten

5.15 . . . unto whom *I have fastened* pillars of gladness . . .

Pronunciation notes:
(**Dee—A mip zi*) Three syllables. The *A* stands alone.

Amiran (am-ir-an)* *pron.* Yourselves

3.63 Lift up, I say, *yourselves*.

Pronunciation notes:
(**Dee—Amiran*) I suggest three syllables.

Amma (am-a)* *adj.* Cursed

9.35 *Cursed* are they whose iniquities they are.

Pronunciation notes:
(**Dee—Am ma*) Two syllables. The two *m*'s combine into a single sound, as in the English word *summer*.

Note:
This word is a palindrome. It is spelled the same forward as it is spelled backward.

Amzes (am-zes) *n.?* Those That Fear God(?)

Note:
See the *Five Books*, pp. 324–25. Here Kelley sees what the *Book of Loagaeth* looks like from the outside. It is covered in blue silk, and has the title *Amzes naghezes Hardeh* painted upon it in gold. Kelley says this signifies "the universal name of Him that created universally be praised and extolled forever."
However, also see *TFR*, p. 174, where the Angel Ave reveals that the title of Enoch's book was "Let Those That Fear God, and Are Worthy, Read." (Dee, at that point, notes, "The title of Enoch's books expounded into English.") If this happens to be the real translation, then perhaps *Amzes* indicates "Those That Fear God." (Also see *Hoxmarch*—Fear of God.)

Pronunciation notes:
(*Dee—Amzes naghezes Hardeh—Note this to be pronounced roundly together.*) Perhaps this means the three words should be pronounced as if they were one?

Ananael (an-AN-ee-el)* *n.* Secret Wisdom

3.80 . . . partakers of *the secret wisdom of* your creation.

Pronunciation notes:

(**Dee—Ananael*) Dee gives us little clue here. The word is likely four syllables.

(**Dee—anánæl*) See the *48 Claves*. Dee shows an accent over the second syllable. Also, note that the final *ae* is written as *æ* (called an *ash*)—indicating that the two letters combine to form one sound. I believe, in this case, the ash indicates a long "e" sound (as in the English spelling of the word *encyclopædia*).

Note:

The similarity between this word and the name of the Archangel of Venus, *Anael* (or *Annael*). Annael was the first Angel contacted by Dee and Kelley (see the *Five Books*), which initiated the transmission of the entire Angelic system of magick.

Possible shared root:

Nanaeel (nay-NAY-ee-el) — (My) Power

Anetab (ay-NEE-tayb)* *n.* — (In) Government

6.25 . . . and are *in government* and continuance as . . .

Pronunciation notes:

(**Dee—A né tab*) Three syllables, with an accent on the second. Based on the other versions of this word (see below), I have given the *a* in the final syllable a long sound.

(**Dee—anétab*) See the *48 Claves*. The accent is again shown on the second syllable.

Also:

Gnetaab (nee-TAY-ab)	(Your) Governments
Netaab (nee-TAY-ab)	Governments
Netaaib (nee-TAY-ay-ib)	Government
Tabaam (tay-BAY-an)	Governor
Tabaord (tay-BAY-ord)	(Let) Be Governed
Tabaori (tay-BAY-oh-rii)	Govern
"Tabas" (tay-BAS)	Govern
Cab (kab)	Rod/Scepter
Caba (ka-BA)	To Govern

Angelard (an-jee-lard)* *n.* Thoughts

10.64 . . . even as the heart of man doth *his thoughts* . . .

Pronunciation notes:

(**Dee—An ge lard*) Three syllables. The *e* should take its long sound.

(**Dee—angêlard*) See the *48 Claves*. Here, Dee placed a circumflex over the *e*—confirming its long sound.

Aoiveae (ay-oy-VEE-ay)* *n.* Stars

30.139 . . . until *the stars* be numbered.

Pronunciation notes:

(**Dee—A oi vé ae*) This appears to be four syllables, with an accent on the third. The initial *A* stands alone. The Early Modern English letter combination *oi* (or *oy*) makes an "oy" sound—as in the words *boil* or *toy*. The *e* in the third syllable likely takes a long sound.

(**Dee—Aoivéâe*) See the *48 Claves*. Here, Dee again placed the accent over the *e* in the third syllable. He also placed a circumflex over the second *a* to indicate its long sound.

Apachana (ap-AY-kay-na)* *n.* The Slimy Things Made of Dust**

Pronunciation note:

(**Dee—ap-á-cha-na*) See the *Five Books*, p. 320. Four syllables, with an accent on the second. The second and third *a*'s seem to take the long sound.

From *Loagaeth*:

(***Dee—The slimy things made of dust.*) See the *Five Books*, p. 320.

"Apila" (ap-ii-la) *v.* — To Live

Compounds:

Odapila (ohd-ap-ii-la) [Od + "Apila"] — And Liveth

Note:

Also see *Hom* (To Live).

Aqlo (AY-kwah-loh)* *pron.* — Thy (Your)

18.19 . . . is called *in thy* kingdom Joy.

Pronunciation notes:

(*Dee—A q lo quu*) Three syllables. The initial *A* and the *q* stand alone. Dee shows that the *q* should sound like "quu" (or "qw")—making the sound of "kwah." The final *o* should likely take a long sound.

(*Dee—á-q-lo*) See the *48 Claves*. This note is essentially the same as that in *TFR*. However, Dee here placed an accent over the first syllable.

Possible shared root:

Bolp (bohlp) — Be Thou
Yls (yils) — Thou
Ylsi (yil-sii) — Thee
L (el) — First
"Lo" (loh) — First

Ar (ar)* *pron.* — That

12.16 Bring down your train 3363 *that* the Lord may be magnified . . .

Pronunciation notes:

(*Dee—Ar*) One syllable.

Compounds:

Arcaosgi (ar-kay-OZH-ii) [Ar + Caosgi] — To(?) the Earth
Arcoazior (ar-koh-ay-zhor) [Ar + "Coazior"] — That Increase
Artabas (ar-tay-bas) [Ar + "Tabas"] — That Govern

Note:

The word *Ar* (That) is a conjunction, while the word *Ds* (Which/That) is a pronoun.

Compare from *Loagaeth*:

Ar, Arh

"Ar" (ar) *v.?* To Van?

Compounds:

Arcaosgi (ar-kay-OZH-ii) ["Ar" + Caosgi] (To Van?) the Earth

Note:

The English word *van* is—by one definition—a shortened form of the word *vanguard*, the front part of an advancing army. Its use here in the Keys—as part of the phrase *to van the earth*—appears to treat it as a verb. A more proper definition of "Ar" may be "to advance upon (especially with hostile intent)."

Arcaosgi (ar-kay-OZH-ii)* ["Ar" + Caosgi] *comp.* (To Van?) the Earth

6.17 . . . fiery darts *to van the earth* . . .

Pronunciation notes:

(**Dee—Ar ca ós gi*) Four syllables, with an accent on the third syllable. See pronunciation notes at *Caosgi* (Earth) for more information.

(**Dee—arcaósgi*) See the *48 Claves*. Note the accent again on the third syllable.

Note:

Literally, this compound should translate: "That (the) Earth." There is no indication of the word for *to van* in the Key, and *Ar* is properly defined as "that." Could it be that an identical Angelical word *Ar* might translate as "to van"? Also see note at "Ar."

Arcoazior (ar-koh-ay-zhor)* [Ar + "Coazior"] *comp.* That Increase

30.129 . . . Bring forth with those *that increase* . . .

Pronunciation notes:

(**Dee—Ar co a zior*) Likely four syllables. The *a* in the third syllable stands alone. The *zi* in the fourth syllable likely sounds similar to the *ti* and *si* in the English word endings *-tion* and *-sion* (as in the English words *aggression*, *tradition*, etc.). I have represented this sound in my pronunciation with "zh."

Argedco (ar-JED-koh)* *v.* — With Humility We Call Thee, with Adoration of the Trinity.**

Pronunciation note:

(**Dee—argédco*) See the *Five Books*, p. 310. Dee places an accent over the *e*.

From *Loagaeth*:

(***Dee—With humility we call thee, with adoration of the Trinity.*) See the *Five Books*, p. 310.

Compare from *Loagaeth*:

Argednon

Arn (arn) *prop. n.* — "The Second Aethyr"

30.3 . . . which dwell in *the second aethyr* . . .

Note:

This (word 30.3) is the single space in the Key of the Aethyrs, which must be changed for each invocation—replacing word 30.3 with the name of the appropriate Aethyr. No established definitions were given for these names.

Arn contains the three Parts of the Earth *Doagnis*, *Pacasna*, and *Dialioa*.

Arphe (ar-fay) *v.* — I Desire Thee, O God*

From *Loagaeth*:

(**Dee—I desire thee, O God.*) See the *Five Books*, p. 320.

Artabas (ar-tay-bas)* [Ar + "Tabas"] *comp.* That Govern

30.123 . . . govern those *that govern* . . .

Pronunciation notes:
(**Dee—Ar ta bas*) Three syllables. The *a* in the second syllable appears to be long.

Arzulgh (ar-zulj) *prop. n.* Spirit Opposing *Befafes**

From *Loagaeth*:
(**Dee—This is the name of the spirit contrary to Befafes*) See the *Five Books*, p. 310. *Befafes* is an Angel of the *Heptarchia*.

Compare from *Loagaeth*:
Arzusen

Ascha (ask-a) n/a?*

From *Loagaeth*:
(**Dee—Gohed, pronounced as Iohed, signifieth One Everlasting and all things Descending upon One, and Gohed Ascha is as much to say as One God.*) See the *Five Books*, p. 304. The word *Gohed* means "One Everlasting . . ." (referring to God), so it is not clear exactly what *Ascha* adds in the phrase *Gohed Ascha* ("One God" or "One Everlasting God").

Pronunciation note:
The *sch* letter combination should sound like "sk" (as in *school*). Note, also, that in the *Book of Loagaeth*, Dee gives the pronunciation for the word *Zuresch* as "zuresk"—further indicating the "sk" sound for *sch*.

Also see:
Masch

Compare from *Loagaeth*:
Asch, Ascha, Aschah, Aschal, Ascham, Asche, Aschedh, Aschem, Ascheph, Aschi, Aschin, Aschma, Aschol, *and probably* Dasch, Gascheth, Hasche, Pasch, Pascha, Pascheph, *and maybe* Iemasch, Surascha, Vascheth

Asobam (ay-SOH-bam)* *pron.* (On) Whom

9.60 . . . *on whom* they frown not . . .

Pronunciation notes:

(**Dee—A so bam*) Dee originally wrote this word as *Asobama*—but he dropped the final *a* in his phonetic note *and* in the *48 Claves*. So the word is only three syllables long. The initial *A* stands alone. The *o* should take its long sound.

(**Dee—a-sóbam*) See the *48 Claves*. Here, Dee placed an accent over the second syllable.

Also:

"Saba" (SAY-bay)	Whose
Soba (SOH-bay)	Whose
Sobam (SOH-bam)	Whom
Sobca (SOB-kay)	Whose
"Sobha" (SOB-hay)	Whose
"Sobo" (SOH-boh)	Whose
Sobra (SOB-ray)	Whose
"Sola" (SOH-lay)	Whose

Asp (asp) *prop. n.* "The Twenty-First Aethyr" (Quality?)

30.3 . . . which dwell in *the twenty-first aethyr* . . .

Note:

This (word 30.3) is the single space in the Key of the Aethyrs, which must be changed for each invocation—replacing word 30.3 with the name of the appropriate Aethyr. No established definitions were given for these names.

Asp contains the three Parts of the Earth *Chirzpa*, *Toantom*, and *Vixpalg*.

Possible shared root:

Aspian (as-pii-an) Qualities (i.e., "Characteristics")

Aspian (as-pii-an)* *n.* Qualities (Characteristics)

30.77 . . . let them differ in *their qualities*.

Pronunciation notes:
(**Dee—As pi an*) Three syllables. The *i* should take its long sound.

Possible shared root:
Asp (asp) "The Twenty-First Aethyr"

Note:
Compare to the name of the Part of Earth (and its Angelic Governor), *Aspiaon*.

Aspt (aspt)* *prep.* Before, In Front

30.144 . . . and appear *before* the covenant of his mouth . . .

Pronunciation notes:
(**Dee—Aspt*) One syllable.

Note:
Could there be a relationship between this word and the name of the *Apst*, an Angel of medicine of the Northern Watchtower?

Astel (as-tel) n/a

Note:
See *Five Books*, p. 366. The Angel Illemese appears to Dee and Kelley with a bundle of empty boxes that he calls virtuous. When Dee asks for an explanation, Illemese says, "Will you have my bill? [. . .] I will show it. Serve it, where you list. *Iudra galgol astel.*" Dee states that he and Kelley do not understand, and wish to know how it can be served. But Illemese never offers definitions for these Angelical words.

Also see:
Garnastel (gar-nas-tel) n/a

Asymp (ay-simp)* *pron.* or *adj.* Another

30.82 . . . no one creature equal with *another.*

Pronunciation notes:

(**Dee—A symp*) Two syllables. The *A* stands alone.

Also:

Symp (simp) Another

Probable shared root:

"Smnad" (sem-en-ad) Another

Note:

The root here may be "sm" or "sym."

Atraah (ay-tray-a)* *n.* Girdles

12.10 . . . bind up *your girdles* and visit us.

Pronunciation notes:

(**Dee—A tra ah*) Three syllables. The first *a* stands alone. In Early Modern English, a double *a* indicates a long sound—which Dee indicates for the second syllable in his phonetic note.

(**Dee—atraâh*) See the *48 Claves*. Here Dee placed a circumflex over the *third a*. Dee seems to have used *âh* to indicate a vowel sound similar to what we hear in the English words *father* and *fall.*

Audcal (od-kal) *n.* Gold (the Mercury of the Philosopher's Stone)*

From the *Alchemical Cipher*:

See *TFR*, pp. 387–89. The Angel Levanael says of Audcal, "It is Gold. [. . .] *Audcal* is his Mercury. *Darr*, (in the Angelical tongue), is the true name of the Stone." Therefore *Audcal* (Gold) is here described as the alchemical Mercury (or essence) of the Philosopher's Stone.

Note:

(**Dee—We know that the Philosopher's Stone being left by metal, with metal, and upon metal, etc . . .*) Dee is here speaking of touching base metals with the Philosopher's Stone, which would turn them into gold.

Pronunciation note:

The *au* letter combination should make a short "o" sound (as in *auburn* or *autumn*).

"Avav" (ay-vav) *n.* Pomp

Compounds:

Avavox (ay-vay-voks) ["Avav" + Tox] His Pomp

Possible shared root:

Avavago (av-AY-vay-go) Thunders (of Increase)

Note:

Perhaps there is something of the concept of "pomp," in the "Thunders of Increase"—as in a mighty king or god preceded by thunderous sounds and trumpets. This is, after all, the nature of the Thunders and Voices described in *Merkavah* (and related) literature such as St. John's Revelation.

Avavago (av-AY-vay-go)* *prop. n.* Thunders (of Increase)

4.8 . . . are not *the Thunders of Increase* numbered . . .?

8.36 . . . *The Thunders* have spoken . . .

Pronunciation notes:

(**Dee 4.8—Ava va go*) Four syllables. The second and third *a*'s are long.

(**Dee 8.36—A uá ua go*) Four syllables, accent on the second syllable. The first *a* seems to stand alone in word 8.36—but such is not indicated in other notes for this word. Next, Dee shows in word 4.8 that the *u*'s should actually sound like *v*'s. Finally, the *g* should take a hard sound when preceding an *o*.

(**Dee 4.8—avávâgo*) See the *48 Claves*. Accent on the second syllable. The third *a* carries a circumflex—indicating its long sound.

(**Dee 8.36—audvâgo*) See the *48 Claves*. This note matches the previous note.

Note:
The generic Angelical word for "thunder" is likely *Const*. The Thunders mentioned here and elsewhere in the Keys are groups of Angels. See *Coraxo* (Thunders) and *Sapah* (Mighty Sounds). Also note the Thunders, Lightnings, and Voices which proceeded from the Divine Throne in the vision of St. John (Book of Revelation). The Avavago are mentioned only in Keys Four and Eight—both of which seem to relate to the Southern Quarter of the Universe.

Possible shared root:
Avavox (ay-VAY-voks) ["Avav" + Tox] His Pomp

Avavox (ay-VAY-voks)* ["Avav" + Tox] *comp.* His Pomp

30.94 The work of man and *his pomp* . . .

Pronunciation notes:
(**Dee—A ua vox*) Dee spelled this word *Auavox*. However, the *u*/*v* preceding a vowel should take the "v" sound—which I have used in the spelling *Avavox*. The initial *A* stands alone. I have taken the accent from *Avavago* (Thunders of Increase).
(**Dee—auâuox*) See the *48 Claves*. Here, Dee placed a circumflex over the second *a* to indicate its long sound.

Possible shared root:
Avavago (av-AY-vay-go) Thunders (of Increase)

Note:
See note at "Avav."

Aviny (ay-VII-nee)* *n.* Millstones

9.42 . . .are *millstones* greater than the earth . . .

Pronunciation notes:

(**Dee—A vi ny*) Three syllables. The *i* should take its long sound. The *y* at the end of a word should take the long "e" sound.

(**Dee—auíny*) See the *48 Claves*. Here, Dee placed an accent over the second syllable.

"Azia" (ay-ZII-ay) *prep.* Like (unto)

Compounds:

Aziagiar (ay-zii-AY-jii-er) ["Azia" + "Giar"] Like unto the Harvest

Also:

Aziazor (ay-ZII-ay-zor) Likeness of

Note:

Also see Pugo (as unto).

Aziagiar (ay-zii-AY-jii-er)* ["Azia" + "Giar"] *comp.* Like unto the Harvest

8.19 . . .and *like unto the harvest of* a widow.

Pronunciation notes:

(**Dee—A zi á gi er*) Five syllables, with an accent on the third syllable. Both *a*'s stand alone. Both *i*'s likely take the long sound. The *g* should take a soft sound before an *i*.

(**Dee—aziágîer*) See the *48 Claves*. Dee again placed an accent on the third syllable. He also added a circumflex over the second *i* to indicate its long sound.

Also:

Aziazor (ay-ZII-ay-zor) Likeness of

Aziazor (ay-ZII-ay-zor)* *n.* Likeness of

10.7 . . . *in the likeness of* an oak . . .

Pronunciation notes:

(*Dee—A zí a zor*) Four syllables, with an accent on the second syllable. Both *a*'s stand alone, and the *i* likely takes its long sound.

(*Dee—aziâzor*) See the *48 Claves*. Here, Dee again placed an accent over the *i* in the second syllable. He also placed a circumflex over the second *a* to indicate its long sound.

Note:

It appears that "azia" is the root here. Note that an *o* is suffixed onto the root word, which sometimes indicates "of." (The further addition of an *r* is an anomaly.) "Azia" appears in what might be a compound word below.

Possible Root or Compound:

Aziagiar (ay-zii-AY-jii-er) ["Azia" + "Giar"] Like unto the Harvest

Azien (az-EEN)* *n.* Hands

3.6 . . . *on whose hands* stand 12 . . .

Pronunciation notes:

(*Dee—Azien*) I assume there should be two syllables here. The Early Modern English letter combination *ie* can make a long "e" sound. (It can also make a long "i" sound—but usually in combination with *ght*. So I have settled on the long "e" sound instead.)

I have adopted the accent from *Ozien* (hand).

Also:

Ozien (oh-ZEEN) (Mine Own) Hand

Zien (zeen) Hands

Probable shared root:

Ozol (oh-ZOHL) Hands

Zol (zohd-OL) Hands

Note:

There is no indication at this time that *Azien* (hands) and *Azia* (likeness) are related concepts.

Pa (B)

Bab (bab) *n.* Dominion

From *Corpus Omnium*:

Found in the post-Deluge portion of the Table, in the phrase *Zna Bab Iad* (Moving Dominion of God).

Note:

This word is a palindrome. It is spelled the same forward as it is spelled backward.

Possible shared root:

Ababalond (ay-BAY-bay-lond)	Harlot
Babage (bay-BAY-jee)	South
Babagen (bay-BAY-jen)	South
Babalon (bay-BAY-lon)	Wicked

Note:

Perhaps the Heptarchic Angels *Babalel* (king of Tuesday), *Bobogel* (king of Sunday), and *Bablibo* (lunar Governor of Sunday) share *Bab/Bob* as a root. (See *Babalon* for more on King Babalel, and *Babagen* for more on King Bobagel.)

Compare from *Loagaeth*:

Babalad, Babna

Babage (bay-BAY-jee)* *n.* South

4.3 I have set my feet *in the south* . . .
12.3 O you that reign *in the south* . . .

Pronunciation notes:

(*Dee 4.3—Ba bage*) Two syllables. The final *e* should make the second *a* long and the *g* soft. The first *a* also seems to be long.
(*Dee 12.3—Ba ba ge*) Seems to be three syllables. Both *a*'s long.

(*Dee 4.3—babâge*) See the *48 Claves*. Here, Dee placed a circumflex over the second *a* to indicate its long sound. There is no such indication for the first *a*.

I have adopted the accent from *Bablon* (wicked).

Also:

Babagen (bay-BAY-jen) — South

Possible shared root:

Bab (bab) — Dominion

Babalon (bay-BAY-lon) — Wicked

Ababalond (ay-BAY-bay-lond) — Harlot

Note:

If baba or *bab* is a shared root between these words, then I am unsure of the reason for this apparent bias against the southern angle of the Heavens/compass in the Angelical language. The poetry of the Keys also tends to lean toward an anti-northern angle bias.

Compare from *Loagaeth*:

Babalad, Babna

Babagen (bay-BAY-jen)* *n.* — South

13.2 O you swords of *the south* . . .

Pronunciation notes:

(**Dee—B ba gen jen*) Three syllables. For some reason, Dee forgets the *a* in the first syllable in his phonetic note. (Or, this could be a minor error in *TFR*.) However, other versions of this word suggest it should be a long "a" sound. Dee does indicate that the *g* in the third syllable should take the softer "j" sound.

(**Dee—Babâgen*) See the *48 Claves*. Dee placed a circumflex over the second *a* to indicate its long sound.

I have adopted the accent from *Bablon* (wicked).

Also:

Babage (bay-BAY-jee) — South

Possible shared root:

Bab (bab) Dominion

Babalon (bay-BAY-lon) Wicked

Ababalond (ay-BAY-bay-lond) Harlot

Note:

See the "Compare from *Loagaeth*" section for the word *Bobagen*, which may be related to *Babagen*. If this is the case, then also compare to the name of the Angel *Bobogel*, the Heptarchic King of Sunday. Perhaps *Bobogel* is related to the South because the Sun at midday (its zenith) is associated with the South in astrology.

Compare from *Loagaeth*:

Babalad, Babna, Bobagen

Babalon (bay-BAY-lon)* *n.* or *adj.* Wicked

6.11 . . . a torment to *the wicked* . . .

Pronunciation notes:

(**Dee—Babálon*) Likely three syllables, with an accent on the second syllable. Both *a*'s likely take their long sound—which is supported by the pronunciation of Ababalond (harlot).

(**Dee—babálon*) See the *48 Claves*. This note matches that from *TFR*.

Note:

Wicked is usually an adjective, but it is used here as a noun.

Also:

Ababalond (ay-BAY-bay-lond) Harlot

Note:

Notice the similarity between this word and the name of the ancient empire of Babylon. (The famous Temple to Marduk even appears in the Genesis 11 as the "Tower of Babel"—where the confusion of tongues took place.) Beginning with *1 Enoch* (likely written during the Judaic captivity in Babylon), the kingdom of Babylon has been a biblical symbol of iniquity. Also see note at *Ababalond* (harlot).

Also compare to the name of the Angel *Babalel*, the Heptarchic King of Tuesday. As the King of Tuesday and Mars, perhaps "The Wicked" (or even "The Wicked of God") is a fitting title for this Angel.

Possible shared root:

Bab (bab) Dominion
Babage (bay-BAY-jee) South
Babagen (bay-BAY-jen) South

Compare from *Loagaeth*:

Babalad, Babna

Baeovib (bee-oh-vib) *prop. n.* Righteousness

15.14 . . . knowest the great name *righteousness* . . .

Pronunciation notes:

(**Dee—Bæôuib*) See the *48 Claves*. The ash (*æ*) in Dee's phonetic notation can indicate a short *a* or a long "e" sound. (I assume the long *e* in this case.) Dee placed a circumflex over the *o* to indicate its long sound. The *u* is somewhat unsure, although I have assumed it should make the sound of *v* when preceding a vowel. (I have also spelled the word with a *v*.) This should be a word of three syllables.

Note:

The transmission of Key Fifteen is missing from Dee's journals. We only have the English for this Key given later (see *TFR*, p. 193). Plus, the word appears in this location in Dee's *48 Claves*.

It appears this is a proper noun—likely a Name of God. See also *Baltoh*, *Baltle*, and *Samvelg* (all forms of "righteous").

Bag (bag) *prop. n.* "The Twenty-Eighth Aethyr" (Fury?)

30.3 . . . which dwell in *the twenty-eighth aethyr* . . .

Note:

This (word 30.3) is the single space in the Key of the Aethyrs, which must be changed for each invocation—replacing word 30.3 with the name of the appropriate Aethyr. No established definitions were given for these names.

Bag contains the three Parts of the Earth *Labnixp*, *Pocisni*, and *Oxlopar*.

Possible shared root:

Bagie (bag-EE) Fury

Note:

The names of the Heptarchic Angels *Bagenol* (prince of Friday) and *Bagnole* (solar Governor of Friday). If the word *Bag* is a root indicating "fury," this could indicate an etymology for these Angels.

Bagie (bag-EE)* *n.* Fury

14.2 O you sons of *fury* . . .

Pronunciation notes:

(**Dee—bagíe*) See the *48 Claves*. The only phonetic clue Dee gives us is the accent mark. I am assuming two syllables here. The *a* might take the short sound in the first syllable. In Early Modern English, the *ie* letter combination should make a long "e" sound (as in the English word *believe*).

Note:

The transmission of Key Fourteen is missing from Dee's journals. We only have the English for this Key given later (see *TFR*, p. 193). Plus, the word appears in this location in Dee's *48 Claves*.

See also Baltim (extreme justice, or fury).

Possible shared root:

Bag (bag) "The Twenty-Eighth Aethyr"

Bagle (BAY-gayl)* *conj.* For (Wherefore, Because)

4.36 . . . *For* I am the Lord . . .
5.53 . . . *For why?* Our Lord and Master is One.
7.42 . . . *For*, to this remembrance . . .
8.35 . . . *For* the Thunders have spoken . . .
8.39 . . . Come away, *for* the crowns of the temple . . .
9.62 . . . *For why?* The God if Righteousness . . .
9.70 . . . *For* the time is such . . .
10.18 . . . Laid up *for* the earth . . .**
10.74 . . . *For* her iniquity is great . . .
11.32 . . . *For* I have prepared for you . . .
30.103 . . . *For why?* It repenteth me . . .

Note:
***Bagle* at 10.18 is the only instance where the word is not synonymous with "because" or the older "wherefore" (or "for why?").

Pronunciation notes:
(**Dee 4.36; 7.42; 8.35, 39; 9.62, 70; 10.18—Ba gle*) Two syllables. Long *a*. Also note that the final letters *le* following a consonant usually make an "ayl" sound in Angelical. (See *Baltle* and *Cicle* for examples.)
(**Dee 5.53—Ba' gle*) Accent on the first syllable.
(**Dee 10.74; 11.32; 30.103—Bagle*)
(**Dee 5.53—Bágle*) See the *48 Claves*. The accent is again shown on the first syllable.

Also:
Baglen (BAY-gayl-en) Because

Note:
Aso see Lap (for) and Darsar (wherefore).

Compare from *Loagaeth*:
Baged

Baglen (BAY-gayl-en)* *conj.* Because

30.110 . . . *Because* she is the bed of an harlot . . .

Pronunciation notes:

(**Dee—Baglen*) Dee does not leave us much of a clue. However, I suggest three syllables, accent on the first syllable, based on the pronunciation notes for Bagle.

Also:

Bagle (BAY-gayl)	For (Wherefore, Because)

Note:

Also see Lap (for) and Darsar (wherefore).

Bahal (BAY-hal)* *v.* — To Cry Loudly (i.e., To Yell)

11.14 . . . the Eagle spake and *cried with a loud voice* . . .

Pronunciation notes:

(**Dee—Ba hal*) Two syllables. The first *a* appears to take its long sound.
(**Dee—báhal*) See the *48 Claves*. Here, Dee placed an accent upon the first syllable.

Note:

See also Faaip (voices).

Shared root:

Bia (bii-a)	Voices
Bial (bii-al)	Voice
Bien (bii-en)	(My) Voice

Balit (bal-it) *n.* — The Just

**16.10 . . . shall comfort *the just* . . .

Note:

**The transmission of the first twelve words of Key Sixteen is missing from Dee's journals. We only have the English given for it on *TFR*, p. 194. However, they do appear in Dee's *48 Claves*.

The phrase *the just* has an implied noun: *people*. In the complete phrase *the just people*, the word *just* is an adjective.

Also:

Balt (balt) — Justice
Baltan (bal-tan) — Justice
Baltim (bal-tim) — Extreme Justice (or Fury)

Note:

See also Baltoh (*righteousness*).
Also compare to the name of the Angel *Baligon*, the Heptarchic King of Friday. The Just may be a root for his name. If his name is a compound, perhaps it is (Balit + Gono), "Faith (of) the Just."

Possible shared root:

Baltle (bal-tayl) — Righteousness
Balzarg (bal-zarj) — Stewards
Balzizras (bal-zii-sras) — Judgment

Balt (balt)* *n.* — Justice

1.6 . . . sayeth the God of *Justice* . . .
3.57 . . . become the skirts of *justice* . . .
**16.4 . . . the house of *Justice* . . .

Pronunciation notes:

(**Dee 1.6; 3.57—Balt*)

Note:

**The transmission of the first twelve words of Key Sixteen is missing from Dee's journals. We only have the English given for it on *TFR*, p. 194. However, they do appear in Dee's *48 Claves*.

Also:

Balit (bal-it) — The Just
Baltan (bal-tan) — Justice
Baltim (bal-tim) — Extreme Justice (or Fury)

Compounds:

Baltoh (bal-toh) [Balt + Toh] — Righteousness

Baltoha (bal-toh-ha) [Balt + "Toha"] (My) Righteousness
Iadbaloth (ii-ad-BAL-toh) [Iad + Balt + Toh] God of Righteousness

Possible shared root:
Baltle (bal-tayl) Righteousness
Balzarg (bal-zarj) Stewards
Balzizras (bal-zii-sras) Judgment

Baltan (bal-tan)* *n.* Justice

30.150 . . . sworn to us *in his justice* . . .

Pronunciation notes:
(**Dee—Baltan*) Likely two syllables.

Also:
Balit (bal-it) The Just
Balt (balt) Justice
Baltim (bal-tim) Extreme Justice (or Fury)

Note:
See also Baltoh (*righteous*).

Possible shared root:
Baltle (bal-tayl) Righteousness
Balzarg (bal-zarj) Stewards
Balzizras (bal-zii-sras) Judgment

Baltim (bal-tim) *n.* Extreme Justice (or Fury)

14.24 . . . called amongst you *fury* (or *extreme justice*) . . .

Note:
The transmission of Key Fourteen is missing from Dee's journals. We only have the English for this Key given later (see *TFR*, p. 193). Plus, the word appears in this location in Dee's *48 Claves*.

Also:

Balit (bal-it) — The Just
Balt (balt) — Justice
Baltan (bal-tan) — Justice

Note:

Bagie (fury).

Possible shared root:

Baltle (bal-tayl) — Righteousness
Baltoh (bal-toh) — Righteous
Balzarg (bal-zarj) — Stewards
Balzizras (bal-zii-sras) — Judgment

Baltle (bal-tayl)* *n.* — Righteousness

1.70 . . . balance of *righteousness* and truth . . .

Pronunciation notes:

(**Dee—Baltale to be sounded*) Should be two syllables. The letters *le*, following a consonant, combine to form the "ayl" sound at the end of the word. (See *Cicle* and *Bagle*.)

Also:

Baltoh (bal-toh) — Righteousness

Possible shared root:

Balit (bal-it) — The Just
Balt (balt) — Justice
Baltan (bal-tan) — Justice
Baltim (bal-tim) — Extreme Justice (or Fury)
Balzarg (bal-zarj) — Stewards
Balzizras (bal-zii-sras) — Judgment

Note:

See also "Piamol." See also *Baeouib* and *Samvelg* (both are forms of "righteous").

Baltoh (bal-toh)* [Balt + Toh] *comp.* Righteousness

2.22 . . . the chamber of *righteousness* . . .

Pronunciation notes:

(**Dee—Baltoh*) Likely two syllables.

Also:

Baltle (bal-tayl) Righteousness

Compounds:

Baltoha (bal-toh-ha) [Balt + "Toha"] (My) Righteousness

Iadbaloth (ii-ad-BAL-toh) [Iad + Balt + Toh] God of Righteousness

Note:

Also see Baeouib (righteousness) and Samvelg (the righteous).

Possible shared root:

Balit (bal-it) The Just

Balt (balt) Justice

Baltan (bal-tan) Justice

Baltim (bal-tim) Extreme Justice (or Fury)

Balzarg (bal-zarj) Stewards

Balzizras (bal-zii-sras) Judgment

Baltoha (bal-toh-ha)* [Balt + "Toha"] *comp.* (My) Righteousness

8.12 . . . which I have prepared for *my own righteousness* . . .

Pronunciation notes:

(**Dee—Bal to ha*) Three syllables. The *o* takes a long sound (likely due to the *oh* letter combination).

(**Dee—baltôha*) See the *48 Claves*. Here Dee placed a circumflex over the *o* to indicate its long sound.

Also:

Baltle (bal-tayl) Righteousness

Compounds:

Baltoh (bal-toh) [Balt + Toh] — Righteousness

Iadbaloth (ii-ad-BAL-toh) [Iad + Balt + Toh] — God of Righteousness

Note:

Also see *Baeouib* (righteousness) and *Samvelg* (the righteous).

Balye (bay-lii-ee)* *n.* — Salt

9.19 . . . and of the marrow of *salt* . . .

Pronunciation notes:

(**Dee—Ba ly e*) Three syllables. I suggest a long *a* in the first syllable. I have given the *y* a long "i" sound in the second syllable. Finally, the *e* stands alone in the third syllable.

Balzarg (bal-zarj)* *n.* — Stewards

3.30 . . . I made you *stewards* and placed you . . .

Pronunciation notes:

(**Dee—BALZARG arg as in barge*) I suggest two syllables. Dee indicates a soft *g* at the end.

Note:

Saying *steward* is another manner of saying *caretaker*. It could indicate a "Governor."

Possible shared root:

Balit (bal-it) — The Just

Balt (balt) — Justice

Baltan (bal-tan) — Justice

Baltim (bal-tim) — Extreme Justice (or Fury)

Baltoh (bal-toh) — Righteousness

Balzizras (bal-zii-sras) — Judgment

Balzizras (bal-zii-sras)* *n.* — Judgment

30.9 . . . execute *the Judgment* of the Highest.

Pronunciation notes:

(*Dee—Bal zi zras*) Three syllables. I assume a long *i* at the end of the second syllable.

Possible shared root:

Balit (bal-it) — The Just
Balt (balt) — Justice
Baltan (bal-tan) — Justice
Baltim (bal-tim) — Extreme Justice (or Fury)
Baltoh (bal-toh) — Righteousness
Balzarg (bal-zarj) — Stewards

Bams (bams)* *v.* — To Forget

30.90 . . . let them *forget* their names . . .

Pronunciation notes:

(*Dee—Bams*) One syllable.

Barees (bar-ees) *n.*? — n/a

Note:

See the *Five Books*, p. 188. The Ruling Prince of the *Heptarchia*, Hagonel (not to be confused with the Son of the Sons of Light with the same name) presents his Seal—which is identical to the common symbol of the Sun (a circle with a dot in the center)—and calls it *Barees*. No definition is given.

Basgim (bas-jim)* *n.* — Day

10.24 . . . which burn night and *day* . . .

Pronunciation notes:

(**Dee—Bas gim*) Two syllables. The vowels are all short. The *g* should take its soft sound when preceding an *i*.

Shared root:

Bazemlo (bas-em-loh) Midday the First
"Bazem" (bas-em) Midday

Note:

These words apparently share "bas/baz" as a root.

"Bazem" (bas-em) *n.* Midday

Compounds:

Bazemlo (bas-em-loh) ["Bazem" + "Lo"] Midday the First

Shared root:

Basgim (bas-jim) Day

Note:

These words apparently share "bas/baz" as a root.

Also:

Compare the names of the Heptarchic Angels *Baspalo* (Mercury Governor of Monday), *Basledf* (Venus Governor of Monday), and *Bazpama* (Mars Governor of Wednesday). Also compare the name of the Part of the Earth (and its Angelic Governor) *Bazchim*.

Bazemlo (bas-em-loh)* ["Bazem" + "Lo"] *comp.* Midday the First

8.1 *The midday the first* is as the third heaven . . .

Pronunciation notes:

(**Dee—Baz me lo*) Dee originally wrote this word as *Bazmelo*. However, see *TFR*, p. 200, where Illemese corrects this:
(*Illemese—Basem lo, or Basemlo*) Three syllables.
(**Dee—Bazmêlo*) See the *48Keys*. Dee preserved the *Bazmelo* spelling of the word here. He even placed a circumflex over the *e* to indicate a long sound. However, I have settled upon the correction made by Illemese.

Shared root:

Basgim (bas-jim) — Day

Note:

These words apparently share *bas / baz* as a root.

Also:

Compare the name of the Heptarchic Angel *Basmelo*, the solar Governor of Thursday. See the pronunciation note—as this might explain why Dee originally wrote Bazemlo as "Basmelo" instead. I suggest the Governor's name should be pronounced as Dee describes above—with a long "e" sound (bas-mee-loh).

Befafes (bef-ay-fes) *prop. n.* — Light From Light,* *Heptarchic* Prince of Tuesday, Mars

Note:

(**Dee—Befafes his etymology is as much to say "Light from the Light."*) See the *Five Books*, p. 310. However, see *Ialpirt* (light)—which I assume refers to a different kind of Light than expressed in Befafes' name.

I have not included most of the Heptarchic names and those derived from tablets and magick squares elsewhere in the Angelical system in this Lexicon. However, the name of the Prince of Tuesday, *Befafes*, plays an important role between *Loagaeth* and the forty-eight Keys.
Also see *Obelison* (Pleasant Deliverer), a name of Befafes.

Also:

Befes (bef-es) — Heptarchic Prince of Tuesday (vocative)

Compare from *Loagaeth*:

Bef, Befas

Befes (BEF-es)* *n.* — Heptarchic Prince of Tuesday (vocative)**

Pronunciation note:

(**Dee—Béfes*) See the *Five Books*, p. 310. Dee places an accent over the first *e*.

From *Loagaeth*:

(***Dee—Befes the vocative case of Befafes. Befafes O, is to call upon him as on God. Befafes O, is as much to say, "Come Befafes and bear witness." Befafes his etymology is as much to say "Light from the Light."*) See the *Five Books*, p. 310. *Befafes* is the Heptarchic Prince of Tuesday.

Also:

Befafes (bef-ay-fes) — Heptarchic Prince of Tuesday, Mars

Compare from *Loagaeth*:

Bef

Bia (bii-a)* *n.* — Voices

2.30 . . . mightier are *your voices* than the manifold winds . . .

Pronunciation notes:

(**Dee—Bia*) Likely two syllables with a long *i*. See pronunciation note for *Bien* (my voice). I believe the final *a* should take the short sound, as Dee did not write it by itself.

Also:

Bial (bii-al) — Voice

Bien (bii-en) — (My) Voice

Shared root:

Bahal (BAY-hal) — Cry with a Loud Voice

Note:

The *Bia* family of words seem to indicate the physical speaking voice. See also *Faaip* (voices/psalms) and *Farzem* (uplifted voices)—both of which seem to indicate the action of speaking or singing.

Biab (bii-ab)* *v.* To Stand

3.7 . . . on whose hands *stand* 12 kingdoms.

Pronunciation notes:
(**Dee—Biab*) Likely two syllables with a long *i*, as in the English word *dial*.

Note:
Why would this word seem to share a root with the words for "voice" (*Bial*, *Bien*, etc.)?

Bial (bii-al) *n.* Voice

14.18 Behold *the voice* of God . . .

Pronunciation notes:
Likely two syllables with a long *i*. See pronunciation note for *Bien* (my voice).

Note:
The transmission of Key Fourteen is missing from Dee's journals. We only have the English for this Key given later (see *TFR*, p. 193). Plus, the word appears in this location in Dee's *48 Claves*.

Also:

Bia (bii-a) — Voices
Bien (bii-en) — (My) Voice

Note:
See also Faaip (voices/psalms) and Farzem (uplifted voices).

Shared root:

Bahal (BAY-hal) — Cry with a Loud Voice

Bien (bii-en)* *n.* (My) Voice

6.33 . . . hearken unto *my voice*.

Pronunciation notes:

(**Dee—Bi en*) Two syllables. The *i* is likely a long vowel.

Also:

Bia (bii-a) Voices

Bial (bii-al) Voice

Note:

See also *Faaip* (voices / psalms) and *Farzem* (uplifted voices).

"Bigl" (big-el) *n.* Comforter?

Compounds:

Bigliad (big-lii-ad) ["Bigl" + Iad?] (In Our) Comforter

Note:

It is not certain that *Bigliad* should be a compound, or if *Iad* is merely a root in this word.

Pronunciation notes:

See *Crpl* (but one) for a similar pronunciation.

Possible shared root:

"Bliard" (blii-ARD) Comfort

Blior (blii-OR) Comfort

Bliora (blii-OH-ra) Comfort

Bliorax (blii-OH-raks) To Comfort

Bliorb (blii-ORB) Comfort

Bliors (blii-ORS) Comfort

"Bliort" (blii-ORT) Comfort

Pibliar (pib-lii-AR) Places of Comfort

Bigliad (big-lii-ad)* ["Bigl" + Iad?] *comp.* (In Our) Comforter

7.49 . . . our strength waxeth strong *in our comforter* . . .

Pronunciation notes:

(**Dee—Big li ad*) Three syllables. The *i* at the end of the second syllable takes a long sound.

(*Dee—Biglîad*) See the *48 Claves*. Here, Dee adds a circumflex over the *i* to indicate its long sound.

Note:

Bigliad is a direct reference to God. It would seem to be a compound of *Iad* (God) and *Blior* (comfort)—though note the radical change from *Blior* to *"Bigl."* I'm not sure what the root would be in this case.

Blans (blanz)* *v.* — To Harbor

10.5 . . . and *are harboured* in the north . . .

Pronunciation notes:

(*Dee—Blans*) One syllable. The *a* is likely short.

"Bliard" (blii-ARD) *n.* — Comfort

Pronunciation note:

I have adopted the accent from *Bliora* (comfort).

Compounds:

Fbliard (ef-blii-ard) [F + "Bliard"] Visit (with) Comfort

Also:

"Bigl" (big-el)	Comforter
Blior (blii-OR)	Comfort
Bliora (blii-OH-ra)	Comfort
Bliorax (blii-OH-raks)	To Comfort
Bliorb (blii-ORB)	Comfort
Bliors (blii-ORS)	Comfort
"Bliort" (blii-ORT)	Comfort
Pibliar (pib-lii-AR)	Places of Comfort

Blior (blii-OR)* *n.* — Comfort

9.74 . . . as requireth *comfort* . . .

Pronunciation notes:

(**Dee—Bli or*) Two syllables. I have adopted the accent from *Bliora* (comfort).

Also:

"Bigl" (big-el)	Comforter
"Bliard" (blii-ARD)	Comfort
Bliora (blii-OH-ra)	Comfort
Bliorax (blii-OH-raks)	To Comfort
Bliorb (blii-ORB)	Comfort
Bliors (blii-ORS)	Comfort
"Bliort" (blii-ORT)	Comfort
Pibliar (pib-lii-AR)	Places of Comfort

Compounds:

Tablior (TAY-blii-or) [Ta + Blior]	As Comforters

Possible compounds:

Bigliad (big-lii-ad) ["Bigl" + Iad?]	(In Our) Comforter

Bliora (blii-OH-ra)* *n.* Comfort

5.49 . . . visit us in peace and *comfort* . . .

Pronunciation notes:

(**Dee—Bli ó ra*) Three syllables, with the accent on the second syllable. The *o* stands alone.

(**Dee—blíora*) See the *48 Claves*. Again the accent is shown on the second syllable.

Also:

"Bigl" (big-el)	Comforter
"Bliard" (blii-ARD)	Comfort
Blior (blii-OR)	Comfort
Bliorax (blii-OH-raks)	To Comfort
Bliorb (blii-ORB)	Comfort
Bliors (blii-ORS)	Comfort
"Bliort" (blii-ORT)	Comfort
Pibliar (pib-lii-AR)	Places of Comfort

Bliorax (blii-OH-raks)* *v.* Shalt Comfort (or To Comfort)

16.9 . . . and *shalt comfort* the just . . .

Note:

The transmission of the first twelve words of Key Sixteen is missing from Dee's journals. We only have the English given for it on *TFR*, p. 194. However, they do appear in Dee's *48 Claves*.

Also:

Note this could be an example of the *-ax* affix, indicating action.

Pronunciation notes:

(**Dee—bliôrax*) See the *48 Claves*. Dee placed a circumflex over the *o* to indicate a long sound. The accent is taken from *Bliora* (comfort). See other versions of this word for further pronunciation notes.

Also:

"Bigl" (big-el) Comforter
"Bliard" (blii-ARD) Comfort
Blior (blii-OR) Comfort
Bliora (blii-OH-ra) Comfort
Bliorb (blii-ORB) Comfort
Bliors (blii-ORS) Comfort
"Bliort" (blii-ORT) Comfort
Pibliar (pib-lii-AR) Places of Comfort

Compounds:

Tablior (TAY-blii-or) [Ta + Blior] As Comforters

Bliorb (blii-ORB)* *n.* Comfort

30.17 . . . God, the beginning of *comfort* . . .

Pronunciation notes:

(**Dee—Bliórb*) Likely two syllables, with an accent on the second syllable.

Also:

“Bigl” (big-el) Comforter
“Bliard” (blii-ARD) Comfort
Blior (blii-OR) Comfort
Bliora (blii-OH-ra) Comfort
Bliorax (blii-OH-raks) (Shalt) Comfort
Bliors (blii-ORS) Comfort
“Bliort” (blii-ORT) Comfort
Pibliar (pib-lii-AR) Places of Comfort

Bliors (blii-ORS)* *n.* Comfort

8.51 . . . to the terror of the earth, and *to our comfort* . . .
18.5 . . . burning flame of *comfort* . . .

Pronunciation notes:

(**Dee 8.51—Bli ors*)
(**Dee 18.5—B liors*) Two syllables. Based on other versions of this word, I suspect that Dee's note at word 18.5 is a misprint. I have taken my pronunciation from the note at 8.51. The *i* at the end of the first syllable should likely take a long sound.
I have adopted the accent from *Bliora* (comfort).

Also:

“Bigl” (big-el) Comforter
“Bliard” (blii-ARD) Comfort
Blior (blii-OR) Comfort
Bliora (blii-OH-ra) Comfort
Bliorax (blii-OH-raks) To Comfort
Bliorb (blii-ORB) Comfort
“Bliort” (blii-ORT) Comfort
Pibliar (pib-lii-AR) Places of Comfort

“Bliort” (blii-ORT) *n.* Comfort

Pronunciation note:

I have adopted the accent from *Bliora* (comfort).

Compounds:

Comobliort (koh-moh-blii-ort) ["Como" + "Bliort"] — Window of Comfort

Also:

"Bigl" (big-el) — Comforter
"Bliard" (blii-ARD) — Comfort
Blior (blii-OR) — Comfort
Bliora (blii-OH-ra) — Comfort
Bliorax (blii-OH-raks) — To Comfort
Bliorb (blii-ORB) — Comfort
Bliors (blii-ORS) — Comfort
Pibliar (pib-lii-AR) — Places of Comfort

Bobagelzod (boh-bay-JEL-zohd)* *n.?* — Heptarchic King of Sunday, Sol?

From *Loagaeth*:

See the *Five Books*, p. 313. This would appear to be the name of the Heptarchic King of Sunday and Sol, *Bobagel*. Perhaps this is a formal vocative case of his name? (See the "Angelical Linguistics" chapter.)

Pronunciation note:

(**Dee—Bobagélzod*) See the *Five Books*, p. 313. Dee places an accent over the *e*. I have given the first *a* and *o* their long sounds based on similar words (see *Babagen*, *Babalon*, etc.).

Compare from *Loagaeth*:

Bobagen

Bogpa (bog-pa)* *v.* — To Reign

1.66 . . . and *reigneth* amongst you . . .

Pronunciation notes:

(**Dee—Call it Bogpa*) I assume two syllables.

Note:

See also *Sonf* (reign).

Bolp (bulp)* *v.?* or *pron.* — (Be) Thou

18.24 *Be thou* a window of comfort unto me.

Pronunciation notes:

(**Dee—Bolp*) One syllable. I assume this word sounds similar to the English word *gulp*.

Probable shared root:

Aqlo (AY-kwah-loh)	Thy
Yls (yils)	Thou
Ylsi (yil-sii)	Thee
L (el)	First
Ol (ohl)	I, Myself

Note:

If *Ol* (myself) is the root here, then the pre- and suffixed letters (*B* and *p*) alter it to its antonym (thou). Also see the word *I* (is / are), which goes through a similar antonymic change into *Ip* (not).

I also note that this word seems to indicate action, even though *thou* is technically a personal pronoun.

Booapis (boh-OH-ay-pis)* *v.* — To Serve

30.63 . . . as a handmaid *let her serve them.*

Pronunciation notes:

(**Dee—B o o a p i S*) This is a very confusing note, and I doubt that Dee intended every one of these letters to stand alone. (To make sense of this, I have taken the pronunciation notes for *Aboapri* into account.) I have combined the initial *B* and the first *o*, and left the second *o* to stand alone. This makes a word of four syllables.

I have applied the accent to the second syllable based on *Aboapri* (to serve).

Also:

Aboapri (ay-BOH-ay-prii) — To Serve

Note:

It would appear that *boap/booap* serves as the common root between these two words.

Bornogo (bor-noh-goh) *prop. n.* — Heptarchic Prince of Sunday, Sol

From *Loagaeth*:

This name appears in a star pattern on the ninth Table of *Loagaeth*. *Bornogo* is the Heptarchic Prince of Sunday and Sol. Interestingly, it would seem a version of the name *Bobgel* (the King of Sunday) also appears in *Loagaeth*. (See *Bobogelzod*.)

Bransg (branzh)* *n.* — Guard

9.2 A mighty *guard of* fire with two-edged swords . . .

Pronunciation notes:

(**Dee—Bransg*) This word is likely one syllable. All of these letters fit naturally together in English. The *a* should take its short sound. The *sg* should make the sound of "sj" (a kind of "zhuh" sound)—which I have represented as *zh*. (See *Vorsg* for another example.)

Note:

A *guard*, as the word is used in Key Nine, refers to troops who have been assigned to something specific—such as an honor guard assigned to carry a flag. The *mighty guard* in Key Nine is like a defensive platoon.

Brgda (burj-da)* *v.* — To Sleep

3.25 . . .which *sleep* and shall rise.

Pronunciation notes:

(**Dee—as Burgda as burgen to bud*) Apparently two syllables, with a soft "g" (or "j") sound followed immediately by a *d*. (Almost like a hard "j" or "dg" sound—as in *fudge* and *budge*.) As is often the case, the *r* nested between two incompatible consonants adopts an "ur" sound.

"Brin" (brin) *v.* Have

Compounds:

Dsbrin (dee-es-brin) [Ds + "Brin"] Which Have

Also:

"Brint" (brint) Has

Brints (brints) To Have

Note:

"Brin" is likely the root word for *Brints* and its related words.

"Brint" (brint) *v.* Has

Compounds:

Odbrint (ohd-brint) [Od + "Brint"] And Has

Also:

"Brin" (brin) Have

Brints (brints) To Have

Note:

"Brin" may represent the root word here.

Brints (brints)* *v.* To Have

18.15 . . . 6332 *have* their abiding . . .

Pronunciation notes:

(**Dee—Brints*) All one syllable. The *i* is likely short.

Also:

"Brin" (brin) Have

"Brint" (brint) Has

Note:
"Brin" may represent the root word here.

Compare from *Loagaeth*:
Brtnc

Brita (brit-a)* *v.* To Speak of

6.34 *I have talked of you* and I move you . . .

Pronunciation notes:
(**Dee—Brita*) Likely two syllables.

Note:
Also see *Camliax* (Spake).

Busd (buzd)* *n., adj.* Glory, Glorious

8.23 . . . in *the glory* of the earth . . .
**16.7 . . . thy beginning *in glory* . . .

Pronunciation notes:
(**Dee 8.23—Bufd*) One syllable. I notice "Bufd" is spelled with an *f* while every other version of the word (*Busdir, Busdirtilb*) is spelled with an *s*. In Dee's English, elongated *s*'s were often used that highly resemble *f*'s. Therefore, it is likely that this word should read *Busd*. (See *Casasam*/"Cafafam" for a similar example.)
(**Dee 8.23—busd*) See the *48 Claves*. Here, Dee confirms that the *f* in *TFR* should actually be an *s*.

Note:
**The transmission of the first twelve words of Key Sixteen is missing from Dee's journals. We only have the English given for it on *TFR*, p. 194. However, they do appear in Dee's *48 Claves*.

Also:
Busdir (buz-der) Glory

Note:

Busd would seem to indicate *glory* in the sense of "wondrous." See also *Ialpirgah* (flames of the first glory), which properly relates to light and fire—and possibly the light (glory) of the rising Sun. And *Adgmach* (glory), which appears to indicate "adoration, praise." Also see "Lzirn" (wonders) and *Sald* (wonder).

Also compare *Busd* to the Heptarchic Angel *Busduna*, the lunar Governor of Tuesday. Apparently, *Busduna* contains an etymology of "glorious."

Busdir (buz-der)* *n.* Glory

18.8 . . . openest *the glory* of God.

Pronunciation notes:

(**Dee—Bus dir*) Two syllables.

Also:

Busd (buzd) Glory

Compounds:

Busdirtilb (buz-der-tilb) [Busdir + Tilb] Glory (of) Her

Note:

See note at *Busd*.

Busdirtilb (buz-der-tilb)* [Busdir + Tilb] *comp.* Glory (of) Her

30.50 . . . that *the glory of her* may be . . .

Pronunciation notes:

(**Dee—Bus dir tilb*) Three syllables.

Butmon (but-mon)* *n.* Mouth

7.9 . . . the Lord *hath opened his mouth* . . .

Pronunciation notes:

(**Dee—But mon*) Two syllables. Both vowels are probably short.

Also:

Butmona (but-moh-na) — Mouth
Butmoni (but-moh-nii) — Mouths

Note:

Compare to the name of the Angel *Butmono*, the Heptarchic Prince of Thursday. If the *-o* affix (of) applies here, Butmono's name means "of the mouth"—like the mouth of God.

Butmona (but-moh-na)* *n.* — Mouth

30.146 . . . the covenant of *his mouth* which he hath sworn . . .

Pronunciation notes:

(**Dee—But mo na*) Three syllables. The *o* likely takes a long sound.
(**Dee—butmôna*) See the *48 Claves*. Here, Dee placed a circumflex over the *o*—thus confirming its long sound.

Also:

Butmon (but-mon) — Mouth
Butmoni (but-moh-nii) — Mouths

Note:

See note at *Butmon*.

Butmoni (but-moh-nii)* *n.* — Mouths

9.46 . . . and *from their mouths* run seas of blood.

Pronunciation notes:

(**Dee—BUT MO NI*) Three syllables. It is unclear why Dee wrote this word in all caps. The *o* in the second syllable should take its long sound. Likewise for the *i* in the final syllable.

(**Dee—butmôni*) See the *48 Claves*. Here, Dee placed a circumflex over the *o* to indicate its long sound.

Also:

Butmon (but-mon)	Mouth
Butmona (but-moh-na)	Mouth

Note:

See note at *Butmon*.

Veh (C/K)

Ca (see-ay)* *adv.* Therefore

1.74 Move, *therefore* . . .
2.43 Move, *therefore* . . .
5.42 *Therefore*, come you and obey . . .
11.36 Move, *therefore* . . .

Pronunciation notes:
(**Dee 1.74—Call it C A [two syllables]*) Each letter here stands alone.
(**Dee 2.43—Ca*)
(**Dee 5.42—Ca Sa*) This note suggests one syllable, with the *C* taking the sound of "S."
(**Dee 1.74—c-a*) See *48 Claves*. Two syllables are again indicated.

Note:
See also "Ca" (*as*).

Compare from *Loagaeth*:
Ca

"Ca" (kay) *prep.* As?

Compounds:
Icorsca (ii-KORS-kay) [I + Cors + "Ca"] Is Such as

Also:
Ta (tay) As

Note:
The English word *as* is generally translated as *Ta*. However, there is precedent elsewhere in the Keys for this switch from *T* to *C*. See *Cab* (scepter) and *Caba* (govern).

Cab (kab) *n.* Rod/Scepter

1.44 . . . delivered you *a rod* with the arc of knowledge . . .

Note:

This word obviously means *scepter*—such as a ruling king would carry. It is intimately connected with the word *Caba* (govern), which precedes *Cab* in the Key by a few words.

Also:

Caba (ka-BA) Govern

Shared root:

Tabaam (tay-BAY-an) Governor
"Tabas" (tay-BAS) Govern

Note:

Note that the *T* (of the Taba root) becomes a *C* here. Note also the word Icorsca (*is such as*)—which uses *Ca* for *as* rather than the normal *Ta*. There does seem to be some relationship between the letters *T* and *C* in the Angelical.

Caba (ka-BA)* *v.* To Govern

1.40 . . . a law *to govern* the holy ones . . .

Pronunciation notes:

(**Dee—call it Caba*) Should be two syllables.
(**Dee—cabá*) See *48 Claves*. The accent is on the second syllable.

Also:

Cab (kab) Govern

Shared root:

Tabaam (tay-BAY-an) Governor
"Tabas" (tay-BAS) Govern

Note:

See note with Cab (scepter) and "Ca" (as?). Also see *Tabaam*.

Cabanladan (kab-an-lad-an) n/a

Note:

See *TFR*, pp. 34–35. This session is recorded entirely in Latin. Here we find this Angelical phrase spoken by "a Voice": *Garil zed masch, ich na gel galaht gemp gal noch Cabanladan.* No translation or context is offered.

Cacacom (kay-SAY-som)* *v.* To Flourish

3.66 . . . his mercies *flourish* . . .

Pronunciation notes:

(**Dee—Ca ca com*) Three syllables. See *Casasam* (abiding)—indicating the *c*'s in Cacacom (except for the initial *C*) should also take the soft "s" sound.

(**Dee—ca-cá-com*) See the *48 Claves*. Here, Dee indicates the accent on the second syllable.

Also:

"Cacocasb" (kay-KOH-kasb) Another While
Cacrg (KAY-kurg) Until
Casasam (kay-SAY-sam) Abiding

Possible shared root:

Acocasb (ay-KOH-kasb) Time
Capimali (kay-pii-MAY-lii) Successively
"Capimao" (kay-pii-MAY-oh) While
Capimaon (kap-ii-MAY-on) Number of Time
Capmiali (kap-mii-AY-lii) Successively
Cocasb (KOH-kasb) Time
Cocasg (KOH-kazh) Times
Qcocasb (kwah-KOH-kasb) Contents of Time

Note:

Also see *Pild* (continually).

"Cacocasb" (kay-KOH-kasb) *n.* — Another While

Pronunciation note:

I have adopted the accent from other versions of this word.

Compounds:

Odcacocasb (ohd-kay-KOH-kazb) [Od + "Cacocasb"] — And Another While

Also:

Acocasb (ay-KOH-kasb)	Time
Cacacom (kay-SAY-som)	Flourish
Cacrg (KAY-kurg)	Until
Cocasb (KOH-kasb)	Time
Cocasg (KOH-kazh)	Times
Qcocasb (kwah-KOH-kasb)	Contents of Time

Probable shared root:

Casasam (kay-SAY-sam)	Abiding
Capimali (kay-pii-MAY-lii)	Successively
"Capimao" (kay-pii-MAY-oh)	While
Capimaon (kap-ii-MAY-on)	Number of Time
Capmiali (kap-mii-AY-lii)	Successively

Note:

Also see *Pild* (continually).

Cacrg (KAY-kurg)* *prep.* or *conj.* — Until

8.28 . . . shall not see death *until* this house fall . . .

30.138 . . . add and diminish *until* the stars be numbered . . .

Pronunciation notes:

(**Dee 8.28—Ca curg*)

(**Dee 30.138—Ca crg cúrg*) Two syllables. The *r* takes the "ur" sound. With word 30.138, Dee seems to indicate the second syllable carries the accent (over the *úr*).

(**Dee 8.28—cacarg*) See the *48 Claves*. Here, Dee uses an *a* in the second syllable instead of a *u* to indicate the implied vowel sound. (This *a* and the corresponding *u* are strictly phonetic glosses.)
(**Dee 30.138—cácrg*) See the *48 Claves*. Here, Dee placed the accent upon the first syllable. (I have adopted this in my own pronunciation.)

Also:

Cacacom (kay-SAY-som)	Flourish
"Cacocasb" (kay-KOH-kasb)	Another While

Probable shared root:

Acocasb (ay-KOH-kasb)	Time
Casasam (kay-SAY-sam)	Abiding
Capimali (kay-pii-MAY-lii)	Successively
"Capimao" (kay-pii-MAY-oh)	While
Capimaon (kap-ii-MAY-on)	Number of Time
Capmiali (kap-mii-AY-lii)	Successively
Cocasb (KOH-kasb)	Time
Cocasg (KOH-kazh)	Times
Qcocasb (kwah-KOH-kasb)	Contents of Time

Note:
Also see *Pild* (continually).

"Cafafam" n/a

Note:
See *Casasam* (abiding).

Calz (kalz)* *n.* Firmaments (i.e., Heavens)

1.8 . . . above *the firmaments* of wrath . . .

Pronunciation notes:
(**Dee—Calz*) One syllable.

Note:
See also *Piripsol* (Heavens).

Camascheth (kam-ask-eth) n/a

Note:

See *TFR*, p. 22. Here, the guardian Angel of Lord Lasky of Poland says a prayer on Lasky's behalf, which ends with, "Grant this *Camascheth galsuagath garnastel zurah logaah luseroth.*" No translation is offered.

Compare from *Loagaeth*:

Vascheth

Camikas (kam-ii-kas) n/a

Note:

See the *Five Books*, p. 276. Here, Kelley is once again convinced the Angels are evil devils sent to lead humans astray. The Archangel Raphael holds his hands to Heaven (in what appears to be exasperation) and exclaims, "*Camikas Zure!*" No translation is suggested.

Camliax (kam-lii-aks)* *v.* Spake (i.e., Spoke)

11.12 . . . the Eagle *spake* and cried . . .

Pronunciation notes:

(*Dee—Cam li ax*) Three syllables. The *i* likely takes its long sound.

(*Dee—camlîax*) See the *48 Claves*. Here, Dee placed a circumflex over the *i* to indicate its long sound.

Note:

This could be an example of the suffix *-ax* indicating action.

Also see:

Brita (To Speak of).

Canal (san-al)* *n.* (Continual) Workmen

6.20 . . . and 7699 *continual workmen* whose courses . . .

Pronunciation notes:

(**Dee—Canal Sanal*) Two syllables. The initial *C* takes a soft sound (as in *circle* or *cereal*).

Canse (kan-say) *adj.* Mighty*

Note:

(**Dee—Canse signifieth mighty, and Cruscanse more mighty.*) See *Five Books*, p. 304. *Cruscanse* (more mighty) is found in *Loagaeth*, but *Canse* (mighty) was mentioned only in a marginal note.

See also *Micaolz* (mighty), *Micalp* (mightier)

Also:

Cruscanse (krooz-kan-say) Very Mighty

Compare from *Loagaeth*:

Can, Cans

Caosg (kay-OZH)* *n.* Earth

3.53 . . . on *the earth* continually . . .

5.9 . . . looking with gladness upon *the earth* . . .

**16.12 . . . walkest upon *the earth* with feet . . .

Pronunciation notes:

(**Dee 3.53—Caosg*)

(**Dee 5.9—Ca ósg*) Two syllables, accent on the second syllable. Also note that an *a* followed by an *o* usually appears to take its long sound (as in the English word *chaos*).

I assume that the final *sg* letter combination makes a soft "j" or "zhuh" sound. I have represented this sound with the letters *zh*. (See *Vorsg* and *Cocasg* for this same sound.)

(**Dee 3.53—caósg*) See the *48 Claves*. The *o* again carries the accent.

(**Dee 5.9—ca-ósg*) See the *48 Claves*. This note matches the one in *TFR*.

Note:
**The transmission of the first twelve words of Key Sixteen is missing from Dee's journals. We only have the English given for it on *TFR*, p. 194. However, it does appear in Dee's *48 Claves*.

Also:
Caosga (kay-OS-ga) Earth
Caosgi (kay-OZH-ii) Earth
Caosgin (kay-OS-jin) Earth
Caosgo (kay-OS-go) Of the Earth
Caosgon (kay-OS-gon) Unto the Earth

Caosga (kay-OS-ga)* *n.* Earth

30.43 . . . *the earth*, let her be governed . . .

Pronunciation notes:
(**Dee—Ca ós ga*) Likely three syllables—with the accent on the second syllable. The *g* should take the hard sound before an *a*—as in the English words *gave* and *gantry*. Finally, the *a* in the first syllable should be long, because it precedes an *o*.
(**Dee—Caósga*) See the *48 Claves*. Here, Dee again placed an accent upon the second syllable.

Also:
Caosg (kay-OZH) Earth
Caosgi (kay-OZH-ii) Earth
Caosgin (kay-OS-jin) Earth
Caosgo (kay-OS-go) Of the Earth
Caosgon (kay-OS-gon) Unto the Earth

Compounds:
Fcaosga (ef-kay-OS-ga) [F + Caosga] Visit the Earth

Caosgi (kay-OZH-ii)* *n.* Earth

5.22 . . . vessels to water *the earth* . . .
6.23 . . . visit with comfort *the earth* . . .

10.19 . . . laid up for *the earth* . . .
**15.9 . . . weave *the earth* with dryness . . .
30.26 . . . for the government of *the earth* . . .

Note:
**The transmission of Key Fifteen is missing from Dee's journals. We only have the English for this Key given later (see *TFR*, p. 193). Plus, the word appears in this location in Dee's *48 Claves*.

Pronunciation notes:
(**Dee 5.22—Ca ós gi*)
(**Dee 6.23—Ca os gi kaosgi*)
(**Dee 10.19; 30.26—Ca os gi*) In these notes, Dee indicates three syllables, with an accent on the second syllable. He also gives the initial *C* its hard ("K") sound. The *a* preceding an *o* should take the long sound (as in the English word *chaos*), and the *g* preceding an *i* likely takes its soft sound. Finally, because the *g* is soft, it likely combines with the *s* to make a kind of "zhuh" sound—which I have indicated in my pronunciation as *zh*.
(**Dee 5.22; 30.26—caósgi*) See the *48 Claves*. Note the accent again on the second syllable.
(**Dee 15.9—caôsgi*) See the *48 Claves*. Note the circumflex over the *o*, indicating its long sound.

Compounds:
Arcaosgi (ar-kay-OZH-ii) ["Ar" + Caosgi] — To(?) the Earth

Also:
Caosg (kay-OZH) — Earth
Caosga (kay-OS-ga) — Earth
Caosgin (kay-OS-jin) — Earth
Caosgo (kay-OS-go) — Of the Earth
Caosgon (kay-OS-gon) — Unto the Earth

Caosgin (kay-OS-jin)* *n.* — Earth

9.44 . . . millstones greater than *the earth* . . .

Pronunciation notes:

(**Dee—Ca os gin*) Three syllables. The *a* in the first syllable should be long. The *g* should take a soft sound when preceding an *i*.

(**Dee—caósgin*) See the *48 Claves*. Here, Dee placed an accent over the second syllable.

Also:

Caosg (kay-OZH)	Earth
Caosga (kay-OS-ga)	Earth
Caosgi (kay-OZH-ii)	Earth
Caosgo (kay-OS-go)	Of the Earth
Caosgon (kay-OS-gon)	Unto the Earth

Caosgo (kay-OS-go)* *prep. phrase* Of the Earth

8.24 . . . in the glory *of the earth* . . .
8.49 . . . to the terror *of the earth* . . .
9.30 . . . the moss *of the earth* . . .
**14.12 . . . all creatures *of the earth* . . .
18.11 . . . to the center *of the earth* . . .
30.6 . . . mighty in the parts *of the earth* . . .

Pronunciation notes:

(**Dee 8.24—Ca, or Ka os go*)
(**Dee 8.49—Ca as go Ka*)
(**Dee 9.30; 18.11—Ca os go*)
(**Dee 30.6—Ca ós go*) These notes indicate three syllables, an accent on the second syllable. The *C* takes a hard sound, and so does the *g*. (The *g* took a soft sound in *Caosg*, but the final *o* changes the sound.) Finally, I assume a long sound for the *a* because it precedes an *o*.

(**Dee 8.24, 49; 9.30; 14.12; 18.11; 30.6—caósgo*) See the *48 Claves*. Here, Dee indicates an accent on the second syllable.

Note:

**The transmission of Key Fourteen is missing from Dee's journals. We only have the English for this Key given later (see *TFR*, p. 193). Plus, the word appears in this location in Dee's *48 Claves*.

Also:

Caosg (kay-OZH) — Earth
Caosga (kay-OS-ga) — Earth
Caosgi (kay-OZH-ii) — Earth
Caosgin (kay-OS-jin) — Earth
Caosgon (kay-OS-gon) — Unto the Earth

Caosgon (kay-OS-gon)* *prep. phrase* — Unto the Earth

10.73 . . . woe *be to the earth* . . .

Pronunciation notes:

(**Dee—Ca ós gon*) Three syllables. The accent mark is placed in the middle of the second syllable. The *a* should be long, followed by a short *o* (as in the English word *chaos*). The *g* preceding an *o* should take the hard sound.

(**Dee—Caósgon*) See the *48 Claves*. Again, Dee shows an accent over the second syllable.

Also:

Caosg (kay-OZH) — Earth
Caosga (kay-OS-ga) — Earth
Caosgi (kay-OZH-ii) — Earth
Caosgin (kay-OS-jin) — Earth
Caosgo (kay-OS-go) — Of the Earth

Capimali (kay-pii-MAY-lii)* *adv.* — Successively

4.25 . . . also *successively* are the number of time . . .

Pronunciation notes:

(**Dee—Ca pi ma li*) Four syllables.

(**Dee—Capimáli*) See the *48 Claves*. Accent on the third syllable.

Also:

"Capimao" (kay-pii-MAY-oh) — While (period of time)
Capimaon (kap-ii-MAY-on) — Number of Time
Capmiali (kap-mii-AY-lii) — Successively

Possible shared root:

Acocasb (ay-KOH-kasb) — Time
Cacacom (kay-SAY-som) — Flourish
"Cacocasb" (kay-KOH-kasb) — Another While
Cacrg (KAY-kurg) — Until
Casasam (kay-SAY-sam) — Abiding
Cocasb (KOH-kasb) — Time
Cocasg (KOH-kazh) — Times
Qcocasb (kwah-KOH-kasb) — Contents of Time

Compare from *Loagaeth*:

Cap

Note:

Also see *Pild* (continually).

"Capimao" (kay-pii-MAY-oh) *n.* — While (period of time)

Pronunciation note:

I have adopted the accent from *Capimali* (successively).

Compounds:

Lcapimao (el-ka-PII-may-oh) [L + "Capimao"] — One While

Also:

Capimaon (kap-ii-MAY-on) — Number of Time
Capimali (kay-pii-MAY-lii) — Successively
Capmiali (kap-mii-AY-lii) — Successively

Possible shared root:

Acocasb (ay-KOH-kasb) — Time
Cacacom (kay-SAY-som) — Flourish
"Cacocasb" (kay-KOH-kasb) — Another While
Cacrg (KAY-kurg) — Until
Casasam (kay-SAY-sam) — Abiding
Cocasb (KOH-kasb) — Time
Cocasg (KOH-kazh) — Times
Qcocasb (kwah-KOH-kasb) — Contents of Time

Compare from *Loagaeth*:
Cap

Note:
Also see *Pild* (continually).

Capimaon (kap-ii-MAY-on)* *n.* Number of Time

4.27 . . . also successively are the *number of time* . . .

Pronunciation notes:
(**Dee—Capi ma on*) Four syllables. The first *a* seems to be short in this case. I have adopted the accent from *Capimali* (successively).

Also:

Capimali (kay-pii-MAY-lii)	Successively
"Capimao" (kay-pii-MAY-oh)	While (period of time)
Capmiali (kap-mii-AY-lii)	Successively

Possible shared root:

Acocasb (ay-KOH-kasb)	Time
Cacacom (kay-SAY-som)	Flourish
"Cacocasb" (kay-KOH-kasb)	Another While
Cacrg (KAY-kurg)	Until
Casasam (kay-SAY-sam)	Abiding
Cocasb (KOH-kasb)	Time
Cocasg (KOH-kazh)	Times
Qcocasb (kwah-KOH-kasb)	Contents of Time

Compare from *Loagaeth*:
Cap

Note:
Also see *Pild* (continually).

Capmiali (kap-mii-AY-lii)* *adv.* Successively

3.38 . . . power *successively* over 456 . . .

Pronunciation notes:

(**Dee—Capmiali*) Likely four syllables. See pronunciation notes for *Capimaon* and *Capimali*.

(**Dee—Cap-mi-áli*) See the *48 Claves*. Dee places an accent on the third syllable. Both *i*'s likely take their long sound.

Also:

Capimali (kay-pii-MAY-lii)	Successively
"Capimao" (kay-pii-MAY-oh)	While
Capimaon (kap-ii-MAY-on)	Number of Time

Possible shared root:

Acocasb (ay-KOH-kasb)	Time
Cacacom (kay-SAY-som)	Flourish
"Cacocasb" (kay-KOH-kasb)	Another While
Cacrg (KAY-kurg)	Until
Casasam (kay-SAY-sam)	Abiding
Cocasb (KOH-kasb)	Time
Cocasg (KOH-kazh)	Times
Qcocasb (kwah-KOH-kasb)	Contents of Time

Compare from *Loagaeth*:

Cap

Note:

Also see *Pild* (continually).

Carbaf (kar-baf)* *v.* To Sink (i.e., To Stoop, To Dive)

8.33 . . . until this house fall and the dragon *sink*.

Pronunciation notes:

(**Dee—Car baf*) Two syllables.

Note:

This word is used to describe the dragon *stooping*—or diving to attack prey. The word *stoop* can also mean to descend from superior rank or moral standing—both of which make sense when applied to the dragon (or Satan).

Probable shared root:
"Abai" (a-bay) — Stooping

Carma (kar-ma) *v.* — To Come Out/To Arrive From/To Arise

Note:
See *TFR*, p. 32. Here, Dee is speaking with the Angel Madimi. Suddenly, Madimi halts the session and demands, "*Carma geta Barman.*" Dee asks her what this means, and she replies (in Latin, which roughly translates to:) "Come out of there, *Barma*." Madimi's command exorcises fifteen spirits from the body of Edward Kelley, the chief of whom is named Barma. After a short exchange (see *Gil*, etc.), Madimi banishes all fifteen spirits back to Hell "until the last cry." (That is, until the End Times.) Also see *Niis* (Come), *Nissa* (Come away!). *Carma Geta* is likely intended as an exorcism phrase, and not something one would use with the Angels. *Niis*, *Niisa*, etc. are appropriate for use with celestial beings.

Possible shared root:
Carmara (kar-mar-a) — n/a

Compare from *Loagaeth*:
Csrmax, Armax, Cardax

Carmara (or Marmara) (kar-mar-a) *prop. n.* — n/a

Possible shared root:
Carma (kar-ma) — To Come Out/To Arise

Note:
See the *Five Books*, pp. 184 and 187. *Carmara* is the title of the ruling King of the *Heptarchia*. In Dee's lifetime, the Heptarchic King of Venus—Baligon—held the title. Today, I presume it should be the King of Mercury—Bnaspol—though I do not know if he would hold the same title.
(Also see *Ga*, *Galvah*, *Hagonel*, *Mapsama*, *Murifri*, *Nalvage*, *Vaa*, and *Za*.)

Compare from *Loagaeth*:
Csrmax, Armax, Cardax

Casarm (kay-SARM)* *pron.* Whom

1.38 . . . *to whom* I made a law . . .
5.14 . . . *unto whom* I fastened pillars . . .

Pronunciation notes:
(**Dee—Casarm*) I assume just two syllables here. Also see *Casarmg*, *Casarman*, and *Casarmi*—which indicate the first *a* is long, and the accent is on the second syllable.

Also:

Casarma (kay-SAR-ma)	Whom
Casarman (kay-SAR-man)	Whom/(Under) Whose
Casarmg (kay-SAR-mij)	In Whom
Casarmi (kay-SAR-mij)	(Under) Whom

Also see:
Soba (whose)

Casarma (kay-SAR-ma)* *pron.* Whom

2.13 . . . *whom* I have prepared . . .

Pronunciation notes:
(**Dee—Casarma*)
(**Dee—Cas-arma*) See *48 Claves*. I assume three syllables here. Also see *Casarmg*, *Casarman*, and *Casarmi*, which indicate the first *a* is long. Other versions of this word indicate an accent on the second syllable.

Also:

Casarm (kay-SARM)	Whom
Casarman (kay-SAR-man)	Whom/(Under?) Whose
Casarmg (kay-SAR-mij)	In Whom
Casarmi (kay-SAR-mij)	(Under) Whom

Also see:
Soba (whose)

Casarman (kay-SAR-man)* *pron.* or *adj.* Whom/(Under) Whose

11.22 . . . *of whom* it is measured . . .
**15.4 . . . *under whose* wings . . .

Pronunciation notes:
(*Dee 11.22—Ca sar man*) Three syllables. The first *a* is likely long.
(*Dee 11.22—Ca-sár-man*) See the *48 Claves*. Here, Dee places an accent upon the second syllable.

Note:
The *of* in the above translation (11.22) seems to be implied. The word *under* (in 15.4) is something more of a problem. At first it seems to be a mistake—however, there is also the instance of *Casarmi* (under whom) in Key Four.

**The transmission of Key Fifteen is missing from Dee's journals. We only have the English for this Key given later (see *TFR*, p. 193). Plus, the word appears in this location in Dee's *48 Claves*.

Also:

Casarm (kay-SARM)	Whom
Casarma (kay-SAR-ma)	Whom
Casarmg (kay-SAR-mij)	In Whom
Casarmi (kay-SAR-mij)	(Under) Whom

Also see:
Soba (whose).

Casarmg (kay-SAR-mij)* *pron.* In Whom

3.72 . . . *in whom* we say . . .
4.20 . . . *in whom* the second beginning of things . . .
7.14 . . . *in whom* the strength . . .
8.7 . . . made of hyacinth pillars, *in whom* the Elders . . .

18.12 . . . *in whom* the secrets . . .

Pronunciation note:

(**Dee 3.72; 8.7—Casarmg*)
(**Dee 4.20—Casarmg the g as in seurge*) Final *g* takes the soft "j" sound.
(**Dee 7.14—Ca sarmg. The g as dg armg*) Again, a soft "g" sound. Also, the first *a* appears long.
(**Dee 18.12—ca sar mg*) Three syllables. Again the *a* seems to take the long sound. Usually the *m* and the *g* would have to stand alone—as they do not combine naturally in English. However, in order to give the *g* its soft sound as Dee indicates, it is necessary to insert a vowel sound between the *m* and *g*. I suggest "mij."
(**Dee 3.72—Casármg*) See the *48 Claves*. Dee placed an accent on the second syllable.

Note:

The Angelical affix-word G (you) is not apparently intended in this spelling of *Casarmg*.

Also:

Casarm (kay-SARM) — Whom
Casarma (kay-SAR-ma) — Whom
Casarman (kay-SAR-man) — Whom/(Under) Whose
Casarmi (kay-SAR-mij) — (Under) Whom

Also see:

Soba (whose).

Casarmi (kay-SAR-mij)* *pron.* — (Under) Whom

4.13 . . . *under whom* I have placed 9639 . . .

Pronunciation notes:

(**Dee—Ca sarmi*) Here, we are likely seeing one of Dee's typical substitutions of the letter *i* (that is—*j*) for the letter *g*. Both *Casarmg* and *Casarmi* are probably identical when spoken. However, note that Dee does not show the *i* as a separate syllable—so I have combined the *m* and *i* into the sound of "mij."

(**Dee—Casármi*) See the *48 Claves*. Dee places an accent on the second syllable.

Note:

What is confusing here is the addition of *under* to the word's definition. It repeats in Key Fifteen with the word *Casarman* (under whose).

Also:

Casarm (kay-SARM)	Whom
Casarma (kay-SAR-ma)	Whom
Casarman (kay-SAR-man)	Whom/(Under) Whose
Casarmg (kay-SAR-mij)	In Whom

Also see:

Soba (whose).

Casasam (kay-SAY-sam)* *n.* Abiding

18.16 . . . 6332 have *their abiding* . . .

Pronunciation note:

(**Dee—Ca fa fam*) Three syllables. I suspect that "Cafafam" is a mistake for *Casasam*. In Dee's English, *f* was often written in an elongated fashion that highly resembles an *s*. (I find this highly likely, because we also have the word *Cacacom* [flourish], which uses two *C*s instead of *S*s. Those *C*s could easily take the soft "s" sound.)

(**Dee—casâsam*) See the *48 Claves*. Here, Dee confirms that the *f*s shown in this word in *TFR* should be *s*'s instead. He also placed a circumflex over the second *a* to indicate its long sound.

I have adopted the accent from *Cacacom* (flourish).

Note:

Abiding seems to be used in this case as a noun, to mean "period of existence."

Also:

Cacacom (kay-SAY-som)	Flourish

Probable shared root:

Acocasb (ay-KOH-kasb)	Time

Cacrg (KAY-kurg) — Until
"Cacocasb" (kay-KOH-kasb) — Another While
Capimali (kay-pii-MAY-lii) — Successively
"Capimao" (kay-pii-MAY-oh) — While
Capimaon (kap-ii-MAY-on) — Number of Time
Capmiali (kap-mii-AY-lii) — Successively
Cocasb (KOH-kasb) — Time
Cocasg (KOH-kazh) — Times
Qcocasb (kwah-KOH-kasb) — Contents of Time

Note:
Also see *Pild* (continually).

Kelpadman (kel-pad-man) — n/a*

Note:
See the *Five Books*, p. 413. Kelley overhears many voices singing a song at some distance, and these are the words Dee recorded: *Pinzu-a lephe ganiurax kelpadman pacaph*. No translations are suggested.

Ceph (kef)* *prop. n.* — Letter Z

Note:
The name of the Angelical letter for Z. It is likely that these letter names have translations of their own. (For instance, note the Hebrew alphabet: the letter Z is named *Zain*, but *Zain* also translates as "sword.") However, such translations for the Angelical letters are never given. (See the *Five Books*, p. 270.)

Pronunciation notes:
(**Dee—Sounded like keph.*)

Compare from *Loagaeth*:
Cheph

Chiis (kiis)* *v.* — Are (They)

9.36 . . . cursed *are they* . . .

Pronunciation notes:

(**Dee—Chiis*) One syllable. In Early Modern English, a double *i* indicated the long vowel sound. This is further supported by Dee's phonetic notes for *Chis* (are). I suspect the second *i* in this word is a phonetic gloss.

Also:

Chis (kiis)	Are
"Chisda" (kiis-da)	Are There
Chiso (kiis-oh)	Shall Be
"Gchis" (jee-kiis)	Are
"Ichis" (jay-kiis)	Are
Zchis (zohd-kiis)	(They) Are

Note:

Note the usage of the letter *I* (Angelical for "is") through these words. Because both *I* and *Chis* are forms of "to be," it is possible that *I* forms the root of the *Chis* family of words.

Also see *Zchis* (they are).

Chirlan (kir-lan)* *v.* — To Rejoice

7.16 . . .in whom the strength of men *rejoiceth* . . .
9.64 The God of Righteousness *rejoiceth* in them.

Pronunciation notes:

(**Dee 7.16; 9.64—Chir lan Kir*) Two syllables. The *Ch* in the first syllable is given the harder "K" (or "Kh") sound. Both vowels are likely short.

Chis (kiis)* *v.* — Are

2.24 Stronger *are* your feet . . .
2.29 . . . mightier *are* your voices . . .
3.10 . . . six *are* the seats of . . .
3.14 . . . the rcst *are* as sharp sickles . . .
3.20 . . . *are*, to are not, except by the hands . . .
4.22 . . . *are*, and wax strong . . .
4.26 . . . successively *are* the number of time . . .

4.29 . . . powers *are* as the first 456 . . .
6.3 . . . spirits of the fourth angle *are* nine . . .
8.9 . . . Elders *are* become strong . . .
9.15 . . . whose wings *are* of wormwood . . .
9.41 . . . in their eyes *are* millstones . . .
9.56 . . . upon their heads *are* marble . . .
10.2 . . . *are* numbered and harboured . . .
10.11 . . . *are* 22 nests of lamentation . . .
12.5 . . . and *are* 28 lanterns . . .
**15.6 . . . under whose wings *are* 6739 . . .
17.5 . . . whose wings *are* thorns . . .
30.19 . . . whose eyes *are* the brightness . . .

Pronunciation notes:

(**Dee 2.24—Chis [as Xis]*) The *X* is actually a Greek *Chi*—indicating the *Ch* has a "K" sound.

(**Dee 2.29—Chis [the I long]*) This note shows a long vowel sound for the *i*.

(**Dee 3.10—Chis as Kisse*) The *ss* represents a single "s" sound—as in *Kise*. The final *e* gives the *i* its long sound. We also see again that the *Ch* has a "K" sound.

(**Dee 3.14—Chis as Kis*)

(**Dee 3.20; 4.22, 26—Chis Kis*)

(**Dee 4.29; 6.3; 8.9; 9.15, 41, 56; 10.2, 11; 12.5; 17.5—Chis*)

(**Dee 30.19—Chis Kiss*)

(**Dee 2.29—chís*) See the *48 Claves*. I am unsure why Dee placed an accent on a single-syllable word—unless he had originally intended this particular instance to compound with the word before or after it.

Note:

**The transmission of Key Fifteen is missing from Dee's journals. We only have the English for this Key given later (see *TFR*, p. 193). Plus, the word appears in this location in Dee's *48 Claves*.

Compounds:

Chisholq (KIIS-hohl-kwa) [Chis + Holq]	Are Measured
Chismicaolz (kiis-mii-KAY-ohlz) [Chis + Micaolz]	Are Mighty
Chista (kiis-tay) [Chis + Ta]	Are as
Chistad (kiis-tad) [Chis + Ta + D]	Are as the Third
Dschis (dee-es-kiis) [Ds + Chis]	Which Are

Irgilchisda (ir-jil-KIIS-da) ["Irgil" + Chis + "Da"] How Many Are There

Odchis (ohd-kiis) [Od + Chis] And Are

Unalchis (yew-nal-kiis) [Unal + Chis] These Are

Also:

Chiis (kiis) Are (They)

"Chisda" (kiis-da) Are There

Chiso (kiis-oh) Shall Be

"Gchis" (jee-kiis) Are

"Ichis" (jay-kiis) Are

Zchis (zohd-kiis) (They) Are

Note:

See note at *Chiis*.

Also see *Geh* (are / art)—which may be a more formal term.

"Chisda" (kiis-da) [Chis + "Da"] *comp.* Are There

Compounds:

Irgilchisda (ir-jil-KIIS-da) ["Irgil" + Chis + "Da"] How many Are There

Chisholq (KIIS-hohl-kwa)* [Chis + Holq] *comp.* Are Measured

9.24 . . . *are measured* with their ministers . . .

Pronunciation notes:

(**Dee—Chis hol q*) Three syllables. The final *q* stands alone. See *Chis* for further pronunciation notes.

(**Dee—chis hôlq*) See the *48 Claves*. Here, Dee placed an accent over the first syllable. He also placed a circumflex over the *o* to indicate its long sound.

Chismicaolz (kiis-mii-KAY-ohlz)* [Chis + Micaolz] *comp.* Are Mighty

30.4 . . . *are mighty* in the parts of the earth . . .

Pronunciation notes:

(**Dee—Chis Micáolz Kis*) Four syllables, with an accent on the third syllable. (See *Micaolz*, where Dee places the accent on the same part of the word.) Dee also reminds us that the *Ch* has a "Kh" sound. See *Chis* for the long "i" sound in the first syllable. See *Micaolz* for the long "i" sound in the second syllable.

(**Dee—chis Micaólz*) See the *48 Claves*. Here, Dee indicates the accent on the fourth syllable instead. However, based on other versions of *Micaolz* (mighty), I have settled upon placing the accent over the third syllable.

Chiso (kiis-oh)* *v.* Shall Be

10.78 . . . her iniquity is, was, and *shall be* great . . .

Pronunciation notes:

(**Dee—Chi so K*) Two syllables. Dee indicates that the *Ch* should take the hard "K" (or "Kh") sound. Also, the *i* appears to take the long sound—which is supported by the long "i" sound in other versions of this word.

Note:

Also see *Trian* (shall be).

Also:

Chis (kiis)	Are
Chiis (kiis)	Are (They)
"Chisda" (kiis-da)	Are There
"Gchis" (jee-kiis)	Are
"Ichis" (jay-kiis)	Are
Zchis (zohd-kiis)	(They) Are

Note:

Often, an *o* affix indicates "of." However, it does not appear to hold true in this case.

Chista (kiis-tay)* [Chis + Ta] *comp.* Are as

5.37 . . . whose numbers *are as* the first . . .

Pronunciation notes:

(**Dee—Chis ta . . .Kista*) Two syllables. The *Ch* takes a hard "Kh" sound. See *Chiis* for the long "i" sound.

Chistad (kiis-tad)* [Chis + Ta + D] *comp.* Are as the Third

7.26 . . . *are as the third* and fourth . . .

Pronunciation notes:

(**Dee—Chis tad Kis*) Two syllables. Dee indicates that the *Ch* in the first syllable should take the harder "K" (or "Kh") sound. Also see the pronunciation notes for *Chis*.

Chr (kar)* *prop. n.* "The Twentieth Aethyr" (To Be / Exist?)

30.3 . . . which dwell in *the twentieth aethyr* . . .

Note:

(**Dee—kar in palato very much.*) This means the *Ch* in this word is guttural (a hard sound made "in palato"—the back of the roof of the mouth, just at the throat)—a raspy "kh" sound. This (word 30.3) is the single space in the Key of the Aethyrs, which must be changed for each invocation—replacing word 30.3 with the name of the appropriate Aethyr. No established definitions were given for these names. However, if *Chr* means "to be / exist," do not confuse this with the verb *I* ("to be"—"is / are").

Chr contains the three Parts of the Earth *Zildron*, *Parziba*, and *Totocan*.

Possible shared root:

Chramsa (kraym-sa) Be It Made with Power

Christeos (kris-TEE-os) Let There Be

Chramsa (KRAYM-sa)* *v.* Be It Made with Power**

Pronunciation note:

(**Dee—chrámsa —the first "a" very long.*) See the *Five Books*, p. 307. Dee adds an accent over the first *a*.

From *Loagaeth*:

(***Dee—A reverent word, [. . .] and is, be it made with power.*) See the *Five Books*, p. 307.

Possible shared root:

Chr (kar) "The Twentieth Aethyr"
Christeos (kris-TEE-os) Let There Be

Compare from *Loagaeth*:

Cramsa, Chramsa

Christeos (kris-TEE-os)* *v.* Let There Be . . .

30.47 . . . *let there be* division in her . . .
30.68 . . . and *let there be* no one creature equal . . .
30.79 . . . *let there be* no creature upon or within her . . .

Pronunciation notes:

(**Dee 30.47—Chris té os*)

(**Dee 30.68, 79—Chris te os*) Three syllables, with an accent on the second syllable. I assume a long "e" sound at the end of the second syllable. The *Ch* should take the "Kh" sound, as in the word *Christian.*

(**Dee 30.47, 68—christéos*) See the *48 Claves*. In these places, Dee again indicates an accent on the second syllable.

(**Dee 30.79—christêos*) See the *48 Claves*. Here, Dee used a circumflex over the *e* to indicate its long sound.

Note:

The similarity between this word and the word *Christ* in Greek (*Christos*)—meaning "the Anointed One." In ancient Gnosticism, the *Christos*—as distinct from Jesus—was the source of all life. The *Christos* was also known as the Word (*Logos*)—the agent of creation. (See John 1.) In Genesis 1, the first words spoken by the Creator are, "Let there be Light!"

Possible shared root:

Chr (kar) "The Twentieth Aethyr"
Chramsa (kraym-sa) Be It Made with Power

CIAL (sii-al)* 9996

9.26 . . . are measured with their ministers *9996*.

Pronunciation notes:

(**Dee—Ci al*) Two syllables. The *C* preceding an *I* should make a soft "s" sound—as in the English words *circle* and *circus*.

Note:

This word was not originally given with Key Nine. It was added later when Nalvage transmitted the English for the Key (see *TFR*, p. 191). This seems to have been the case with many of the numbers mentioned in the Keys.

Ciaofi (sii-ay-oh-fii)* *n.* Terror

8.48 . . . appear *to the terror* of the earth . . .

Pronunciation notes:

(**Dee—C I A O fi*) Dee's note is somewhat confusing. There is no *ao* letter combination in Early Modern English. Therefore, both letters should be sounded separately (as in the English word *chaos*). This leaves the initial *Ci*—which Dee writes as if they should each stand alone. However, these two letters do make a natural sound in English (as in *circle* and *circus*). Therefore, I suggest four syllables for this word, rather than the five Dee indicates in his phonetic note.

Cicle (sii-kayl)* *n.* Mysteries

1.78, (RFP), 30.152 Open *the mysteries of* your creation . . .

Pronunciation notes:

(**Dee 1.78—Call it Cicle*)

(**Dee 30.152—Cicle*) Dee gives us little to work with. I assume the initial *C* followed by an *i* should make an "s" sound (as in *circus* and *circle*). The *i* should take a long sound (based on Dee's phonetic note for *Cicles*).

Then, the final *le* following a consonant likely makes the "ayl" sound. (See the pronunciation notes for *Baltle* and *Bagle*.)

Also:

Cicles (sii-kayls) Mysteries

Cicles (sii-kayls)* *n.* Mysteries

5.52 Conclude us as receivers *of your mysteries* . . .

Pronunciation notes:

(**Dee—Ci cles*) Two syllables. I assume the initial *C* followed by an *i* should make an "s" sound (as in *circus* or *circle*). Also, the *cle* should make the sound of "kayl." (See the pronunciation notes for *Baltle* and *Bagle*.)

Also:

Cicle (sii-kayl) Mysteries

Cinxir (sinks-ir)* *v.* To Mingle

10.31 . . . live sulphur *myngled with* poison.

Pronunciation notes:

(**Dee—Cynx ir*) Two syllables. The initial *C* should take the "S" sound when preceding an *i*. Both vowels are short.

CLA (kla)* 456

3.40 . . . over *456*, the true ages of time . . .

4.31 . . . are as the first *456*.

Pronunciation notes:

(**Dee 3.40; 4.31—Cla*) Dee appears to suggest one syllable.

Cnila (see-NII-la)* *n.* Blood

9.49 . . . from their mouths run seas of *blood*.

Pronunciation notes:

(**Dee—Cni la*) This appears to be two syllables. However, it is unlikely that the *C* should blend with the *n*. (See *Cnoqod*, etc.) Therefore, it is more likely three syllables. The *i* should take its long sound.

(**Dee—Cníla*) See the *48 Claves*. Here, Dee placed an accent over the *i* in the second syllable.

Cnoqod (see-NOH-kwod)* *n.* (Unto) Servants

2.44 . . . move, therefore, *unto his servants* . . .

Pronunciation notes:

(**Dee—as C Nó Quod*) Three syllables, with an accent on the second syllable. Dee added a *u* in his note as a phonetic gloss—indicating the "kwah" sound.

(**Dee—c-nó-qod*) See *48 Claves*. This note agrees with the note in *TFR*.

Also:

Cnoquodi (see-noh-KWOH-dii) (With) Ministers
Cnoquol (see-NOH-kwol) Servants
Noco (NOH-kwoh) Servant

Note:

Also see *Lang* (Those Who Serve).

Cnoquodi (see-noh-KWOH-dii)* *n.* (With) Ministers

9.25 . . . are measured *with their ministers* 9996 . . .

Pronunciation notes:

(**Dee—Cno quo di*) Dee seems to indicate three syllables. However, other version of this word indicate the initial *C* should stand alone. Therefore, it is likely four syllables instead. The *u* in *Cnoquodi* and *Cnoquol* is likely a phonetic gloss. (It does not appear in *Cnoqod*, except in Dee's pronunciation note.)

(**Dee—Cnoquódi*) See the *48 Claves*. Dee placed an accent on the third syllable.

Also:

Cnoqod (see-NOH-kwod)	(Unto) Servants
Cnoquol (see-NOH-kwol)	Servants
Noco (NOH-kwoh)	Servant

Note:
Also see *Lang* (Those Who Serve).

Cnoquol (see-NOH-kwol)* *n.* Servants

7.33 *O you servents of* mercy . . .

Pronunciation notes:
(**Dee—Cno quol kol*) Dee indicates that the *q* sounds like a "k" (as in the English words *kick* and *kite*). The *u* in *Cnoquol* and *Cnoquodi* is likely a phonetic gloss—making the *q* take more of a "kwah" sound. (The *u* does not appear in *Cnoqod*, except in Dee's pronunciation note.) See pronunciation note at *Cnoqod* for the accented syllable.

Also:

Cnoqod (see-NOH-kwod)	(Unto) Servants
Cnoquodi (see-noh-KWOH-dii)	(With) Ministers
Noco (NOH-kwoh)	Servant

Note:
Also see *Lang* (Those Who Serve).

"Coazior" (koh-ay-zhor) *v.* To Increase

Compounds:

Arcoazior (ar-koh-ay-zhor) [Ar + "Coazior"]	That Increase

Note:
It is a long shot, but I suspect a connection between this word and the name of the Angel *Hecoa*, one of the Sons of Light. (Perhaps "Coa" is a root word.) This would give his name an etymology similar to his brother *Dmal*, whose name may contain *Mal* (increase).

Cocasb (KOH-kasb)* *n.* — Time

3.42 . . . the true ages of *time* . . .
10.55 . . . know any *time* there . . .

Pronunciation notes:

(**Dee 3.42—Cocasb*)

(**Dee 10.55—Co casb*) Two syllables. The *o* at the end of the first syllable should be long. The *a* appears to be short in this case.

I have adopted the accent from other versions of this word.

Also:

Acocasb (ay-KOH-kasb)	Time
"Cacocasb" (kay-KOH-kasb)	Another While
Cocasg (KOH-kazh)	Times
Qcocasb (kwah-KOH-kasb)	Contents of Time

Possible shared root:

Cacacom (kay-SAY-som)	Flourish
Cacrg (KAY-kurg)	Until
Casasam (kay-SAY-sam)	Abiding
Capimali (kay-pii-MAY-lii)	Successively
"Capimao" (kay-pii-MAY-oh)	While
Capimaon (kap-ii-MAY-on)	Number of Time
Capmiali (kap-mii-AY-lii)	Successively

Note:

Also see *Pild* (continually).

Cocasg (KOH-kazh)* *n.* — Times

10.37 . . . that 5678 *times* . . .
10.46 . . . thousand *times* as many . . .

Pronunciation notes:

(**Dee 10.37—Co casg g as dg*) Two syllables, with a soft final *g*. The *sg* likely blends into a soft *j* or "zhuh" sound. See *Vorsg* (over you) and *Caosg* (earth), where I also use the "zhuh" digraph in relation to the final letters *sg*. I indicate this rare digraph in my pronunciation as "zh."

(**Dee 10.46—Co Casg . . .gao dg*) Two syllables again. It is unclear what *gao* indicates.

I have adopted the accent from other versions of this word.

Also:

Acocasb (ay-KOH-kasb)	Time
"Cacocasb" (kay-KOH-kasb)	Another While
Cocasb (KOH-kasb)	Time
Qcocasb (kwah-KOH-kasb)	Contents of Time

Possible shared root:

Cacacom (kay-SAY-som)	Flourish
Cacrg (KAY-kurg)	Until
Casasam (kay-SAY-sam)	Abiding
Capimali (kay-pii-MAY-lii)	Successively
"Capimao" (kay-pii-MAY-oh)	While
Capimaon (kap-ii-MAY-on)	Number of Time
Capmiali (kap-mii-AY-lii)	Successively

Note:

Also see *Pild* (continually).

Collal (kol-lal)* *n.* — Sleeves / Sheaths

9.58 . . . upon their (hands) are marble *sleeves*.

Pronunciation notes:

(**Dee—Col lal*) Two syllables. Both vowels should take their short sounds.

Note:

This word indicates *sheaths*—so that these "sleeves" are in fact gloves of a sort.

Commah (KOM-mah)* *v.* — To Truss Together (Join)

1.25 . . . and *trussed you together* like the palms of my hands . . .

Pronunciation notes:

(**Dee—COMMAH*) Dee gives us little clue here. In Early Modern English, a double consonant generally combined into one sound. This word likely has two syllables. I have adopted the accent from *Comselh* (circle).

Possible shared root:

Comselh (KOM-sel) Circle

Comselh (KOM-sel)* *n.* Circle

3.5 I am *a circle* on whose hands . . .

Pronunciation notes:

(**Dee—Com Selh*) Two syllables. I assume the final *h* is very faint if not entirely silent.

(**Dee—cómselh*) See *48 Claves*. Note the accent on the first syllable.

Possible shared root:

Commah (KOM-mah) Trussed Together

"Como" (koh-moh) *n.* Window

Compounds:

Comobliort (koh-moh-blii-ort) ["Como" + "Bliort"]
Window of Comfort

Comobliort (koh-moh-blii-ort)* ["Como" + "Bliort"] *comp.*
Window of Comfort

18.25 . . . be thou a *window of comfort* . . .

Pronunciation notes:

(**Dee—Co mo bli ort*) Four syllables. The *o*'s in the first and second syllables should both take their long sound. The *i* is also long.

Congamphlgh (KONG-am-filj)* *n.* Faith / Holy Ghost**

Pronunciation notes:

(**Dee—CÓNGAM-PHLGH —phlgh = filgh.*) See the *Five Books*, p. 316. Three syllables. Dee adds an accent over the *o*.

From *Loagaeth*:

(***Dee—Faith that revereth man's breast, the Holy Ghost.*) See the *Five Books*, p. 316.

Note:

Also see *Gono* (faith).

Conisbra (koh-NIS-bra)* *n.* The Work of Man

30.92 *The work of man* and his pomp . . .

Pronunciation notes:

(**Dee—Co nis bra*) Three syllables. I assume the *o* takes a long sound, because Dee placed the *n* at the head of the second syllable instead of at the end of the first.

(**Dee—Conísbra*) See the *48 Claves*. Here, Dee placed an accent over the *i* in the second syllable.

Note:

Neither of the usual Angelical words for "work" ("Aath" or *Vaun*) or mankind (*Cordziz*) appear within this word. Since Conisbra at least shares some common letters with *Cordziz*, I would assume *Conisbra* has "mankind" as its root.

Possible shared root:

Cordziz (KORD-ziz) Mankind

Const (konst)* *n.* Thunders

10.34 . . . These be *the Thunders* . . .

Pronunciation notes:

(**Dee—Const K*) One syllable. Dee indicates the *C* should take its harder "K" sound.

Note:

This is probably the generic Angelical word for "thunder"; however, the Key is referring to a group of Angels—referred to earlier in the Key as the *Coraxo* (Thunders)—rather than weather. Also see *Sapah* (Mighty Sounds), *Avavago* (Thunders), and *Coraxo* (Thunders).

Coraxo (koh-RAYKS-oh)* *prop. n.* Thunders of Judgment and Wrath

10.1 . . . *The Thunders of Judgment and Wrath* are numbered . . .
11.6 . . . They were five *Thunders* which flew into the East . . .

Pronunciation notes:

(**Dee 10.1—Co rax o*)

(**Dee 11.6—Co ráx o*) Three syllables, with an accent on the second syllable. Both *o*'s are long. Also, the Angel Illemese gives further information:

(**Illemese—Coraaxo*) See *TFR*, p. 200. The double *a* here shows that the *a* should also be long.

(**Dee 10.1; 11.6—Coráxo*) See the *48 Claves*. Dee again shows the accent over the second syllable.

Note:

The generic Angelical word for "thunder" is likely *Const*. The Thunders mentioned here and elsewhere in the Keys are groups of Angels. See *Avavago* (Thunders) and *Sapah* (Mighty Sounds). Note the Thunders, Lightnings, and Voices that proceeded from the Divine Throne in the vision of St. John (Book of Revelation). The Coraxo are mentioned only in Keys Ten and Eleven—both of which seem to relate to the Northern Quarter of the Universe.

Cordziz (KORD-ziz)* *n.* Mankind

30.83 . . . *the reasonable creatures of earth (or men)*, let them vex . . .

Pronunciation notes:

(**Dee—Cord ziz*) Two syllables. I've kept the accent on the same syllable as in *Olcordziz* (made mankind).

Compounds:

Olcordziz (ohl-KORD-ziz) [Oln + Cordziz]   Made Mankind

Possible shared root:

Consibra (koh-NIS-bra)   Work of Man

Note:

Also see *Ollog* (men).

Cormf (kormf)* *n.*   Number

11.29 . . . whose *number* is 31 . . .

Pronunciation notes:

(**Dee—Cormf*) Note that this word sometimes ends with an *f* and sometimes with a *p*. I suspect this means that—in both cases—the *ph* digraph is intended. Dee seems to indicate one syllable here.

Also:

Cormfa (korm-FA)   Numbers
Cormp (kormf)   Numbered
Cormpo (korm-FOH)   Hath (Yet) Numbered
Cormpt (kormft)   Numbered

Shared root:

Sagacor (say-GAY-kor)   In One Number

Possible shared root:

Coronzom (kor-on-zom)   Satan, the Devil, the Enemy

Cormfa (korm-FA)* *n.*   Numbers

5.36 . . . whose *numbers* are as the first . . .

Pronunciation notes:
(**Dee—Cormfa*) Note that this word sometimes ends with an *f* and sometimes with a *p*. I suspect this means that—in both cases—the *ph* digraph is intended.

I have adopted the accent from *Cormpo* (hath numbered).

Also:
Cormf (kormf) — Number
Cormp (kormf) — Numbered
Cormpo (korm-FOH) — Hath (Yet) Numbered
Cormpt (kormft) — Numbered

Shared root:
Sagacor (say-GAY-kor) — In One Number

Possible shared root:
Coronzom (kor-on-zom) — Satan, the Devil, the Enemy

Cormp (kormf)* *v.* — To Number

4.9 . . . *numbered* 33 . . .
10.3 . . . are *numbered* and harboured . . .

Pronunciation notes:
(**Dee 4.9; 10.3—Cormp*) Note that this word sometimes ends with an *f* and sometimes with a *p*. I suspect this means that—in both cases—the *ph* digraph is intended.

Also:
Cormf (kormf) — Number
Cormfa (korm-FA) — Numbers
Cormpo (korm-FOH) — Hath Numbered, Yet Numbered
Cormpt (kormft) — Numbered

Shared root:
Sagacor (say-GAY-kor) — In One Number

Possible shared root:
Coronzom (kor-on-zom) — Satan, the Devil, the Enemy

Cormpo (korm-FOH)* *v.* — Hath (Yet) Numbered

4.18 . . . none *hath yet numbered* but one . . .

Note:

The *-o* affix should indicate the word "of." Thus, the literal translation might be "of number"—meaning something that has been numbered. If so, then the proper English definition should be "hath numbered," and the "yet" is simply implied.

Pronunciation notes:

(**Dee—Corm po*) Two syllables. Note that this word sometimes ends with an *f* and sometimes with a *p*. I suspect this means that—in both cases—the *ph* digraph is intended.

(**Dee—cormpó*) See the *48 Claves*. Accent placed on the last syllable.

Also:

Cormf (kormf) — Number

Cormfa (korm-FA) — Numbers

Cormp (kormf) — Numbered

Cormpt (kormft) — Numbered

Shared root:

Sagacor (say-GAY-kor) — In One Number

Possible shared root:

Coronzom (kor-on-zom) — Satan, the Devil, the Enemy

Cormpt (kormft)* *v.* — (Are) Numbered

30.140 . . . until the stars *be numbered*.

Pronunciation notes:

(**Dee—Cormpt*) Note that this word sometimes ends with an *f* and sometimes with a *p*. I suspect this means that—in both cases—the *ph* digraph is intended. Dee seems to indicate just one syllable for this word.

Also:

Cormf (kormf) — Number

Cormfa (korm-FA) — Numbers

Cormp (kormf) Numbered
Cormpo (korm-FOH) Hath (Yet) Numbered

Shared root:
Sagacor (say-GAY-kor) In One Number

Possible shared root:
Coronzom (kor-on-zom) Satan, the Devil, the Enemy

Coronzom (kor-on-zom) *prop. n.* Satan, the Devil, the Enemy

Note:
See *TFR*, p. 92. Here Gabriel is discussing Adam's loss of the Angelical language when he fell from Paradise. In this telling, Gabriel refers to Satan as *Coronzom*: "So that in innocency the power of [Adam's] partaking with God, and with us [God's] good Angels, was exalted, and so became holy in the sight of God. Until that *Coronzom* (for so is the true name of that mighty Devil), envying his felicity, [. . .] began to assail him, and so prevailed."
The name *Coronzom* may predate Dee's journals in some form. Translator Rob Thomas (aka *Zadkiel*) has recorded his own search for a Barbarous Name found in the *Picatrix*: *Hacoronoz*—said in the text to be Greek. However, as Mr. Thomas notes, the name is likely a corruption of *ha Kronos* (the Chronos). *Chronos* is the Greek god of time, and the use of *ha* as "the" is drawn from Hebrew. (See the online discussion at http://groups.yahoo.com/group/solomonic/message/10778.)
I note that "succession of time" is an important subject in the Angelical Keys (see Cocasg and related words). Time, an aspect of the created realm, may be the principal domain of *Coronzom*.
Also note that this name appears incorrectly as *Coronzon* (with a final *n*) in *TFR*. The correct spelling can be found in Cotton Appendix 46, Part 1, folio 91.
Also see *Githgulcag* (likely a name for Lucifer) and *Telocvovim* (likely a name for the fallen Satan).

Possible shared root:
Cormfa (korm-FA) Numbers
Cormp (kormf) Numbered
Cormpo (korm-FOH) Hath (Yet) Numbered

Cormpt (kormft) Numbered
Sagacor (say-GAY-kor) In One Number

Cors (kors)* *adj.* Such

2.35 . . . a building *such* as is not but in the mind . . .

Pronunciation note:
(*Dee—Cors*) One syllable.

Also:
Corsi (kor-sii) Such

Compounds:
Icorsca (ii-KORS-kay) [I + Cors + Ca] Is Such as
Corsta (kors-tay) [Cors + Ta] Such as

Corsi (kor-sii)* *adj.* Such

8.53 . . . our comfort and *of such* as are prepared.

Pronunciation note:
(*Dee—Cor si*) Two syllables. The final *i* is likely a long vowel.

Also:
Cors (kors) Such

Corsta (kors-tay)* [Cors + Ta] *comp.* Such as

7.20 . . . *such as* work wonders . . .
30.125 . . . cast down *such as* fall . . .

Pronunciation notes:
(*Dee 7.20—Cors ta*)
(*Dee—Cor sta*) Two syllables.

Note:
Also see *Icorsca* (is such as).

Crip (krip)* *conj.* But

10.81 Come away, *but* not your noises.

Pronunciation notes:

(**Dee—Crip*) One syllable. Based on other versions of this word, I assume the *i* is a phonetic gloss.

Also:

"Crp" (krip) But

Note:

Crip (but) is usually a conjunction. Also see *Oq* (but), which is a preposition.

Croodzi (kroh-OD-zii)* *n.* Beginning (of Things)

4.21 . . . in whom *the second beginning of things* are . . .

Note:

There is no indication of the word *second* in *Croodzi*. Interestingly, the English for Key Four makes more sense without adding the word *second* here.

Pronunciation notes:

(**Dee—Cro od zi*) Three syllables.

(**Dee—croódzi*) See the *48 Claves*. An accent is placed on the second syllable.

Also:

Acroodzi (ak-roh-OD-zii) Beginning

Note:

Also see *Iaod* (beginning), *Iaodaf* (in the beginning), *Amgedpha* (I will begin anew), and *Nostoah* (it was in the beginning).

"Crp" (krip) *conj.* But

Compounds:

Crpl (krip-el) ["Crp" + L] But One

Also:

Crip (krip) — But

Note:

Crip (but) is a conjunction. However, for some reason, "Crp" is used in *Crpl* as a preposition. Also see *Oq* (but), a preposition.

Crpl (krip-el)* ["Crp" + L] *comp.* — But One

4.19 . . . none hath yet numbered *but one* . . .

Pronunciation notes:

(**Dee—CRPL*) Dee gives us little clue here. See the pronunciation note for Crip (but). Based on that, I suggest two syllables, with the *l* standing alone.

(**Dee—c-rp-l*) See the *48 Claves*. Dee seems to indicate three syllables here. However, I have settled on the two-syllable pronunciation.

Also:

Crip (kirp) — But

"Crus" (kroos)* *adj.* — More, Greater (?)**

Note:

(***Dee—Canse signifieth mighty, and Cruscanse more mighty.*) See *Five Books*, p. 304. *Cruscanse* (more mighty) is found in *Loagaeth*, and *Canse* (mighty) was mentioned in a marginal note. *"Crus"* was not mentioned by itself, but it may indicate "more" or "greater."

Pronunciation note:

(**Dee—Pronounce as we do cruse a cup.*) See the *Five Books*, p. 306. Dee made this marginal note next to the entire word *Cruscanse*, but it obviously only indicates the first syllable *"Crus." Cruse a cup* is an archaic phrase, but the word cruse likely rhrymes with the English word *cruise*.

Also:

Cruscanse (kroos-kan-say) — More Mighty

Cruscanse (KROOS-kan-say) [*"Crus"* + *Canse*]* *comp.* More Mighty**

Pronunciation note:

(***Dee—crúscanse*) See the *Five Books*, p. 304. Dee adds an accent over the first *a*.

From *Loagaeth*:

(**Dee—Canse signifieth mighty, and Cruscanse more mighty.*) See *Five Books*, p. 304. *Cruscanse* (more mighty) is found in *Loagaeth*, but *Canse* (mighty) was mentioned only in a marginal note.

Note:

See also *Micaolz* (mighty), *Micalp* (mightier)

Kures (kyew-res) n/a (?)

Note:

See *TFR*, p. 32. Here, the Angel Madimi has just interrupted the session to exorcise several demons from the body of Kelley. (See *Carma*.) These spirits came out of Kelley violently, scratching each other in the face and swarming about Madimi. To her, the spirits spoke in Angelical, "*Gil de pragma kures helech.*" Dee asks Madimi what this means, and she replies in Latin, which roughly translates as: "We want to live here in our [friends]." (*Madimi* does not offer definitions for the individual words.)

When Dee asks who these "friends" are supposed to be, the spirits indicate Kelley as their place of habitation (probably meaning both Dee and Kelley). Madimi then banishes these spirits.

Pronunciation note:

I feel the *Ku* might make a "q" sound similar to "cu" in words like *cure* or *cute*.

Gal (D)

D (dee) * *n.* or *adj.* — Third

6.30 . . . the second and *the third* . . .

Pronunciation notes:

(**Dee—d*) A single letter standing alone sounds like the English name of the letter.

Note:

This is the word for "third," but not the number 3. It is a noun when something is referred to as "the third." However, it becomes an adjective when used with another noun, as in "the Third Flame."

Compounds:

Chistad (kiis-tad) [Chis + Ta + D] — Are as (the) Third
Dialprt (dii-AL-purt) [D + "Ialprt"] — Third Flame
Duiv (DOO-iv) [D + Div] — Third Angle

"Da" (dah) *pron.* — There

Compounds:

Irgilchisda (ir-jil-KIIS-da) ["Irgil" + Chis + "Da"] — How Many Are There
"Chisda" (kiis-da) [Chis + "Da"] — Are There

Note:

Also see *Geta* (There)

Damploz (DAM-ploz)* *n.* — Variety

30.30 . . . and her unspeakable *variety* . . .

Pronunciation notes:

(**Dee—Dám ploz*) Two syllables, accent on the first syllable.
(**Dee—dámploz*) See the *48 Claves*. Dee again placed the accent on the first syllable.

DAOX (day-oks)* 5678

10.36 . . . thunders that *5678* times . . .

Pronunciation notes:

(**Dee—"Da" ox*) Two syllables. The *A* should be long.

(**Dee—dâox*) See the *48 Claves*. Here, Dee placed a circumflex over the *A* to confirm its long sound.

Note:

This word was not originally given with Key Ten. (It does appear there—see *TFR*, p. 131—but Dee may have added it at a later time.) It was added later when Nalvage transmitted the English for the Key (see *TFR*, p. 192). This seems to have been the case with many of the numbers mentioned in the Keys.

Darbs (darbs)* *v.* To Obey

5.45 . . . come you and *obey* your creation.

Pronunciation notes:

(**Dee—Darbs—one Syllable*) One syllable.

DARG (darj)* 6739

15.7 . . . whose wings are *6739* which weave . . .

Note:

The transmission of Key Fifteen is missing from Dee's journals. We have only the English given on *TFR*, p. 193. On that same page, Nalvage gives the phonetic note included in the following pronunciation notes.

Pronunciation notes:

(**Nalvage—Darg At large*) See *TFR*, p. 193. I assume this indicates that the final *g* should take a short sound, as in the English word *large*.

Darr (dar) *n.* The Philosopher's Stone

From the *Alchemical Cipher*:

See *TFR*, pp. 387–89. The Angel Levanael says of this word, "*Audcal* is his Mercury. *Darr*, (in the Angelical tongue), is the true Name of the Stone." *Audcal* (gold) is here described as the alchemical Mercury (or essence) of the Philosopher's Stone.

Pronunciation note:

The *rr* is likely a hard "r" sound.

Darsar (dar-sar)* *adv.* Wherefore / Therefore

6.31 *Wherefore*, hearken unto my voice.

Pronunciation notes:

(**Dee—Darsar*) Likely two syllables.

Note:

See also *Bagle* (for, wherefore, because) and *Lap* (for).

"Dax" (daks) *n.* Loins

Compounds:

Daxil (daks-il) ["Dax" + "Yl"] Thy Loins

Daxil (daks-il)* ["Dax" + "Yl"] *comp.* Thy Loins

17.17 Gird up *thy loins* and harken.

Pronunciation notes:

(**Dee—Dax il*) Two syllables. I suspect the *i* takes the sound of a short *i* in this case, rather than the "y" sound of *Yls*, *Ylsi*, etc.

Dazis (daz-IS)* *n.* Heads

9.50 *Their heads* are covered with diamond . . .
10.27 . . . vomit out *the heads of* scorpions.

Pronunciation notes:
(**Dee 9.50—Daz is*)
(**Dee 10.27—Daz ís*) Two syllables. The accent is placed on the second syllable.
(**Dee—dazís*) See the *48 Claves*. Here, Dee again places the accent on the second syllable.

De (dee)* *prep.* Of

3.47 . . . the corners *of* your governments . . .

Pronunciation notes:
(**Dee—De, is my name*) In other words, the word *De* (of) should sound just like Dee's own name. The *e* takes the long sound.

Note:
There is only this one instance of the word *of* in the literal Angelical Keys. In a few other cases, the word of seems to be indicated by an *-o* affix (i.e., see Caosgo). Meanwhile, in the vast majority of cases the word *of* is absent from the Angelical, implied strictly by context.

Also see *TFR*, p. 32. Here, the Angel Madimi has just interrupted the session to exorcise several demons from the body of Kelley. (See *Carma.*) To Madimi, the spirits spoke in Angelical, "*Gil de pragma kures helech.*" (Note the word *De.*) Dee asks the Angel what this phrase means, and she replies in Latin, which roughly translates as, "We want to live here in our [friends]." (Madimi does not offer definitions for the individual words.)

Compare from *Loagaeth*:
De

Deo (dee-oh) *prop. n.* "The Seventh Aethyr"

30.3 . . . which dwell in *the seventh aethyr* . . .

Note:

This (word 30.3) is the single space in the Key of the Aethyrs, which must be changed for each invocation—replacing word 30.3 with the name of the appropriate Aethyr. No established definitions were given for these names.

Deo contains the three Parts of the Earth *Opmacas*, *Genadol*, and *Aspiaon*.

Des (des) *prop. n.* "The Twenty-Sixth Aethyr"

30.3 . . . which dwell in *the twenty-sixth aethyr* . . .

Note:

This (word 30.3) is the single space in the Key of the Aethyrs, which must be changed for each invocation—replacing word 30.3 with the name of the appropriate Aethyr. No established definitions were given for these names.

Des contains the three Parts of the Earth *Pophand*, *Nigrana*, and *Bazchim*.

Dialprt (dii-AL-purt)* [D + "Ialprt"] *comp.* Third Flame

17.2 O thou *third flame* . . .

Pronunciation notes:

(**Dee—Di al pert*) Three syllables. The *i* seems to take a long sound. The *r* takes its extended "ur" (or "er") sound. I have adopted the accent from similar words.

Dilzmo (dilz-moh)* *v.* To Differ

30.76 . . . *let them differ* in their qualities.

Pronunciation notes:

(**Dee—Dil zmo*) Dee indicates two syllables. However, I am unsure why he places the *z* in the second syllable—as that *should* indicate the *z* and likely the *m* both stand alone. However, that would make for three or four syllables. Dee likely intended *Dilz mo* instead.

Div (DII-vee) *n.* — Angle

Pronunciation note:

I have adopted the accent from *Sdiu* (fourth angle).

Compounds:

Sdiu (es-DII-vee) [S + Div] — Fourth Angle
Vivdiv (viv-DII-vee) [Viv + Div] — Second Angle
Duiv (DOO-iv) [D + Div] — Third Angle

Dlasod (dee-lay-sod) *n.* — Sulfur

From the *Alchemical Cipher*:

See *TFR*, pp. 387–89. The Angel Levanael says of this word, "*Dlasod* is Sulfur."

Note:

Also see *Salbrox* (Live Sulfur). Where Salbrox is the kind of sulfur one would find on a match, *Dlasod* refers to alchemical sulfur.

Dluga (dee-LOO-ga)* *v.* — To Give

3.35 . . . *giving unto* every one of you . . .

Pronunciation notes:

(**Dee—Dluga*) See pronunciation note at *Idlugam* (is given). I assume the *D* in this word should stand alone, making three syllables.

Also:

"Dlugam" (dee-LOO-gam) — Given
Dlugar (dee-LOO-gar) — To Give

"Dlugam" (dee-LOO-gam) *v.* Given

Compounds:

Idlugam (id-LOO-gam) [I + "Dlugam"] Is given

Also:

Dluga (dee-LOO-ga) To Give

Dlugar (dee-LOO-gar) To Give

Dlugar (dee-LOO-gar)* *v.* To Give

5.19 . . . and *gave them* vessels . . .

6.15 . . . *giving unto them* fiery darts . . .

Pronunciation notes:

(**Dee 5.19; 6.15—Dlugar*) See pronunciation note at Idlugam (is given). I assume the *D* in this word should stand alone, making three syllables.

Also:

Dluga (dee-LOO-ga) To Give

"Dlugam" (dee-LOO-gam) Given

Doalim (doh-ay-lim)* *n.* Sin

13.8 . . . to stir up wrath of *sin* . . .

Pronunciation notes:

(**Dee—Do a lim*) Three syllables. The *o* takes its long sound, and the *a* stands alone (instead of the two combining into one sound). The *i* appears to be short.

(**Dee—doâlim*) See the *48 Claves*. Here, Dee places a circumflex over the *a* to indicate its long sound.

Dobix (dob-iks)* *v.* To Fall

30.126 Cast down such as *fall*.

Pronunciation notes:

(**Dee—Dobix*) Likely two syllables. Both vowels appear to take their short sounds.

Note:

Also see *Loncho* (to fall).

Dodpal (dod-pal)* *v.* To Vex

30.84 . . . *let them vex* and weed out one another.

Pronunciation notes:

(**Dee—Dod pal*) Two syllables.

Also:

Dodrmni (dod-rum-nii)	Vexed
Dods (dods)	To Vex
Dodsih (dod-sih)	Vexation

Dodrmni (dod-rum-nii)* *adj.* Vexed

30.55 . . . may be always drunken and *vexed* in itself . . .

Pronunciation notes:

(**Dee—Dod rm ni Dodrumni*) Three syllables. Plus, Dee has added an extra clue, showing us that *rm* should take a sound like *rum*.

Also:

Dodpal (dod-pal)	To Vex
Dods (dods)	To Vex
Dodsih (dod-sih)	Vexation

Dods (dods) *v.* To Vex

14.10 . . . *vexing* all creatures of the earth with age.

Note:

The transmission of Key Fourteen is missing from Dee's journals. We only have the English for this Key given later (see *TFR*, p. 193). Plus, the word appears in this location in Dee's *48 Claves*.

Also:

Dodpal (dod-pal) — (Let) Vex
Dodrmni (dod-rum-nii) — Vexed
Dodsih (dod-sih) — Vexation

Dodsih (dod-sih)* *n.* — Vexation

17.8 . . . to stir up *vexation* and . . .

Pronunciation notes:

(*Dee—Dod sih*) Two syllables. Both vowels seem to take their short sounds.

Also:

Dodpal (dod-pal) — To Vex
Dodrmni (dod-rum-nii) — Vexed
Dods (dods) — To Vex

Don (don) *prop. n.* — Letter *R*

Note:

The name of the Angelical letter for *R*. It is likely that these letter names have translations of their own. (For instance, note the Hebrew alphabet: the letter *R* is named *Resh*, but *Resh* also translates as "head" or "beginning.") However, such translations for the Angelical letters are never given. (See the *Five Books*, p. 270.)

"Donasdoga" (doh-NAS-dog-ay) — n/a

From *Loagaeth*:

See note at *Donasdogamatastos*.

Compounds:

Donadogamatastos (doh-NAS-dog-ay-MAT-az-tos)

[*"Donasdoga"* + *"Matastos"*] "Hellfire"

Donasdogamatastos (doh-NAS-dog-ay-MAT-az-tos)**

[*"Donasdoga"?* + *"Matastos"?*] *n.* "Hellfire"*

From *Loagaeth*:

(**Dee—The furious and perpetual fire enclosed for the punishment of them that are banished from the glory.*) See the *Five Books*, p. 321. This is likely a reference to the place of punishment prepared for the fallen Angels known as the Watchers in *1 Enoch*.

Pronunciation notes:

(****Dee—do násdoga mátastos—One word of 7 syllables: 4 in the first part and 3 in the last.*) See the *Five Books*, p. 321. Dee seems to indicate the first *o* and the second *a* should each be long. He places two accents in the word.

Note:

The fact that Dee places two accents in this word leads me to suspect this is a compound word. This may also explain why Dee points out that the first four syllables make up the "first part" and the final three the "last."

Compare from *Loagaeth*:

Donadocha, Doncha

Dooain (doh-OH-ay-in)* *n.* Name

3.68 . . . and (his) *Name* is become mighty . . .

12.20 . . . whose *name* amongst you is wrath.

Pronunciation notes:

(**Dee 3.68—Do o a in*)

(**Dee 12.20—Do ó a in*) Four syllables. The second *o* stands alone as the second syllable, and has the accent. The *a* also stands alone.

(**Dee 3.68—do-o-â-in*) See the *48 Claves*. Dee added a circumflex over the *a* to indicate the long vowel.
(**Dee 12.20—dooâin*) See the *48 Claves*. Dee shows the circumflex over the *a* again.

Also:

Dooaip (doh-OH-ay-ip) — In the Name
Dooiap (doh-OH-ii-ap) — In the Name

Possible shared root:

Omaoas (oh-may-OH-as) — Names

Dooaip (doh-OH-ay-ip)* *n.* — (In the) Name

4.40 *In the name of* the Creator . . .

Pronunciation notes:

(**Dee—Do oa ip*) This appears to be three syllables. However, see the *48 Claves*:
(**Dee—Do-ó-â-io*) See the *48 Claves*. Here, Dee shows four syllables. There is an accent on the second syllable, and the *a* (standing alone) is given a circumflex to indicate its long sound. (Note that Dee also mistakenly wrote a final *o* on this word instead of the final *p*.)

Also:

Dooain (doh-OH-ay-in) — Name
Dooiap (doh-OH-ii-ap) — (In the) Name

Possible shared root:

Omaoas (oh-may-OH-as) — Names

Dooiap (doh-OH-ii-ap)* *n.* — (In the) Name

3.59 *In the name of* the same your God . . .

Pronunciation notes:

(**Dee—Do o i ap*) Four syllables. The second *o* and the *i* each stand alone.

(**Dee—do-ó-î-ap*) See the *48 Claves*. Four syllables, with an accent on the third syllable. Dee also shows a circumflex over the *i* to indicate its long sound.

Also:

Dooaip (doh-OH-ay-ip) (In the) Name
Dooain (doh-OH-ay-in) Name

Possible shared root:

Omaoas (oh-may-OH-as) Names

Dorpha (dor-fa)* *v.* To Look About

4.5 . . . and *have looked about me* saying . . .

Pronunciation notes:

(**Dee—Dor pha*) Two syllables.

Also:

Dorphal (dor-fal) To Look Upon (with Gladness)

Dorphal (dor-fal)* *v.* To Look Upon (with Gladness)

5.8 . . . *looking with gladness upon* the earth . . .

Pronunciation notes:

(**Dee—Dorphal*) Likely two syllables.

Note:

I do not see *with gladness* indicated in the Angelical. If this were a compound, then the *L* (meaning "the first/one") would make this word mean "looking upon one." Instead, the word *Dorphal* is not a compound, and seems to have a tone of benevolence built into its definition—as to look over someone as a loved one.

Also:

Dorpha (dor-fa) To Look About

Dosig (doh-sig)* *n.* Night

10.22 . . . which burn *night* and day . . .

Pronunciation notes:

(**Dee—Do sig*) Two syllables. I assume the *o* should take its long sound. I also assume the final *g* takes its hard sound.

Drilpa (dril-pa)* *adj.* Great

10.79 . . . is, was, and shall be *great*.
16.18 *Great* art thou in the God of . . .

Pronunciation notes:

(**Dee 10.79; 16.18—Dril pa*) Two syllables. The *i* takes a short sound.

Also:

Drilpi (dril-pii) Greater Than

Drilpi (dril-pii)* *adj.* Greater Than

9.43 . . . millstones *greater than* the earth . . .

Pronunciation notes:

(**Dee—Dril pi*) Two syllables. The first *i* appears to take its short sound, while the final *i* takes a long sound.

Also:

Drilpa (dril-pa) Great

Drix (driks)* *v.* To Bring Down

12.13 *Bring down* your train . . .

Pronunciation notes:

(**Dee—Drix*) One syllable.

Droln (drohln)* *adj.* or *adv.* Any

10.53 . . . neither know *any* (long) time here.

Pronunciation notes:

(**Dee—droln*) One syllable. I suggest a long sound for the *o*.

Drux (drooks)* *prop. n.* Letter *N*

Note:

The name of the Angelical letter for *N*. It is likely that these letter names have translations of their own. (For instance, note the Hebrew alphabet: the letter *N* is named *Nun*, but *Nun* also translates as "fish.") However, such translations for the Angelical letters are never given. (See the *Five Books*, p. 270.)

Pronunciation notes:

(**Dee—In sound, drovx.*) Dee uses a *v* here instead of a *u*. The word would look like *droux* in modern English. The *ou* letter combination could produce a long *o* or a long "u" sound. I have adopted the long *u*, because the word *Drux* is actually spelled with a *Van* (*U*).

Compare from *Loagaeth*:

*Adrux, Drux, Druz***

Note:

***Druz* was given in the margin of *Loagaeth*, Table One, side A, line 1—as an alternate form of *Drux*.

Ds (dee-es)* *pron.* Which/That

1.19 . . . *which* measureth your garments . . .
1.53 . . . him *that* liveth . . .
1.60 . . . *which* shineth as a flame . . .
5.32 . . . *which* are garnished with . . . lamps . . .
10.20 . . . *which* burn night and day . . .
10.35 . . . thunders *that* 5678 times . . .

10.49 . . . surges *which* rest not . . .
11.7 . . . thunders *which* flew into the east . . .
13.19 . . . power *which* is called amongst you . . .
**14.5 . . . *which* sit upon 24 seats . . .
**15.11 . . . *which* knowest the great name . . .
***16.5 . . . *which* hast thy beginning in glory . . .
18.6 . . . *which* openest they glory . . .
18.17 . . . *which* is called in thy kingdom joy . . .
30.22 . . . *which* provided you for the government . . .
30.147 . . . *which* hath sworn unto us . . .

Pronunciation notes:

(**Dee 1.19—DS*)

(**Dee 11.7; 18.6, 17; 30.22, 147—Ds*)

(**Dee 5.32; 10.20, 35, 49; 13.19—ds*) Likely a word of two syllables. Each letter pronounced on its own.

Note:

**The transmissions of Keys Fourteen and Fifteen are missing from Dee's journals. We only have the English for them given later (see *TFR*, p. 193). Plus, these words appear in these locations in Dee's *48 Claves*.

Note:

***The transmission of the first twelve words of Key Sixteen is missing from Dee's journals. We only have the English given for it on *TFR*, p. 194. However, they do appear in Dee's *48 Claves*.

Compounds:

Dsabramg (dee-say-bray-mig) [Ds + Abramg]	Which Prepared
Dsbrin (dee-es-brin) [Ds + "Brin"]	Which Have
Dschis (dee-es-kiis) [Ds + Chis]	Which Are
Dsi (dee-sii) [Ds + I]	Which Is
Dsinsi (dee-sin-sii) [Ds + "Insi"]	Which Walkest
Dsium (dee-sii-um) [Ds + "Ium"]	Which (Is) Called
Dsoado (dee-soh-ay-doh) [Ds + "Oado"]	Which Weave
Dsom (dee-som) [Ds + Om]	That Understand
Dsonf (dee-sonv) [Ds + Sonf]	Which Reign
Dspaaox (dee-SPAY-ay-oks) [Ds + Paaox]	Which Remain
Dspraf (dee-es-praf) [Ds + "Praf"]	Which Dwell

Also:

Dst (dee-es-tee) Which

Note:

The word *Ar* (that) is a conjunction, while the word *Ds* (which / that) is a pronoun.

Further:

Ds (dee-es) *conj.* And(?)

1.34 . . . *and* beautified your garments . . .
1.42 . . . *and* delivered you a rod . . .

Note:

It is difficult to accept that the word *and* is intended in these two instances. The word *which* does fit in both cases—even if it doesn't allow the English to sound quite as smooth. For the proper Angelical word for *and*, see *Od*.

Dsabramg (dee-say-bray-mig)* [Ds + Abramg] *comp.* Which Prepared

8.11 . . . *which I have prepared* for my own righteousness . . .

Pronunciation notes:

(*Dee—Dsabramg [g not as dg]*) Dee only tells us that the final *g* should take the hard sound rather than the soft "dg" (as in *hedge*) or "j" sound (as in *jump* and *just*). Otherwise, I assume the initial *D* should stand alone, while the *s* combines with the following vowel. (Further supporting this, see the pronunciation notes for *Dsi*.) Four syllables total.
(*Dee—dsa-bramg*) See the *48 Claves*. Here, Dee may be indicating a long sound for the first *a*. See notes for *Abramig* and *Abramg*, where we find that both *A*s should take the long sound.

Dsbrin (dee-es-brin)* [Ds + "Brin"] *comp.* Which Have

9.6 . . . *which have* vials 8 . . .
13.3 . . . *which have* 42 eyes . . .
**14.14 . . . *which have* under you 1636 . . .

Pronunciation notes:

(**Dee 9.6; 13.3—Ds brin*) This should be three syllables. (See the pronunciation of *Ds*.)

Note:

**The transmission of Key Fourteen is missing from Dee's journals. We only have the English for this Key given later (see *TFR*, p. 193). Plus, the word appears in this location in Dee's *48 Claves*.

Dschis (dee-es-kiis)* [Ds + Chis] *comp.* Which Are

8.25 . . . *which are*, and shall not see death . . .
13.12 . . . making men drunken *which are* empty . . .

Pronunciation notes:

(**Dee8.25; 13.12—Ds chis*) I assume three syllables here. See the pronunciation notes for *Ds* (which) and *chis* (are).

Dsi (dee-sii)* [Ds + I] *comp.* Which Is

4.38 . . . God, *which is*, and liveth . . .

Pronunciation notes:

(**Dee—D SI*) I assume two syllables here—as Dee likely only intended for the *D* to stand alone. The *si* join to make a sound together.

Dsinsi (dee-sin-sii) [Ds + "Insi"] *comp.* Which Walkest

16.11 . . . *which walkest upon* the earth . . .

Note:

The transmission of the first twelve words of Key Sixteen is missing from Dee's journals. We only have the English given for it on *TFR*, p. 194. However, they do appear in Dee's *48 Claves*.

Dsium (dee-sii-um) [Ds + "Ium"] *comp.* Which (Is) Called

14.22 . . . *which is called* amongst you . . .

Note:

The transmission of Key Fourteen is missing from Dee's journals. We only have the English for this Key given later (see *TFR*, p. 193). Plus, the word appears in this location in Dee's *48 Claves*.

Dsoado (dee-soh-ay-doh)* [Ds + "Oado"] *comp.* Which Weave

15.8 . . . *which weave* the earth with dryness . . .

Note:

The transmission of Key Fifteen is missing from Dee's journals. We only have the English for this Key given later (see *TFR*, p. 193). Plus, the word appears in this location in Dee's *48 Claves*.

Pronunciation notes:

(**Dee—dsoâdo*) See the *48 Claves*. Likely four syllables. The initial *D* should stand alone, as it precedes a consonant (*s*) it does not naturally combine with in English. The *so* should form the second syllable, making the *o* take its long sound. The *a* takes a long sound, as Dee indicated with the circumflex.

Dsom (dee-som)* [Ds + Om] *comp.* That Understand

16.15 . . . *that understand* and separate creatures . . .

Pronunciation notes:

(**Dee—dsom*) Dee does not give us much of a clue. However, other compounds involving *Ds* (which) suggest that the initial *D* should stand alone, and the *som* should combine to form a second syllable.

Dsonf (dee-sonv)* [Ds + Sonf] *comp.* Which Reign

4.11 . . . *which reign in* the second angle . . .

12.2 . . . *that reign in* the south . . .

Pronunciation notes:

(**Dee—Dsonf*) The *D* should stand alone. However, the *s* blends into the rest of the word in a single syllable. See the pronunciation notes for *Sonf* (reign).

Dspaaox (dee-SPAY-ay-oks)* [Ds + Paaox] *comp.* Which Remain

8.22 . . . *which remain* in the glory . . .

Pronunciation notes:

(**Dee—Dspá a ox*) This is likely four syllables, as the *D* should most likely stand alone. The *sp* combine their sounds, as in the English words *spot* or *special*. The accent is on the second syllable. The first *a* takes a long sound, likely due to the letter combination *aa*. (Double vowels often indicated long vowel sounds in Early Modern English.)

(**Dee—ds pá-â-ox*) See the *48 Claves*. Dee again shows the accent on the first *a*. He also added a circumflex over the second *a* to indicate its long sound. This note seems to indicate that the *s* and the *p* do not combine together—although I have decided to stick with Dee's note from *TFR*.

Dspraf (dee-es-praf)* [Ds + "Praf"] *comp.* Which Dwell

30.2 . . . *which dwell* in the "1st Aethyr" . . .

Pronunciation notes:

(**Dee—Ds praf*) *Ds* should be two syllables, then "Praf" seems to have just one.

Dst (dee-es-tee)* *pron.* Which (Also)

3.24 . . . *which* sleep and shall rise . . .
4.24 . . . *which also* successively are . . .

Pronunciation notes:

(**Dee 3.24; 4.24—DST*) Most likely three syllables, each letter standing alone. Elsewhere, Dee indicates that *Ds* (that/which) has two syllables.

Also:

Ds (dee-es) Which/That

Note:

Also see *Ar* (that).

Duiv (DOO-iv)* [D + Div] *comp.* Third Angle

5.3 . . . have entered into *the third angle* . . .

Pronunciation notes:

(**Dee—Du iv*) Two syllables. Likely a long *u* followed by a short *i*.

(**Dee—du-i-v*) See the *48 Claves*. Here Dee seems to indicate three syllables. However, I have settled upon the two-syllable version in my pronunciation.

I have adopted the accent from *Sdiu* (fourth angle).

Note:

Duiv is not D + Viv—which would mean "third second." However, combining *D* (third) and *Div* (angle) only results in *Div*. (The repeated letter *D* would vanish.) The *u* is included to differentiate the word, although I am not sure why *u* is chosen.

Graph (E)

Eai* (ee-AY-ii) *prep.* — Amongst

Alternate spelling:

(**Dee 1.67—AAI The first a may be an A an O or an e*) Thus, there are two alternate spellings for *Aai* (amongst).

Pronunciation notes:

See *Aai* (amongst), which Dee indicates has three syllables.

Also:

Aai (ay-AY-ii) — Amongst (You)
Aaf (ay-AF) — Amongst
Aaiom (ay-AY-om) — Amongst (Us?)
Aao (ay-ay-OH) — Amongst
Oai (oh-AY-ii) — Amongst

"Ecrin" (EE-krin) *n.* — Praise

Compounds:

Odecrin (oh-dee-KRIN) [Od + "Ecrin"] — And the Praise (of)

Also:

Oecrimi (oh-EE-krim-ii) — To Sing Praises

Ednas (ed-nas)* *n.* — Receivers

5.51 Conclude us as *receivers of* your mysteries.

Pronunciation notes:

(**Dee—Ed nas*) Two syllables. Both vowels appear to take their short sounds.
(**Dee—ed-nas*) See the *48 Claves*. This note matches that from *TFR*.

Note:

This may also be the verb *to receive*. However, it is used in Key Five as a noun.

Ef (ef)* *v.* To Visit

12.12 . . . bind up your girdles and *visit us* . . .

Pronunciation notes:

(**Dee—Ef*) One syllable. The *E* is likely a phonetic gloss. (See *F*).

Also:

F (ef) Visit

Efafafe (ee-FAY-fay-fee)* *n.* Vials

9.7 . . . which have *vials* 8 of wrath . . .

Pronunciation notes:

(**Dee—E fa fa fe*) Four syllables. The initial *E* stands alone. The two *a*'s are each long vowels. The final *e* is uncertain—as it could be silent, or it could make a long "e" sound. I have chosen the long *e*.

(**Dee—efáfâfe*) See the *48 Claves*. Dee placed an accent on the second syllable. He also placed a circumflex over the second *a* to indicate its long sound.

Note:

This word is a palindrome. It is spelled the same forward as it is spelled backward.

Also:

Ofafafe (oh-FAY-fay-fee) Vials

El (el)* *prop. n.* The First

6.8 . . . whom *the First* hath planted . . .

Pronunciation notes:

(**Dee—el*) One syllable. The *E* is likely a phonetic gloss.

Compounds:

Gohel (GOH-hel) [Goho + El] Sayeth the First

Lel (el-el) [L + El] Same

Note:

This reminds me of the Hebrew Name of God: *El*.

Also compare to the name of the Angel *El* (or *L*), one of the Sons of the Sons of Light. His name literally translates as "The First."

Also:

"Lo" (loh) — The First
L (el) — The First
La (lah or el-ah) — The First
Lu (loo) — From One

"Elzap" (el-ZAP) *n.* — Course

Compounds:

Elzaptilb (el-ZAP-tilb) ["Elzap" + Tilb] — Her Course

Also:

"Lzar" (el-ZAR) — Courses

Elzaptilb (el-ZAP-tilb)* ["Elzap" + Tilb] *comp.* — Her Course

30.57 *Her course*, let it run with the heavens . . .

Pronunciation notes:

(**Dee—El zap tilb*) Three syllables. As we can see in the word "Lzar," (course) the *E* in *Elzaptilb* is a phonetic gloss only.

(**Dee—Elzáptilb*) See the *48 Claves*. Here, Dee placed an accent over the second syllable.

Em (em)* *n.* — Nine

6.4 The spirits of the fourth angle are *nine* . . .

Pronunciation notes:

(**Dee—Em*) One syllable. The *E* is not likely a phonetic gloss—see *M* (except).

Note:
I assume this is the word for "nine" rather than the actual number 9.

Emetgis (em-et-jis) *n.* Seal

15.16 . . . righteousness and *the seal of* honour.

Note:
The transmission of Key Fifteen is missing from Dee's journals. We only have the English for this Key given later (see *TFR*, p. 193). Plus, the word appears in this location in Dee's *48 Claves*.

Also note that the first four letters of this word are *Emet* (Hebrew for "truth"). This matches the name of Dee's Seal of Truth—or *Sigillum Dei Emet*. Perhaps this Seal of Truth and the Seal of Honor are one and the same.

Pronunciation note:
I assume the *g* takes the soft sound, as it precedes an *i* (as in the English words *giant* or *gibberish*).

Emna (em-na)* *n.* Here

10.56 . . . neither know any (long) time *here*.

Pronunciation notes:
(**Dee—Em na*) Two syllables.

Note:
Also see *Sem* (in this place).

EMOD (ee-mod)* 8763

16.14 . . . with feet *8763* that understand . . .

Pronunciation notes:
(**Dee—E mod*) Two syllables. The initial *E* stands alone.

Note:

This word was not originally given with Key Sixteen. It was added later when Nalvage transmitted the English for the Key (see *TFR*, p. 194). This seems to have been the case with many of the numbers mentioned in the Keys.

Enay (en-ay)* *n.* Lord

7.8 . . . wherein *the Lord* hath opened His mouth . . .
12.17 . . . 3663 that *the Lord* may be magnified . . .

Pronunciation notes:

(**Dee 7.8—Enay*)

(**Dee12.17—E nay*) Two syllables. Dee indicates here (word 12.17) that the *E* can stand alone (ee-nay). However, consider that the spelling of *Enay* is actually a phonetic gloss. The word is one and the same with *NA* (en-ay). Dee's phonetic notes seem to indicate that either pronunciation is acceptable—although I have settled upon the "en-ay" version.

Compounds:

Zirenaiad (zii-er-NAY-ad) [Zir + Enay + Iad] I am the Lord (Your) God

Also:

NA (en-ay) Lord

Eol (ee-OHL)* *v.* Made

3.29 In the first, *I made you* stewards . . .

Pronunciation note:

(**Dee—EOL)* Dee gives us little clue here.

(**Dee—E-ól)* See the *48 Claves*. Two syllables, with an accent on the second syllable. The initial *E* stands alone.

Also:

Eolis (ee-OH-lis) Making
Oln (ohln) Made (of)

Note:
Also see *Ozazm* (to make) and *Ozazma* (to make).

Eolis (ee-OH-lis)* *v.* To Make

13.9 . . . *making* men drunken . . .

Pronunciation note:
(**Dee—E o lis*) Three syllables. The *E* and *o* each stand alone.
(**Dee—eôlis*) See the *48 Claves*. Here, Dee placed a circumflex over the *o* to indicate its long sound.
I have adopted the accent from *Eol* (made).

Also:
Eol (ee-OHL) Made
Oln (ohln) Made (of)

Note:
Also see *Ozazm* (to make) and *Ozazma* (to make).

Eophan (ee-oh-fan)* *n.* Lamentation

10.14 . . . 22 nests of *lamination* and weeping . . .

Pronunciation notes:
(**Dee—E o phan*) Three syllables. The intial *E* and the *o* each stand alone.
(**Dee—eôphan*) See the *48 Claves*. Here, Dee places a circumflex over the *o* to indicate its long sound.

"Eors" (ee-ORS)* n/a

Note:
This word appears nowhere in the Angelic system as of yet. It was originally dictated in the tenth Key as the word "thousand." However, this was corrected on page 192 of *TFR* with the word *Math* (10.45). "Eors" may have been merely a mistake on Kelley's part, and not an Angelical word at all (there were many difficulties in the reception of Key Ten).

Other such interferences with the transmission of the Keys were attributed to demonic spirits—see *Piamol*.

Pronunciation notes:
(**Dee—E órs*) Two syllables, with an accent on the second syllable. The initial *E* stands alone.

ERAN (ee-RAN)* 6332

18.14 . . . the secrets of truth *6332* have their abiding . . .

Pronunciation notes:
(**Dee—E ran*) Two syllables. The initial *E* stands alone.
(**Dee—erán*) See the *48 Claves*. Here, Dee placed an accent over the second syllable.

Note:
This word was not originally given with Key Eighteen. It was added later when Nalvage transmitted the English for the Key (see *TFR*, p. 194). This seems to have been the case with many of the numbers mentioned in the Keys.

Erm (erm) *n.* Ark/Refuge/Haven

1.45 . . . delivered you a rod with *the ark of* knowledge.

"Es" (es) *n.* Fourth

Compounds:
Odes (ohd-es) [Od + "Es"] And Fourth

Also:
S (es) Fourth

Note:
The *E* in "Es" is a phonetic gloss.
Also note this is the word for "fourth," but not the number 4. The word *fourth* could be a noun or adjective, but is used here as a noun.

Compare from *Loagaeth*:

Es

Esiasch (ee-sii-ash)* *n.* Brothers

5.26 . . . they are *the brothers of* the first and second . . .

Pronunciation notes:

(**Dee—E siach*) I suggest three syllables here. The initial *E* stands alone. Note that Dee indicates the sound of "ach" for *asch*. I assume this means the *ch* makes the "tch" sound (as in the English word *church*) instead of the harder "kh" sound. However, the preceding *s* would give the *ch* an extra soft sound, almost like a hard "sh."

(**Dee—esîach*) See the *48 Claves*. Note the circumflex over the *i*—indicating the long sound.

Ethamz (ee-THAM-zohd)* *v.* To Cover

9.51 Their heads *are covered with* diamond . . .

Pronunciation notes:

(**Dee—E tham Zod*) Three syllables. The initial *E* and the final *z* each stand alone. The *a* should take a short sound.

(**Dee—ethámz*) See the *48 Claves*. Here, Dee placed an accent over the second syllable.

"Etharzi" (eth-AR-zii) *n.* Peace

Compounds:

Fetharzi (feth-AR-zii) [F + "Etharzi"] Visit (Us) in Peace

Or (F)

F (ef) *v.* To Visit

Compounds:
Fbliard (ef-blii-ard) [F + "Bliard"] Visit (with) Comfort
Fcaosga (ef-kay-OS-ga) [F + Caosga] Visit the Earth
Fetharzi (feth-AR-zii) [F + "Etharzi"] Visit in Peace

Also:
Ef (ef) To Visit

Faaip (fay-AY-ip)* *n.* Voices (Voicings / Psalms?)

2.5 . . . understand your *voices* of wonder . . .

Pronunciation notes:
(**Dee—Fa á ip*) Dee indicates three syllables, the second *a* standing alone and accented.
(**Dee—Fa-á-ip*) See *48 Claves*. This note matches the one from *TFR*.

Possible shared root:
Farzem (farz-em) Uplifted Voices
Bia (bii-a) Voice

Note:
The word *Bia* appears to be Angelical for "voice"—as in one's speaking voice. *Faaip*, however, has the connotation of something that is said (as in to voice an opinion), or perhaps sung. Key Two gives me the impression that the Faaip ("voices" of wonder) are actually "songs" (or "voicings") of wonder—something akin to Psalms.
Also see *Luiahe* (song of honor).

Faboan (fay-boh-an)* *n.* Poison

10.32 . . . live sulphur myngled with *poison*.

Pronunciation notes:

(**Dee—Fa bo an*) Three syllables. The first *a* and the *o* take their long sounds.

(**Dee—fabôan*) See the *48 Claves*. Here, Dee placed a circumflex over the *o* to indicate its long sound.

Note:

See also *Tatan* (Wormwood).

Fafen (fay-fen)* *n.* Intent

3.43 . . . true ages of time, *to the intent that* from your highest . . .

Pronunciation notes:

(**Dee—Fafen*) The *e* likely gives the *a* a long sound.

Also:

Fafen (fay-fen)** Train

12.14 Bring down *your train* . . .

Pronunciation notes:

(***Dee—Fa fen*) Two syllables.

Note:

This is one of the few instances were a single Angelical word *appears* to have two completely separate definitions. The "train" in Key Twelve appears to have a triple meaning: (1) The poetry suggests the train of a royal robe or wedding gown. (2) It also suggests the meaning of "retinue"—so the Key is asking the Angels to descend with their servants and ministers. Finally, (3) a "train" can be defined as a "succession of events" or "consequences"—which best suits the word *Fafen* as a synonym of "intention." (As in a "train of thought.")

Fam (fam) *prop. n.* Letter *S* / *Sh*

Note:

The name of the Angelical letter for *S* / *Sh*. It is likely that these letter names have translations of their own. (For instance, note the Hebrew alphabet:

the letter *S/Sh* is named *Shin*, but *Shin* also translates as "tooth.") However, such translations for the Angelical letters are never given. (See the *Five Books*, p. 270.)

Compare from *Loagaeth*:
Fam

Faonts (fay-onts)* *v.* — To Dwell (within)

5.11 . . . and *dwelling within* the brightness of the heavens . . .

Pronunciation notes:
(**Dee—Fa onts*) Two syllables. There is no *ao* letter combination in Early Modern English—each letter makes a separate sound—as in the English word *chaos*. The *a* is likely long.

Shared root:
Fargt (farj-et) — Dwelling Places
"Faorgt" (fay-or-jet) — Dwelling Place

"Faorgt" (fay-or-jet) *n.* — Dwelling Place

Compounds:
Odfaorgt (ohd-fay-or-jet) [Od + "Faorgt"] — And the Dwelling Place

Also:
Fargt (farj-et) — Dwelling Places
Faonts (fay-onts) — To Dwell (within)

Fargt (farj-et)* *n.* — Dwelling Places

30.89 And *the dwelling places*, let them forget . . .

Pronunciation notes:
(**Dee—Farg t Gad*) Two syllables. Dee's notation appears to indicate a hard *g* at the end of the first syllable, and the *t* stands alone. However, see the pronunciation for *Odfaorgt*, where we find the *g* can be soft, and combines with the *t* to indicate the sound of "dgt"—or "jet."

Also:

"Faorgt" (fay-or-jet) Dwelling Place

Faonts (fay-onts) To Dwell (within)

Farzm (farz-em) *v.* Uplifted Voices (To Speak up)

1.48 . . . *you lifted up your voices* and swore . . .

Possible shared root:

Faaip (fay-AY-ip) Voices (Psalms?)

Bia (bii-a) Voices

Fbliard (ef-blii-ard)* [F + "Bliard"] *comp.* Visit (with) Comfort

6.22 . . . *visit with comfort* the earth . . .

Pronunciation notes:

(*Dee—F bli ard*) Three syllables. The initial *F* stands alone. The *i* is likely long (as in the English words *dial* and *trial*).

(*Dee—f-bliard*) See the *48 Claves*. This note shows the *F* standing alone.

Fcaosga (ef-kay-OS-ga)* [F + Caosga] *comp.* Visit the Earth

4.35 . . . arise you sons of pleasure and *visit the earth* . . .

Pronunciation notes:

(*Dee—F gaos ga*) Four syllables. Dee originally wrote this word as "Fgaosga"—which is apparently a mistake for *Fcaosga* (see *Caosga*). Therefore, the *g* in the second syllable is likely a *c* instead.

(*Dee—F caósga*) See the *48 Claves*. Note the accent on the third syllable.

Fetharzi (feth-AR-zii)* [F + "Etharzi"] *comp.* Visit in Peace

5.47 . . . *visit us in peace* . . .

Pronunciation notes:

(*Dee—Feth ár zi*) Three syllables, with an accent on the second.

Dee originally had "Sfetharzi" written for this word—although his phonetic note excludes the *S*. (The Angelical itself does not require the *S* at all, as the word *F* indicates "visit.") It is possible that the *S* was merely held over from the end of the previous word (*Qaas*).
(**Dee—Feth-ar-zi*) See the *48 Claves*. This note essentially matches that from *TFR*.

Fifalz (fii-falz)* *v.* Weed Out

30.86 . . . let them vex and *weed out* one another.

Pronunciation notes:
(**Dee—Fi falz*) Two syllables.

Fisis (FIS-iis)* *v.* To Execute (i.e., Carry Out)

30.8 . . . and *execute* the judgment of the Highest.

Pronunciation notes:
(**Dee—fisise*) This appears to indicate two syllables. The final *e* in Dee's phonetic note indicates a long *i* in the second syllable.
(**Dee—fisis*) See the *48 Claves*. Here, Dee placed an accent over the *i* in the first syllable.

Ged (G/J)

Ga (gay) *prop. n.* n/a

Pronuncation Note:

I have chosen the long "a" sound based upon the likely pronunciation of *Za*. (See *Za*.)

Note:

See *TFR*, pp. 228–29. The names of most of the Angels encountered by Dee and Kelley can be found in other parts of the Angelic system—such as the *Heptarchia* or Great Table (Watchtower) systems. However, *Ga* is one of the few entirely unique Angels that appeared to the two men. It was very late in the Angelical journals, after all of the essential Angelic magick had been transmitted. One day, Kelley saw three little creatures running around the floor of the room. It turned out that they were Angels from the Great Table (Watchtowers)—but their names were *not* derived according to the instructions Ave had previously given to Dee.

Ga says of himself: "I am the midst of the third [Tablet],* and the last of the spirit of life.** Understand in this temporal controversy, and conflict of man's soul. But not according to his eternal and immeasurable proportion." Dee notes, in Latin: "*Ga*—The Last of the Spirit of Life."

The three Angels, apparently jointly, say, "For even as the father, son and holy spirit are one, but of themselves and being dilated, is full of power, and many. So are we one particularly in power,*** but separated. Notwithstanding, spiritually of, and amongst, others, and dilated in the will of God, and into the branches of his determinations. But, particularly living, and jointly praising God."

Note:

*Dee notes the Angels are numbering the Watchtowers in an odd fashion. So that in this case, he points out, the numbering should follow: First = Eastern, Second = Western, Third = Southern, and Fourth = the Northern Watchtower. In the above text, I have added the bracketed [Tablet] in order to clarify the speech.

***Ga*'s name is found as the last two letters on the Line of the Holy Spirit (the horizontal arm of the Great Cross) of the Southern Watchtower Tablet.
(***On the next page Dee notes: *The three names make one name of 7 letters —Gazavaa.*)

I further note that all three of these names begin with capital letters on the Great Table (Watchtowers). Also, each one of them terminates once it hits the Great Cross, Black Cross, or the end of the Watchtower. We may have discovered an entirely new Angelic system in the Watchtowers.
(See *Vaa*, and *Za*. Also see *Carmara, Galvah, Hagonel, Mapsama, Murifri*, and *Nalvage*.)

Compare from *Loagaeth*:
Ga

"GA" (gah) — 31

Compounds:
Iga (ii-gah) [I + "GA"] — Is 31

Note:
This word was not originally given with Key Eleven. It was added later when Nalvage transmitted the English for the Key (see *TFR*, p. 193). This seems to have been the case with many of the numbers mentioned in the Keys.

Jabes (jay-bes) — n/a

Note:
See the *Five Books*, p. 298, where the Angels use the phrase *Ne Ne Ne na Jabes*. But no definitions of these words are offered.

Pronunciation note:
The final *e* should make the *a* long.

Gah (jah)* *n.* Spirits

6.1 *The spirits of* the fourth angle . . .

Pronunciation notes:

(**Dee—Gah*) One syllable.

(**Dee—Iah.*) See the *Five Books*, p. 302. In most cases, a *g* followed by an *a* makes the hard "guh" sound. However, when this word appears in *Loagaeth*, Dee notes in the margin that it should begin with the soft "juh" sound. (Remember that *i* and *j* are interchangeable in Dee's English.)

Possible root for:

Gahoachma (jah-hohk-ma) I Am That I Am

Gahire (jah-hii-er) (A Name of God?)

Note:

The way the term *spirits* is used in Key Six indicates that this word does not indicate lower spirits, demons, fairies, etc. This is further supported by the appearance of this word as a root in two Names of God. Therefore, Gah would represent "pure spirits" or Angels—used in the same sense as we might describe the Holy "Spirit."

See *Tohcoth* (nature spirits).

Compare from *Loagaeth*:

Gah

Gahire (jah-hii-er) *prop. n.?* (A Name of God?)

Possible shared root:

Gah (jah) Spirits

Gahoachma (jah-hohk-ma) I Am That I Am

Note:

See *TFR*, p. 3. The Angel Murifri here speaks a prayer in Angelical, and Kelley can only overhear a few of the words: *Oh Gahire Rudna gephna oh Gahire.* It is unclear whether this represents a single Angelical phrase, or if they are disconnected words recorded by Dee as Kelley overheard them here and there in the prayer. No translations are suggested.

It seems likely, at least, that *Oh Gahire* is intended as a repeated phrase. *Oh* may indicate "Come and Bear Witness" and *Gahire* is likely a Name of God associated by root with *Gahoachma* (I Am That I Am). Therefore, *Oh Gahire* is likely an invocation of some aspect of God.

Gahoachma (jah-hohk-ma) *prop. n.* — I Am That I Am*

Possible shared root:

Gah (jah) — Spirits

Gahire (jah-hii-er) — (A Name of God?)

Note:

(**Dee—Gahoachma = I Am That I Am, Edward Kelley expounded it.*) See the *Five Books*, p. 322. The first words spoken by the Angelic voice in this session were, "I AM. Gahoachma." This is likely a proper Name of God, based upon the Hebrew name given to Moses at the Burning Bush: *Eheieh asher Eheieh* (I Am That I Am). It represents the pure and essential Divine Consciousness, without personality or duality.

I note that *Gah* (Spirit) seems to be the root of *Gahoachma*. I also note a similarity between the -hoachma portion of the word and the Hebrew *Hochmah* (Wisdom).

Gal (gal) *prop. n.* — Letter *D*

Note:

The name of the Angelical letter for *D*. It is likely that these letter names have translations of their own. (For instance, note the Hebrew alphabet: the letter *D* is named *Daleth*, but *Daleth* also translates as "door.") However, such translations for the Angelical letters are never given. (See the *Five Books*, p. 270.)

Also see *TFR*, pp. 34–35. This session is recorded entirely in Latin. Here we find this Angelical phrase spoken by "a Voice": *Garil zed masch, ich na gel galaht gemp gal noch Cabanladan*. (Note the word *gal*.) No translation or context is offered.

Compare from *Loagaeth*:
Gal

Galaht (gal-aht) n/a

Note:
See *TFR*, pp. 34–35. This session is recorded entirely in Latin. Here we find this Angelical phrase spoken by "a Voice": *Garil zed masch, ich na gel galaht gemp gal noch Cabanladan*. No translation or context is offered.

Galgol (gal-gol) n/a

Note:
See *Five Books*, p. 366. The Angel Illemese appears to Dee and Kelley with a bundle of empty boxes that he calls virtuous. When Dee asks for an explanation, Illemese says, "Will you have my bill? [. . .] I will show it. Serve it, where you list. *Iudra galgol astel*." Dee states that he and Kelley do not understand, and wish to know how it can be served. But Illemese never offers definitions for these Angelical words.

I note a similarity between this word and the Hebrew word for "whirling," *Galgal*. The *Galgalim* are an order of Angels also known as the Wheels (*Auphanim*).

Galsagen (GAL-saj-en)* *prop. n.* or *v.?* Divine Power Creating the Angel of the Sun**

Pronunciation note:
(**Dee—gálsagen*) See the *Five Books*, p. 307. Dee places an accent over the first *a*.

From *Loagaeth*:
(***Dee—The Divine power creating the Angel of the Sonne.*) See *Five Books*, p. 307. The word *Sonne* almost certainly means "Sun." See the *Five Books*, pp. 81–82, where Dee and Kelley meet an Angel named Salamian, who claims to be "mighty in the Sonne." There is ample evidence that Salamian is an

Angel of the Sun. Dee notes that his name can be found in the *Heptameron*, with that grimoire's "Call of Sunday." Later in the same session, the Archangel Raphael tells Dee to contact the Olympic solar Angel *Och*. (See the *Arbatel of Magic* for *Och*.) Then, still during the same session, Michael (Archangel of the Sun) claims that Salamian is under his direction.

Galsuagath (gals-vay-gath) n/a

Note:

See *TFR*, p. 22. Here, the guardian Angel of Lord Lasky of Poland says a prayer on Lasky's behalf, which ends with, "Grant this *Camascheth galsuagath garnastel zurah logaah luseroth*." No translation is offered.

Pronunciation note:

I have opted to pronounce the *u* as a *v* in this case, as it immediately precedes another vowel.

Galvah (gal-VAH)* *prop. n.* The End (or *Omega*)**

Pronunciation notes:

(**Dee, recording the words of Galvah—"My name is Galua'h"*) See *TFR*, p. 12. Galvah is likely two syllables, with the accent shown in the middle of the second syllable. The *u* takes the harder "v" sound.

Note:

(***Dee, recording the words of Galvah—"My name is Galua'h, in your language I am called Finis. [. . .] I am Finis, I am a beam of that Wisdom which is the end of man's excellency."*) See *TFR*, pp. 12–14. *Finis* is Latin for "the end." Galvah arrived after forty-eight Tables of *Loagaeth* had been delivered already, and it was her job to deliver the final Table. (Thus, seeing the Book through to its end.)

On p. 13, *Galvah* reveals that she is the Mother of the Daughters and the Daughters of the Daughters of Light. (This makes Her one and the same with "I AM," the mother of the Daughter of the Daughters named Madimi. See *TFR*, p. 27.)

On p. 14, we learn that *Galvah* is a proper name, and not the general word for "the end." (*Galvah: Understand my name particularly, and not generally.*)

Later on the same page, the Angel Ilemese refers to Galvah as "Wisdom." All of this information indicates that this entity is no less than *Sophia* of the Gnostics, the *Sheckinah* of Judaism, the Soul of the World of the Hermeticists, the Bride of God. "I AM" (a shortened form of the Name of God given to Moses: *I Am That I Am*) is likely her truest name. *Galvah*, therefore, is a specific title. It likely relates to the Greek *Omega* in the biblical phrase: "I Am the *Alpha* and the *Omega*." (See Revelation Ch 1:8.)

(Also see *Carmara, Ga, Hagonel, Mapsama, Murifri, Nalvage, Vaa*, and *Za* .)

Note:
See *Ul* for the general Angelical word for "the end."

Ganiurax (gan-ii-ur-ax) n/a

Note:
See the *Five Books*, p. 413. Kelley overhears many voices singing a song at some distance, and these are the words Dee recorded: *Pinzu-a lephe ganiurax kelpadman pacaph*. No translations are suggested.
Note that *Ganiurax* may have the *-ax* suffix, indicating action.

Garil (gar-il) n/a

Note:
See *TFR*, pp. 34–35. This session is recorded entirely in Latin. Here we find this Angelical phrase spoken by "a Voice": *Garil zed masch, ich na gel galaht gemp gal noch Cabanladan*. No translation or context is offered.

Garmal (gar-mal) n/a

Note:
See the *Five Books*, p. 415. This is part of a prayer recited jointly by the Archangels Michael, Raphael, and Uriel: "*Huseh Huseh Huseh garmal, Peleh Peleh Peleh pacaduasam.*" No translations are suggested.

Compare from *Loagaeth*:
Garmah, Garmes

Garnastel (gar-nas-tel) n/a

Note:
See *TFR*, p. 22. Here, the guardian Angel of Lord Lasky of Poland says a prayer on Lasky's behalf, which ends with, "Grant this *Camascheth galsuagath garnastel zurah logaah luseroth.*" No translation is offered.

Also see:
Astel (ast-el) n/a

Gascampho (gas-KAM-foh)* *interr.* Why Didst Thou So?**

Pronunciation note:
(**Dee—gascámpho* or *gáscampho*) See the *Five Books*, p. 310. Dee places an accent over the second *a*, and then offers the alternative of placing the accent over the first *a* in a footnote. I have settled on the first option.

From *Loagaeth*:
(***Dee—"Why didst thou so?": as God said to Lucifer. The word hath 64 significations.*) See the *Five Books*, p. 310. This is likely a reference to Lucifer's rebellion in Heaven, or (more precisely) to the judgment of Lucifer afterward.

Gazavaa (gah-zah-vay) *prop. n.?* n/a*

Note:
(**Dee—The three names make one name of 7 letters—Gazavaa.*)
See *TFR*, pp. 228–29. A compound word made from the three Angels Ga, Za, and Vaa—who appear upon the Great Table (Watchtowers), but represent some hitherto unknown system of name-derivation. Dee created the compound *Gazavaa* when the three Angels told him, "For even as the father, son and holy spirit are one, but of themselves and being dilated,* is full of power, and many. So are we one particularly in power, but separated."

It is unclear if *Gazavaa* is a true Angelical word, or if Dee was merely taking the above words of the three Angels too literally. It appears to me that many further Angelical names might be derived from the Watchtowers, as we see with *Ga*, *Za*, and *Vaa*.

For a full account, see the notes with *Ga*, *Za*, and *Vaa*.

Note:

*"Dilated" would mean "spread out." In this case, it indicates the separation of the One God into the Trinity.

"Gchis" (jee-KIIS) *v.* — Are

Compounds:

Gchisge (jee-KIIS-jee) ["Gchis" + "Ge"] — Are Not

Also:

Chis (kiis) — Are
Chiis (kiis) — Are (They)
"Chisda" (kiis-da) — Are There
Chiso (kiis-oh) — Shall Be
"Ichis" (jay-kiis) — Are
Zchis (zohd-kiis) — (They) Are

Note:

"Gchis" and "Ichis" should be the same word—both are spelled the same in Angelical characters, with an initial Ged (*J*). See note at *Gchisge*.

Gchisge (jee-KIIS-jee)* ["Gchis" + "Ge"] *comp.* — Are Not

4.7 . . . *Are not* the Thunders of Increase numbered . . .?

Pronunciation notes:

(**Dee—G Chis ge*) Three syllables. The *i* and *j* are interchangeable in Dee's English. The *j* makes a soft "juh" sound, which is likely what Dee was hearing in both *Gchisge* and *Ichisge*. It is likely that both words begin with the Angelical Letter Ged (*J*).

Since Dee capitalized the second syllable, it *may* indicate the accent there. Also, see *Chis* and *Chiis* (are) for the long "i" sound.

(*Dee—G-chisge*) See the *48 Claves*. This looks like two syllables. However, three syllables are indicated elsewhere (including the word *Ichisge*).

Also:

Ichisge (jay-KIIS-jee) Are Not

"Ge" (jee) *adv.* Not

Compounds:

Gchisge (jee-KIIS-jee) ["Gchis" + "Ge"] Are Not
Ichisge (jay-KIIS-jee) ["Ichis" + "Ge"] Are Not
Tage (tayj) [Ta + "Ge"] As (Is) Not

Compare from *Loagaeth*:

Ge, Ie

Note:

See also *Ip* (not), "Pam" (not), and *Ag* (none).

Gebofal (jeb-oh-fal) *n.* "The Practice of the 49 Gates of Understanding"*

Note:

(**Dee recording the words of Levanael—"Now to the work intended, which is called in the Holy Art Gebofal. Which is not, (as the philosophers have written), the first step supernatural, but it is the first supernatural step naturally limited unto the 48 Gates of Wisdom; where your Holy Book beginneth."*) See *TFR*, p. 373. The Holy Book in question, of course, is the *Book of Loagaeth*. *Gebofal*, therefore, must be the Angelical name of the practice of opening the forty-eight Gates.

Ged (jed) *prop. n.* Letter *G/J**

Note:

The name of the Angelical letter for *G/J*. It is likely that these letter names have translations of their own. (For instance, note the Hebrew alphabet: the letter *G/J* is named *Gimel*, but *Gimel* also translates as

"camel.") However, such translations for the Angelical letters are never given. (See the *Five Books*, p. 270.)
(**Dee—After that he said, One, One, One, Great, Great, Great!*) This does not appear to be a definition of Ged, but an invocation associated with the word in some way. See the letter *Med*, where another invocation is made along with the delivery of a letter.

Compare from *Loagaeth*:
Ged, Ied

Geh (jay)* *v.* Art (i.e., Are)

16.19 Great *art* thou in the God of . . .

Pronunciation notes:
(**Dee—Geh jeh*) One syllable. Dee indicates that the *G* should take a soft "j" sound. In Early Modern English, the *eh* would have combined to form a long "a" sound.

Note:
See also *Chis* (are). Perhaps *Geh* (art) is a term of formality or respect?

Compare from *Loagaeth*:
Geh, Ieh

Geiad (jej-AYD)* *prop. n.* Lord and Master

5.54 . . . *our Lord and Master* is all one . . .

Pronunciation notes:
(**Dee—Ge jad ie in as ien,** the iad as iade*) The word *Geiad* only appears in Dee's *48 Claves*. It is missing from *TFR* (perhaps from damage to the text?)—but Dee's slightly confusing phonetic note is still there. Based on this note, I believe Dee originally wrote *Geiad* in his journal (*TFR*) as "Ie iad"—divided into two syllables. The first syllable (*ie* or *ge*) sounds similar to "ien" ("jen")—that is, the *i* sounds like *j*, and the *e* takes its short sound. The second syllable (*iad*) must sound like the English word *jade*—with the *i* again taking the "j" sound.

I have adopted the accent from similar words.

Note:
**I believe that "ie in as ien" should be "ie *as in* ien."

Ge is translated elsewhere as "not"—though it is obviously not intended in this case.

Also:

Gohed (joh-ED) — One Everlasting . . .
Iad (yad) — God
"Iadoias" (jad-oh-JAS) — Eternal God
Iadpil (ii-AD-pil) — (To) Him
Iaida (jay-II-da) — The Highest
Iaidon (jay-II-don) — All Powerful
Ioiad (joh-JAD) — Him That Liveth Forever
Oiad (oh-ii-AD) — Of God
Piad (pii-AD) — Your God

Gel (jel) — n/a

Note:
See *TFR*, p. 35. This session is recorded entirely in Latin. Here we find this Angelical phrase spoken by "a Voice": *Garil zed masch, ich na gel galaht gemp gal noch Cabanladan.* No translation or context is offered.

Compare from *Loagaeth*:
Gel, Geld

Gemeganza (jeem-gan-za) — Your Will Be Done / As You Wish*

Note:
(**Dee—gemeganza = your will be done*) See the *Five Books*, p. 314. Dee here asks if he and Kelley can leave off for the night, as it is getting late. A voice responds, "*Gemeganza.*"

Gemp (jemp) n/a

Note:

See *TFR*, pp. 34–35. This session is recorded entirely in Latin. Here we find this Angelical phrase spoken by "a Voice": *Garil zed masch, ich na gel galaht gemp gal noch Cabanladan.* No translation or context is offered.

Gephna (jef-na) n/a

Note:

See *TFR*, p. 3. The Angel *Murifri* here speaks a prayer in Angelical, and Kelley can only overhear a few of the words: *Oh Gahire Rudna gephna oh Gahire.* It is unclear whether this represents a single Angelical phrase, or if they are disconnected words recorded by Dee as Kelley overheard them here and there in the prayer. No translations are suggested.

Ger (jer)* *prop. n.* Letter *Q/Qu*

Note:

The name of the Angelical letter for *Q/Qu*. It is likely that these letter names have translations of their own. (For instance, note the Hebrew alphabet: the letter *Q/Qu* is named *Qoph*, but *Qoph* also translates as "ear.") However, such translations for the Angelical letters are never given. (See the *Five Books*, p. 270.)

Pronunciation notes:

(**Dee—In sound, gierh.*) In Dee's notation *gierh*, the *gi* may be the same as *gj*—to indicate a soft "g" (or "j") sound. This is the pronunciation I have chosen for the word. However, it is also possible that the *ie* is intended to make an "ee" sound—so the word would sound like "jee-rr."

Compare from *Loagaeth*:

Ger

Geta (jet-a) *adv.* There

Note:

See *TFR*, p. 32. Here, Dee is speaking with the Angel Madimi. Suddenly, Madimi halts the session and demands, *"Carma geta Barman."* Dee asks her what this means, and she replies (in Latin, which roughly translates to): "Come out of there, *Barma*." Madimi's command exorcises fifteen spirits from the body of Edward Kelley, the chief of whom is named *Barma*. After a short exchange (see *Gil*, etc.), Madimi banishes all fifteen spirits back to Hell until the last cry. (That is, until the End Times.)

Carma Geta is likely intended as an exorcism phrase to command lesser spirits, and not something one would use with the Angels.

Note:

Also see "Da" (there).

Compare from *Loagaeth*:

Get

Gethog (jeth-og) *prop. n.* "A Divine Name From the *Sigillum Emeth*"

Note:

See the *Five Books*, p. 161 (*Hamuthz Gethog*). Kelley is having a vision of the Seven Biblical Days of Creation at this point—during which the Seven Ensigns of Creation are revealed. Oddly, the reception of one Ensign was interrupted by the reception of another. This interruption was marked by the sudden speaking of the words *Hamuthz Gethog*. (Dee does not attribute these words to any particular Angel. Much of the content of these sessions are merely attributed to "a Voice.") The "woman" who appears at these words creates the Sun, Moon, and Stars, and then presents her Ensign. (This happens to be the Ensign from which is drawn one of the Seals of the Watchtowers.) She then exits, and the interrupted vision continues.

No translation is given for *Hamuthz*, but *Gethog* is recognizable as one of the Divine Names encoded upon the Seal of Truth.

Compare from *Loagaeth*:

Gethgol

"Giar" (jii-ar) *n.* Harvest

Compounds:

Aziagiar (ay-zii-AY-jii-ar) ["Azia" + "Giar"] Like unto the Harvest

Pronunciation notes:

The vowel sound made by *ia* is unclear. However, we can find it in words like *dial*, *dialect*, or *William*. Based on this, I have assumed the sound should be a long *i* followed by a short *a*.

Gigipah (jij-ii-pah)* *n.* (Living) Breath

3.12 Six are the seats of *living breath* . . .

Pronunciation notes:

(**Dee—Gi gi pah*) Three syllables.

(**Dee—Gigîpah*) See *48 Claves*. Note that Dee places a circumflex over the second *i*—indicating its long sound. Thus, I assume the first *i* takes its short sound.

Gil (jil) n/a

Note:

See *TFR*, p. 32. Here, the Angel Madimi has just interrupted the session to exorcise several demons from the body of Kelley. (See *Carma*.) These spirits came out of Kelley violently, scratching each other in the face and swarming about Madimi. To her, the spirits spoke in Angelical, "*Gil de pragma kures helech*." Dee asks Madimi what this means, and she replies (in Latin, which roughly translates as:) "We want to live here in our [friends]." (Madimi does not offer definitions for the individual words.)

When Dee asks who these "friends" are supposed to be, the spirits indicate Kelley as their place of habitation (probably meaning both Dee and Kelley). Madimi then banishes these spirits.

Gisg (gizh) *prop. n.* Letter *T*

Note:

The name of the Angelical letter for *T*. It is likely that these letter names have translations of their own. (For instance, note the Hebrew alphabet: the letter *T* is named *Teth*, but *Teth* also translates as "serpent.") However, such translations for the Angelical letters are never given. (See the *Five Books*, p. 270.)

Githgulcag (jith-gul-kag) *prop. n.* Lucifer, Satan(?)

Note:

See *TFR*, p. 6. Here, an Angel (who is later identified as the Daughter of Light named *Aath*) tells Dee, "It is written that Pride was the first offense. *Githgulcag* knew not himself. Therefore he was ignorant. [. . .] You will grant me that pride is the greatest sin. Pride was the cause he knew not himself. Therefore Pride is the cause of Ignorance. Ignorance was the nakedness wherewithal you were first tormented,* and the first Plague that fell onto man was the want of Science." *Aath* appears to first explain the reason for Lucifer's Fall, and then ends her speech with a very Hermetic interpretation of the Fall from Eden.

Could *Githgulcag* have some indication of "ignorance"?

Note:

*See Genesis 3:7, "And the eyes of them both were opened, and they knew that they were naked."

Also see *Coronzom* (the Devil, Satan) and *Telocvovim* (likely a name for the fallen Lucifer).

Givi (jiv-ii)* *adj.* Stronger

2.23 . . . *stronger* are your feet than the barren stone.

Pronunciation notes:

(**Dee—Giui*) The letter *u* should probably sound like "v" when surrounded by vowels. The initial *G* should have a soft sound when preceding an *i*, and the final *i* likely has the long sound.

Note:

Also see *Umadea* (strong towers), *Umplif* (strength) and *Ugeg* (become strong).

Gizyax (jiz-wii-aks)* *n.* — Earthquakes

10.43 . . . a hundred mighty *earthquakes* . . .

Pronunciation notes:

(**Dee—Giz y ax*) Three syllables. The initial *G* should take the soft ("j") sound when preceding an *i*. The y stands alone.

Gmicalzo (jee-mii-KAYL-zoh)* *n.* — In Power (and Presence?)

6.37 . . . I move you *in power and presence* . . .

Pronunciation notes:

(**Dee—G-ni cál zo*) Likely four syllables, with an accent on the second syllable. Dee here indicates that the initial *G* stands alone. The *i* and *a* should take their long sounds (see *Micalzo*). Also note that Dee wrote an *n* in his phonetic note, but this is likely a mistake for *m*.
(**Dee—g-micálzo*) See the *48 Claves*. The initial *G* is again standing alone. The accent is again on the third syllable.

Compounds:

Gmicalzoma (jee-mii-KAYL-zoh-ma)
[Gmicalzo + "Oma"] — With a Power of Understanding

Also:

Micalp (mii-KALP) — Mightier
Micalzo (mii-KAYL-zoh) — Mighty
Micaoli (mii-KAY-oh-lii) — Mighty

Micaolz (mii-KAY-ohlz or mii-KAY-ohl-zohd) Mighty
Omicaolz (oh-mii-KAY-ohl-zohd) (Be) Mighty

Possible shared root:

Miketh (mii-KETH) "The True Measure of the Will of God in Judgment, Which Is by Wisdom"(?)

Note:

Also see *Umadea* (strong towers), *Umplif* (strength), *Ugeg* (become strong), *Vohim* (mighty), and *Nanaeel* (my power).

Gmicalzoma (jee-mii-KAYL-zoh-ma)* [Gmicalzo + "Oma"] *comp.*
Power of Understanding

30.33 . . . with *a power of understanding* to dispose all things . . .

Pronunciation notes:

(*Dee—Gmi cál zo ma*) Likely five syllables, with an accent on the third syllable. The *G* should stand alone, and the *i* and *o* should take their long sounds. Also, the first *a* is likely a long vowel—see *Micalzo* (mighty/ power).

(*Dee—gmicálzôma*) See the *48 Claves*. Here, Dee again placed the accent upon the third syllable. He also placed a circumflex over the *o* to indicate its long sound.

Gnay (nay)* *v.* Doth (i.e., Does)

9.33 . . . as the rich man *doth* his treasure.
10.63 . . . as the heart of man *doth* his thoughts.

Pronunciation notes:

(*Dee 9.33; 10.63—Gnay*) One syllable. In Early Modern English, the digraph *Gn* began to take the sound of a hard *n*—such as in the English words *gnat* and *gnash*.

Gnetaab (nee-TAY-ab)* *n.* (Your) Governments

3.48 . . . the corners of *your governments* . . .

Pronunciation notes:

(**Dee—Gnetaab*) In Early Modern English, the letters *Gn* became a digraph that sounds like *n*. See *Netaab* (government) for further pronunciation notes.

(**Dee—gne-táab*) See the *48 Claves*. Likely three syllables, with an accent on the second syllable. The *e* likely takes a long sound.

Also:

Anetab (ay-NEE-tayb) — (In) Government
Netaab (nee-TAY-ab) — Your Governments
Netaaib (nee-TAY-ay-ib) — Government
Tabaam (tay-BAY-an) — Governor
Tabaord (tay-BAY-ord) — (Let) Be Governed
Tabaori (tay-BAY-oh-rii) — Govern
"Tabas" (tay-BAS) — Govern

Further:

Cab (kab) — Rod/Sceptor
Caba (ka-BA) — To Govern

Gnonp (non-pee) *v.* — To Garnish

1.31 Whose seats *I garnished with* the fire . . .

Gohed (joh-ED)* *prop. n.?* — "One Everlasting, All Things Descending Upon One"**

Pronuncation Note:

(**Dee—Gohed, pronounced as Iohed . . .*) See the *Five Books*, p. 304. Dee here shows the pronunciation of *Iohed*—showing the soft *G* (or *j*) sound. I have adopted the accent from similar words.

From *Loagaeth*:

(***Dee—Gohed, pronounced as Iohed, signifieth One Everlasting and all things Descending upon One, and Gohed Ascha is as much to say as One God.*) See the *Five Books*, p. 304.

Also:

Geiad (jej-AYD) — Lord and Master
Iaisg (hay-IZH) — Everlasting One . . . God
Ioiad (joh-JAD) — Him That Liveth Forever
"Iadoias" (jad-oh-JAS) — Eternal God

Gohel (GOH-hel)* [Goho + El] *comp.* — Sayeth the First

2.41 . . . arise, *sayeth the First* . . .

Pronunciation notes:

(**Dee—Go hel*) Two syllables, and the *h* is audible. I assume the *e* is a phonetic gloss, as it is in the word *El* (The First).
(**Dee—góhel*) See *48 Claves*. The first syllable is given an accent.

Note:

I am uncertain why the final *o* of *Goho* was dropped here. Angelical usually only drops a letter in a compound if it is repeated twice. Note, for example, the compound *Zirenaiad*, formed of the words *Zir*, *Enay*, and *Iad*. We can see that the final *y* of *Enay* and the initial *I* of *Iad* combine into one letter in the compound.

Gohia (goh-HII-a)* *v.* — (We) Say

3.73 . . . in whom *we say*, move . . .

Pronunciation notes:

(**Dee—Gohia*) I assume three syllables, with a long *i*. I have adopted the accent from other versions of this word.

Note:

Although this word is similar to the compound word *Gohoiad* (sayeth god), it is apparent that *Iad* does not serve as a root here at all.

Also:

Goho (goh-HOH) — To Say
Gohol (goh-HOHL) — To Say
Gohon (goh-HON) — Have Spoken

Gohulim (goh-HOO-lim) It Is Said
Gohus (goh-US) (I) say

Goho (goh-HOH)* *v.* To Say

1.4 . . . *sayeth* the God of Justice . . .
3.2 Behold, *sayeth* your God . . .

Pronunciation notes:

(**Dee 1.4—GOHO*)

(**Dee 3.2—Goho*) Dee gives us little clue here. The initial *G* should take a hard sound when preceding an *o*. I suspect both *o*'s take a long sound.

(**Dee 1.4; 3.2—Gohó*) See *48 Claves*. The accent is shown on the second syllable.

Compounds:

Gohoiad (goh-HOH-ii-ad) [Goho + Iad] Sayeth God
Gohel (GOH-hel) [Goho + El] Sayeth the First

Also:

Gohia (goh-HII-a) (We) Say
Gohol (goh-HOHL) To Say
Gohon (goh-HON) Have Spoken
Gohulim (goh-HOO-lim) It Is Said
Gohus (goh-US) (I) say

Compare from *Loagaeth*:

Goho, Gohor

Gohoiad (goh-HOH-ii-ad)* [Goho + Iad] *comp.* Sayeth the Lord

8.13 . . . *sayeth the lord*, whose long continuance . . .

Pronunciation notes:

(**Dee—Go hó i ad*) This appears to be four syllables—though I find that it sounds more like three when spoken fluently. (Elsewhere, the word *Iad* is given the single-syllable pronunciation of "yad.") There is an accent on the second syllable.

(*Dee—gohó î-ad*) See the *48 Claves*. Dee again placed the accent on the second syllable. He also indicates that the *i* stands alone. (The circumflex over the *i* further indicates the long vowel sound.)

Gohol (goh-HOHL)* *v.* To Say

4.6 . . . *saying*, are not the thunders . . .
30.42 . . . rose up in the beginning, *saying* . . .

Pronunciation notes:
(*Dee 4.6—Go hol*)
(*Dee 30.42—Go hól*) Two syllables. The *G* before an *o* should take a hard sound (as in the English words *going* and *gone*). In the phonetic note for word 30.42, Dee places the accent on the second syllable.
(*Dee 4.6; 30.42—Gohól*) See the *48 Claves*. Accent again on the second syllable.

Also:

Gohia (goh-HII-a)	(We) Say
Goho (goh-HOH)	To Say
Gohon (goh-HON)	Have Spoken
Gohulim (goh-HOO-lim)	It Is Said
Gohus (goh-US)	(I) say

Compare from *Loagaeth*:
Goho

Goholor (goh-HOH-lor)* *v.* Lift Up

3.61 *Lift up*, I say, yourselves . . .

Pronunciation notes:
(*Dee—Goholor*) I suggest three syllables here. The *G* preceding an *o* is likely hard.
(*Dee—Gohólor*) See the *48 Claves*. Dee places the accent on the second syllable.

Note:

It is uncertain why this word "seems" to have *Goho* (to say) as a root. It may be a rare case of coincidentally similar spelling between unrelated Angelical words. Unfortunately, the English sense is not "uplifted voices" (see *Farzem*).

Compare from *Loagaeth*:

Gohor

Gohon (goh-HON)* *v.* — Have Spoken

8.37 . . . the thunders *have spoken* . . .

Pronunciation notes:

(**Dee—Go hón*) Two syllables. The accent mark is placed on the second syllable. The first *o* should take its long sound.

(**Dee—gohón*) See the *48 Claves*. This note essentially matches that from *TFR*.

Also:

Gohia (goh-HII-a)	(We) Say
Goho (goh-HOH)	To Say
Gohol (goh-HOHL)	To Say
Gohulim (goh-HOO-lim)	(It Is) Said
Gohus (goh-US)	(I) say

Compare from *Loagaeth*:

Goho, Gohonp

Gohulim (goh-HOO-lim)* *v.* — (It Is) Said

30.12 . . . to you *it is said*, behold . . .

Pronunciation notes:

(**Dee—Go hú lim*) Three syllables, with an accent on the second syllable.

(**Dee—gohúlim*) See the *48 Claves*. Here, Dee again placed an accent over the second syllable.

Also:

Gohia (goh-HII-a) — (We) Say
Goho (goh-HOH) — To Say
Gohol (goh-HOHL) — To Say
Gohon (goh-HON) — Have Spoken
Gohus (goh-US) — (I) say

Compare from *Loagaeth*:

Goho

Gohus (goh-US)* *v.* — (I) Say

3.62 Lift up, *I say*, yourselves!
12.24 Move, *I say*, and show yourselves.

Pronunciation notes:

(**Dee 3.62—Gohus*) Two syllables. I suggest a short "u" sound.
(**Dee—gohús*) See the *48 Claves*. Dee placed an accent on the second syllable.

Also:

Gohia (goh-HII-a) — (We) Say
Goho (goh-HOH) — To Say
Gohol (goh-HOHL) — To Say
Gohon (goh-HON) — Have Spoken
Gohulim (goh-HOO-lim) — (It Is) Said

Compare from *Loagaeth*:

Goho

Gon (gon) *prop. n.* — Letter *I*/Y

Note:

The name of the Angelical letter for *I*/ *Y*. It is likely that these letter names have translations of their own. (For instance, note the Hebrew alphabet: the letter *I* is named *Yod*, but *Yod* also translates as "hand.") However, such translations for the Angelical letters are never given. (See the *Five Books*, p. 270.)

Gono (gon-oh) *n.* Faith (Trust/Loyalty)

1.51 . . . and swore obedience *and faith* to him . . .

Note:

Also see *Congamphlgh* (Faith/Holy Ghost).

Gosaa (goh-say-ay)* *n.* Stranger

30.109 . . . let her be known, and another while *a stranger.*

Pronunciation notes:

(**Dee—Go sa a*) Three syllables. The final *a* stands alone. The other two vowels also appear to take their long sounds.

(**Dee—gosâa*) See the *48 Claves*. Here, Dee placed a circumflex over the first *a* to indicate its long sound.

Graa (gray)* *n.* Moon

1.16 . . . *the moon* is a through-thrusting fire . . .

Pronunciation notes:

(**Dee—GRAA*) Dee gives us little clue here. Likely, the double *a* indicates a long vowel, as we see in Early Modern English.

Compare from *Loagaeth*:

Gra

Graph (grakh-fa)* *prop. n.* Letter *E**

Note:

The name of the Angelical letter for *E*. It is likely that these letter names have translations of their own. (For instance, note the Hebrew alphabet: the letter *E* is named *Aleph*, but *Aleph* also translates as "ox/bull.") However, such translations for the Angelical letters are never given. (See the *Five Books*, p. 270.)

Pronunciation note:

(**Dee—The sound as Grakpha, in the throat.*) Dee adds the *k* in the center of this word, likely to indicate a throaty "kh" sound just before the "f" sound. I normally pronounce the word along the lines of "grah-fa."

Grosb (grozb)* *n.* or *v.* (Bitter) Sting

13.22 . . . is called amongst you *a bitter sting* . . .

Note:

Words 13.21 and 13.22 are both missing from Dee's journals. We only have the English given for this Key on *TFR*, p. 193. However, they do appear in Dee's *48 Claves*.

Note that the word *sting* should be a verb ("to sting"), but it is used in this case as a noun ("a sting").

Pronunciation notes:

(**Dee—GROSB*) Likely one syllable.

Shared root:

"Quasb" (kwazb) Destroy

Grsam (gur-sam)* *n.* Admiration

1.37 . . . beautified your garments with *admiration* . . .

Pronunciation notes:

(**Dee—as Gursam*) Usually, the *G* and *r* would combine to form a "Gr" sound. However, this should be followed by a vowel—such as in the words *great* and *grant*. In the case of *Grsam*, the first two letters are followed by a consonant. Therefore, the first two letters stand as a syllable of their own ("gur"), followed by the second syllable ("sam").

Gru (groo) *n.* or *v.?* To Cause, Bring About, Result

From *Corpus Omnium*:

Found in the post-Crucifixion portion of the Table, in the phrase *Gru Sor Iad* (Cause of the Actions of God).

Na (H)

Hagonel (hag-on-el) *prop. n.* n/a

Note:

See the *Five Books*, pp. 188–91. Hagonel is the title of the ruling Prince of the *Heptarchia*. (Not to be confused with the Son of the Sons of Light of the same name.) In Dee's lifetime, the Heptarchic Prince of Venus—Bagenol—held the title. Today, I presume it should be the Prince of Mercury—Blisdon—though I do not know if he would hold the same title.

(Also see *Carmara*, *Ga*, *Galvah*, *Mapsama*, *Murifri*, *Nalvage*, *Vaa*, and *Za* .)

Hamuthz (ham-oothz) n/a

Note:

See the *Five Books*, p. 161 (*Hamuthz Gethog*). Kelley is having a vision of the Seven Biblical Days of Creation at this point—during which the Seven Ensigns of Creation are revealed. Oddly, the reception of one Ensign was interrupted by the reception of another. This interruption was marked by the sudden speaking of the words *Hamuthz Gethog*. (Dee does not attribute these words to any particular Angel. Much of the content of these sessions are merely attributed to "a Voice.") The "woman" who appears at these words creates the Sun, Moon, and stars, and then presents her Ensign. (This happens to be the Ensign from which is drawn one of the Seals of the Watchtowers.) She then exits, and the interrupted vision continues.

No translation is given for *Hamuthz*, but *Gethog* is recognizable as one of the Divine Names encoded upon the Seal of Truth.

Hardeh (har-day) *v.?* To Read (?)

Pronunciation notes:

(*Dee—Amzes naghezes Hardeh—Note this to be pronounced roundly together.*)

Perhaps this means the three words should be pronounced as if they were one.

Note:

See the *Five Books*, pp. 324–25. Here Kelley sees what the *Book of Loagaeth* looks like from the outside. It is covered in blue silk, and has the title *Amzes naghezes Hardeh* painted upon it in gold. Kelley says this signifies "the universal name of Him that created universally be praised and extolled forever."

However, also see *TFR*, p. 174, where the Angel Ave reveals that the title of Enoch's book was "Let Those That Fear God, and Are Worthy, Read." (Dee here notes: *The title of Enoch's books expounded into English.*) If this happens to be the real translation, then perhaps *Hardeh* indicates "to read."

Harg (harg)* *v.* To Plant

6.9 . . . the first *hath planted* a torment . . .

Pronunciation notes:

(**Dee—Harg argenton*) One syllable. Dee's phonetic note seems to be a form of the Latin *argentum* (silver). Both Patricia Shaffer (*DeesPronunciationNotes.rtf*) and my Latin dictionary suggest that *g* in Latin always takes the hard sound. Thus Harg has the sound of "arg" rather than "arj."

Helech (hel-ek) n/a (?)

Note:

See *TFR*, p. 32. Here, the Angel Madimi has just interrupted the session to exorcise several demons from the body of Kelley. (See *Carma*.) These spirits came out of Kelley violently, scratching each other in the face and swarming about Madimi. To her, the spirits spoke in Angelical, "*Gil de pragma kures helech.*" Dee asks Madimi what this means, and she replies (in Latin), "We want to live here in our [friends]." (Madimi does not offer definitions for the individual words.)

When Dee asks who these "friends" are supposed to be, the spirits indicate Kelley as their place of habitation (probably meaning both Dee and Kelley.) Madimi then banishes these spirits.

Hoath (hohth)* *n.* True Worshiper

(RFP . . . *a true worshiper* of the highest.)

Pronunciation notes:

(**Dee—Call it Hoath.*) One syllable, rhyming with the English word *both*. The *oa* letter combination in Early Modern English makes a long "o" sound—as in the English words *boat* and *coat*.

Holdo (hol-doh)* *v.* To Groan

11.2 The mighty seat *groaned* . . .

Pronunciation notes:

(**Dee—Hol do*) Two syllables. The first *o* is short, while the second *o* takes its long sound.

Holq (HOL-kwah)* *v.* To Measure

1.20 . . . which *measureth* your garments . . .
11.23 . . . of whom *it is measured* . . .

Pronunciation notes:

(**Dee 1.20—HOLQ as Holquu*) The double *u* is literally a *w*. So, *quu* sounds like "kwah."

(**Dee 11.23—Hól q*) This note lets us know the word *Holq* has two syllables, with an accent on the first syllable.

(**Dee 1.20; 11.23—hol-q*) See *48 Claves*. Shows two syllables, with the *q* standing alone.

Compounds:

Chisholq (KIIS-hohl-kwa) [Chis + Holq] Are Measured

Hom (hom) *v.* To Live

1.54 . . . to him that *liveth* and triumpheth . . .

Shared root:

Homil (hom-il) — Ages

Homin (hom-in) — Age

Note:

Also see "Apila" (to live).

Homil (hom-il)* *n.* — (True) Ages

3.41 . . . over 456, the *true ages of* time . . .

Pronunciation notes:

(**Dee—Homil*) Likely two syllables.

Also:

Homin (hom-in) — Age

Shared root:

Hom (hom) — To Live

Homin (hom-in)* *n.* — Age

14.13 . . . vexing all creatures of the earth *with age* . . .

Pronunciation notes:

Likely two syllables.

Note:

The transmission of Key Fourteen is missing from Dee's journals. We only have the English for this Key given later (see *TFR*, p. 193). Plus, the word appears in this location in Dee's *48 Claves*.

Also:

Homil (hom-il) — Ages

Shared root:

Hom (hom) — To Live

Hoxmarch (hoks-mark) *v.* Fear (Stand in Awe of) God

Note:

See *TFR*, pp. 18–19. The Mother Galvah appears to Kelley in a rather dressed-up fashion. Dee asks her if she has put on her holiday clothes, but this is apparently not the case. She replies: "FEAR GOD. My Garment is called *HOXMARCH*, which in your speech is called . . ." Dee then replies, "It is Just Wisdom to fear the Lord. We acknowledge it to be an old and a true Lesson, and also the first step of the pathway to felicity." Galvah then goes on to reveal the final Table of *Loagaeth*.

Take special note that Dee's use of the word *fear* in this sense (as with the King James Bible, published at the same period of history), indicates "to stand in awe." The concept of "fear = terror" is not indicated by this.

Hubaio (hoo-BAY-ii-oh)* *n.* Lanterns

12.7 . . . 28 *the lanterns of* sorrow . . .

Pronunciation notes:

(*Dee—Hubá i o*) Four syllables, with an accent on the second. The *a* seems to take a long sound. The *i* and the final *o* each stand alone. The long *u* is indicated in the phonetic note for *Hubaro*.

(*Dee—hubíâo*) See the *48 Claves*. Dee seems to have switched the letters *a* and *i* in this notation. However, he does place an accent over the second syllable, and the circumflex over the *a* indicates its long sound. Based on the other versions of this word, I have settled upon the spelling found in *TFR*.

Also:

Hubar (hoo-BAR) Lamps

Hubaro (hoo-BAY-roh) (Living) Lamps

Compare from *Loagaeth*:

Hubra, Lubrah, Ubrah-ax, Vbrah, Subracah, Zubra, Zubrah

Hubar (hoo-BAR)* *n.* Lamps

5.33 . . . which are garnished with *continually burning lamps* . . .

Pronunciation notes:

(**Dee—Hubar*) Likely two syllables. The long *u* is indicated in the phonetic note for *Hubaro*. I have adopted the accent from other versions of this word.

Also:

Hubaio (hoo-BAY-ii-oh) Lanterns
Hubaro (hoo-BAY-roh) (Living) Lamps

Compare from *Loagaeth*:

Hubra, Lubrah, Ubrah-ax, Vbrah, Subracah, Zubra, Zubrah

Hubaro (hoo-BAY-roh)* *n.* (Living/Burning) Lamps

17.11 . . . and hast 7336 living lamps going before . . .

Pronunciation notes:

(**Dee—Hu ba ro*) Three syllables. I suggest long *u*, *a*, and *o* sounds—as both of them fall as the very end of their syllables. I have adopted the accent from *Hubaio* (lanterns).

(**Dee—hubâro*) See the *48 Claves*. Here, Dee placed a circumflex over the *a* to indicate the long sound.

Also:

Hubaio (hoo-BAY-ii-oh) Lanterns
Hubar (hoo-BAR) Lamps

Compare from *Loagaeth*:

Hubra, Lubrah, Ubrah-ax, Vbrah, Subracah, Zubra, Zubrah

Hucacha (hoo-kay-cha) n/a

Note:

See the *Five Books*, p. 310. Spoken during a longer prayer offered by "many voices": "It is good, O God, for you are goodness itself. And great because of the size of greatness itself. *Adgmach, adgmach, adgmach*! I am, and this pace is, holy. *Adgmach, adgmach, adgmach hucacha*."

Dee notes that "*Adgmach adgmach adgmach* = *Much Glory,*" but he offers no definition for *Hucacha*. Could *Hucacha* mean "This Place Is Holy"?

Huseh (hoo-say) n/a

Note:

See the *Five Books*, p. 415. Part of a prayer recited jointly by the Archangels Michael, Raphael, and Uriel: *Huseh Huseh Huseh garmal, Peleh Peleh Peleh pacaduasam.* No translations are suggested.

Gon (*I/Y*)

Note that several words in this section begin with *Ged* (G, *J*) rather than *Gon* (*I/Y*). However, Dee spelled these particular words in English with an initial *I*, as that was an acceptable alternative to *J* in Early Modern English (John = Iohan, Justice = Iustice. In fact, the *J* as we know it is simply an elongated *I*.) Because of this, I have included those words in this section.

I (ii)* *v.* Is/Are

1.13 . . . the sun *is* as a sword . . .
10.76 . . . *is*, was, and shall be . . .

Pronunciation notes:

(**Dee 1.13—a word by itself*)
(**Dee 10.76—I*) As we pronounce the word *I*.

Compounds:

Dsi (dee-sii) [Ds + I] Which Is
Icorsca (ii-KORS-kay) [I + Cors + "Ca"] Is Such as
Idlugam (id-LOO-gam) [I + "Dlugam"] Is Given
Iga (ii-ga) [I + "GA"] Is 31
Il (ii-el) [I + L] Is One
Inoas (in-OH-as) [I + Noas] Are Become
Isalman (ii-SAYL-man) [I + Salman] Is a House
Ita (ii-tay) [I + Ta] Is as
Ivonph (ii-VONV) [I + Vonph] Is Wrath
Ivonpovnph (ii-VON-foh-unv)
[I + "Vonpo" + "Vnph"] Is Wrath in Anger
Pii (pii-ii) ["Pi" + I] She Is
Ti (tii) ["T" + I] It Is

Shared root:

Ip (ip) Not
Ipam (ip-am) Is Not
Ipamis (ip-am-is) Can Not Be

Note:
The word *I* (is/are) appears to be a form of the verb "to be." Also see *Zir* (am, were, was).
Also see *Chis* (are) and *Geh* (art).

Also note the Angel *I*, one of the Sons of Light. His name literally translates as "is," "to be," or "to exist." (Perhaps "The Existent"?)

Ia (yah) n/a?

From *Loagaeth*:
This word is never given a definition. However, I have found it to be such a vital root word in the Angelical language, I decided to give it its own entry. It appears several times in *Loagaeth*. See *Iad* (God), *Iadnah* (Knowledge), *Ialprg* (Flame), etc. *Ia* appears to indicate many celestial or sacred concepts.

Note:
The similarity between this word and the Hebrew *Ia* (or *Yah*—God).

Compare from *Loagaeth*:
Iad, Iads, Ia-dron, Iaisg

Iad (yad)* *prop. n.* God

1.5 . . . sayeth *the God of* Justice . . .

Pronunciation notes:
(**Dee—Iad, as Yad*) The *I* has the sound of "y" rather than "j."

Compounds:
Bigliad (big-lii-ad) ["Bigl" + Iad?] (God) Our Comforter
Gohoiad (goh-HOH-ii-ad) [Goho + Iad] Sayeth the Lord
Iadbaloth (ii-ad-BAL-toh) [Iad + Balt + Toh] God (of) Righteousness
Iadoiasmomar (jad-oh-JAS-moh-mar)*
["Iadoias" + "Momar"] God Eternally Crowned
Sobaiad (soh-BAY-ad) [Soba + Iad] Whose God
Zirenaiad (zii-er-NAY-ad) [Zir + Enay + Iad] I Am the Lord (Your) God

Also:

Geiad (jej-AYD)	Lord and Master
"Iadoias" (jad-oh-JAS)	Eternal God
Iadpil (ii-AD-pil)	(To) Him
Iaida (jay-II-da)	The Highest
Iaidon (jay-II-don)	All Powerful
Iaisg (jay-IZH)	Everlasting One and Indivisible God
Ioiad (joh-JAD)	Him That Liveth Forever
Oiad (oh-ii-AD)	Of God
Piad (pii-AD)	Your God

Note:

See notes for *Iadbaltoh* (God of Righteousness).
Also see *Mad* (god, in the non-specific sense).

Probable root:

Ia (yah)	n/a

Iad as root? (Not referring to God):

Iadnah (yad-nah)	Knowledge
Iaiadix (yay-II-ad-iks)	Honor
Laiad (lay-II-ad)	Secrets of Truth

Note:

While this final group of words does not refer to God, the use of *Iad* as a root may indicate the lofty nature of these ideas.

Compare from *Loagaeth*:

Ia, Iad, Iads, Ia-dron

Compare from *Corpus Omnium*:

Iad appears in all four portions of the Table—taking up the cells in the outer corners. This is likely symbolic of the Horned Altars in the Tabernacle of Moses and the Temple of Solomon. (The same symbolism can be found upon Dee's Holy Table—which has the Angelical letter *Veh* [B] at the four corners.)

Iadbaltoh (ii-ad-BAL-toh)* [Iad + Balt + Toh] *comp.*

(Triumphant) God of Righteousness

9.63 . . . The God of Righteousness rejoiceth in them.

Pronunciation notes:

(**Dee—I ad bal toh*) Four syllables. The initial *I* stands alone—although it tends to blend with the second syllable when this word is spoken fluently. The *oh* in the last syllable makes a long "o" sound. The other syllables are all short.

(*Dee—Iadbáltoh) See the 48 Claves. Here, Dee placed an accent over the third syllable.

Also:

Baltle (bal-tayl) Righteousness

Note:

The similarity between *Iadbaltoh* and the ancient Gnostic name and title for the Creator: *Ialdabaoth*, the God of Righteousness.

Iadnah (yad-nah)* *n.* Knowledge

1.46 . . . ark of knowledge . . .

Pronunciation notes:

(**Dee—yadnah*) The *I* in this case takes the "y" sound. (Also see the pronunciation given for *Iad*).

(**Dee—Jadnah*) See *48 Claves*. Here Dee indicates the "j" sound. I have settled upon the "y" sound instead, as it is closer to the sound of related words (as we can see in each of the following compounds and related words).

Compounds:

Iadnamad (yad-nay-mad) [Iadnah + Mad?] Pure Knowledge

Probable root:

Ia (yah) n/a

Iad (yad) God

Probable shared root:

Iaiadix (yay-II-ad-iks) — Honor

Laiad (lay-II-ad) — Secrets of Truth

Compare from *Loagaeth*:

Ia, Iad

Iadnamad (yad-nay-mad)* [Iadnah + Mad?] *comp.?* — Pure Knowledge

30.157 . . . make us partakers of undefiled knowledge.

Pronunciation notes:

(**Dee—Iad na mad*) Three syllables. The *a* in the second syllable is likely long.

(**Dee—Iadnâmad*) See the *48 Claves*. Here, Dee places a circumflex over the second a to indicate its long sound.

Note:

This compound literally translates as "knowledge," "God," or "Godly Knowledge" (see *Mad*).

"Iadoias" (jad-oh-JAS) *prop. n.* — Eternal God

Compounds:

Iadoiasmomar (jad-oh-JAS-moh-mar)
["Iadoias" + "Momar"] — God Eternally Crowned

Also:

Ioiad (joh-JAD) — Him That Liveth Forever

Shared root:

Geiad (jej-AYD) — Lord and Master

Gohed (joh-ED) — One Everlasting . . .

Ia (yah) — n/a

Iad (yad) — God

Iadpil (ii-AD-pil) — (To) Him

Iaida (jay-II-da) — The Highest

Iaidon (jay-II-don) — All Powerful

Oiad (oh-ii-AD) (Of) God
Piad (pii-AD)
Your God

Iadoiasmomar (jad-oh-JAS-moh-mar)* ["Iadoias" + "Momar"] *comp.*
God Eternally Crowned

8.44 . . . *God is, was, and shall be crowned.*

Pronunciation notes:

(**Dee—Iad o i as mo mar*) This word appears to be six syllables—though I suspect it is only five. The first *o* stands alone. The *I* likely takes the hard "j" sound—as we see in *Ioiad* (Him That Liveth Forever)—thus I have used a Ged (J) in the Angelical spelling. Finally, the second *o* takes its long sound.

(**Dee—Jad-oiás-mômar*) See the *48 Claves*. Dee here indicates a "j" sound for the initial *I*—thus I have used a Ged (J) for this letter well. He places the accent over the second *a*, and a circumflex over the second *o* to indicate its long sound.

Iadpil (ii-AD-pil)* *prop. n.* (Unto) Him

1.52 . . . faith *to Him* that liveth . . .

Pronunciation notes:

(**Dee—Call it IADPIL accent ad*) This note is haphazard. However, Dee seems to indicate that the letters *ad* stand as their own (accented) syllable. This means the *I* stands alone, and this word has three syllables.

(**Dee—Iädpil*) See *48 Claves*. There is a dieresis over the *a*, to indicate that it does not combine its sound with the initial *I*.

Also:

Geiad (jej-AYD) Lord and Master
Iad (yad) God
"Iadoias" (jad-oh-JAS) Eternal God
Iaida (jay-II-da) The Highest
Iaidon (jay-II-don) All Powerful
Ioiad (joh-JAD) Him That Liveth Forever

Oiad (oh-ii-AD) — (Of) God
Piad (pii-AD) — Your God

Probable root:

Ia (yah) — n/a

Iaiadix (yay-II-ad-iks)* *n.* — Honor

15.17 . . . seal of *honour* . . .

Note:

The transmission of Key Fifteen is missing from Dee's journals. We only have the English for this Key given later (see *TFR*, p. 193). Plus, the word appears in this location in Dee's *48 Claves*.

Pronunciation notes:

(**Dee—iaiâdix*) See the *48 Claves*. Dee placed an accent over the second *i*—which I assume is the second syllable. He also placed a circumflex over the second *a* to indicate its long sound. Compare to the pronunciation of *Laiad* (secrets of truth).

Probable shared root:

Ia (yah) — n/a
Iad (yad) — God
Iadnah (yad-nah) — Knowledge
Laiad (lay-II-ad) — Secrets of Truth

Iaial (jay-yal)* *v.* — To Conclude (To Judge)

5.50 . . . *conclude us as* receivers of your mysteries . . .

Note:

"Conclude" or "judge"—especially in the sense of Divine Judgment. In this place in the Keys, the speaker is asking the Angels to judge him worthy of the higher mysteries.

Pronunciation notes:

(*Dee—Ia ial*) Two syllables. Other words similar to *Iaial* seem to indicate a "j" sound for the first syllable—thus I have spelled this word with an initial Ged (J). (See Iaida, Iaidon, etc.)

(*Dee—ia-ial*) See the *48 Claves*. This note matches that from *TFR*.

Possible compound:

Oxiayal (ox-jay-al) [Tox? + Iaial] "The Mighty Seat" (i.e., Divine Throne)

Compare from *Loagaeth*:

Iaialgh

Iaida (jay-II-da)* *prop. n.* The Highest

(RFP) . . . the true worshiper of *the Highest* . . .

30.10 . . . the judgment of *the Highest* . . .

Pronunciation notes:

(*Dee 1.86—A word, Jaida*)

(*Dee 30.10—Ia—í da Ya*) There seem to be two pronunciations here—one taking the hard "j" sound and the other taking the soft "y" sound. I have settled on the "j" version in my pronunciation—along with an initial Ged (J) in the Angelical lettering—as that sound is found in many similar words. The note at 30.10 indicates three syllables, with the accent on the second syllable. Dee added the *Ya* to his notation to indicate the "y" sound for the initial *I* in that case.

(*Dee 1.RFP—Jaida*) See *48 Claves*. Dee indicates the "j" sound again.

(*Dee 13.RFP; 14.RFP; 15.RFP; 17.RFP; 18.RFP—Iaïda*) See the *48 Claves*. In these places, Dee added a dieresis over the second *i*, indicating that it should not join its sound with the previous vowel.

(*Dee 16.RFP; 30.10—Iaída*) See the *48 Claves*. Here, Dee again placed an accent on the *i* in the second syllable.

Also:

Geiad (jej-AYD) Lord and Master

Iad (yad) God

"Iadoias" (jad-oh-JAS) Eternal God

Iadpil (ii-AD-pil) (To) Him

Iaidon (jay-II-don)	All Powerful
Ioiad (joh-JAD)	Him That Liveth Forever
Oiad (oh-ii-AD)	Of God
Piad (pii-AD)	Your God

Possible compound:

Qadah (kwah-AY-dah) [Qaa + Iaida?]	Creator

Probable root:

Ia (yah)	n/a

Compare from *Loagaeth*:

Ia-dron

Iaidon (jay-II-don)* *prop. n.* The All Powerful

2.39 . . . mind of *the All Powerful* . . .

Pronunciation note:

(**Dee—Ia í don*) Three syllables, with an accent on the second syllable. (**Dee—Ja-í-don*) See *48 Claves*. Same as in *TFR*. Note the "j" sound for the first syllable, and the initial Ged (J) in the Angelical lettering.

Also:

Geiad (jej-AYD)	Lord and Master
Iad (yad)	God
"Iadoias" (jad-oh-JAS)	Eternal God
Iadpil (ii-AD-pil)	(To) Him
Iaida (jay-II-da)	The Highest
Ioiad (joh-JAD)	Him That Liveth Forever
Oiad (oh-ii-AD)	Of God
Piad (pii-AD)	Your God

Probable root:

Ia (yah)	n/a

Compare from *Loagaeth*:

Ia-dron

Iaisg (jay-IZH)* *prop. n.* Everlasting One and Indivisible God**

Pronunciation note:

*(*Dee—ia-ísg)* See the *Five Books*, p. 307. Two syllables, with an accent on the second. This word likely begins with the "j" sound (see *Ioiad*), thus I have spelled it in Angelical with an initial Ged (J).

From *Loagaeth*:

(***Dee—Everlasting One and Indivisible God.*) See the *Five Books*, p. 307.

Also:

Geiad (jej-AYD) Lord and Master
Gohed (joh-ED) One Everlasting, All Things Descending Upon One
Ioiad (joh-JAD) Him That Liveth Forever
"Iadoias" (jad-oh-JAS) Eternal God

Probable root:

Ia (yah) n/a

Compare from *Loagaeth*:

Ia, Ia-dron

Ialpirgah (YAL-pur-jah)* ["Ialprt" + "Pirgah"] *comp.* "Flames of the First Glory"

7.6 . . . amongst *the Flames of the First Glory* . . .

Pronunciation notes:

(**Dee—IAL pir gah Yal*) Three syllables. The first syllable likely takes an accent. Dee indicates that *Ial* should sound like "Yal." The *g* should take a soft "j" sound, as seen in other versions of the word *Prge*.

(**Dee—ial-pîrgah*) See the *48 Claves*. Dee places a circumflex over the second *i* to indicate a long sound. However, the long *i* does not appear in any other phonetic notes, for this or related words.

Note:

"Pirgah" is obviously a form of the word *Prge* (fire), and must mean "the First Glory" (i.e., the Light of Divinity, and possibly a reference to the rising Sun).

Also see *Ialpirt* (light), which seems to indicate Light from celestial beings.
Also see *Busd* (glory), which seems to indicate glory as in "wondrous."
Also see *Adgmach* (glory), which seems to indicate "adoration, praise."

Ialpirt (YAL-pert)* *n.* Light

18.3 . . . thou mighty *light* and burning flame . . .

Pronunciation notes:
(**Dee—Ol pirt*) The actual Angelical spelling of this word is not shown in Dee's journals. We only have his phonetic note, which shows the first syllable as *Ol*. However, this is corrected by Illemese later in the journals:
(*Illemese—al part*) See *TFR*, p. 200. Two syllables. This word is obviously the same as "Ialprt" (flame). Illemese drops the initial *I* (though I have retained it in my pronunciation, with the sound of "y"). The second *i* should be a phonetic gloss—which Illemese indicates with an *a* in his note.
I have adopted the accent from similar words.

Also:

Ialpon (YAL-pon)	Burn
Ialpor (YAL-por)	Flaming
"Ialprt" (YAL-pert)	Flame

Note:
These words (including compounds with "Ialprt") are used in the Keys to indicate Light as from a celestial being. The common-use nouns for a fire are *Vep* (flame) and *Prge* (fire). For verb forms, see *Ialpor* (flaming) and *Ialpon* (burn).

Ialpon (YAL-pon)* *v.* To Burn

10.21 . . . which *burn* night and day . . .

Pronunciation notes:

(*Dee—Jal pon Yal*) Two syllables. Dee appears to indicate that the initial *I* can take the "j" or "y" sound. I have settled upon the "y" sound, as it better matches other versions of this word. I have adopted the accent from similar words.

Also:

Ialpor (YAL-por) Flaming
"Ialprt" (YAL-pert) Flame
Ialpirt (YAL-pert) Light

Note:

Ialpon (to burn) is a verb. *Ialpor* (flaming) is an adjective. The "Ialprt" / *Ialpirt* family of words (flame, light) are nouns—specifically referring to the Light of celestial beings. The common-use nouns for a fire are *Vep* (flame) and *Prge* (fire).

Compare from *Loagaeth*:

Ia, Alpon

Ialpor (YAL-por)* *adj.* Flaming

9.5 . . . two edged swords *flaming* . . .

Pronunciation notes:

(*Dee—I AL por yal*) Dee indicates three syllables. However, the *I* must take the "y" sound. Because of this, it tends to blend with the second syllable (*al*) to make "yal." Therefore, I have given the word only two syllables in my pronunciation. (Further supporting this, see the pronunciation notes for *Ialpon*.)
I have adopted the accent from similar words.

Also:

Ialpon (YAL-pon) Burn
"Ialprt" (YAL-pert) Flame
Ialpirt (YAL-pert) Light

Note:

See note at *Ialpon*.

Also compare the name of the Part of the Earth (and its Governor), *Yalpamb*. This could even be a compound (Ialpor + Pambt), or "Unto the Flame."

Compare from *Loagaeth*:
Ia

Ialprg (YAL-purj)* ["Ialprt" + "Prg"] *comp., prop. n.* — Burning Flame

18.4 . . . *burning flame* of comfort . . .

Pronunciation notes:
(**Dee—Ial purg*) Two syllables. The *r* takes its elongated "ur" sound. See "Prg", *Prge*, etc. for evidence that the final *g* should be soft. See *Ialpurg* for the accented first syllable.

Also:
Ialpurg (YAL-purj) ["Ialprt" + "Purg"] — Burning Flame(s)

Note:
The *u* in Ialpurg is a phonetic gloss.

"Ialprt" (YAL-pert) *n.* — Flame

Compounds:
Dialprt (dii-AL-purt) [D + "Ialprt"] — Third Flame
Lialprt (el-YAL-purt) [L + "Ialprt"] — First Flame
Vivialprt (viv-ii-AL-purt) [Viv + "Ialprt"] — Second Flame

Further compounds:
Ialprg (YAL-purj) ["Ialprt" + "Prg"] — Burning Flame(s)
Ialpirgah (YAL-pur-jah) ["Ialprt" + "Pirgah"] — Flames of the First Glory
Ialpurg (YAL-purj) ["Ialprt" + "Purg"] — Burning Flame(s)

Also:
Ialpirt (YAL-pert) — Light
Ialpon (YAL-pon) — Burn
Ialpor (YAL-por) — Flaming

Note:

All of these words are nouns, and they are all used to indicate Light as if from a celestial being. The common-use nouns for a fire are Vep (flame) and Prge (fire). For a verb form, see Ialpon (to burn). See Ialpor (flaming) for an adjective.

Ialpurg (YAL-purj)* ["Ialprt" + "Purg"] *comp., prop. n.* Burning Flame(s)

2.10 . . . *burning flames* have formed . . .

Pronunciation notes:

(*Dee—Ial purg*) Two syllables. The final *g* is likely soft—see the pronunciation notes for Prge (fire).

(*Dee—Iál-prg*) See *48 Claves*. Two syllables, with an accent on the first syllable. As we can see, the *u* is a phonetic gloss.

Also:

Ialprg (YAL-purj) ["Ialprt" + "Prg"] Burning Flame(s)

Compare from *Loagaeth*:

Ia

Iaod (YAY-ohd)* *n.* Beginning

5.30 . . . *the beginning of* their own seats . . .

30.16 . . . *the beginning of* comfort . . .

Pronunciation notes:

(*Dee 5.30; 30.16—I á od*) This would appear to have three syllables. However, also see *Iaodaf* (in the beginning), which indicates the initial *Ia* stand together. The accent is placed on the first syllable.

(*Dee 5.30—iáod*) See the *48 Claves*. Accent on the first syllable.

(*Dee 30.16—Jáod*) See the *48 Claves*. Dee seems to indicate the "j" sound for the initial *I*. However, see *Iaodaf* (in the beginning), which clearly indicates a "y" sound instead.

Also:

Iaodaf (YAY-oh-daf) (In the) Beginning

Note:

Also see *Acroodzi* (beginning), *Croodzi* (beginning of things), *Nostoah* (it was in the beginning).

Compare from *Loagaeth*:

Ia

Iaodaf (YAY-oh-daf)* *n.* (In the) Beginning

30.41 . . . rose up *in the beginning* . . .

Pronunciation notes:

(**Dee—Ia o daf Y*) Dee here indicates three syllables, and shows that the initial *I* takes the "y" sound. The first *a* seems to take its long sound. (Note also that it is followed by an *o*—as in the English word *chaos*.) Plus, see the pronunciation notes for *Iaod* (beginning).

(**Dee—iáodaf*) See the *48 Claves*. Here, Dee placed an accent upon the first syllable.

Also:

Iaod (YAY-ohd) Beginning

Note:

Also see *Acroodzi* (beginning), *Croodzi* (beginning of things), *Nostoah* (it was in the beginning).

Yarry (YAR-ee)* *n.* Providence

30.37 . . . *the providence of* Him who sits upon the Holy Throne.

Pronunciation notes:

(**Dee—Yar ry*) Two syllables. The initial *Y* should take the "yuh" sound, and the final *y* should take the "ee" sound. In Early Modern English, a double *r* is a regular "r" sound.

(**Dee—yárry*) See the *48 Claves*. Here, Dee indicates an accent on the first syllable.

Ich (ik)* *prop. n.* "The Eleventh Aethyr"

30.3 . . . which dwell in *the eleventh aethyr* . . .

Note:
This (word 30.3) is the single space in the Key of the Aethyrs, which must be changed for each invocation—replacing word 30.3 with the name of the appropriate Aethyr. No established definitions were given for these names.

Ich contains the three Parts of the Earth *Molpand*, *Usnarda*, and *Ponodol*.

Also see *TFR*, pp. 34–35. This session is recorded entirely in Latin. Here we find this Angelical phrase spoken by "a Voice": "*Garil zed masch, ich na gel galaht gemp gal noch Cabanladan.*" No translation or context is offered. (Note the word *Ich*.)

Pronunciation notes:
(**Dee—ik.*) This means the *ch* in this word is hard, making a "kh" sound (as in the English word *ache*).

"Ichis" (jay-kiis) *v.* Are

Compounds:
Ichisge (jay-KIIS-jee) ["Ichis" + "Ge"] Are Not

Also:
Chis (kiis) Are
Chiis (kiis) Are (They)
"Chisda" (kiis-da) Are There
Chiso (kiis-oh) Shall Be
"Gchis" (jee-kiis) Are
Zchis (zohd-kiis) (They) Are

Note:
"Ichis" and "Gchis" are likely the same word—thus I have spelled this word with an initial Ged (J). See note at *Ichisge*.
Also see *Chis* (are).

Ichisge (jay-KIIS-jee)* ["Ichis" + "Ge"] *comp.* Are Not

3.21 . . . who are, *to are not*, except mine own hand . . .

Pronunciation notes:

(**Dee—I Chisge Kis*) Likely three syllables. Dee is not clear on the proper sound of the initial *I*—which could take the sound of "y" or "j." However, see *Gchisge* (are not), which indicates that both *Ichisge* and *Gchisge* should start with a soft "g" or "j" sound. (Note I have spelled the word with an initial Ged [J].) Finally, Dee indicates the *ch* should take the harder "k" sound.

(**Dee—i-chis-ge*) See the *48 Claves*. This note confirms three syllables for this word.

See *Gchisge* (are not) for the accented syllable.

Also:

Gchisge (jee-KIIS-jee) ["Gchis" + "Ge"] Are Not

Note:

The ungrammatical English phrase here—*to are not*—is probably a mistake on the part of Dee or Kelley. Apparently, the word *to* should read *and*, or perhaps *or*. However, the missing conjunction (*and/or*) is merely implied in the Angelical.

Also see *Chis* (are).

Icorsca (ii-KORS-kay)* [I + Cors + "Ca"] *comp.* Is Such as

9.72 . . . for the time *is such as* requireth comfort.

Pronunciation notes:

(**Dee—I cors ca Ka*) Three syllables. Dee indicates that the *c* in the last syllable should take the hard "k" sound. The initial *I* stands alone.

(**Dee—icórsca*) See the *48 Claves*. Here, Dee placed an accent over the second syllable.

Note:

See the similar *Corsta* (such as). Note that *ta* becomes *ca* here. For more info, see *Tabaam* (Governor), which becomes *Caba* in Key One. Also see *Ta* (as).

Idlugam (id-LOO-gam)* [I + "Dlugam"] *comp.* Is Given

7.44 . . . this remembrance *is given* power . . .

Pronunciation notes:

(**Dee—Id lú gam*) Three syllables, with an accent on the second syllable. The *I* does not stand alone in Dee's note, and we know it takes the vowel sound ("i" rather than "j"), because it precedes a consonant.

(**Dee—idlúgam*) See the *48 Claves*. The accent is again shown on the second syllable.

Idoigo (ii-dee-oy-go)* *prop. n.* "Him Who Sits Upon the Holy Throne"

30.38 . . . the providence of *Him who sits upon the Holy Throne*.

Pronunciation notes:

(**Dee—I d oi go*) Dee seems to indicate four syllables here—with the initial *I* and *d* each standing alone. The *oi* should make an "oy" sound—as in the English words *oil* and *boil*.

Note:

This word appears as a Name of God upon the Eastern Watchtower of the Great Table of the Earth, ruling the Angels of medicine. Also, the title "Him Who Sits Upon the Throne" is common in biblical and *Merkavah* literature—such as *1 Enoch* and related texts like the Book of Revelation 4:9, 7:10, etc.

Iehusoz (jay-US-os)* *n.* (God's) Mercies

3.65 . . . *his mercies* flourish . . .

Pronunciation notes:

(**Dee—Jehusoz*) Three syllables. The initial *I* takes the consonant "J" sound—and I have thus spelled it with an initial Ged (J). The *eh* likely makes a long "a" sound, as in Early Modern English. No further long vowel sounds are indicated.

(**Dee—Iehúsoz*) See the *48 Claves*. Dee placed an accent on the second syllable.

Note:

The similarity between this word and Jesus in Greek (*Iesous*) and Hebrew (*Ieshuah*).

See also *Rit*, which probably stands for the more generalized concept of mercy.

Compare from *Loagaeth*:

Ihehudetha, Ihehudz, Ihehusch, Iehuscoth, Iehusa, Iehuded, Gehudan

Iga (ii-ga)* [I + "GA"] *comp.* Is 31

11.30 . . . whose number *is 31*.

Pronunciation notes:

(**Dee—I ga*) Two syllables. The *I* stands alone, and the *g* likely takes its hard sound.

Il (ii-el)* [I + L] *comp.* Is One

5.55 . . . our Lord and Master *is all one*.

Note:

Do not confuse this compound with the singular word "Yl" (thy).

Pronunciation notes:

(**Dee—i l*) Two syllables—both letters stand alone.

(**Dee—i-L*) See the *48 Claves*. This note matches that from *TFR*.

"Yl" (yil) *pron., sing.* Thy

Compounds:

Daxil (daks-il) ["Dax" + "Yl"] Thy Loins

Pronunciation note:

The "I" in this word element should sound like "y." Both letters form one syllable together. See *Yls*, *Ylsi*, etc.

Also:

Yls (yils) Thou

Note:

Do not confuse this word with the compound *Il* (is one).

Ili (Il-lii)* *n.* (The) First/(At) First

3.28 *In the first* I made you . . .

Pronunciation note:

(**Dee—ILI)* Dee give us little clue here.

(**Dee—í-lí)* See the *48 Claves*. Dee indicates two syllables. For some reason, he has accent marks on both *I*s. (I have left the accent on the first syllable in my pronunciation.) Both *I*s are likely long vowels.

Note:

This word is a palindrome, spelled the same forward and backward. Also see *La* (the First).

Probable root:

L (el) First, One

Yls (yils)* *pron., sing.* Thou

15.1 *O thou* the governor . . .

**16.1 *O thou* second flame . . .

16.20 . . . great art *thou* . . .

17.1 *O thou* third flame . . .

18.1 *O thou* mighty light . . .

Pronunciation notes:

(**Dee 17.1—ILS*)

(**Dee 16.20—Yls as Yils*)

(**Dee 18.1—Ils*) One syllable. Dee sometimes wrote this word with an initial *I*. However, he shows us in word 16.20 that the "Y" sound is intended. (I have used the *Y* in all versions of the word in this Lexicon.)

Note:

**The transmission of the first twelve words of Key Sixteen is missing from Dee's journals. We have only the English given on *TFR*, p. 194. Illemese also gives word 16.1 later, on *TFR*, p. 200. Plus, the word appears in Dee's *48 Claves*.

Also:

"Yl" (yil)	Thy
Ylsi (yil-sii)	Thee

Note:

These words indicate "you" in a singular sense—such as, "I am speaking to you." Also see *Nonci*, which indicates "you" in the plural sense—such as, "I am speaking to all of you."

Probable root:

L (el)	First

Possible shared root:

Aqlo (AY-kwah-loh)	Thy
Bolp (bohlp)	Be Thou

Ylsi (yil-sii)* *pron.* Thee

7\~ꕃ7

17.13 . . . living lamps going before *thee* . . .

Pronunciation notes:

(**Dee—Yl si*) Two syllables. The first syllable sounds like "yil," as shown with the phonetic notes for the word *Yls* (thou). The final *i* should take a long sound.

Also:

"Yl" (yil)	Thy
Yls (yils)	Thou

Note:

These words indicate "you" in a singular sense.
Also see *Nonci*, which indicates "you" in the plural sense.

Probable root:

L (el) — First, One

Possible shared root:

Aqlo (AY-kwah-loh) — Thy
Bolp (bohlp) — Be Thou

Imvamar (im-vay-mar)* *v.* — To Apply unto

3.77 . . . and *apply yourselves unto us* as unto partakers . . .

Pronunciation notes:

(**Dee—It is Im ua mar*) Likely three syllables. The *u* preceding an *a* likely takes the hard "v" sound.
(**Dee—Im-uâ-mar*) See the *48 Claves*. Dee places a circumflex over the first *a* to indicate the long vowel sound.

Note:

To "apply" something is to "bring it into action" or "put it into operation." Perhaps even more important here, it also means "to employ diligently or with close attention." (As in "to apply yourself to your studies.") Both of these senses of the word fit perfectly in Angelic invocations such as the Keys.

Inoas (in-OH-as)* [I + Noas] *comp.* — Are/Have Become

7.11 . . . and *they are become* 28 living dwellings . . .

Pronunciation notes:

(**Dee—In ó as*) Three syllables, with an accent upon the second syllable. In Early Modern English, the *oa* letter combination makes a long "o" sound (as in the English words *boat* and *coat*). Dee represents this by having the *o* stand alone in his phonetic note.
(**Dee—inóas*) See the *48 Claves*. The accent is again shown on the second syllable.

"Insi" (in-sii) *v.* To Walk

Compounds:

Dsinsi (dee-sin-sii) [Ds + "Insi"] Which Walkest

Ioiad (joh-JAD)* *prop. n.* Him That Liveth Forever

2.52 . . . I am of *Him that liveth forever* . . .

Pronunciation notes:

(**Dee—Ioiad*) Dee does not indicate a "y" sound here, nor does the *I* stand alone. Also note the existence of *Geiad* and *Gohed*—both starting with a soft "g" or "j" sound. Therefore I assume a "j" sound is intended for *Ioiad*, and I have spelled the word in Angelical with an initial Ged (J).

I have adopted the accent from similar words.

Also:

"Iadoias" (jad-oh-JAS) Eternal God

Note:

I have found the title "He Who Lives Forever" attributed to God in *1 Enoch*, 6:1.

Probable root:

Ia (yah) n/a

Iad (yad) God

Shared root:

Geiad (jej-AYD) Lord and Master

Gohed (joh-ED) One Everlasting . . .

Iadpil (ii-AD-pil) (To) Him

Oiad (oh-ii-AD) (Of) God

Piad (pii-AD) Your God

Yolcam (yol-kam)* *v.* Bring Forth (i.e., To Bear)

30.127 *Bring forth* with those that increase.

Pronunciation notes:

(**Dee—Yol cam*) Two syllables.

Also:

Yolci (yol-sii) To Bring Forth

Yolci (yol-sii)* *v.* To Bring Forth

10.58 One rock *bringeth forth* 1000 . . .

Pronunciation notes:

(**Dee—Yol Ci*) Two syllables. The *c* likely takes the softer "s" sound, as it precedes an *i* (as in the English words *circle* and *circus*).

Also:

Yolcam (yol-kam) Bring Forth

Yor (yor)* *v.* To Roar

10.40 . . . *roar* with a hundred mighty earthquakes . . .

Pronunciation notes:

(**Dee—Yor*) One syllable, with an initial "Y" sound.

Ip (ip)* *adv.* Not

9.68 Come away, and *not* your vials.
10.82 Come away, but *not* your noises.

Pronunciation notes:

(**Dee 9.68; 10.82—Ip*) One syllable. The *I* should be short.

Compounds:

Odipuran (ohd-II-pew-ran) [Od + Ip + "Puran"] And Shall Not See
Pageip (pay-jee-ip) ["Page" + Ip] Rest Not

Probable root:

I (ii) Is

Note:

The word *Ip* appears to be a conjugation of *I*. The addition of the *p* accomplishes the transmutation of "to be"—or "is"—into "not be." See also *Ul* (end)—an antonymic transmutation of *L* (the first).

Probable root for:

Ipam (ip-am) [I + "Pam"] Is Not
Ipamis (ip-am-is) [I + "Pamis"] Can Not Be
Ripir (rii-PIR) No Place

Note:

Also see "Ge" (not), Ag (none), "Pam" (not) and "Pamis" (cannot).

"Ip" (ip) *pron.* Her

Compounds:

Ixomaxip (iks-oh-MAKS-ip) ["Ix" + Omax + "Ip"] Let Her Be Known

In this example, the "Ip" obviously doesn't indicate *not*. It is uncertain, but it may indicate *her*. There is only one relative example (see below), which is itself just as uncertain.

Also:

"Pi" (pii) She
Pii (pii-ii) ["Pi" + I] She Is

Note:

Also see *Tilb* (her).

Ipam (ip-am) [I + "Pam"] *comp.* Is Not

1.57 . . . whose *beginning is not* . . .

The Angelical for "beginning" (*Croodzi*) does not appear here.

Also:

Ipamis (ip-am-is) [I + "Pamis"] Cannot Be

Note:

The word *I* (is/are) very likely stands for "is" in Ipam, and "be" in *Ipamis*. The change from "Pam" to "Pamis" seems to change the tense, and therefore the usage of *I*.

Probable shared root:

Ip (ip) — Not

Ipamis (ip-am-is)* [I + "Pamis"] *comp.* — Cannot Be

1.59 . . . nor end *cannot be* . . .

Pronunciation notes:

(**Dee—the A pronounced short*)

(**Dee—Ipâmis*) See *48 Claves*. Note the circumflex over the *a*—which should indicate a long sound. However, this conflicts with the short *a* Dee noted in *TFR*.

Also:

Ipam (ip-am) [I + "Pam"] — Is Not

Note:

The word *I* (is/are) very likely stands for "is" in *Ipam*, and "be" in *Ipamis*. The change from "Pam" to "Pamis" seems to change the tense.

Probable shared root:

Ip (ip) — Not

"Ipuran" (II-pew-ran) [Ip + "Puran"] *comp.* — Shall Not See

Compounds:

Odipuran (ohd-II-pew-ran) [Od + Ip + "Puran"] — And Shall Not See

"Irgil" (ir-jil) *comp.* — How Many

Compounds:

Irgilchisda (ir-jil-KIIS-da) ["Irgil" + Chis + "Da"] — How Many Are There

Note:

Also see *Plosi* (as many).

Irgilchisda (ir-jil-KIIS-da)* ["Irgil" + Chis + "Da"] *comp.* How Many Are There

8.21 . . . *how many are there* which remain . . .

Pronunciation notes:

(**Dee—Ir gil chís da*) Four syllables, with an accent on the third syllable. Also see *Chis* (are) for more pronunciation notes.

(**Dee—Irgil chís da*) See the *48 Claves*. Dee again indicates the accent on the third syllable.

Yrpoil (yur-POY-il)* *n.* Division

30.48 . . . and let there be *division* in her . . .

Pronunciation notes:

(**Dee—Yr pó il*) Three syllables, with an accent on the second syllable. The *r* should likely take the "ur" sound. In Early Modern English, the *oi* letter combination should make an "oy" sound (as in the words *oil* and *boil*). See pronunciation notes for *Poilp* (divided).

(**Dee—yrpóil*) See the *48 Claves*. Here, Dee again placed the accent on the second syllable.

Also:

Poilp (poylp) Divided

Isalman (ii-SAYL-man)* [I + Salman] *comp.* Is a House

7.2 . . . *is a house* of virgins . . .

Pronunciation notes:

(**Dee—I Sal man*) Three syllables. The *I* stands alone. The capital *S may* indicate the accent.

(**Dee—isâlman*) See the *48 Claves*. Dee placed a circumflex over the first *a* to indicate its long sound.

Isro (iz-roh)* *comp.* Promise of

13.15 . . . Behold *the promise of* God . . .

Pronunciation notes:
(**Dee—Is ro*) Two syllables. I have represented the *s* as a *z* in my pronunciation, for a sound similar to the English word *is*. The final *o* is likely a long vowel.

Also:
Aisro (ay-ii-sroh) Promise of

Note:
It is possible that the *-o* affix (of) is in use here.
Also see *Sibsi* (covenant), *Surzas* (sworn), and *Znrza* (swore).

Ita (ii-tay)* [I + Ta] *comp.* Is as

8.2 . . . *is as* the 3rd heaven . . .

Pronunciation notes:
(**Dee—I ta*) Two syllables. The initial *I* stands alone.

Iudra (jood-ra) n/a

Note:
See *Five Books*, p. 366. The Angel Illemese appears to Dee and Kelley with a bundle of empty boxes that he calls virtuous. When Dee asks for an explanation, Illemese says, "Will you have my bill? [. . .] I will show it. Serve it, where you list. *Iudra galgol astel.*" Dee states that he and Kelley do not understand, and wish to know how it can be served. But Illemese never offers definitions for these Angelical words.

Pronunciation notes:

Because the initial *I* precedes a *u*, I suspect this word should begin with the "j" consonant sound. I have spelled the word in Angelical with an initial Ged (J).

"Ium" (jay-um) *v.* (Is) Called

Compounds:

Dsium (dee-sii-um) [Ds + "Ium"] Which Is Called

Also:

Iumd (jay-umd) (Is) Called

Note:

"Ium" / *Iumd* is translated as "is called." However, it is unlikely that this is a compound word, and thus the *I* should not stand for "is." (The pronunciation of the *i* as "j" may support this.) I have spelled this word in Angelical with an initial Ged (J).

Iumd (jay-umd)* *v.* (Is) Called

13.20 . . . which *is called* amongst you . . .
18.18 . . . which *is called* in thy kingdom . . .

Pronunciation notes:

(**Dee 13.20—J umbd*)

(**Dee 18.18—I umd*) Two syllables. The note Dee gave us with word 13.20 is the most useful. It lets us know that the initial *I* actually takes a "J" sound. For that reason, I have spelled this word in Angelical with an initial Ged (J). Then, Dee shows us that the first part of the second syllable sounds like "umb"—as in the English words *dumb* and *numb*. Therefore, the *u* takes its short sound.

Also:

"Ium" (jay-um) (Is) Called

Note:

See the note at "Ium."

Ivonph (ii-VONV)* [I + Vonph] *comp.* Is Wrath

12.22 . . . whose name amongst you *is wrath* . . .

Pronunciation notes:

(*Dee—I vonph*) Two syllables. The initial *I* stands alone. The *nph* should be similar to the *nf* in *Sonf* (reign). I have represented the sound in my pronunciation with an *nv*—where the *v* indicates a sound somewhere between a hard *f* and a very soft *v*.

I have adopted the accent from *Ivonpovnph* (is wrath in anger).

Ivonpovnph (ii-VON-foh-unv)* [I + "Vonpo" + "Vnph"] *comp.*

Is Wrath in Anger

17.15 . . . whose God *is wrath in anger* . . .

Pronunciation notes:

(*Dee—I von po vnph*) Four syllables. The initial *I* stands alone. The *p* in the third syllable is likely a *ph* digraph (see *Vonph*, *Vonpho*). The *o* in the third syllable is likely long. In the fourth syllable, Dee originally wrote a *v*—although it should take the "u" sound before a consonant. (Therefore, the *vn* should create the sound of "un"—with a short *u*.) Finally, the last three letters, *nph*, should be similar to the *nf* in words like *Sonf* (reign). I have written this sound as *nv* in my pronunciation—indicating a sound somewhere between a hard *f* and a very soft *v*.

(*Dee—i vónpôvnph*) See the *48 Claves*. Here, Dee placed an accent over the initial *o* in the second syllable. He also placed a circumflex over the second *o* to confirm its long sound.

Note:

This word is translated literally as "is wrath of wrath." The word *anger* is not actually indicated by the Angelical; it is simply a gloss to make the English make more sense. The basic idea is "intense wrath."

Further compounds:

Ivonph (ii-VONV) [I + Vonph] Is Wrath

Iurehoh (jur-AY-hoh)* *n.?* "What Christ Did in Hell"**

Pronunciation notes:

*(*Dee—iuréhoh)* Because the initial *I* precedes a *u*, I suspect this word should begin with the "J" consonant sound. Thus, I have spelled this word in Angelical with an initial Ged (J). Then, the *eh* should make a long "a" vowel sound. Finally, the *oh* should combine to form a long "o" sound. Dee placed and accent over the *e*.

From *Loagaeth*:

(***Dee—This last word was hid a pretty while with a rim like a thin bladder before it. And when it was perfectly seen then there appeared a bloody cross over it. It is a word signifying what Christ did in hell.*) See the *Five Books*, p. 323. This is a reference to an obscure Christian legend (called *Descensus Ad Inferos*) in which Christ—during his three days in the Tomb—actually descended into Hell. While there, he literally stormed the place—smashing open gates, knocking down bridges, and liberating a number of souls who had been wrongly entrapped there. This is a controversial legend, mentioned in passing in the Apostles' Creed.

Iusmach (jus-mak) *adj.?* Begotten*

From *Loagaeth*:

(**Dee—Begotten.*) See the *Five Books*, p. 319.

Pronunciation notes:

Because the initial *I* precedes a *u*, I suspect this word should begin with the "J" consonant sound. Thus, I have spelled it in Angelical with an initial Ged (J).

"Ix" (iks) *v.* Let

Compounds:

Ixomaxip (iks-oh-MAKS-ip) ["Ix" + Omax + "Ip"] Let Her Be Known

Ixomaxip (iks-oh-MAKS-ip)* ["Ix" + Omax + "Ip"] *comp.*

Let Her Be Known

30.107 . . . one while *let her be known* . . .

Pronunciation notes:

(*Dee—Ix o máx ip*) This is likely four syllables, with an accent on the third syllable. The *o* stands alone.

Note:

While the word for "her" (*Tilb*) does not appear here, and the *-ip* obviously can't stand for "not," I should point out that the word for "she" appears as *Pi* in another isolated case.

Also note that the *omax* (knowest) element of this word has the *-ax* suffix to indicate action.

Izazaz (ii-zay-zaz)* *v.* To Frame (i.e., To Form)

2.11 . . . burning flames *have framed* within the depths of my jaws . . .

Pronunciation notes:

(*Dee—Izazaz*) Dee gives us little clue here.

(*Dee—I-zâ-zaz*) See *48 Claves*. Three syllables. The initial *I* stands alone. The first *a* has a circumflex, indicating that it takes its long sound.

Izizop (iz-is-op)* *n.* (Your?) Vessels

3.44 . . . that *from your highest vessels* and the corners . . .

Pronunciation notes:

(*Dee—Izizop*) Apparently three syllables. As we see in the pronunciation notes for *Zizop* (vessels), the second *z* takes on an "s" sound.

Note:

This is not a compound word, so the *I* does not indicate "is." I have noted that the word *I* can sometimes conjugate Angelical words in various ways. Therefore, perhaps the addition of *I* in this case indicates "your"?

Also:

Zizop (zis-op) Vessels

Ur (L)

L (el)* *prop. n.*	The First, One

2.8 . . . o you the second of *the first* . . .
5.27 . . . brothers of *the first* and second . . .

Pronunciation notes:

(**Dee 2.8—A word*)
(**Dee5.27—L*) Pronounced as we would the name of the letter *L*.

Compounds:

Agltoltorn (ag-el-tol-torn) [Ag + L + "Toltorn"]	No One Creature
Crpl (krip-el) ["Crp" + L]	But One
Il (ii-el) [I + L]	Is One
Lcapimao (el-ka-PII-may-oh) [L + "Capimao"]	One While
Lel (el-el) [L + El]	Same
Lialprt (el-YAL-purt) [L + "Ialprt"]	First Flame
Lnibm (el-nib-em) [L + "Nibm"]	One season
Lpatralx (el-PAY-tralks) [L + "Patralx"]	One Rock
Lsmnad (els-mad) [L + "Smnad"]	One Another

Also:

El (el)	The First
La (lah or el-ah)	The First
"Lo" (loh)	The First
Lu (loo)	From One

Note:

Compare to the name of the Angel *L* (or *El*), one of the Sons of the Sons of Light. His name literally translates as "The First."

Possible root for:

Aqlo (AY-kwah-loh)	Thy
Bolp (bohlp)	Be Thou
Daxil (daks-il)	Thy Loins
Ili (ii-EL-ii)	At First
Yls (yils)	Thou
Lil (el-il)	"The First Aethyr"

Ol (ohl) — I
Qaal (kwah-AY-el) — Creator
Ul (yewl) — End
Uls (yewls) — Ends

La (lah *or* el-ah)* *n.* — The First

5.38 . . . *the first*, ends, and contents of time . . .

Pronunciation notes:

(**Dee—La*) Dee seems to indicate one syllable here. However, other words that have *L* (the first) as their root tend to pronounce the *L* as if it stands alone. I have offered both options in my pronunciation.

Also:

L (el) — The First
El (el) — The First
"Lo" (loh) — The First
Lu (loo) — From One

Note:

Also see *Ili* (at first).

Laiad (lay-II-ad)* *n.* — Secrets of Truth

18.13 . . . in whom *the secrets of truth* . . .

Pronunciation notes:

(**Dee—La i ad*) Three syllables. The first *a* is likely long. The *i* stands alone.
(**Dee—Laíad*) See the *48 Claves*. Here, Dee placed an accent over the *i* in the second syllable.

Note:

Compare to the name of the Angel *Laidrom*, an Elder of the Southern Watchtower. It is possible that *Laidrom* is a compound of *Laiad* (secrets of truth) and *Om* (understand)—"He Who Understands the Secrets of Truth." (Unless, of course, *Rom* is a word unto itself.)

Probable root:

Ia (yah) — n/a

Iad (yad) — God

Probable shared root:

Iadnah (yad-nah) — Knowledge

Iaiadix (yay-II-ad-iks) — Honor

Lang (lang) *prop. n.* — Those Who Serve

From *Corpus Omnium*:

Associated with the post-Deluge quadrant of the Table. Translated in Latin as *Ministrantes* (Those Who Serve).

Compare from *Loagaeth*:

Lang, Langed

Note:

Also see *Cnoqod* (servants).

Lansh (lonsh)* *n.* — Exalted Power

1.7 . . . *in power exalted above* the firmaments . . .

Pronunciation notes:

(**Dee—LANSH as Lonsh*)

Also:

Lonsa (lon-sha) — Power

Lonshi (lon-shii) — Power

"Lonshin" (lon-shin) — Powers

Note:

Also see *Micalzo* (power/mighty), *Naneel* (my power).

Lap (lap)* *conj.* — For (Because)

(RFP) *For*, I am the servant . . .

2.32 *For*, you are become a building . . .

2.50 *For*, I am of him . . .

Pronunciation notes:

(**Dee 1.81—Call it Lap*)

(**Dee 2.32, 50—Lap*)

Note:

Also see *Bagle* (for), *Darsar* (wherefore)

Compare from *Loagaeth*:

Lap

Larag (lay-rag)* *conj.* Neither/Nor

10.51 . . . rest not *neither* know any (long) time here.

Pronunciation notes:

(**Dee—La rag*) Two syllables. The *a* is likely long. The final *g* is likely hard, as in the English words *rag* and *bag*.

Note:

The word *neither* can be a conjunction, adjective, or pronoun depending on use. Here in Key Ten, it is used as a conjunction.

"Las" (las) *adj.* Rich

Compounds:

Lasollor (las-OHL-or) ["Las" + "Ollor"] Rich Man

Compare from *Loagaeth*:

Las, Laz

Lasdi (las-dii)* *n.* (My) Feet

4.2 . . . I have set *my feet* in the south . . .

Pronunciation notes:

(**Dee—Las di*) Two syllables. The final *i* is likely a long vowel.

Also:

Lusd (lus-dee) Feet

Lusda (lus-da) Feet

Lusdan (lus-dan) Feet

Lasollor (las-OHL-or)* ["Las" + "Ollor"] *comp.* Rich Man

9.32 . . . as the *rich man* doth his treasure . . .

Pronunciation notes:

(**Dee—Las ol lor*) Three syllables. The *o* is likely long, while the other two vowels remain short. The two *l*s combine into a single sound, as in the English word *lesson*.

(**Dee—las óllor*) See the *48 Claves*. Here, Dee placed an accent over the second syllable.

Lava (lav-ah) *n.* Fervency / Humility?*

Note:

(**Dee—Laua Zuraah = Use humility in prayers to God, that is fervently pray. It signifieth, Pray Unto God.*) See the *Five Books*, p. 324. Between lines 46 and 47 of Table One of *Loagaeth*, some kind of stormy interference erupted in the shewstone. A voice then said the phrase "*Laua Zuraah.*" The two men then prayed as instructed, and the interference cleared. It would appear that *Laua* indicates a specific attitude in prayer, which might mean fervency or humility. I don't believe *Laua* would be the standard Angelical word for either "fervent" or "humility."

Also compare this word to the name of the Part of the Earth (and its Angelic Governor), *Lauacon*.

Compare from *Loagaeth*:

Lauax

Lcapimao (el-kay-PII-may-oh)* [L + "Capimao"] *comp.* One While

30.106 . . . *one while* let her be known . . .

Pronunciation notes:

(**Dee—L ca pí ma o*) Five syllables, with an accent on the third syllable. The initial *L* and the final *o* each stand alone. Finally, I assume the *a* in the fourth syllable is long, because it is followed by an *o*.

(**Dee—L capîmao*) See the *48 Claves*. Here, Dee placed a circumflex over the *i* to indicate its long sound.

Lea (lee-ay) *prop. n.* "The Sixteenth Aethyr"

30.3 . . . which dwell in *the sixteenth aethyr* . . .

Note:

This (word 30.3) is the single space in the Key of the Aethyrs, which must be changed for each invocation—replacing word 30.3 with the name of the appropriate Aethyr. No established definitions were given for these names.

Lea contains the three Parts of the Earth *Cucarpt*, *Lauacon*, and *Sochial*.

Lel (el-el)* [L + El] *adv.* Same

30.73 . . . no creature upon or within her *the same* . . .

Pronunciation notes:

(**Dee—Lel*) Dee gives us little clue here. This could be a word of one or two syllables, depending on whether or not the initial *L* should stand alone. Since I have assumed this is a compound involving the word *L* (first), I have decided to allow the initial *L* to stand alone. (Note I have also assumed the *e* is a phonetic gloss.)

Note:

The basic concepts behind *L*/*El* are both "beginning" and "singularity." Thus, I feel it is important that it appears twice in this word—to indicate that two (or more) things are actually "one" (the same).

The word *same* can be an adjective, pronoun, or adverb, depending on use. Here in Key Thirty, it is used as an adverb.

Note:

Also see *Parach* (equal).

Lephe (leef-ay) n/a*

Note:

(**Dee—Life Lephe Lurfando is a strong charge to the wicked to tell the truth. This [the Angel] said to my demand of this phrase whereof I had mention many years since.*) See the *Five Books*, p. 308. *Life Lephe Lurfando* is a perfect phrase for use in goetic evocations, but we are never given specific definitions for each word.

(**Dee—Pinzu-a lephe ganiurax kelpadman pacaph.*) See the *Five Books*, p. 413. Kelley overhears many voices singing a song at some distance, and these are the words Dee recorded. No translations are suggested.

Compare from *Loagaeth*:

Lefa, Lefe, Leph, Life

Levithmong (lev-ith-mong)* *n.* Beasts of the Field

30.99 Let them become caves for *the beasts of the field.*

Pronunciation notes:

(**Dee—Levith mong*) Three syllables. I assume *mong* rhymes with the English word *song.*

Note:

The similarity between this word and *Leviathan*. Leviathan is a mythical sea creature mentioned in biblical literature (especially *1 Enoch*), who is destined to battle a mighty land creature named *Behemoth* during the End Times (apparently representing a clash of land and sea). It would appear that *Levithmong* (beasts of the field) is a combination of the *Leviathan* and *Behemoth* concepts.

Lialprt (el-YAL-purt)* [L + "Ialprt"] *comp.* First Flame

15.3 . . . the governer of *the First Flame* . . .

Note:

The transmission of Key Fifteen is missing from Dee's journals. We only have the English given for the Key on *TFR*, p. 193. However, Illemese gives the pronunciation later on *TFR*, p. 200. Plus, the word appears in Dee's *48 Claves*.

Pronunciation notes:

(**Illemese—L al purt*) See *TFR*, p. 200. Three syllables. Though Illemese seems to have dropped the sound of the *i*, I think this is merely because it barely makes a sound when this word is spoken fluently. I have retained it (sounding as "y") in my pronunciation.

(**Dee—Liálprt*) See the *48 Claves*. Here, Dee placed an accent over the *a* in the second syllable.

Life (liif) n/a*

Note:

(**Dee—Life Lephe Lurfando is a strong charge to the wicked to tell the truth. This [the Angel] said to my demand of this phrase whereof I had mention many years since.*) See the *Five Books*, p. 308. *Life Lephe Lurfando* is a perfect phrase for use in goetic evocations, but we are never given specific definitions for each word.

Compare from *Loagaeth*:

Lefa, Lefe, Leph, Life

Lil (el-il)* *prop. n.* "The First Aethyr"

30.3 . . . which dwell in *the first aethyr* . . .

Pronunciation notes:

(**Dee—Lil*) Dee gives us little clue here. This could be a word of one or two syllables—depending on if the initial *L* should stand alone. Because this word indicates the First Aethyr and likely has *L* (the first) as its root, I will assume the *L* should stand alone.

Note:

Lil is the name—probably of a descriptive nature—of the first of the thirty Aethyrs. It holds the single space in the Key of the Aethyrs, which must be changed for each invocation, replacing Lil with the name of the next Aethyr, and then the next, and so on.

Lil contains the three Parts of the Earth *Occodon*, *Pascomb*, and *Valgars*.

Probable root:
L (el) — First

Lilonon (lii-loh-non)* *n.* — Branches

10.10 . . . whose *branches* are 22 nests . . .

Pronunciation notes:
(**Dee—Li lo non*) Three syllables. The *i* and the first *o* both appear to take their long sounds.
(**Dee—Lilônon*) See the *48 Claves*. Here, Dee uses a circumflex over the first *o* to indicate its long sound.

Limlal (lim-lal)* *n.* — Treasure

9.34 . . . as the rich man doth *his treasure*.

Pronunciation notes:
(**Dee—Lim lal*) Two syllables. Both vowels appear to take their short sounds.

Lin (lin) *prop. n.* — "The Twenty-Second Aethyr"

30.3 . . . which dwell in *the twenty-second aethyr* . . .

Note:
This (word 30.3) is the single space in the Key of the Aethyrs, which must be changed for each invocation—replacing word 30.3 with the name of the appropriate Aethyr. No established definitions were given for these names.

Lin contains the three Parts of the Earth *Ozidaia*, *Paraoan*, *Calzirg*.

Lit (lit) *prop. n.* "The Fifth Aethyr"

30.3 . . . which dwell in *the fifth aethyr* . . .

Note:

This (word 30.3) is the single space in the Key of the Aethyrs, which must be changed for each invocation—replacing word 30.3 with the name of the appropriate Aethyr. No established definitions were given for these names.

Lit contains the three Parts of the Earth *Lazdixi*, *Nocamal*, and *Tiarpax*.

Lnibm (el-nib-em)* [L + "Nibm"] *comp.* One Season

30.64 . . . *one season*, let it confound another . . .

Pronunciation notes:

(**Dee—L nib m*) Three syllables. The *L* and *m* each stand alone.

"Lo" (loh) *n.* The First

Compounds:

Bazemlo (bas-em-loh) [Bazem + "Lo"] The Midday the First
Talo (tay-el-oh) [Ta + "Lo"] As the First

Also:

L (el) First
El (el) The First
La (lah or el-ah) First
Lu (loo) From One

Possible root for:

Aqlo (AY-kwah-loh) Thy
Bolp (bohlp) Be Thou
Ol (ohl) I

Loagaeth (loh-gah)* *n.* Speech from God**

Pronunciation note:

(**Dee, recording the words of Galvah—"Touching the Book, it shall be called Logah: which in your language signifieth Speech from God. Write [it] after this sort: L O A G A E T H: it is to be sounded Logah. This word is of great signification, I mean in respect of the profoundness thereof."*) See *TFR*, p. 19. In Early Modern English, the *oa* letter combination makes a long "o" sound (as in the English words *boat* and *coat*). Dee recorded Galvah's phonetic explanation by dropping the *a* (*it shall be called Logah*). At the same time, we see that the final *eth* are entirely silent.

Note:

**This is the name of the Holy Book of forty-nine Tables transmitted to Dee and Kelley by the Archangel Raphael. It also appears as the first word of the forty-ninth Table in the Holy Book (see "Compare from *Loagaeth*" below).

Note the similarity between the Angelical *Loagaeth*, the Greek *Logos* (Word), and the Hebrew *Eth* (Spirit). It is interesting that both *Loagaeth* and *Logos* indicate "word/speech" and both are used in the biblical sense (as a reference to the God-Christ—see John 1, "In the Beginning was the Word . . . and the Word was God.").

Possible shared root:

Logaah (loh-gay-ah) n/a

Compare from *Loagaeth*:

Loagaeth, Loangah, Loggahah

Loe (loh-ee) *prop. n.* "The Twelfth Aethyr"

30.3 . . . which dwell in *the twelfth aethyr* . . .

Note:

This (word 30.3) is the single space in the Key of the Aethyrs, which must be changed for each invocation—replacing word 30.3 with the name of the appropriate Aethyr. No established definitions were given for these names.

Loe contains the three Parts of the Earth *Tapamal, Gedoons*, and *Ambriol.*

Logaah (loh-gay-ah) — n/a

Possibly also:

Loagaeth (loh-gah) — Speech from God

Note:

See *TFR*, p. 22. Here, the guardian Angel of Lord Lasky of Poland says a prayer on Lasky's behalf, which ends with, *"Grant this Camascheth galsuagath garnastel zurah logaah luseroth."* No translation is offered.

Loholo (LOH-hoh-loh)* *v.* — To Shine

1.61 . . . which *shineth as* a flame . . .

Pronunciation notes:

(**Dee—Call it Loholo. Long, the first syllable accented*) I assume that Dee intended all the *o*'s in this word to be long.

(**Dee—lóhôlo*) See *48 Claves*. The accent and circumflex match Dee's note from *TFR*.

"Lolcis" (LOL-sis) *n.* — Bucklers

Compounds:

Talolcis (tay-LOL-sis) [Ta + "Lolcis"] — As Bucklers

Loncho (lon-koh)* *v.* — To Fall

8.30 . . . until this house *fall* and the dragon sink.

Pronunciation notes:

(**Dee—Lon cho or ko*) Two syllables. Dee indicates that the *ch* takes the harder "k" (or "kh") sound.

Note:

Also see *Dobix* (to fall).

Compare from *Loagaeth*:
Onchen

Londoh (lon-DOH)* *n.* Kingdoms

7.24 Whose *kingdoms* and continuance are as . . .

Pronunciation notes:
(**Dee—Lon dóh*) This appears to be two syllables, with an accent upon the second syllable.
(**Dee—londóh*) See *48 Claves*. Accent still on the second syllable.

Compounds:
Oslondoh (os-LON-doh) [Os + Londoh] 12 Kingdoms

Note:
The similarity between this word and the word *London*. Dee was very dedicated to the cause of the English empire—and many scholars suspect this word of bias on Dee's part rather than the Angels. For a parallel case, see *Madrid* (iniquity).

Also:
Adohi (ay-DOH-hii) Kingdom

Compare from *Loagaeth*:
Doh, Dohoh

Lonsa (lon-sha)* *n.* Power

3.37 . . . *power* successively over 456 . . .

Pronunciation notes:
(**Dee—Lonsa*) Likely two syllables. Based on the other versions of this word, I assume the *s* should make the *sh* digraph.

Also:
Lansh (lonsh) Exalted Power
Lonshi (lon-shii) Power
"Lonshin" (lon-shin) Powers

Lonshi (lon-shii)* *n.* Power

7.45 . . . this remembrance is given *power* . . .

Pronunciation notes:

(**Dee—Lon shi*) Two syllables. The *o* should be a short vowel, while the final *i* likely takes a long sound.

Compounds:

Lonshitox (lon-shii-toks) [Lonshi + Tox] His Power

Also:

Lansh (lonsh) Exalted Power

Lonsa (lon-sha) Power

"Lonshin" (lon-shin) Powers

"Lonshin" (lon-shin) *n.* Powers

Compounds:

Odlonshin (ohd-lon-shin) [Od + "Lonshin"] And Powers

Also:

Lansh (lonsh) Exalted Power

Lonsa (lon-sha) Power

Lonshi (lon-shii) Power

Lonshitox (lon-shii-toks)* [Lonshi + Tox] *comp.* His Power

13.18 . . . God and *his power* . . .

Pronunciation notes:

(**Dee—Lon shi tox*) Three syllables. The *i* is the only apparent long vowel.

(**Dee—Lon-shi-tox*) See the *48 Claves*. This note essentially matches that of *TFR*.

Lorslq (lors-el-kwah)* *n.* Flowers

2.1 . . . as *the flowers* in their beauty . . .

Pronunciation notes:

(**Dee—Lors l qua*) Three syllables, with the *l* and the *q* standing alone. (The *q* takes the sound of "kwah.")

(**Dee—lors-l-q*) See *48 Claves*. This note matches Dee's note from *TFR*.

Lpatralx (el-PAY-tralks)* [L + "Patralx"] *comp.* One Rock

10.57 . . . *one rock* bringeth forth 1000 . . .

Pronunciation notes:

(**Dee—L Pá tralx El*) Three syllables. The initial L stands alone, and Dee indicates that it sounds like "El." The first *a* is likely a long vowel. The accent is place on the second syllable.

Lrasd (el-RAZD)* *v.* To Dispose (To Place)

30.34 . . . *to dispose* all things according to . . .

Pronunciation notes:

(**Dee—L rásd*) Two syllables, with an accent on the second syllable. The intial *L* stands alone.

(**Dee—Lrásd*) See the *48 Claves*. Here, Dee again placed an accent on the second syllable.

Lring (el-ring)* *v.* To Stir Up

13.6 . . . 42 eyes *to stir up* wrath of sin . . .

Pronunciation notes:

(**Dee—LRING*) Dee does not indicate that the *r* should take its extended "ur" sound. Therefore, I suspect the *L* should stand alone in this word, making two syllables.

Note:

See also *Zixlay* (to stir up). I am not sure why these two words have the same definition.

Lsmnad (els-mad)* [L + "Smnad"] *comp.* One Another

30.87 . . . vex and weed out *one another* . . .

Pronunciation notes:

(**Dee—Ls mnad*) This note seems confusing at first. Dee indicates two syllables, yet there are still clusters of consonants in each one. In the first syllable, I assume the *l* is pronounced "el"—which allows it to combine naturally with the *s*. In the second syllable, I suspect the *mn* combines to form the same sound as in the English words *column*, *autumn*, and *solemn* (i.e., the *n* is effectively silent).

Note:

Also see *Symp* (another).

Lu (loo) *prep.?* From One*

From *Loagaeth*:

(**Dee—Lu = From one.*) See the *Five Books*, p. 322.

Also:

L (el) The First, One
El (el) The First
La (lah or el-ah) The First
"Lo" (loh) The First

Compare from *Loagaeth*:

Uloh

Luas (loo-akh)* *prop. n.* Those Who Praise (or, the Triumphant)

From *Corpus Omnium*:

Associated with the pre-Deluge quadrant of the Table, translated in Latin as *Laudantes* (Those Who Praise). They can alternately be called *Trimphantes* (Those Who Triumph).

Pronunciation notes:
(**Dee—Luach.*) Dee seems to note here that *Luas*, when spoken, should be ended with a throaty "kh" sound (like the *ch* in ache), instead of an "s" sound.

Compare from *Loagaeth*:
Luah

Lucal (loo-kal)* *n.* North

10.6 . . . harboured *in the north* in the likeness . . .

Pronunciation notes:
(**Dee—Lu cal*) Two syllables. The *u* takes its long sound. I assume the *c* takes its hard ("k") sound.

Luciftian (loo-sif-TII-an)* *n.* (Ornaments of) Brightness

7.19 . . . they are appareled with *ornaments of brightness* . . .

Pronunciation notes:
(**Dee—Lu cif tí an*) Four syllables, with an accent on the third syllable. I assume the *c* takes the soft sound, as in the Latin word *Lucifer*.

Also:
Luciftias (loo-SIF-tii-as) Brightness

Note:
The similarity between this word and the Latin *Lucifer* (light-bearer). See *Luciftias* (brightness) for more info.

Luciftias (loo-SIF-tii-as)* *n.* Brightness

30.20 . . . whose eyes are *the brightness of* the heavens . . .

Pronunciation notes:
(**Dee—Lu cíf ti as*) Four syllables, with an accent on the second syllable. The *c* should take the soft ("s") sound, as in the Latin word *Lucifer*.

(**Dee—Lucíftîas*) See the *48 Claves*. Here, Dee again placed the accent on the second syllable. He also placed a circumflex over the second *i* to indicate its long sound.

Also:

Luciftian (loo-sif-TII-an) (Ornaments of) Brightness

Note:

The similarity between this word and the Latin *Lucifer* (light-bearer). In Roman mythology, Lucifer was the name of the Venus star—which rose in the east just before dawn, thus heralding the approaching Sun. In Christian lore, Lucifer was the first and most beautiful among the Angels, but was cast down for his pride. The Angelical word *Luciftias* still represents brightness in the Heavens, and has no demonic connotations.

Luiahe (loo-JAY-hee)* *n.* Song of Honor

6.40 . . . whose works shall be *a song of honour* . . .

Pronunciation notes:

(**Dee—Lu ía he*) Three syllables, with an accent on the second syllable. Dee does not tell us if the *i* should take the sound of "y" or "j." (I have settled upon the "j" sound., and spelled the word in Angelical with a Ged [J] in this place.) The final *e* is also uncertain. It should remain silent while making the *a* a long vowel. However, Dee's phonetic note indicates three syllables—for which the *e* must make a sound along with the *h*. Whether the *e* should be long or short is unclear, although I have settled upon the long sound.

(**Dee—Lu-iá-he*) See the *48 Claves*. This note matches that from *TFR*.

Note:

Also see *Faaip* (voicing/psalm).

Lulo (loo-loh) *n.* Tartar (Mother of Vinegar)

From the *Alchemical Cipher*:

See *TFR*, pp. 387–89. The Angel *Levanael* says of this word, "*Roxtan* is pure and simple wine in herself. *Lulo* is her mother." Dee replies,

"There may be in these words some ambiguity." So *Levanael* explains more simply, "*Lulo* is Tartar, simply of red wine." (Tartar is Mother of Vinegar.)

It is not likely that *Lulo* is strictly tartar of *red* wine—but *Levanael* had established earlier in this session that red *Roxtan* (wine) was to be used for this alchemical experiment.

Lurfando (lur-fan-doh) n/a*

Note:

(**Dee—Life Lephe Lurfando is a strong charge to the wicked to tell the truth. This [the Angel] said to my demand of this phrase whereof I had mention many years since.*) See the *Five Books*, p. 308. *Life Lephe Lurfando* is a perfect phrase for use in goetic evocations, but we are never given specific definitions for each word.

In at least one case, Dee wrote that a *u* could make the sound of "f"—which was likely an indication of the "v" sound. Therefore, it is possible that *Lurfando* and *Lurvandah* are related.

Compare from *Loagaeth*:

Lurvandah

Lusd (lus-dee)* *n.* (Your) Feet

2.25 . . . stronger are *your feet* than the barren stone.

Pronunciation notes:

(**Dee—Lusd*) It would appear the one syllable is intended here. However, other versions of this word all have two syllables.

Also:

Lasdi (las-dii)	(My) Feet
Lusda (lus-da)	(Their) Feet
Lusdan (lus-dan)	(With) Feet

Lusda (lus-da)* *n.* (Their) Feet

9.21 . . . have settled *their feet* in the west . . .

Pronunciation notes:
(**Dee—Lus da*) Two syllables.

Also:
Lasdi (las-dii) (My) Feet
Lusd (lus-dee) (Your) Feet
Lusdan (lus-dan) (With) Feet

Lusdan (lus-dan)* *n.* (With) Feet

16.13 . . . which walkest upon the earth *with feet* 876 . . .

Pronunciation notes:
(**Dee—Lus dan*) Two syllables.

Also:
Lasdi (las-dii) (My) Feet
Lusd (lus-dee) (Your) Feet
Lusda (lus-da) (Their) Feet

Luseroth (lus-er-oth) n/a

Note:
See *TFR*, p. 22. Here, the guardian Angel of Lord Lasky of Poland says a prayer on Lasky's behalf, which ends with, "Grant this *Camascheth galsuagath garnastel zurah logaah luseroth*." No translation is offered.

Compare from *Loagaeth*:
Luseth, Luza, Luzan, Luzath, Luzed, Lusaz, Luzez, Uzed

"Lzar" (el-ZAR) *n.* — Courses

Compounds:

Sobolzar (soh-BOL-zar) ["Sobo" + "Lzar"] — Whose Courses

Also:

"Elzap" (el-ZAP) — Course

"Lzirn" (el-zirn) *n.* — Wonders

Compounds:

Vaulzirn (VOL-zern) ["Vau" + "Lzirn"] — Work Wonders

Note:

See also *Sald* (wonder), *Busd* (glory), and *Peleh* (Worker of Wonders?).

Also compare to the name of the Angel *Lzinopo*, an Elder of the Southern Watchtower. Perhaps his name means something akin to "He Who Works Wonders." Also compare to the name of the Angel *Iznr* or *Izinr*, an Angel of medicine also of the Southern Watchtower.

Tal (M)

M (em)* *conj.* or *prep.* Except

3.22 . . . *except (by)* mine own hand . . .

Pronunciation notes:

(*Dee—EM it is a word*) Likely just one syllable.

Note:

See Oq (but), "Crp" (but).

Maasi (may-ay-sii)* *v.* Laid Up (i.e., Stored Up)

10.17 . . . and weeping *laid up* for the earth . . .

Pronunciation notes:

(*Dee—Ma a si*) Three syllables. The double *a* should represent a long "a" sound in Early Modern English. Dee's note indicates two long *a*'s, but they nearly blend into one when this word is spoken fluently. The final *i* is likely long.

(*Dee—maâsi*) See the *48 Claves*. Here, Dee places a circumflex over the second *a* to indicate its long sound.

Mabberan (MAB-er-an) *adv.* How Now(?)*

Pronunciation notes:

The first *a* of *Mabberan* is accented in Dee's journal. Also, I assume the first *a* takes its short sound, because it is followed by a double *b* (similar to the *a* in the English words *rabble* or *babble*).

Note:

(* *Vors Mabberan = how now: what hast thou to do with us?*) See the *Five Books*, p. 311. Here, several spirits appear and demand of Dee and Kelley, "*Vors Mabberan?*"—to which Dee makes his marginal notation above. Given the known definition of *Vors* (over, especially in a hierarchy), I assume this phrase is a challenge, as if to say, "What authority do you have over us?" On its own, it is possible that *Mabberan* has some meaning akin to "What do you want?" or "Why have you bothered us?"

Mabza (MAB-za)* *n.* — Coat

8.43 . . . and *the coat of* him that is . . .

Pronunciation notes:

(**Dee—Mab za*) Two syllables.

(**Dee—mábza*) See the *48 Claves*. Here, Dee adds an accent to the first syllable.

Mad (mad)* *n.* — (Your) God, Pure/Undefiled

(RFP) . . . servant of *the same your God* . . .
3.60 . . . in the name of *the same your God* . . .
6.42 . . . the praise of *your God* . . .
13.16 . . . behold the promise of *God* . . .
30.15 . . . behold the face of *your God* . . .

Pronunciation notes:

(**Dee 1.84—Call it Mad.*)

(**Dee 3.60; 6.42; 13.16, 30.15—Mad.*)

Compounds:

Madzilodarp (mad-ZII-loh-darp) [Mad + "Zilodarp"] — God of Conquest

Iadnamad (yad-nay-mad) [Iadnah + Mad?] — Pure Knowledge

Probable root for:

"Madriax" (MAY-drii-yaks) — Heavens

Madriiax (MAY-drii-yaks) — Heavens

Madrid (MAY-drid) — Iniquity

Note:

The proper Name of God in Angelical is *Iad*. *Mad*, on the other hand, indicates *god* in the generic sense. The word *your* is not directly indicated by the Angelical—though the change in spelling adequately suggests *some other god* as opposed to Iad Himself.

At the same time, note that Mad is used as a root in several cases to indicate things celestial or divine (*Iadnamad*, *"Madriax,"* and the antonymic *Madrid*).

Also see *Piad* (your God).

"Madriax"* (MAY-drii-yaks) *n.* Heavens

Note:

(**Dee—I think this word wanted as may appear by Madriax, about 44 words from the end.*) "Madriax" does not appear with this spelling in the Keys in *TFR*. Apparently, Dee did not receive the first word of the Key of the Aethyrs (word 30.1) until sometime after its transmission. (Illemese, who revealed this Key, gave only the English "O you heavens," but gave no Angelical for the phrase.) Dee found the proper word later in the Key—*Madriiax* (word 30.116). After adding *Madriiax* (with the *double i*) into space 30.1, Dee made the above note in the margin, spelling the word as *Madriax* (with a *single i*). However, also note the word *Oadriax* (lower Heavens) which also uses a single *i*—so this spelling, *Madriax*, is likely acceptable.

Pronunciation notes:

(**Dee 30.1—Madrîax*) See the *48 Claves*. Here, Dee spelled the word with only one *i*. He also placed a circumflex over the *i* to indicate its long sound.

See pronunciation notes for *Madriiax* (Heavens).

Also:

Madriiax (MAY-drii-yaks) Heavens

Oadriax (oh-AY-drii-aks) Lower Heavens

Probable root:

Mad (mad) (Your) God, "Pure/Undefiled"

Madriiax (MAY-drii-yaks)* *n.* Heavens

30.1 *O you heavens* that dwell in the first Aethyr . . .

30.116 *O you heavens*, arise!

Pronunciation notes:

(**Dee 30.116—Má dri iax yax*) Three syllables, accent on the first syllable. The double *i* probably results in a long "i" sound in the second syllable. Dee places a "y" sound at the beginning of the third syllable, but it is barely audible when the word is spoken fluently.

(**Dee 30.1—Madrîax*) See the *48 Claves*. Here, Dee spelled the word with only one *i*. (See note at "Madriax.") He also placed a circumflex over the *i* to indicate its long sound.

(**Dee 30.116—Mádrîiax*) See the *48 Claves*. Here, Dee again placed an accent over the first syllable. He also placed a circumflex over the first *i* to indicate its long sound.

Note:

Note that the Heavens, in this case, are being addressed as living creatures. This is common in mystical systems such as Gnosticism or the Qabalah—where the Heavens (*Aeons*, *Sephiroth*) are treated as *both* celestial spheres and intelligent beings.

The Key of the Aethyrs is the only place where the Heavens are addressed as intelligent. Elsewhere, the standard word for "the Heavens" is *Piripsol/Piripson*.

Also see *Calz* (firmaments).

Also:

"Madriax" (MAY-drii-yaks)	Heavens
Oadriax (oh-AY-drii-aks)	Lower Heavens

Probable root:

Mad (mad)	(Your) God, Pure/Undefiled

Note:

Also see *Piripsol/Piripson* (The Heavens).

Madrid (MAY-drid)* *n.* Iniquity

9.38 Cursed are they whose *iniquities* they are.

10.75 . . . for *her iniquity* is, was, and shall be great.

Pronunciation notes:

(*Dee 9.38; 10.75—Ma drid*) Two syllables. The *a* should take a long sound. The *dr* combine into a single sound, as in the English words *drive* and *drop*.

I have adopted the accent from similar words.

Probable root:

Mad (mad) (Your) God, "Pure / Undefiled"

Note:

The similarities between this word and the city of Madrid, the capital of Spain. Dee was very dedicated to the cause of the English empire, and Spain was in contention with England, as Dee recorded his journals. Therefore, many scholars suspect this word of bias on Dee's part rather than the Angels. For a parallel case, see *Londoh* (kingdom).

Madzilodarp (mad-ZII-loh-darp)* [Mad + "Zilodarp"] *comp.*

God of Conquest

16.21 . . . great art thou in *the God of stretch forth and conquer* . . .

Pronunciation notes:

(*Dee—Mad zí lo darp*) Four syllables, with an accent on the second syllable. The *i* and the *o* each take their long sounds.

Note:

I have simplified "stretch forth and conquer" into the obvious definition of "conquest."

"Mal" (mal) *n.* Thrust, Arrow, Increase

Compounds:

Malprg (mal-purj) ["Mal" + "Prg"] Through-thrusting Fire (i.e., Fiery Arrow)

Malpurg (mal-purj) ["Mal" + "Purg"] Fiery Arrows

Malpirgi (mal-per-jii) ["Mal" + "Pirgi"] Fires of Life and Increase

Note:

These words appear to show that "Mal" indicates the idea of arrows, rising, shooting, increase, etc.
Also see *Coazior* (increase).

Also note the Angel *Dmal*, one of the Sons of Light. "Mal" (arrow, increase) appears to be the root of his name.

Compare from *Loagaeth*:
Mal

Malpirgi (mal-per-jii)* ["Mal" + "Pirgi"] *comp.* — Fires of Life and Increase

3.52 . . . pouring down *the Fires of Life and Increase* . . .

Pronunciation notes:

(**Dee—Malpirgi*) Likely three syllables, with a long *i* at the end. Also, the first *i* in *Malpirgi* is likely a phonetic gloss. See *Malprg* and *Malpurg*.

Also:

Malprg (mal-purj) ["Mal" + "Prg"] — Through-thrusting Fire (i.e., Fiery Arrow)
Malpurg (mal-purj) ["Mal" + "Purg"] — Fiery Arrows

Malprg (mal-purj)* ["Mal" + "Prg"] *comp.* — Through-thrusting Fire (i.e., Fiery Arrow)

1.18 . . . the moon is *a through-thrusting fire* . . .

Pronunciation notes:

(**Dee—Malprg, as Malpurg*) Dee here shows us where to place the vowel sound. *Malprg* is likely the radical spelling of this word. See *Malpurg*, *Prge*, and *Malpirgi* for phonetic glosses. (The case of *Prge*—which follows the *g* with an *e* phonetic gloss—gives the final *g* its soft sound.)

Also:

Malpirgi (mal-per-jii) ["Mal" + "Pirgi"] — Fires of Life and Increase
Malpurg (mal-purj) ["Mal" + "Purg"] — Fiery Darts (Arrows)

Malpurg (mal-purj)* ["Mal" + "Purg"] *comp.* Fiery Darts/Arrows

6.16 . . . *fiery darts* to van the earth . . .

Pronunciation notes:

(**Dee—Mal purg*) Two syllables. The *u* is likely a phonetic gloss, and the final g should be soft. See pronunciation notes for *Malprg* and *Malpirgi.*

Also:

Malpirgi (mal-per-jii) ["Mal" + "Pirgi"] Fires of Life and Increase
Malprg (mal-purj) ["Mal" + "Prg"] Through-thrusting Fire (i.e., Fiery Arrow)

Mals (Makhls)* *prop. n.* Letter *P/Ph*

Note:

The name of the Angelical letter for *P/Ph*. It is likely that these letter names have translations of their own. (For instance, note the Hebrew alphabet: the letter *P/Ph* is named *Peh*, but *Peh* also translates as "mouth.") However, such translations for the Angelical letters are never given. (See the *Five Books*, p. 270.)

Pronunciation notes:

(**Dee—In sound machls.*) This is likely a soft "kh" sound (like the *ch* in *ache*, only softer) made just before the *"l"* sound. However, *Mals* is only one syllable. I tend to pronounce this word along the lines of "mahls."

Compare from *Loagaeth*:

Mals

Manin (man-in)* *n.* (In the) Mind

2.38 . . . but *in the mind of* the All Powerful.

Pronunciation note:

(**Dee—Manin*) Likely two syllables.

Maoffas (may-AHF-fas)* *adj.* Measureless

18.23 . . . in thy kingdom Joy, and *not to be measured.*

Pronunciation notes:

(**Dee—ma óf fas*) Three syllables, with an accent on the second syllable. The first *a* should be long and the *o* should be short, as in the English word *chaos*. The two *f*'s should combine into one sound, as we see in Early Modern English.

(**Dee—maóffas*) See the *48 Claves*. Here, Dee again indicated the accent on the second syllable.

MAPM (map-em)* 9639

4.15 I have placed *9639* whom none hath yet . . .

Pronunciation notes:

(**Dee—Map m*) Two syllables, the final *m* stands alone.

Mapsama (map-sam-a) *prop. n.* He That Speaks*

Note:

(**Dee records the words of Mapsama: "My name is called He That Speaks. I am one under Gabriel, and the name of Jesus I know and honour. My name is Mapsama."*) See *TFR*, pp. 138–39, 145ff. The names of most of the Angels encountered by Dee and Kelley can be found in other parts of the Angelic system—such as the Heptarchia or Great Table (Watchtower) systems. However, Mapsama is one of the few entirely unique Angels to appear to the two men. Mapsama appears to be connected to the political ambitions of Lord Lasky of Poland. He is also the Angel who delivered the instructions for the Book of Silver, which Dee never accomplished. (See also *Ga, Galvah, Murifri, Nalvage, Vaa,* and *Za.*)

Marb (marb)* *adj.* According to

30.36 . . . all things *according to* the providence . . .

Pronunciation notes:

(*Dee—Marb*) One syllable.

Marmara (mar-mar-a) *prop. n.* n/a

Note:

This is a variation of Carmara, the title of the ruling King of the *Heptarchia*. See the entry for *Carmara*.

Possible shared root:

Carma (kar-ma) To Come Out/To Arise

Masch (mask) n/a

Note:

See *TFR*, pp. 34–35. This session is recorded entirely in Latin. Here we find this Angelical phrase spoken by "a Voice": "*Garil zed masch, ich na gel galaht gemp gal noch Cabanladan.*" No translation or context is offered.

Pronunciation note:

The *sch* letter combination should sound like "sk" (as in *school*). Note, also, that in the *Book of Loagaeth*, Dee gives the pronunciation for the word *Zuresch* as "zuresk"—further indicating the "sk" sound for *sch*.

Compare from *Loagaeth*:

Iemasch, Asch, Ascha, Aschah, Aschal, Ascham, Asche, Aschedh, Aschem, Ascheph, Aschi, Aschin, Aschma, Aschol, and probably *Dasch, Gascheth, Hasche, Pasch, Pascha, Pascheph, and maybe Iemasch, Surascha, Vascheth*

"Matastos" (MAT-az-tos) n/a

From *Loagaeth*:

See note at *Donasdogamatastos*.

Compounds:

Donadogamatastos (doh-NAS-dog-ay-MAT-az-tos)

["*Donasdoga*" + "*Matastos*"] "Hellfire"

Matb (may-teb) *n.* One Thousand (1000)

10.45 . . . and *a thousand* times as many surges . . .
10.59 One rock bringeth forth *1000* . . .

Pronunciation notes:

Dee provided no phonetic notes for this word. See the pronunciation notes for *Matorb* (long, as in "period of time").

Note:

I suspect this is the word for "one thousand" rather than the numeral *1000*. Compare to *Torb* (one hundred) and *Matorb* (long period of time).

This word was not originally given with Key Ten. It was added later when Nalvage transmitted the English for the Key (see *TFR*, p. 192). This seems to have been the case with many of the numbers mentioned in the Keys.

Compounds:

Matorb (may-torb) [Matb + Torb] Long (Period of Time)

Matorb (may-torb)* [Matb + Torb] *comp.* Long (Period of Time)

10.54 . . . neither know any *(long)* time here.

Pronunciation notes:

(**Dee—Ma torb*) Two syllables. The *a* should take its long sound.

Note:

There was no English given for *Matorb* in Dee's journals. However, it appears that the word is a compound of *Matb* (one thousand) and *Torb* (one hundred)—thus suggesting that the word is intended to indicate "a very long time." Similar, perhaps, to the Egyptian phrase "millions of years," which can indicate an eternity.

Maz (maz) *prop. n.* "The Sixth Aethyr"

30.3 . . . which dwell in *the sixth aethyr* . . .

Note:
This (word 30.3) is the single space in the Key of the Aethyrs, which must be changed for each invocation—replacing word 30.3 with the name of the appropriate Aethyr. No established definitions were given for these names.

Maz contains the three Parts of the Earth *Saxtomp*, *Vavaamp*, and *Zirzird*.

Compare from *Loagaeth*:
Maz, Mazad

Med (med) *prop. n.* Letter *O*

Note:
The name of the Angelical letter for *O*. It is likely that these letter names have translations of their own. (For instance, note the Hebrew alphabet: the letter *O* is named *Vav*, but *Vav* also translates as "stake" or "nail.") However, such translations for the Angelical letters are never given. (See the *Five Books*, p. 270.)
(*Dee—He said, Great is His Glory.*) This is not likely a translation of the word *Med*. See the letter *Ged*, where another invocation is made along with the delivery of a letter.

Miam (mii-AM)* *n.* Continuance

6.27 . . . in government and *continuance*.

Pronunciation notes:
(**Dee—Miam*) This is likely two syllables. Dee gives us little clue, but I assume the *i* should take a long sound.
(**Dee—miám*) See the *48 Claves*. Here, Dee places an accent over the *a* in the second syllable.

Compounds:
Odmiam (ohd-mii-AM) [Od + Miam] And Continuance

Also:

"Mian" Continuance

Note:

Seems to indicate "lifespan" or "continued existence."

"Mian" (mii-AN) *n.* Continuance

Pronunciation note:

I have adopted the accent from *Miam* (continuance).

Compounds:

Solamian (soh-LAY-mii-an) ["Sola" + "Mian"] Whose Continuance

Also:

Miam (mii-AM) Continuance

MIAN (mii-AN)* 3663

12.15 . . . bring down your train *3663* that the Lord . . .

Pronunciation notes:

(**Dee—Mi an*) Two syllables. The *I* likely takes its long sound.

Note:

This word was not originally given with Key Twelve. It was added later when Nalvage transmitted the English for the Key (see *TFR*, p. 193). This seems to have been the case with many of the numbers mentioned in the Keys.

Do not confuse this word with "Mian" from *Solamian* (whose continuance).

Micalp (mii-KALP)* *adj.* Mightier

2.28 . . . *mightier* are your voices . . .

Pronunciation notes:

(**Dee—Mi calp*) Two syllables. The *i* is likely a long vowel. Also see *Micalzo*, where the accent is placed on the second syllable.

Also:

Gmicalzo (jee-mii-KAYL-zoh) Power
Micalzo (mii-KAYL-zoh) Mighty
Micaoli (mii-KAY-oh-lii) Mighty
Micaolz (mii-KAY-ohlz or mii-KAY-ohl-zohd) Mighty
Omicaolz (oh-mii-KAY-ohl-zohd) (Be) Mighty

Possible shared root:

Miketh (mii-KETH) "The True Measure of the Will of God in Judgment, Which Is by Wisdom"(?)

Note:

Also see *Umadea* (strong towers), *Umplif* (strength), *Ugeg* (become strong), *Vohim* (mighty).

Micalzo (mii-KAYL-zoh)* *n. or adj.* Mighty / Power

2.46 . . . show yourselves *in power* . . .
6.5 . . . *mighty in* the firmaments of waters . . .
**18.2 . . . thou *mighty* light and burning flame . . .

Pronunciation notes:

(**Dee 2.46—Micalzo*)

(**Dee 6.5—Micálzo*) Likely three syllables, with an accent on the second syllable. Also see *Micaolz*, where the *i* of the first syllable and the *a* of the second syllable are long.

(**Dee 6.5—micálzo*) See the *48 Claves*. Again the accent is on the second syllable.

Note:

**Word 18.2 was originally given as *Micaolz* (mighty). However, see *TFR*, p. 200, where Illemese gives the alternate pronunciation of "micalZo" (or *Micalzo*).

Also:

Gmicalzo (jee-mii-KAYL-zoh) Power

Micalp (mii-KALP)	Mightier
Micaoli (mii-KAY-oh-lii)	Mighty
Micaolz (mii-KAY-ohlz or mii-KAY-ohl-zohd)	Mighty
Omicaolz (oh-mii-KAY-ohl-zohd)	(Be) Mighty

Possible shared root:

Miketh (mii-KETH) — "The True Measure of the Will of God in Judgment, Which Is by Wisdom"(?)

Note:

Also see *Umadea* (strong towers), *Umplif* (strength), *Ugeg* (become strong), *Vohim* (mighty).

Micaoli (mii-KAY-oh-lii)* *adj.* — Mighty

9.1 A *mighty* sound . . .

Pronunciation notes:

(**Dee—Mi ca o li*) Four syllables. All of the vowels in this word are indicated as long. They all fall at the ends of their syllables, and the *o* itself stands alone.

(**Dee—Mi-cá-ôli*) See the *48 Claves*. Here, Dee placed an accent on the second syllable. He also placed a circumflex over the *o* to indicate its long sound.

Also:

Gmicalzo (jee-mii-KAYL-zoh)	Power
Micalp (mii-KALP)	Mightier
Micalzo (mii-KAYL-zoh)	Mighty
Micaolz (mii-KAY-ohlz or mii-KAY-ohl-zohd)	Mighty
Omicaolz (oh-mii-KAY-ohl-zohd)	(Be) Mighty

Possible shared root:

Miketh (mii-KETH) — "The True Measure of the Will of God in Judgment, Which Is by Wisdom" (?)

Note:

Also see *Umadea* (strong towers), *Umplif* (strength), *Ugeg* (become strong), *Vohim* (mighty).

Micaolz (mii-KAY-ohlz or mii-KAY-ohl-zohd)* *adj.* — Mighty

3.70 . . . become *mighty* amongst us . . .
**18.2 . . . thou *mighty* light and burning flame . . .

Pronunciation notes:

(*Dee 3.70—Mi ca olz*)

(*Dee 18.2—Mi ca ol zod*) This word can be three or four syllables—depending on whether or not one extends the *z* to "zohd." (This word is further indication that the extended *z* is not a grammatical rule, but a phonetic flourish.) The *i* in the first syllable is likely long.

(*Dee 3.70—mi-cá-olz*) See the *48 Claves*. Dee places the accent on the second syllable.

(*Dee 18.2—Micaólz*) See the *48 Claves*. Here, Dee indicates the accent on the third syllable instead. Also note that he has dropped the extended "z" sound.

Note:

**For word 18.2, the Angel Illemese later gives an alternate pronunciation of "micalZo" (see *Micalzo*).

Compounds:

Chismicaolz (kiis-mii-KAY-ohlz) [Chis + Micaolz] — Are Mighty

Also:

Gmicalzo (jee-mii-KAYL-zoh) — Power
Micalp (mii-KALP) — Mightier
Micalzo (mii-KAYL-zoh) — Mighty*
Micaoli (mii-KAY-oh-lii) — Mighty
Omicaolz (oh-mii-KAY-ohl-zohd) — (Be) Mighty

Possible shared root:

Miketh (mii-KETH) — "The True Measure of the Will of God in Judgment, Which Is by Wisdom" (?)

Note:

Also see *Umadea* (strong towers), *Umplif* (strength), *Ugeg* (become strong), *Vohim* (mighty).

Micma (mik-ma)* *v.* Behold

3.1 . . . *Behold*, sayeth your God . . .
3.64 . . . *Behold*, his mysteries flourish . . .
13.14 . . . *Behold* the promise of God . . .
**14.17 . . . *Behold* the voice of God . . .
30.13 . . . *Behold* the face of your God . . .

Pronunciation notes:

(**Dee 3.1, 64—Micma*)

(**Dee 13.14—Mic ma*) Two syllables.

(**Dee 30.13—Micma Mikma*) The *c* has a hard ("k") sound.

Note:

**The transmission of Key Fourteen is missing from Dee's journals. We only have the English for this Key given later (see *TFR*, p. 193). Plus, the word appears in this location in Dee's *48 Claves*.

Miinoag (mii-ii-noh-ayg)* *n.* Corners (Boundaries)

3.46 . . . and *the corners* of your governments . . .

Pronunciation notes:

(**Dee—Mi i no ag*) This appears to be four syllables. Note that each *i* is pronounced, as we might see in Middle English.

(**Dee—miinoâg*) See the *48 Claves*. Dee placed a circumflex over the *a*, indicating its long sound.

Note:

Also see *Unalah* (skirts).

Miketh (mii-KETH) *n.* "The True Measure of the Will of God in Judgment, Which Is by Wisdom"(?)

Pronunciation note:

I have adopted the accent from similar words, such as *Micaolz* (mighty).

Note:

See the *Five Books*, p. 354. Here, the Angel Illemese says of the *Book of Soyga*, "*Soyga* signifieth not *Agyos. Soyga alca miketh.*" (*Agyos* is Greek for "holiness," and is *Soyga* when spelled backward.) When Dee asked what these words meant, he was told, "The True Measure of the Will of God in Judgment, Which Is by Wisdom." Based on context, I feel that the word *Alca* probably means "to signify"—while *Miketh* (related, perhaps by root, to *Micaolz*) is translated as "the True Measure of the Will of God, etc."

Perhaps this long definition could be shortened to "God's Will in Judgment."

Possible shared root:

Micaolz (mii-KAY-olz *or* mii-KAY-ol-zohd) Mighty

Mir (mir)* *n.* Torment

6.10 . . . hath planted *a torment to* the wicked . . .

Pronunciation notes:

(**Dee—Mir*) One syllable.

Note:

This word appears to be in noun form ("a torment"), rather than in verb form ("to torment").

Mirc (mirk)* *prep.* Upon

9.54 . . . and *upon* their heads are marble . . .

**14.7 . . . which sit *upon* 24 seats . . .

30.70 . . . no creature *upon* or within her . . .

Pronunciation notes:

(**Dee 9.54; 30.70—Mirc Mirk*) One syllable, with a hard *c* at the end.

Note:

**The transmission of Key Fourteen is missing from Dee's journals. We only have the English for this Key given later (see *TFR*, p. 193). Plus, the word appears in Dee's *48 Claves*.

Molvi (mol-vii)* *n.* Surges

10.48 . . . a thousand times as many *surges* . . .

Pronunciation notes:

(**Dee—Mol ui*) Two syllables. The *o* takes its short sound. Dee originally wrote this word with a *u*—but the letter should make a "v" sound when preceding a vowel.

Mom (mom)* *n.* Moss (i.e., Dross?)

9.29 . . . gather up *the moss* of the earth . . .

Pronunciation notes:

(**Dee—Mom*) One syllable. I suggest a short *o*.

Note:

I have seen it suggested that "moss of the earth" is a reference to the dead—but I have not verified that yet. I have found the word *moss* used poetically in many cases, as a synonym for *dross*. (As in, "A rolling stone gathers no moss" or "Clearing the moss from your mind.") In just one case, I have found the phrase "I wish he would gather moss"—which appears to be a reference to death.

Also note this word is a palindrome, reading the same forward and backward.

Momao (MOH-may-oh)* *n.* Crowns

8.40 . . . for *the crowns of* the Temple . . .

Pronunciation notes:

(**Dee—Mo ma o*) Three syllables. Both *o*'s and the *a* should likely take their long sounds.

(**Dee—mómâo*) See the *48 Claves*. Here, Dee added an accent on the first syllable. He also placed a circumflex over the *a* to indicate its long sound.

Also:

"Momar" (MOH-mar) To Crown

"Momar" (MOH-mar) *v.* To Crown

Pronunciation note:

I have adopted the accent from *Momao* (crowns).

Compounds:

Iadoiasmomar (jad-oh-JAS-moh-mar) ["Iadoias" + "Momar"] God Eternally Crowned

Also:

Momao (MOH-may-oh) Crowns

Monasci (mon-ay-sii) *n.* Great Name

15.13 . . . which knowest *the great name* Righteousness . . .

Pronunciation note:

I assume the *sci* letter combination is the same as in the words *science* or *scion*.

Note:

The transmission of Key Fifteen is missing from Dee's journals. We only have the English for this Key given later (see *TFR*, p. 193). Plus, the word appears in this location in Dee's *48 Claves*.

This likely indicates a Name of God.

Also see Dooain, which means *name* in the general sense.

Monons (moh-nons)* *n.* Heart

10.61 . . . *the heart of* man . . .

Pronunciation notes:
(**Dee—Mo nons*) Two syllables. The first *o* takes its long sound.

Moooah (moh-oh-WAH)* *v.* To Repent

30.104 For why? *It repenteth me* I made man.

Pronunciation notes:
(**Dee—Mo o Oah*) Three syllables. The second *o* stands alone. The third syllable is a bit obscure. The *oa* letter combination should make a long "o" sound (as in the English words *boat* and *coat*). However, Dee's phonetic note seems to indicate that the *a* should join with the *h*, leaving the preceding *o* to sound alone. Under that circumstance, the only way *Oah* could form one syllable is to sound like "wah." (Patricia Shaffer makes this suggestion in her *DeesPronunciationNotes.rtf.*)
(**Dee—Mooóâh*) See the *48 Claves*. Here, Dee placed an accent over the third *o* (which should be the third syllable). The *âh* should indicate a short "o" sound (as in the English words *father* and *fall*).

"Mospleh" (mos-play) *n.* Horns

Compounds:
Qmospleh (kwah-mos-play) [Q + "Mospleh"] Or the Horns

Moz (moz *or* moz-ohd)* *n.* Joy, Joy of God

18.21 . . . called in thy kingdom *Joy*.

Pronunciation notes:
(**Dee—Moz*) Dee originally wrote this word as "Qzmoz." However, his phonetic note excludes the letters *qz*. Likewise, Dee recorded the word as "MOZ" in his *48 Claves*.

This exclusion is further supported by the appearance of *Moz* (to rejoice) on the *Corpus Omnium* Table. There, Nalvage reveals that *Moz* can also be pronounced with an extended *z* (see below)—so perhaps "Qzmoz" was a botched attempt to record the extended version of *Moz*.

Also From *Corpus Omnium*:

(**Dee—I pray you, is Mozod, a word of three letters or of five?*
Nalvage: In wrote three, it is larger extended.
Dee: Z extended is Zod.
Nalvage: Moz in itself signifieth Joy, but Mozod extended, signifieth the Joy of God.)

Found in the Pre-Deluge portion of the Table, in the phrase *Zir Moz Iad* (I Am the Joy of God). Apparently, Nalvage pronounced the word *Moz* as "mozod"—prompting Dee to ask how many letters *Moz* should have. Nalvage confirms that it should be written with three letters, but that "Mozod" is an extended pronunciation, expanding the definition of the word from "joy" to "joy of God." This is the first time we see such an extended *z* in Dee's records, although it will recur throughout the *48 Claves*.

Murifri (mur-if-rii) *prop. n.* n/a

Note:

See *TFR*, p. 3. The names of most of the Angels encountered by Dee and Kelley can be found in other parts of the Angelic system, such as the *Heptarchia* or Great Table (Watchtower) systems. However, *Murifri* is one of the few entirely unique Angels that appeared to the two men. He appeared to give further Heptarchic mysteries to Dee and Kelley—nearly the only Heptarchic information in *TFR*, concerning a talisman Dee wished to make for a sick woman. Murifri's name is found among the Tablets of the *Heptarchia*, but he is *not* one of the forty-nine good Angels, nor is the name derived by any instructions that the Angels gave to Dee. (His name appears in Table Three, which is associated with council and nobility.) No etymology is offered for Murifri's name.

(See also *Ga*, *Galvah*, *Mapsama*, *Nalvage*, *Vaa*, and *Za*.)

Drux (N)

NA (en-ay) *prop. n.* The Name of the Trinity,* Lord

From *Loagaeth*:

(**Dee—The Name of the Trinity, One separable for a while.*) This means One God, but temporarily separable into Three. It appears many times throughout *Loagaeth*.

Note:

Also see the *Five Books*, p. 77. The Archangel Michael gives a small wafer marked *NA* as a Eucharist to Dee's Angel of profession.

See Agrippa's *Three Books*, Book III, chapter 11 (Of the Divine Names . . .): ". . . and the Name of God NA (Hebrew: *Nun, Aleph*) is to be invocated in perturbations and troubles."

Also:

Enay (en-ay) Lord

Na (nakh)* *prop. n.* Letter *H*

Note:

See the *Five Books*, p. 270. The name of the Angelical letter for *H*. It is likely that these letter names have translations of their own. (For instance, note the Hebrew alphabet: the letter *H* is named *Heh*, but *Heh* also translates as "window.") However, such translations for the Angelical letters are never given.

Pronunciation notes:

(**Dee—Hath./But in sound Nach as it were in the nose.*) Could *Hath* be what Dee calls the letter *H* in this case? Most of the time, when a word uses the *ch* digraph, it results in a sound like the "ch" in the word *ache* (a "kh" sound made in the throat). However, in this case, Dee tells us to make the sound in the nose, which is a much softer sound. I tend to pronounce the word along the lines of a nasal "nah."

(Note, also, that this pronunciation gives us a good clue that words like *Pa*, *Ga*, *Va*, etc., should have an "ah" vowel sound.)

Note:

Also see the *Five Books*, p. 298. This was at the very end of a session, after the curtain had been pulled to Kelley's vision in the stone. A voice was heard to say, *"Ne ne ne na Jabes."* (Note the word *na.*) This is likely a praise of some sort, but no translation is offered.

Also see *TFR*, pp. 34–35. This session is recorded entirely in Latin. Here we find this Angelical phrase spoken by "a Voice": *"Garil zed masch, ich na gel galaht gemp gal noch Cabanladan."* (Note the word *na.*) No translation or context is offered.

Compare from *Loagaeth*:

Na, Nah

Naghezes (naj-eez-es) *n.?* Worthiness(?)

Pronunciation notes:

(*Dee—Amzes naghezes Hardeh—Note this to be pronounced roundly together.*) Perhaps this means the three words should be pronounced as if they were one.

In the Angelical spelling above, I have assumed the *h* is a phonetic gloss and excluded it.

Note:

See the *Five Books*, pp. 324–25. Here Kelley sees what the *Book of Loagaeth* looks like from the outside. It is covered in blue silk, and has the title *Amzes naghezes Hardeh* painted upon it in gold. Kelley says this signifies "the universal name of Him that created universally be praised and extolled forever."

However, also see *TFR*, p. 174, where the Angel Ave reveals that the title of Enoch's book was "Let Those That Fear God, and Are Worthy, Read." (Dee, at that point, notes: "The title of Enoch's books expounded into English.") If this happens to be the real translation, then perhaps *Naghezes* indicates "to be worthy."

Nalvage (nal-vayj) *prop. n.* Earth-Fleer

Note:

See *TFR*, p. 62ff. The names of most of the Angels encountered by Dee and Kelley can be found in other parts of the Angelic system, such as the *Heptarchia* or Great Table (Watchtower) systems. However, *Nalvage* is one of the few entirely unique Angels that appeared to the two men. He is the Angel who delivered the *Corpus Omnium*, the forty-eight Keys, and the ninety-one Parts of the Earth to Dee and Kelley. He appeared to be an Angel directly under the direction of Gabriel. Later (see *TFR*, p. 68), the Angel Madimi explains that Nalvage is a "close kinsman" of her mother (Galvah) and his name means *Fuga Terrestrium*—"Earth-Fleer" or "Avoidance of Earthly Things."

(See also *Ga, Galvah, Mapsama, Murifri, Vaa,* and *Za.*)

Nanaeel (nay-NAY-ee-el)* *n.* (My) Power

3.50 . . . you might work *my power.*

Pronunciation notes:

(*Dee—Na na e el) Four syllables. The double *ee* actually makes the long "e" sound, followed by the final *l* which sounds like "el."

(*Dee—na-ná-ê-el) See the *48 Claves*. Dee shows an accent on the second syllable. He also placed a circumflex over the first *e*, indicating the long sound.

Note:

This line in Key Three is spoken by God. Nanaeel does *not* represent "power" in the conventional sense of "strength" and "might." (See *Micaolz.*) Instead, Nanaeel is likely related to Ananael (secret wisdom)—meaning that Nanaeel is descriptive of a *kind* of divine power.

Possible shared root:

Ananael (an-AN-ee-el) Secret Wisdom

Nanba (nan-ba)* *n.* Thorns

17.6 . . . whose wings are *thorns* to stir up vexation . . .

Pronunciation notes:

(**Dee—Nan ba*) Two syllables.

Napeai (nay-pee-ay)* *n.* Swords

13.1 . . . O you *swords of* the south . . .

Pronunciation notes:

(**Dee—Na pe ai*) Three syllables. The first *a* and the *e* should take their long sounds. The *ai* (or *ay*) should make a long "a" sound, as in the English words *day* and *play*.

(**Dee—Napêai*) See the *48 Claves*. Here, Dee placed a circumflex over the *e* to indicate its long sound.

Also:

Napta (nap-ta) Two-edged Swords

Nazpsad (nayz-pee-sad) Sword

Closely related root:

Nazarth (nay-zarth) Pillars (of Gladness)

Nazavabh (nay-zay-VAB) (Hyacinth) Pillars

Note:

Apparently the "Naz" root holds some indication of "straightness," while "Nap" indicates "sharpness." The two come together in *Nazpsad* (sword).

Also compare to the name of the Angel *Bnapsen*, the Heptarchic King of Saturday. Perhaps his name contains some etymology of *sword*.

Compare from *Loagaeth*:

Nap, Napo, Napod

Napta (nap-ta)* *n.* (Two-edged) Swords

9.4 . . . with *two-edged swords* flaming . . .

Pronunciation notes:

(**Dee—Nap ta*) Two syllables.

Also:

Napeai (nay-pee-ay) — Swords
Nazpsad (nayz-pee-sad) — Sword

Closely related root:

Nazarth (nay-zarth) — Pillars (of Gladness)
Nazavabh (nay-zay-VAB) — (Hyacinth) Pillars

Note:

See note at *Napeai.*

Compare from *Loagaeth*:

Nap, Napo, Napod

Nazarth (nay-zarth)* *n.* — Pillars (of Gladness)

5.16 . . . I fastened *Pillars of Gladness* . . .

Pronunciation notes:

(**Dee—Na zarth*) Two syllables. The *a* at the end of the first syllable is likely long.

Note:

The similarity between this word and the word *Nazareth*—the town where Jesus supposedly grew up.

Also:

Nazavabh (nay-zay-VAB) — (Hyacinth) Pillars

Closely related root:

Napeai (nay-pee-ay) — Swords
Napta (nap-ta) — Two-edged Swords
Nazpsad (nayz-pee-sad) — Sword

Note:

See note at *Napeai.*

Nazavabh (nay-zay-VAB)* *n.* — (Hyacinth) Pillars

8.5 . . . third heaven made of *hyacinth pillars* . . .

Pronunciation notes:

(**Dee—Na za vábh*) Three syllables, with the accent on the third syllable. The first two *a*'s should be long, while the third *a* takes the short sound. The *bh* makes a soft "b" sound.

(**Dee—nazâvábh*) See the *48 Claves*. Dee placed a circumflex over the *a* in the second syllable to indicate its long sound. He again placed an accent on the last syllable.

Also:

Nazarth (nay-zarth) Pillars (of Gladness)

Note:

Patricia Shaffer has suggested that "hyacinth" may be an indication of the stone lapis lazuli, rather than the plant.

Closely related root:

Napeai (nay-pee-ay) Swords
Napta (nap-ta) Two-edged Swords
Nazpsad (nayz-pee-sad) Sword

Note:

See note at *Napeai*.

Nazpsad (nayz-pee-sad)* *n.* Sword

1.15 . . . the sun is as a *sword* . . .

Pronunciation notes:

(**Dee—NAZPSAD*) Dee gives us little clue here. Most likely, the *p* must stand alone, since it does not make a natural sound when combined with the *z* or the *s* in English. Thus the word might be of three syllables. I have assumed the *a* takes a long sound based upon closely related words.

Also:

Napeai (nay-pee-ay) Swords
Napta (nap-ta) Two-edged swords

Closely related root:

Nazarth (nay-zarth) Pillars (of Gladness)
Nazavabh (nay-zay-VAB) (Hyacinth) Pillars

Note:
There appear to be two roots at work in *Nazpsad*—both "Naz" (straight/pillar) and "Nap" (sword/sharp).

Ne (nee) n/a

Note:
See the *Five Books*, p. 298. This was at the very end of a session, after the curtain had been pulled to Kelley's vision in the stone. A voice was heard to say, "*Ne ne ne na Jabes.*" This is likely a praise of some sort, but no translation is offered.

Compare from *Loagaeth*:
Ne

Netaab (nee-TAY-ab)* *n.* Government

3.34 . . . placed you in 12 seats of *government* . . .

Pronunciation notes:
(**Dee—Netaab*) Dee gives us little clue here. Instead, see his *48 Claves*:
(**Dee—ne-tâ-ab*) See the *48 Claves*. Dee indicates three syllables here. The *e* should take its long sound. The first *a* has a circumflex over it, indicating the long sound. See *Gnetaab* (your governments) for the accent on the second syllable.

Also:

Anetab (ay-NEE-tayb)	(In) Government
Gnetaab (nee-TAY-ab)	(Your) Governments
Netaaib (nee-TAY-ay-ib)	Government
Tabaam (tay-BAY-an)	Governor
Tabaord (tay-BAY-ord)	(Let) Be Governed
Tabaori (tay-BAY-oh-rii)	Govern
"Tabas" (tay-BAS)	Govern

Further:

Cab (kab)	Rod/Scepter
Caba (ka-BA)	To Govern

Netaaib (nee-TAY-ay-ib)* *n.* Government

30.25 . . . provided you *for the government* of the earth . . .

Pronunciation notes:

(**Dee—Ne tá a ib*) Four syllables, with an accent on the second syllable. (**Dee—netáâib*) See the *48 Claves*. Here, Dee again placed the accent on the second syllable. He also placed a circumflex over the second *a* to indicate its long sound.

Also:

Anetab (ay-NEE-tayb)	(In) Government
Gnetaab (nee-TAY-ab)	(Your) Governments
Netaab (nee-TAY-ab)	Governments
Tabaam (tay-BAY-an)	Governor
Tabaord (tay-BAY-ord)	(Let) Be Governed
Tabaori (tay-BAY-oh-rii)	Govern
"Tabas" (tay-BAS)	Govern

Further:

Cab (kab)	Rod/Scepter
Caba (ka-BA)	To Govern

NI (nii)* 28

7.12 . . . they are become *28* living dwellings . . .

Pronunciation notes:

(**Dee—Ni*) Dee seems to indicate a single syllable. I suggest a long "i" sound.

Note:

This word was not originally given with Key Seven. It was added later when Nalvage transmitted the English for the Key (see *TFR*, p. 199). This seems to have been the case with many of the numbers mentioned in the Keys.

Note:

See also *OB* (28).

Nia (nii-a) *prop. n.* "The Twenty-Fourth Aethyr"

30.3 . . . which dwell in *the twenty-fourth aethyr* . . .

Note:

This (word 30.3) is the single space in the Key of the Aethyrs, which must be changed for each invocation—replacing word 30.3 with the name of the appropriate Aethyr. No established definitions were given for these names.

Nia contains the three Parts of the Earth *Orcanir, Chialps*, and *Soageel*.

"Nibm" (nib-em) *n.* Season

Compounds:

Lnibm (el-nib-em) [L + "Nibm"] One Season

Nidali (nii-day-lii)* *n.* Noises

10.83 Come away, but not *your noises*.

Pronunciation note:

(**Dee—Ni da li*) Three syllables. All vowels appear to take their long sounds.

(**Dee—nidâli*) See the *48 Claves*. Here, Dee places a circumflex over the *a* to indicate its long sound.

Niis (nii-IS)* *v.* Come (Here)

5.43 . . . .*come you*, and obey . . .

8.46 . . . *come*, appear to the terror of the earth . . .

Pronunciation notes:

(**Dee 5.43—Ni is*)

(**Dee 8.46—Ni is, small sound of* i) Two syllables. The first *i* appears to take the long sound. Dee's note about the *"small sound of I"* likely indicates a short sound for the *i* in the second syllable.

I have adopted the accent from the other versions of this word.

Also:

Niisa (nii-II-sa) — Come Away

Niiso (nii-II-soh) — Come Away

Niisa (nii-II-sa)* *v.* — Come Away

11.31 . . . *come away*! for I have prepared . . .

Pronunciation notes:

(**Dee—Ni í sa*) Three syllables, with an accent on the second syllable. Both *i*'s take their long sound. The word tends to sound more like two syllables when spoken fluently. (The double *i* would have combined to make a long "i" sound in Early Modern English.)

Also:

Niis (nii-IS) — Come (Here)

Niiso (nii-II-soh) — Come Away

Niiso (nii-II-soh)* *v.* — Come Away

8.34 . . . *come away*! for the Thunders have spoken . . .

8.38 . . . *come away*! for the crowns of the Temple . . .

9.66 . . . *come away*! and not your vials . . .

10.80 . . . *come away*! but not your noises . . .

11.15 . . . *come away*! and they gathered them together . . .

Pronunciation notes:

(**Dee 8.34, 38, 11.15—Ni í so*)

(**Dee 9.66; 10.80—Ni i so*) Three syllables, with an accent on the second syllable. Both *i*'s should take a long sound. The word tends to sound more like two syllables when spoken fluently. (The double *i* would have combined to make a long "i" sound in Early Modern English.)

(**Dee 8.34, 38; 9.66; 11.15—Niíso*) See the *48 Claves*. Dee again shows the accent over the second *i*.

Also:

Niis (nii-IS) Come (Here)

Niisa (nii-II-sa) Come Away

Noaln (noh-aln)* *v.* May Be

30.51 . . . that the glory of her *may be* always drunken

Pronunciation note:

(*Dee—No aln*) Two syllables.

Also:

Noan (noh-an) To Become

Noar (noh-ar) Has Become

Noas (noh-as) Have Become

Noasmi (noh-ays-mii) (Let) Become

Note:

Compare this word to *Noalmr*, a Name of God in the Northern Watchtower, ruling the Angels of medicine. Thus, the name may contain an etymology of "to become."

Noan (noh-AN)* *v.* To Become

2.33 For *you are become* a building . . .

3.5 . . . *you are become* the skirts of justice . . .

Pronunciation note:

(*Dee 2.33—No an*) Two syllables.

(*Dee 3.55—Noan*)

(*Dee 2.33—noán*) See *48 Claves*. The accent is placed on the second syllable.

Also:

Noaln (noh-aln) May Be

Noar (noh-ar) Has Become

Noas (noh-as) Have Become

Noasmi (noh-ays-mii) (Let) Become

Noar (noh-ar)* *v.* (Is) Become

3.69 His name *is become* mighty amongst us.

Pronunciation note:

(*Dee—Noar*) This would appear to rhyme with the English words "roar" and "boar." However, see *Noan* and *Noaln*—both of which are given two syllables.

Also:

Noaln (noh-aln) May Be
Noan (noh-an) To Become
Noas (noh-as) Have Become
Noasmi (noh-ays-mii) (Let) Become

Noas (noh-as)* *v.* To Become

5.5 The mighty sounds . . . *are become* as olives . . .
**11.19 and *became* the house of death.

Pronunciation note:

(*Dee 5.5—Noas*) This would appear to have a sound similar to the English words "toast" or "roast." However, see *Noan* and *Noaln*—both of which are given two syllables.

Note:

**This word was not given during the transmission of Key Eleven. Nor does it appear in Dee's *48 Claves*. We have only the English for the Key given on *TFR*, p. 193. Patricia Shaffer suggests this word here, and I have to agree.

Compounds:

Inoas (in-OH-as) [I + Noas] Are Become

Also:

Noaln (noh-aln) May Be
Noan (noh-an) To Become
Noar (noh-ar) Has Become
Noasmi (noh-ays-mii) (Let) Become

Noasmi (noh-ays-mii)* *v.* (Let) Become

30.97 His buildings, *let them become* caves . . .

Pronunciation note:

(**Dee—No as mi*) Three syllables. The final *i* is given its long sound—like the English word "my."

(**Dee—noâsmi*) See the *48 Claves*. Here, Dee placed a circumflex over the *a* to indicate its long sound.

Also:

Noaln (noh-aln) May Be

Noan (noh-an) To Become

Noar (noh-ar) Has Become

Noas (noh-as) Have Become

Nobloh (noh-bloh)* *n.* Palms (or, Palms of)

1.27 . . . trussed you together as *the palms of* my hands . . .

Pronunciation notes:

(**Dee—Nobloh*)

Note:

There is some possibility that the *-o* affix is in use here. If so, then the final *h* could be a phonetic gloss. Due to lack of evidence, I've stuck with Dee's spelling.

Noch (nok) n/a

Note:

See *TFR*, pp. 34–35. This session is recorded entirely in Latin. Here we find this Angelical phrase spoken by "a Voice": "*Garil zed masch, ich na gel galaht gemp gal noch Cabanladan.*" No translation or context is offered.

Compare from *Loagaeth*:

Nocas, Nochas

Noco (NOH-kwoh)* *n.* Servant

(RFP) . . . I am *a servant of* the same . . .

Pronunciation notes:
(**Dee—Call it Noco*) Two syllables. Note that other versions of this word are spelled with a *q* or *qu*. It is even likely that the word *Noco* should properly be spelled *Noqo*—with a *Ger* (Q) instead of *Veh* (C).
I have adopted the accent from other versions of this word.

Also:

Cnoqod (see-NOH-kwod) (Unto) Servants
Cnoquodi (see-noh-KWOH-dii) (With) Ministers
Cnoquol (see-NOH-kwol) Servants

Note:
"Noquo" or "Noqo" may be the root for all words meaning "servant."

Also see *Lang* (Those Who Serve).

Noib (noh-ib)* *adv.* Yea (Yes)

10.7 . . . woe, woe, *yea* woe be to the earth . . .

Pronunciation notes:
(**Dee—No ib*) Two syllables. The *o* and *i* do not combine into one sound in this case. The *o* should take a long sound, and the *i* is likely short.

Nomig (noh-mig)* *adv.* or *adj.* Even (as)

10.60 . . . bringeth forth 1000 *even as* the heart of man . . .

Pronunciation notes:
(**Dee—No mig big*) Two syllables. The *o* is likely a long vowel. The final *g* seems to take a hard sound, as in the English word *big*.

Nonca (non-sa)* *pron., pl.* (To) You

30.11 . . . *to you* it is said, behold . . .

Pronunciation notes:
(*Dee—Nonca sa*) Two syllables. The *c* takes a soft sound.

Also:

Noncf (non-sef) — You
Nonci (non-sii) — You
Noncp (non-sef) — You

Note:
For *you* singular, see *Yls* (thou).

Noncf (non-sef)* *pron., pl.* — You

30.24 . . . provided *you* for the government . . .
30.32 . . . furnishing *you* with a power . . .

Pronunciation notes:
(*Dee 30.24—Noncf Nonsf*)
(*Dee 30.32—Non cf Nonsf*) Two syllables. Dee shows us here that the *c* takes it soft "s" sound. The *f* likely sounds like "ef," and (based on *Noncp*) I assume the word should end with *Mals* (Ph) rather than *Or* (F).

Also:

Nonca (non-sa) — (To) You
Nonci (non-sii) — You
Noncp (non-sef) — You

Note:
For *you* singular, see Yls (*thou*).

Nonci (non-sii)* *pron., pl.* — You

12.1 . . . *O you* that reign . . .

Pronunciation notes:
(*Dee—Non ci, si*) Two syllables. Dee indicates a soft "s" sound for the *c*. The final *i* is likely a long vowel.

Also:

Nonca (non-sa) — (To) You

Noncf (non-sef) — You

Noncp (non-sef) — You

Note:

For *you* singular, see Yls (*thou*).

Noncp (non-sef)* *pron., pl.* — You

11.34 . . . I have prepared for *you* . . .

Pronunciation notes:

(*Dee—Noncp Nonsp*) Two syllables. Dee shows us here that the *c* takes it soft "s" sound. I suspect the *p* is actually the digraph "ph"—as evidenced by the word *Noncf.*

Also:

Nonca (non-sa) — (To) You

Noncf (non-sef) — You

Nonci (non-sii) — You

Note:

For *you* singular, see Yls (*thou*).

"Nor" (nor) *n.* — Son

Compounds:

Norqrasahi (nor-kra-sa-hii) ["Nor" + "Qrasahi"] — Sons of Pleasure

Also:

"Norm" (norm) — Son/Sons

Noromi (noh-ROM-ii) — Sons

Note:

"Nor" appears to be the root here.

Compare from *Loagaeth*:

Nor

"Norm" (norm) *n.* Son/Sons

Compounds:

Normolap (nor-moh-lap) ["Norm" + "Olap"] Sons of Men

Also:

"Nor" (nor) Son

Noromi (noh-ROM-ii) Sons

Note:

"Nor" appears to be the root here.

Compare from *Loagaeth*:

Nor

Normolap (nor-moh-lap)* ["Norm" + "Olap"] *comp.* Sons of Men

4.47 . . . amongst *the sons of men.*

Pronunciation note:

(*Dee—Nor mo lap*) Three syllables. The second *o* should take the long sound.

(*Dee—Nor-mô-lap*) See the *48 Claves*. Also three syllables. Dee added a circumflex over the second *o* to indicate its long sound.

Note:

"Nor" appears to be the root here.

Compare from *Loagaeth*:

Nor

Noromi (noh-ROM-ii)* *n.* Sons

14.1 *O you sons* of fury . . .

Note:

The transmission of Key Fourteen is missing from Dee's journals. We only have the English for this Key given later (see *TFR*, p. 193). However, Illemese gives the pronunciation later in the journals on *TFR*, p. 200. Plus, the word appears in Dee's *48 Claves*.

Pronunciation notes:

(**Illemese—No Romi.*) See *TFR*, p. 200. I suggest three syllables. The first *o* and the final *i* should take their long sounds.

(**Dee—Norómi*) See the *48 Claves*. Here, Dee placed an accent over the second syllable.

Also:

"Nor" (nor) — Son

"Norm" (norm) — Son/Sons

Note:

"Nor" appears to be the root here.

Compare from *Loagaeth*:

Nor

Norquasahi (nor-kway-SAY-hii)* ["Nor" + "Qrasahi"] *comp.*

Sons of Pleasure

4.33 Arise *you sons of pleasure* and visit the earth . . .

Pronunciation notes:

(**Dee—Nor qua sa hi*) Four syllables. Dee originally wrote this word with an *r* after the *q*. However, he replaced the *r* with a *u* in his phonetic note (indicating that the *q* takes the sound of "kwah"—the *u* is obviously a phonetic gloss). He did the same in the *48 Claves*:

(**Dee—Nor quasáhi*) See the *48 Claves*. Note the accent on the third syllable.

Norz (norz)* *n.*

Six

3.9 *Six* are the seats of living breath . . .

Pronunciation notes:

(**Dee—Norz*) One syllable.

Note:

This appears to be the word for "six" rather than the numeral 6.

Nostoah (nah-stah) *comp.* — It Was in the Beginning*

From *Loagaeth*:

(**Dee—Nostah = It was in the beginning.*) See the *Five Books*, p. 323. "Nostah" is likely the pronunciation of *Nostoah*.

Note:

This seems similar to the Hebrew *Berashith* (It Was in the Beginning), the first word of Genesis. Much importance was placed upon this word in Jewish mysticism. (However, note that the very first word of the Holy *Book of Loagaeth* is *Zuresch*.)

Also see *Acroodzi* (beginning), *Croodzi* (beginning of things), *Iaod* (beginning), *Iaodaf* (in the beginning)

Nothoa (noth-OH-a)* *prep.* — Amidst

1.22 . . . *in the midst of* my vestures . . .

Pronunciation notes:

(**Dee—Nothoa*) Likely three syllables.

(**Dee—nothóa*) See *48 Claves*. The accent is shown on the second syllable.

Note:

Also see *Zomdux* (amidst).

Med (O)

O (oh) 5

11.5 . . . and they were *5* thunders which flew . . .

O (oh) *v.* "Come, and Bear Witness"*

Note:
(**Dee—Befafes O, is to call upon him as on God. Befafes O, is as much to say, Come Befafes and bear witness.*) See the *Five Books*, p. 310. Dee is here using the Angel Befafes as an example. Note that *O*, by itself, seems to indicate "Come and Bear Witness."

Also see the *Five Books*, p. 258. Here, Raphael offers a long prayer, the very end of which is, "How great and innumerable are your [God's] gifts? *O remiges varpax. Kyrie eleyson.*"

Also:
Oh (oh) "Come, and Bear Witness"(?)

Compare from *Loagaeth*:
O, Oh

"Oado" (oh-ay-doh) *v.* To Weave

Compounds:
Dsoado (dee-soh-ay-doh) [Ds + "Oado"] Which Weave

Oadriax (oh-AY-drii-aks)* *n.* Lower Heavens

30.118 . . . *the lower heavens* beneath you . . .

Pronunciation notes:
(**Dee—O ádriax*) Likely four syllables, with an accent on the second syllable. The initial *O* stands alone. The first *a* likely takes its long sound—

based on the sound of similar words. The *i* likely takes a long sound, because it precedes an *a* (as in the English word *dial*).

(**Dee—oádriax*) See the *48 Claves*. Here, Dee again placed an accent over the *a* in the second syllable.

Also:

"Madriax" (MAY-drii-yaks) — Heavens

Madriiax (MAY-drii-yaks) — Heavens

Probable root:

Mad (mad) — (Your) God, "Pure/Undefiled"

Note:

I have suggested that *Mad* is simply a modified form of *Iad*. The *I* of *Iad* (God) became the *M* of *Mad* (your God) to indicate something celestial and divine—yet not quite God Himself. Therefore, *Mad* is the root of "Madriax" (the Heavens). Now, with *Oadriax*, we seem to have a further progression of this same concept. The *M* of *Mad* gives way yet again in favor of the *O*, causing the word to indicate "the lower Heavens."

Oai* (oh-AY-ii) *prep.* — Amongst

Alternate spelling:

(**Dee 1.67—AAI The first a may be an A an O or an e*) Thus, there are two alternate spellings for *Aai* (amongst).

Pronunciation notes:

See *Aai* (amongst), which Dee indicates has three syllables.

Also:

Aai (ay-AY-ii) — Amongst (You)

Aaf (ay-AF) — Amongst

Aaiom (ay-AY-om) — Amongst (Us?)

Aao (ay-ay-OH) — Amongst

Eai (ee-AY-ii) — Amongst

Oali (OH-ay-lii)* *v.* — To Place

4.14 . . . under whom *I have placed* 9639 . . .

Pronunciation notes:

(**Dee—O a li*) Three syllables, the *O* and *a* each standing alone. I have adopted the accent from *Aala* (to place).

Also:

Aala (AY-ay-la) To Place

Probable shared root:

Alar (AY-lar) To Settle/Place
Aldi (AL-dii) Gathering
Aldon (AL-don) Gird Up
Allar (AL-lar) To Bind Up

Oanio (oh-AY-nii-oh)* *n.* Moment

10.39 . . . in the 24th part of *a moment* . . .

Pronunciation notes:

(**Dee—O a' ni o*) Four syllables. All of these vowels are given their long sounds. Accent placed on the second syllable.
(**Dee—oánîo*) See the *48 Claves*. Again, Dee indicates an accent on the second syllable, and a long "i" sound.

Probable shared root:

"Qanis" (kway-nis) Olives
Ooaona (oh-oh-AY-oh-na) Eyes
Ooanoan (oh-oh-AY-noh-an) (In Their?) Eyes

Note:

The similar spelling suggests these three words are connected. This might make sense for *Ooaona* (eyes): the word *Taqanis* (as olives) in Key Five appears to refer to the stars. In biblical literature, the word "eyes" is often used to indicate "stars." (Such as in the visions of St. John and Ezekiel, both of whom saw celestial Angels with wings "full of eyes.") If this is the case, then the shared root here may indicate "small units," which would explain its use to indicate a "moment" (Oanio).

OB (ob)* 28

12.6 . . . and are *28* the lanterns of sorrow . . .

Pronunciation notes:
(**Dee—Ob*) One syllable.

Note:
This word was not originally given with Key Twelve. It was added later when Nalvage transmitted the English for the Key (see *TFR*, p. 193). This seems to have been the case with many of the numbers mentioned in the Keys.
See also NI (28).

Obelison (oh-bel-is-on) *prop. n.* Pleasant Deliverer (a name of *Befafes*)*

Note:
(**Befafes: The Egyptians called me Obelison in respect of my nature.*
Dee: I pray you, what is the etymology of Obelison?
Befafes: A pleasant deliverer.) See the *Five Books*, pp. 234–45 (and the note added later by Dee on p. 201). Dee here encounters the Heptarchic Angel Befafes (Prince of Tuesday), who also claims the title *Obelison* (Pleasant Deliverer).

Also:
Obelisong (oh-bel-is-ong) Pleasant Deliverers

Obelisong (oh-bel-is-ong)* *n.* Pleasant Deliverers

4.44 . . . and show yourselves as *pleasant deliverers* . . .

Pronunciation notes:
(**Dee—Obelisong*) Likely four syllables. I am assuming a hard *g* at the end of the word, as it should combine naturally with the *n*, as in the English words *song* and *wrong*.

Also:
Obelison (oh-bel-is-on) Pleasant Deliverer (a name of *Befafes*)

Obloc (ob-lok)* *n.* Garland

6.13 . . . and *a garland* to the righteous.

Pronunciation notes:
(*Dee—Ob loc*) Two syllables. The initial *O* seems to take the short sound (rather than standing alone).

Also:
Oboleh (OB-oh-lay) Garments

Note:
Both a *garland* and a *garment* are dressings. Also see *Qaa* (garments/creation).

Oboleh (OB-oh-lay)* *n.* Garments

1.36 . . . beautified *your garments* with admiration . . .

Pronunciation notes:
(*Dee—óbôleh*) See *48 Claves*. Likely three syllables, showing the accent on the first syllable. The second *o* carries a circumflex, indicating the long sound.

Also:
Obloc (ob-lok) Garland

Note:
Take special note that the "garments" beautified in this part of Key One are likely the Heavenly Spheres (or celestial orbits). Generally depicted as a set of concentric circles, these could be easily represented poetically as "garlands."
Also see *Qaa* (garments/creation).

Obza (ob-za)* *n.* Half

9.12 . . . for two times and *a half*.

Pronunciation notes:

(**Dee—Ob za*) Two syllables.

Od (ohd *or* od)* *conj.* And

1.24 . . . *and* trussed you together . . .
1.65 . . . *and* reigneth among you . . .
1.71 . . . righteousness *and* truth . . .
RFP . . . *and* show yourselves . . . or . . . *and* appear . . .
2.27 . . . *and* mightier are your voices . . .
2.47 . . . *and* make me a strong seething . . .
3.26 . . . which sleep *and* shall rise . . .
3.31 . . . *and* placed you in 12 seats . . .
3.45 . . . *and* the corners of your government . . .
3.67 . . . *and* name is become mighty . . .
3.76 . . . descend *and* apply yourselves . . .
4.4 . . . *and* have looked around me . . .
4.34 . . . *and* visit the earth . . .
5.4 . . . *and* are become as olives . . .
5.10 . . . *and* dwelling in the brightness . . .
5.18 . . . *and* gave them vessels . . .
5.24 . . . *and* they are the brothers . . .
5.29 . . . *and* the beginning of their own seats . . .
5.40 . . . *and* the contents of time . . .
5.44 . . . come you *and* obey your creation . . .
5.48 . . . in peace *and* comfort . . .
6.12 . . . *and* a garland to the righteous . . .
6.18 . . . *and* 7699 continual workmen . . .
6.26 . . . *and* continuance as the second . . .
6.29 . . . second *and* third . . .
6.35 . . . *and* I moved you . . .
7.10 . . . *and* they are become 28 . . .
7.17 . . . *and* they are appareled . . .
7.29 . . . *and* places of comfort . . .
7.39 . . . *and* be mighty amongst us . . .
7.46 . . . *and* our strength waxeth . . .
8.18 . . . *and* like unto the harvest . . .

8.31 . . . house fall *and* the dragon sink . . .
8.42 . . . the Temple, *and* the coat . . .
8.50 . . . *and* to our comfort . . .
8.52 . . . *and* of such as are prepared . . .
9.11 . . . two times *and* a half . . .
9.17 . . . *and* of the marrow of salt . . .
9.23 . . . *and* are measured of their ministers . . .
9.45 . . . *and* from their mouths run seas . . .
9.53 . . . *and* upon their heads . . .
9.67 . . . Come away, *and* not your vials.
10.4 . . . *and* are harboured in the north . . .
10.15 . . . lamentation *and* weeping . . .
10.23 . . . burn night *and* day . . .
10.25 . . . *and* vomit out the heads of scorpions . . .
10.29 . . . scorpions *and* live sulphur . . .
10.44 . . . *and* a thousand times as many . . .
11.3 . . . *and* they were five thunders . . .
11.10 . . . *and* the Eagle spake . . .
11.13 . . . *and* cried with a loud voice . . .
**11.16 . . . *and* they gathered themselves together . . .
**11.18 . . . *and* became the house of death . . .
11.24 . . . *and* it is as they are . . .
12.4 . . . *and* are 28 lanterns . . .
12.11 . . . *and* visit us . . .
13.17 . . . God *and* His power . . .
***15.15 . . . *and* the seal of honour . . .
****16.8 . . . *and* shalt comfort the just . . .
16.16 . . . understand *and* separate . . .
17.18 . . . *and* hearken . . .
18.22 . . . *and* not to be measured . . .
30.7 . . . *and* execute the judgment . . .
30.27 . . . *and* her unspeakable variety . . .
30.39 . . . *and* rose up in the beginning . . .
30.46 . . . *and* let there be division . . .
30.54 . . . drunken *and* vexed . . .
30.60 . . . *and* as a handmaid . . .
30.67 . . . *and* let there be no creature . . .
30.78 . . . *and* let there be no one creature . . .

30.85 . . . vex *and* weed out . . .

30.88 . . . *and* the dwelling places . . .

30.93 . . . *and* his pomp . . .

30.136 . . . add *and* diminish . . .

30.154 . . . *and* make us partakers . . .

Pronunciation notes:

(**Dee 1.71—OD drawing the O long*)

(**Dee 1.24—As before OD*) Key One was transmitted backward, so 1.71 came before 1.24.

(**Dee 3.31; 8.18, 50, 52—OD*)

(**Dee 30.78—Od Long, or short*)

(**Dee 2.27, 47; 3.45, 67, 76; 4.4, 34; 5.4, 10, 18, 24, 29, 40, 44, 48; 6.12, 18, 35; 7.10, 17, 29, 39, 46; 8. 31, 42; 9.11, 17, 23, 45, 53, 67; 10,4, 15, 23, 25, 29, 44; 11.3, 10, 13, 24; 12.4, 11; 13.17; 16.16; 17.18; 18.22; 30.7, 27, 39, 46, 54, 60, 67, 85, 88, 93, 154—Od*)

(**Dee 6.26, 29—od*) Taking all of these notes together, I suggest a single syllable. The *O* may be long or short, though the long "oh" sound appears to dominate.

Note:

**Words 11.16 and 11.18 do not appear in Dee's journals, nor in the *48 Claves*. We have only the English given for the Key on *TFR*, p. 193. Patricia Shaffer suggests the words for 11.16–19, and I agree with her conclusion.

*** The transmission of Key Fifteen is missing from Dee's journals. We only have the English for this Key given later (see *TFR*, p. 193). Plus, the word appears in this location in Dee's *48 Claves*.

**** The transmission of the first twelve words of Key Sixteen is missing from Dee's journals. We only have the English given for it on *TFR*, p. 194. However, they do appear in Dee's *48 Claves*.

Compounds:

Odapila (ohd-ap-ii-la) [Od + "Apila"] And Liveth

Odbrint (ohd-brint) [Od + "Brint"] And Hast

Odcacocasb (ohd-kay-KOH-kazb) [Od + "Cacocasb"] And Another While

Odchis (ohd-kiis) [Od + Chis] And Are

Odecrin (oh-dee-KRIN) [Od + "Ecrin"] — And the Praise
Odes (ohd-es) [Od + "Es"] — And Fourth
Odfaorgt (ohd-fay-or-jet) [Od + "Faorgt"] — And the Dwelling Place
Odipuran (ohd-II-pew-ran) [Od + Ip + "Puran"] — And Shall Not See
Odmiam (ohd-MII-am) [Od + Miam] — And Continuance
Odlonshin (ohd-lon-shin) [Od + "Lonshin"] — And (Their) Powers
Odquasb (ohd-kwazb) [Od + "Quasb"] — And Destroy
Odugeg (ohd-yew-JEJ) [Od + Ugeg] — And Wax Strong
Odvooan (ohd-vay-ohn) [Od + Vooan] — And Truth
Odzamran (ohd-zam-ran) [Od + Zamran] — And Appear

Also:
Ot (oht) — And

Compare from *Loagaeth*:
Od

Odapila (ohd-ap-ii-la)* [Od + "Apila"] *comp.* — And Liveth

4.39 . . . God which is *and liveth*.

Pronunciation notes:
(**Dee—Od api la*) Likely four syllables. The final *i* in the second syllable is long.
(**Dee—od Apîla*) See the *48 Claves*. Dee added a circumflex over the *i* to indicate its long sound.

Odbrint (ohd-brint)* [Od + "Brint"] *comp.* — And Has

17.9 . . . *and hast* 7336 living lamps . . .

Pronunciation notes:
(**Dee—Od brint*) Two syllables. The initial *O* is likely long (see *Od*), while the *i* is likely short.

Odcacocasb (ohd-kay-KOH-kazb)* [Od + "Cacocasb"] *comp.*
And Another While

30.108 . . . *and another while* a stranger . . .

Pronunciation notes:
(*Dee—Od ca có casb) Four syllables, with an accent on the third syllable. The final letters *sb* can combine to make a sound—though it is an odd one to our modern language. I have rendered the sound in my pronunciation as "zb."
(*Dee—od cacócasb) See the *48 Claves*. Here, Dee again placed an accent over the third syllable.

Note:
See *Cocasb* (time).

Odchis (ohd-kiis)* [Od + Chis] *comp.*
And Are

6.24 . . . *and are* in government and continuance . . .

Pronunciation notes:
(*Dee—Od chif kif) Two syllables. The *ch* takes the harder "k" (or "kh") sound. Dee originally wrote this word as "Odkif." However, we see elsewhere that the Angelical word for *are* is spelled as *Chis*. In Dee's time, the letter *s* was sometimes written in an elongated form that looks similar to a lowercase *f*. (See *Chis* or *Chiis* for further pronunciation notes.)
(*Dee—od chis*) See the *48 Claves*. Here, Dee confirms that the *f* in *TFR* should actually be an *s*.

Odecrin (oh-dee-KRIN)* [Od + "Ecrin"] *comp.*
And the Praise (of)

6.41 . . . a song of honour *and the praise of* your God . . .

Pronunciation notes:
(*Dee—O de crín*) Three syllables. The initial *O* stands alone. The *e* likely takes the long sound, as it rests at the end of its syllable. (Also see the

pronunciation notes for *Oecrimi*.) The accent is placed upon the third syllable.

Odes (oh-DES)* [Od + "Es"] *comp.* And Fourth

7.27 . . . as the third *and fourth* . . .

Pronunciation notes:

(**Dee—O des*) Two syllables. The *O* stands alone—that is, it makes a long sound. The *e* should be a phonetic gloss.

(**Dee—o dés*) See the *48 Claves*. Note the accent over the second syllable.

Odfaorgt (ohd-fay-ORJT)* [Od + "Faorgt"] *comp.* And the Dwelling Place

30.114 . . . the bed of an harlot, *and the dwelling place of* him . . .

Pronunciation notes:

(**Dee—Od fa orgt gt or dgt*) Three syllables. The *a* in the second syllable should be long, as it is followed by an *o* (as in the English word *chaos*). Dee indicates that the *g* in the final syllable should take a softer ("dg") sound.

(**Dee—od faórgt*) See the *48 Claves*. Here, Dee placed an accent upon the third syllable.

Odipuran (ohd-II-pew-ran)* [Od + Ip + "Puran"] *comp.* And Shall Not See

8.26 . . . which are *and shall not see* death . . .

Pronunciation notes:

(**Dee—Odí pu ran*) Four syllables, with an accent on the second syllable. The *i* and the *u* should each take their long sounds. I have given the *u* the sound of "yew"—as in the English words *pure* and *puce*.

(**Dee—odípûran*) See the *48 Claves*. Dee again shows the accent on the second syllable. He also added a circumflex over the *u*—confirming the long vowel sound.

Note:

It seems obvious that *Ip* should stand for "not" or perhaps "shall not" in this word. However, the word *Uran* appears earlier in Key Eight as the word "elders." Therefore, it is unlikely that this word is intended here as "see." It might be that the word is "Puran"—with the two *p*'s (between "Ip" and "Puran") combined as normal for Angelical compounds.

Odlonshin (ohd-lon-shin)* [Od + "Lonshin"] *comp.* And Powers

4.28 . . . *and their powers* are as the first 456 . . .

Pronunciation notes:

(**Dee—Od lonshin*) Three syllables.

Note:

There is no Angelical for *their* in the above.

Odmiam (ohd-MII-am)* [Od + Miam] *comp.* And Continuance

7.25 . . . whose kingdoms *and continuance* . . .

7.32 . . . .seats of mercy *and continuance* . . .

Pronunciation notes:

(**Dee 7.25—Od mi am, or Od Nuám*)

(**Dee 7.32—Od mí am*) I suspect that Dee had some confusion over the sound of word 7.25. However, by word 7.32, he seems to have settled upon his first assumption. Three syllables, with an accent on the second. The *i* should take the long sound.

Odo (od-oh)* *v.* To Open

(RFP), 30.151 *Open* the mysteries of your creation . . .

18.7 . . . which *openest* the glory . . .

Pronunciation notes:

(**Dee 1.77—Call it ODO.*)

(**Dee 18.7; 30.151—Odo*) I suggest two syllables, the last *o* long.

Note:

This word is a palindrome, spelled the same forward and backward.

Odquasb (ohd-kwazb)* [Od + "Quasb"] *comp.* And Destroy

30.130 . . . *and destroy* the rotten . . .

Pronunciation notes:

(*Dee—Od Quasb*) This appears to be two syllables, so "Quasb" must be pronounced together as one syllable. (Also see *Grosb.*) I suspect the *u* is a phonetic gloss. (The Cotton MS of Dee's journals shows a final *z* on this word, but Dee did not include it in his phonetic note or in the *48 Claves*.)

Odugeg (ohd-yew-JEJ)* [Od + Ugeg] *comp.* And Wax Strong

4.23 . . . things are *and wax strong* . . .

Pronunciation notes:

(*Dee—Od Vgeg as Wedge*) There are three syllables here. Dee originally wrote this word with a *v*—however, it should take the "u" sound, as it precedes a consonant (see *Ugeg*). The first *g* should be soft, as it precedes an *e*. Dee notes that the final *g* is soft, as the *dg* in the English word *wedge*. Finally, see *Ugeg* for the accent.

Odvooan (ohd-voo-AN)* [Od + Vooan] *comp.* And Truth

3.58 . . . skirts of justice *and truth* . . .

Pronunciation notes:

(*Dee—Od vooen*) This should be three syllables. The double *o* should result in a long "u" sound—as in the English words *booth* and *shoot*. Dee gives the *a* the sound of "e" in his phonetic note—sounding like a schwa.

(*Dee—od voo*á*n*) See the *48 Claves*. Here, Dee placed an accent upon the final syllable.

Note:

Dere here uses the fallen version of the word *Vooan* (truth). However, it should likely be the dignified version for the purpose of the Call. (See *Vooan* and *Vaoan*.)

Odzamran (ohd-zam-ran)* [Od + Zamran] *comp.* And Appear

4.43 . . . move *and show yourselves* . . .
30.143 . . . move *and appear* . . .

Pronunciation notes:

(**Dee 30.143—Od zamran*) Three syllables.

Oecrimi (oh-EE-kriim-ii)* *v.* To Sing Praises

7.4 . . . a house of virgins *singing praises* amongst . . .
7.37 . . . appear, *sing praises unto* the creator . . .

Pronunciation notes:

(**Dee 7.4—O écri mi*)

(**Dee 7.37—O é crimi*) This appears to be four syllables. The initial *O* and *e* each stand alone. The accent is placed on the second syllable. The first *i* seems to take the long sound.

(**Dee 7.4—oécrîmi*) See the *48 Claves*. Here, Dee again shows the accent on the *e*, and places a circumflex over the first *i* to indicate its long sound.

(**Dee 7.37—oëcrimi*) See the *48 Claves*. Dee placed a dieresis over the *e* to indicate that it does not combine its sound with the preceding *O*.

Also:

"Ecrin" (EE-krin) Praise

Ofafafe (oh-FAY-fay-fee)* *n.* Vials

9.69 Come away, and not *your vials*

Pronunciation notes:

(**Dee—O fa fa fe*) Four syllables. The initial *O* stands alone. The two *a*'s and the final *e* should take their long sounds.

(**Dee—ofáfâfe*) See the *48 Claves*. Here, Dee placed an accent over the *a* in the second syllable. He also placed a circumflex over the second *a* to indicate its long sound.

Also:

Efafafe (ee-FAY-fay-fee) — Vials

Oh (oh) *v.* — Come, and Bear Witness(?)*

Note:

See *TFR*, p. 3. The Angel *Murifri* here speaks a prayer in Angelical, and Kelley can only overhear a few of the words: *Oh Gahire Rudna gephna oh Gahire.* It is unclear whether this represents a single Angelical phrase, or if they are disconnected words recorded by Dee as Kelley overheard them here and there in the prayer. No translations are suggested. (It seems likely, at least, that *Oh Gahire* is intended as a repeated phrase.)

Also:

O (oh) — Come, and Bear Witness*

Note:

(**Dee—Befafes O, is to call upon him as on God. Befafes O, is as much to say, Come Befafes and bear witness.*) See the *Five Books*, p. 310. Dee is here using the Angel Befafes as an example. Note that *O*, by itself, seems to indicate "Come and Bear Witness." The same is likely true of *Oh*, so that *Oh Gahire* is an invocation, likely of an aspect of God. (See *Gahire* for more.)

Compare from *Loagaeth*:

O, Oh

Ohio (oh-hii-oh)* *n.* — Woe

10.65–70, 72 Woe, woe . . . yea woe be to the earth.

Note:

The Angel in Key Ten utters seven woes for the earth.

Pronunciation notes:

(**Dee—O hi o*) Three syllables. Both *O*s stand alone, and the *i* should take a long sound.

(**Dee—Ohîo*) See the *48 Claves*. Here, Dee places a circumflex over the *i*—confirming its long sound.

Ohorela (oh-hor-EL-a)* *v.* To Legislate

1.39 . . . to whom *I made a law* to govern the holy ones . . .

Pronunciation notes:

(**Dee—call it Ohorela*) I assume this should be four syllables.

(**Dee—ohoréla*) See *48 Claves*. The accent is places on the third syllable.

"Oi" (oh-ii) *adj.* or *pron.* This

Compounds:

Oisalman (oh-ii-SAYL-man) ["Oi" + Salman] This House

Note:

This can be a pronoun (as in "this is my cat"), but it is used in this case as an adjective (". . .until this house fall").

Oiad (oh-ii-AD)* *n.* (Of) God

**14.4 . . . the daughters of *the Just* . . .

14.19 . . . behold the voice *of God* . . .

18.9 . . . openest the glory *of God* . . .

Pronunciation notes:

(**Dee 18.9—O i ad*) Three syllables. The *O* and *i* each stand alone.

(**Dee 14.4, 19; 18.9—oîad*) See the *48 Claves*. Dee placed a circumflex over the *i* to indicate its long sound.

I have adopted the accent from similar words.

Note:

The transmission of Key Fourteen is missing from Dee's journals. We only have the English for this Key given later (see *TFR*, p. 193). Plus, the word appears in these locations in Dee's *48 Claves*.

**Others have suggested that word 14.4 should be *Balit* (the just). I would agree that Balit better fits the English in a literal sense. On the other hand, "the Just" in Key Fourteen might be a direct reference to God (as in the God of Justice), so that the English might better read ". . .the daughters of God." If so, then *Oiad* does fit better here.

Also:

Geiad (jej-AYD)	Lord and Master
Iad (yad)	God
"Iadoias" (jad-oh-JAS)	Eternal God
Iadpil (ii-AD-pil)	(To) Him
Ioiad (joh-JAD)	Him That Liveth Forever
Piad (pii-AD)	Your God

Probable root:

Ia (yah) n/a

Oisalman (oh-ii-SAYL-man)* ["Oi" + Salman] *comp.* This House

8.29 . . . until *this house* fall . . .

Pronunciation notes:

(**Dee—O i sal man*) Four syllables. Both the initial *O* and the *i* stand alone. (Rather than making the combined sound of "oy.")

(**Dee—O isâlman*) See the *48 Claves*. Here, Dee placed a circumflex over the first *a* to indicate its long sound.

I have adopted the accent from *Isalman* (is a house).

Ol (ohl)* *pron.* I

1.1 . . . *I* reign over you . . .

Pronunciation notes:

(**Dee—Ol*) One syllable.

Probable root:

L (el) — First, One

Probable shared root:

Aqlo (AY-kwah-loh) — Thy

Bolp (bohlp) — Be Thou

Note:

The pronoun *Ol* (I) is used only once in the Keys—as the very first word of Key One. I should point out, though it may or may not be important, that it is used by God to refer to Himself. It may also appear as a root in words like *Aqlo* (thy) and *Bolp* (be thou).

Compare from *Loagaeth*:

Ol

OL (oh-el)* — 24

10.38 . . . 5678 times *in the 24th part of* a moment . . .

14.8 . . . which sit on seats *24* . . .

Pronunciation notes:

(**Dee—O L*) Seems to be two syllables, each letter standing alone.

Note:

The transmission of Key Fourteen is missing from Dee's journals. We only have the English for this Key given later (see *TFR*, p. 193). Plus, the word appears in this location in Dee's *48 Claves*.

See *Ol* (I) above. These two words do not seem related. Note that *OL* (24) is given a different pronunciation than *Ol* (I).

Olani (oh-el-AY-nii)* *adv.* — Two Times (Twice)

9.10 . . . vials 8 of wrath *for two times* and a half.

Pronunciation notes:

(**Dee—O L a ni*) Four syllables. The *O*, *l*, and *a* each stand alone. It is unclear why the *l* is written as a capital.

(**Dee—oláni*) See the *48 Claves*. Here, Dee placed an accent over the *a* in the third syllable.

Also:

Pala (pay-la) Two, separated
Pola (poh-la) Two, together

Note:

Also see *Viv* (second).

"Olap" (oh-lap) *n.* Men

Compounds:

Normolap (nor-moh-lap) ["Norm" + "Olap"] Sons of Men

Also:

Ollog (ohl-log) Men
"Ollor" (ohl-or) Man
Olora (oh-loh-ra) (Of) Man

Note:

Also see *Cordziz* (mankind).

Olcordziz (ohl-KORD-ziz)* [Oln + Cordziz] *comp.* Made Mankind

30.105 . . . it rependeth me *I made man* . . .

Pronunciation notes:

(**Dee—Ol cord ziz*) Three syllables. All vowels appear to take their short sounds.

(**Dee—olcórdziz*) See the *48 Claves*. Here, Dee placed an accent on the second syllable.

Note:

It is not clear why *Oln* drops its *n* when compounded to *Cordziz*. However, since the English sense of this word is "I made mankind," it may be a play on words between *Oln* (made) and *Ol* (I).

Ollog (ohl-log)* *n.* — Men

13.10 . . . making *men* drunken . . .

Pronunciation notes:

(**Dee—Ol log*) Two syllables. I suggest a long sound for the initial *O*.

Also:

"Olap" (oh-lap) — Men
"Ollor" (ohl-lor) — Man
Olora (oh-loh-ra) — (Of) Man

Note:

Also see *Cordziz* (mankind).

It is a long shot, but perhaps there is a relationship between this word and *Oloag*, a Name of God in the Northern Watchtower, ruling the Angels of medicine. Perhaps this is the God "of Man."

"Ollor" (ohl-lor) *n.* — Man

Compounds:

Lasollor (las-OHL-or) ["Las" + "Ollor"] — Rich Man

Also:

Ollog (ohl-log) — Men
"Olap" (oh-lap) — Men
Olora (oh-loh-ra) — (Of) Man

Note:

Also see *Cordziz* (mankind).

Oln (ohln)* *v.* — Made (of)

8.4 . . . third heaven *made of* hyacinth pillars . . .

Pronunciation note:

(**Dee—Oln*) Dee seems to indicate a single syllable here.

Compounds:

Olcordziz (ohl-CORD-ziz) [Oln + Cordziz] Made Mankind

Note:

See note at *Olcordziz*.

Also:

Eol (ee-OHL) Made

Eolis (ee-OH-lis) Making

Compare from *Loagaeth*:

Olna, Olnah, Olneh, Olnoh

Olora (oh-loh-ra)* *n.* (Of) Man

10.62 . . . as the heart *of man* doth his thoughts.

Pronunciation notes:

(**Dee—O lo ra*) Three syllables. Both *O*s appear to take their long sounds.

(**Dee—olôra*) See the *48 Claves*. Dee here placed a circumflex over the second *o* to indicate its long sound.

Also:

Ollog (ohl-log) Men

"Olap" (oh-lap) Men

"Ollor" (ohl-lor) Man

Note:

Also see *Cordziz* (mankind).

Also:

See note at *Ollog*.

Om (om)* *v.* To Understand/Know

2.4 . . . can the wings of the winds *understand* . . .

10.52 . . . neither *know* at any time . . .

Pronunciation notes:

(**Dee—Om*)

Compounds:

Dsom (dee-som) [Ds + Om] That Understand

Ixomaxip (iks-oh-MAKS-ip) ["Ix" + Omax + "Ip"] Let Her Be Known

Also:

Omax (oh-MAKS) Knowest

"Oma" (oh-ma) (Of) Understanding

"Omp" (omp) Understanding

Compare from *Loagaeth*:

Om

"Oma" (oh-ma) *n.* (Of) Understanding

Compounds:

Gmicalzoma (jee-mii-KAYL-zoh-ma) [Gmicalzo + "Oma"] Power of Understanding

Also:

Om (om) Understand/Know

Omax (oh-MAKS) Knowest

"Omp" (omp) Understanding

Omaoas (oh-may-OH-as)* *n.* Names

30.91 . . . let them forget *their names* . . .

Pronunciation notes:

(**Dee—O ma o as*) Four syllables. Both *O*s stand alone. I suggest a long *a* at the end of the second syllable, because it is immediately followed by an *o*.

(**Dee—omaóas*) See the *48 Claves*. Here, Dee placed an accent on the *o* in the third syllable.

Apparent shared root:

Dooaip (doo-OH-ip) In the Name

Dooain (doo-OH-ay-in) — Name
Dooiap (doo-OY-ap) — In the Name

Note:
I assume that the combination of *oa* forms the root of these words.

Omax (oh-MAKS) *v.* — To Know

15.12 . . . who *knowest* the great name . . .

Pronunciation notes:
(**Dee—ômax*) See the *48 Claves*. Likely two syllables. Dee placed a circumflex over the initial *O* to indicate its long sound. I have adopted the accent from *Ixomaxip* (let her be known).

Note:
The transmission of Key Fifteen is missing from Dee's journals. We only have the English for this Key given later (see *TFR*, p. 193). Plus, the word appears in this location in Dee's *48 Claves*.

This is likely an instance of the *-ax* suffix, indicating action.

Also:
Om (om) — To Understand/Know
"Oma" (oh-ma) — Understanding
"Omp" (omp) — Understanding

Compound:
Ixomaxip (iks-oh-MAKS-ip) ["Ix" + Omax + "Ip"] — Let Her Be known

Omicaolz (oh-mii-KAY-ohl-zohd)* *v.* — (Be) Mighty

7.40 . . . *be mighty* amongst us . . .

Pronunciation notes:
(**Dee—O mi ca ol zod*) Five syllables. The initial *O* stands alone. The *i* should likely take its long sound. The *a* should also take its long sound—as it is followed by an *o* (as in the English word *chaos*). The final *z* stands alone.

I have adopted the accent from other versions of this word.

Also:

Gmicalzo (jee-mii-KAYL-zoh)	Power
Micalzo (mii-KAYL-zoh)	Power/Mighty
Micaoli (mii-KAY-oh-lii)	Mighty
Micaolz (mii-KAY-ohlz or mii-KAY-ohl-zohd)	Mighty
Micalp (mii-KALP)	Mightier

Possible shared root:

Miketh (mii-KETH)	"The True Measure of the Will of God in Judgment, Which Is by Wisdom" (?)

Note:

See also *Vohim* (mighty).

"Omp" (omp) *n.* — Understanding

Compounds:

Omptilb (omp-tilb) ["Omp" + Tilb]	Her Understanding

Also:

Om (om)	To Understand/Know
"Oma" (oh-ma)	(Of) Understanding
Omax (oh-MAKS)	Knowest

Note:

I am unsure if "Omp" is a proper element here, or if the compound should be Om + "Ptilb." (See "Ip" and "Pi"—both versions of "her.")

Omptilb (omp-tilb)* ["Omp" + Tilb] *comp.* — Her Understanding

30.101 . . . confound *her understanding* with darkness . . .

Pronunciation notes:

(**Dee—Omp tilb*) Two syllables. I find that this word, when spoken fluently, has a nearly silent *p*.

Note:

See note at "Omp."

Also:

See *Om* (know).

Ooanoan (oh-oh-AY-noh-an)* *n.* Eyes

9.40 *In their eyes* are millstones . . .

Pronunciation notes:

(**Dee—O o A no an*) Five syllables—though I find the word sounds more like four syllables when spoken fliently. The first two *O*s and the first *a* each stand alone. Dee might have capitalized the *A* to indicate the accent.

(**Dee—oöánôan*) See the *48 Claves*. Here, Dee placed a dieresis over the second *o* to indicate that it does not combine its sound with the previous vowel. He placed an accent over the *a* in the third syllable. Finally, he placed a circumflex over the third *o* to indicate its long sound.

Also:

Ooaona (oh-oh-AY-oh-na) Eyes

Probable shared root:

"Qanis" (kew-ay-nis) Olives

Oanio (oh-AY-nii-oh) Moment

Note:

The similar spelling suggests these four words are connected. This might make sense for *Ooanoan* (eyes): the word *Taqanis* (as olives) in Key Five appears to refer to the stars. In biblical literature, the word "eyes" is often used to indicate "stars." (Such as in the visions of St. John and Ezekiel, both of whom saw celestial Angels with wings "full of eyes.")

If this is the case, then the shared root here may indicate small units, which would explain its use to indicate a moment (*Oanio*).

Also compare the name of the Part of the Earth (and its Angelic Governor), *Ooanamb*.

Ooaona (oh-oh-AY-oh-na)* *n.* Eyes

[Enochian script]

13.5 . . . which have 42 *eyes* to stir up wrath . . .

Pronunciation notes:

(**Dee—O O Ao na.*) Dee indicates here that the two first *O*s should stand alone. Next, there is no *ao* letter combination In Early Modern English. Instead, the letters must make two sounds—as in the word *chaos*. That makes this a word of five syllables (although the double *O*s do tend to blend when this word is spoken fluently). I assume the last *a* is short, and the accent is on the third syllable, as indicated in the word *Ooanoan* (their eyes).

(**Dee—ooáôna*) See the *48 Claves*. Here, Dee placed the accent over the first *a* (which should be the third syllable). He also placed a circumflex over the third *o* to indicate its long sound.

Compounds:

Sabaooaona (say-bay-oh-oh-AY-oh-na) ["Saba" + Ooaona] Whose Eyes

Also:

Ooanoan (oh-oh-AY-noh-an) Eyes

Probable shared root:

"Qanis" (kew-ay-nis) Olives

Oanio (oh-AY-nii-oh) Moment

Ooge (oh-oj)* *n.* Chamber

[Enochian script]

2.21 . . . for *the chamber of* righteousness . . .

Pronunciation notes:

(**Dee—Ooge*) Dee gives us little clue here. Though, the final *e* likely makes the preceding *g* soft.

(**Dee—öoge*) See *48 Claves*. Note the dieresis over the first *O*, showing that its sound does not combine with the following *o*. (I suggest the first *O* takes the long sound, and the second takes the short sound.) Thus, this is likely a word of two syllables.

OP (oh-pee) 22

10.12 . . . are *22* nests of lamentation . . .

Note:
This word was not originally given with Key Ten. It was added later when Nalvage transmitted the English for the Key (see *TFR*, p. 192). This seems to have been the case with many of the numbers mentioned in the Keys.

Oq (oh-kwah)* *prep.* or *conj.* But/Except

2.37 . . . is not *but* in the mind of the all-powerful.

Pronunciation note:
(**Dee—O qua*) Two syllables, each letter stands alone. (The *q* makes the sound of "kwah.")
(**Dee—o-q*) See *48 Claves*. This note matches Dee's note from *TFR*.

Note:
Oq (but) is a preposition. See *Crip* (but), which is a conjunction.

Or (or)* *prop. n.* Letter *F*

Note:
The name of the Angelical letter for *F*. It is likely that these letter names have translations of their own. (For instance, note the Hebrew alphabet: the letter *F* is named *Peh*, but *Peh* also translates as "mouth.") However, such translations for the Angelical letters are never given. (See the *Five Books*, p. 270.)

Pronunciation note:
(**Dee—The voice seemed orh.*) Dee likely added this note to distinguish the sound of *Or* from the sound of *Ur*. (See the note at *Ur*.)

Compare from *Loagaeth*:
Or

Orh (or) *prop. n.* — "A Spirit of Darkness"*

From *Loagaeth*:

(**Dee—The spirit Orh is the second in the scale of imperfections of darkness.*)
See the *Five Books*, p. 310.

Probable shared root:

Ors (ors) — Darkness

Compare from *Loagaeth*:

Orh, Orho

Oroch (oh-ROK) *prep.* — Under

14.15 . . . which have *under you* 1636.

Pronunciation notes:

I have adopted the accent from *Orocha* (beneath).

Note:

The transmission of Key Fourteen is missing from Dee's journals. We only have the English for this Key given later (see *TFR*, p. 193). Plus, the word appears in this location in Dee's *48 Claves*.

Also:

Orocha (oh-ROH-ka) — Beneath

Possible shared root:

Orri (or-ii) — Barren Stone
Ors (ors) — Darkness
Orsba (ors-ba) — Drunken
Orscor (ors-kor) — Dryness
Orscatbl (ors-kat-bel) — Buildings

Orocha (oh-ROH-ka)* *prep.* — Beneath

30.119 . . . the lower heavens *beneath you*, let them serve . . .

Pronunciation notes:

(*Dee—*O ro cha ka*) Three syllables. The *ch* takes a hard "k" (or "kh") sound, as in the English word *ache.*

(*Dee—*orócha*) See the *48 Claves*. Here, Dee placed an accent upon the second syllable.

Also:

Oroch (oh-ROK) Under

Possible shared root:

Orri (or-ii) Barren Stone
Ors (ors) Darkness
Orsba (ors-ba) Drunken
Orscor (ors-kor) Dryness
Orscatbl (ors-kat-bel) Buildings

Orri (or-ii)* *n.* (Barren) Stone

2.26 . . . stronger are your feet than *the barren stone.*

Pronunciation notes:

(*Dee—Orri) Likely two syllables. A double *r* in Early Modern English represents a single "r" sound. The final *i* likely takes the long vowel sound.

Possible shared root:

Oroch (oh-ROK) Beneath
Orocha (oh-ROH-ka) Under
Ors (ors) Darkness
Orsba (ors-ba) Drunken
Orscor (ors-kor) Dryness
Orscatbl (ors-kat-bel) Buildings

Ors (ors)* *n.* Darkness

30.102 Confound her understanding with *darkness.*

Pronunciation notes:

(**Dee—Ors*) One syllable.

Also:

Orh (or) — A Spirit of Darkness

Possible shared root:

Oroch (oh-ROK) — Beneath
Orocha (oh-ROH-ka) — Under
Orri (or-ii) — Barren Stone
Orsba (ors-ba) — Drunken
Orscor (ors-kor) — Dryness
Orscatbl (ors-kat-bel) — Buildings

Compare from *Loagaeth*:

Oarz, Ors, Orse, Orze, Orsa, Orsat, Ors lah

Orsba (ors-ba)* *adj.* — Drunken

13.11 . . . making men *drunken* which are empty.
30.53 . . . may always be *drunken* and vexed . . .

Pronunciation notes:

(**Dee 13.11; 30.53—Ors ba*) Two syllables.

Possible shared root:

Oroch (oh-ROK) — Beneath
Orocha (oh-ROH-ka) — Under
Orri (or-ii) — Barren Stone
Ors (ors) — Darkness
Orscor (ors-kor) — Dryness
Orscatbl (ors-kat-bel) — Buildings

Compare from *Loagaeth*:

Oarz, Ors, Orse, Orze, Orsa, Orsat, Ors lah

Orscatbl (ors-kat-bel)* *n.* — Buildings

30.96 *His buildings*, let them become caves . . .

Pronunciation notes:

(**Dee—Ors cat bl*) Three syllables. In order for the final *bl* to form one syllable, the *l* must sound as "el."

Note:

It would seem that *Ors* (darkness) plays a role in this word—perhaps it is due to the comparison to caves. As far as I can tell, the root letters of *Tilb* (her) are not intended.

Also see *Trof* (a building).

Possible shared root:

Oroch (oh-ROK)	Beneath
Orocha (oh-ROH-ka)	Under
Orri (or-ii)	Barren Stone
Ors (ors)	Darkness
Orsba (ors-ba)	Drunken
Orscor (ors-kor)	Dryness

Compare from *Loagaeth*:

Oarz, Ors, Orse, Orze, Orsa, Orsat, Ors lah

Orscor (ors-kor) *n.* — Dryness

15.10 . . . weave the earth with *dryness* . . .

Note:

The transmission of Key Fifteen is missing from Dee's journals. We only have the English for this Key given later (see *TFR*, p. 193). Plus, the word appears in this location in Dee's *48 Claves*.

Possible shared root:

Oroch (oh-ROK)	Beneath
Orocha (oh-ROH-ka)	Under
Orri (or-ii)	Barren Stone
Ors (ors)	Darkness
Orsba (ors-ba)	Drunken
Orscatbl (ors-kat-bel)	Buildings

Compare from *Loagaeth*:

Oarz, Ors, Orse, Orze, Orsa, Orsat, Ors lah

OS (os) 12

Compounds:

Thilnos (thil-nos) ["Thiln" + Os] 12 Seats

Oslondoh (os-LON-doh) [Os + Londoh] 12 Kingdoms

Compare from *Loagaeth*:

Os

Osf (os-ef) *n.* Discord

From *Corpus Omnium*:

Found in the Tribulation portion of the Table, in the phrase *Osf Ser Iad* (Discord and Sorrow of God).

Oslondoh (os-LON-doh)* [Os + Londoh] *comp.* 12 Kingdoms

3.8 . . . on whose hands stand *12 kingdoms*.

Pronunciation notes:

(**Dee—Os Lon doh [Os signifieth twelve.]*) Dee notes that this is a compound word. It has three syllables.

(**Dee—Os Lón-doh*) See the *48 Claves*. Other versions of *Londoh* show the accent on the "doh" syllable. However, when compounded with *Os*, the accent moves to the "Lon" syllable.

Ot* (ot) *conj.* And

Alternate spelling:

(**Dee 1.75—OD . . . or OT*)

Also:

Od (ohd) And

Othil (oh-THIL)* *n.* or *v.* Seats (of) / To Set

3.11 . . . six are *the seats of* living breath . . .
4.1 . . . *I have set* my feet in the south . . .

Note:
Perhaps Key Four should literally read *"the seats of* my feet are in the south," but this is stated better in English just as it is written in Key Four.

Pronunciation notes:
(**Dee 3.11—Othil*)
(**Dee 4.1—O thil*) Two syllables. The *O* stands alone.
(**Dee 3.11—óthil*) See *48 Claves*. Dee places the accent on the first syllable.
(**Dee 4.1—Othíl*) See *48 Claves*. Here, Dee places the accent on the second syllable. I have adopted this option in my pronunciation.

Compounds:
Othilrit (oh-THIL-rit) (Othil + Rit) Seats of Mercy

Also:
Thil (thil) Seats
Thild (thild) Seats
"Thiln" (thiln) Seats

Othilrit (oh-THIL-rit)* [Othil + Rit] *comp.* Seats of Mercy

7.3 . . . *the seats of mercy* and continuance . . .

Pronunciation notes:
(**Dee—O thil rit*) Three syllables. The *O* stands alone. The *i*'s should both take a short sound.
(**Dee—Othílrit*) See the *48 Claves*. Dee places an accent on the second syllable.

Oucho (oh-yew-choh)* *v.* To Confound

30.65 One season, *let it confound* another.

Pronunciation notes:

(**Dee—O v Cho Chose*) Dee shows us three syllables, with the *O* and the *u*/*v* standing alone. It is unlikely that Dee intended the *u* to sound like "vee," because the letter precedes a consonant. (Further supporting this is the "u" sound in other versions of this word.) Finally, Dee adds "chose"—to show us that the *ch* in the last syllable should make the "tch" sound (as in *church* and *chose*), and the *O* should be long.

Also:

Unchi (un-kii) To Confound
Urch (urk) The Confusers

Note:

It would appear that "uch" serves as a common root between these words.

Ovoars (oh-voh-ars)* *n.* Center

18.10 . . . the glory of God *to the center* of the earth.

Pronunciation notes:

(**Dee—O vo ors*) Three syllables. The initial *O* stands alone. Dee then shows a long "o" sound at the end of the second syllable. He may have mistakenly written an *o* in place of the *a* in the third syllable, or it is an error in *TFR*.

(**Dee—ouôars*) See the *48 Claves*. Dee places a circumflex over the second *o* to indicate its long sound. Note the *a* has returned to the third syllable.

Ovof (oh-vof)* *v.* To Magnify

12.18 . . . the Lord *may be magnified* whose name . . .

Pronunciation notes:
(**Dee—O vof*) Two syllables. The initial *O* stands alone.

OX (oks)* 26

8.6 . . . made of hyacinth pillars *26* in whom . . .

Pronunciation notes:
(**Dee—Ox*) One syllable.

Note:
This word was not originally given with Key Eight. It was added later when Nalvage transmitted the English for the Key (see *TFR*, p. 192). This seems to have been the case with many of the numbers mentioned in the Keys.

Oxex (oks-eks)* *v.* To Vomit (i.e., To Hurl Forth)

10.26 . . . and *vomit out* the heads of scorpions . . .

Pronunciation notes:
(**Dee—Ox ex*) Two syllables. The vowels both appear to take their short sounds.

Note:
This is not the Angelical word for *vomit* (a noun). Instead, this word is a verb, as in a volcano "vomiting" lava or a cannon "vomiting" flame. I notice this word falls just short of the *-ax* suffix, indicating action.
This word may share the masculine "Ox" root with the following:

Possible shared root:

Oxiayal (oks-AY-al) [Tox? + Iaial]	Mighty Seat
Oxo (oks-oh)	"The Fifteenth Aethyr"
Tox (toks)	His

Oxiayal (oks-AY-al)* [Tox? + Iaial] *comp.* Mighty Seat (i.e., Divine Throne)

11.1 *The Mighty seat* groaned . . .

Pronunciation notes:

(**Dee—Ox í Ay al*) Dee heard four syllables, with an accent on the second syllable. However, Illemese corrected this later:

(*Illemese—Ox cai al. Sai*) See *TFR*, p. 200. Three syllables. The *c* used in the second syllable of *Illemese'* phonetic note takes an "s" sound—which I believe indicates the *second half* of the sound of "x." It appears to me that the accented *i* in Dee's phonetic note is not sounded at all in Illemese's version. It is unclear if the *i* should also be removed from the Angelical spelling of the word as well. (I have decided to leave it in.) Next, the letters *ai* or *ay* combine to form a long "a" sound—as in the English words *dais* and *day*. Finally, I have left the accent on the second syllable.

Possible shared root:

Oxex (oks-eks) To Vomit

Tox (toks) His

Note:

This reference to *Iaial* (conclude or judge), combined with the root of *Tox* (him/his), seems to make perfect sense when describing the Holy *Merkavah*—the Throne or "Judgment-Seat" of God.

Oxo (oks-oh) *prop. n.* "The Fifteenth Aethyr"

30.3 . . . which dwell in *the fifteenth aethyr* . . .

Note:

This (word 30.3) is the single space in the Key of the Aethyrs, which must be changed for each invocation—replacing word 30.3 with the name of the appropriate Aethyr. No established definitions were given for these names.

Note that this word is a palindrome, spelled the same forward and backward.

Oxo contains the three Parts of the Earth *Tahamdo*, *Nociabi*, and *Tastoxo*.

Possible shared root:

Oxex (oks-eks) To Vomit

Tox (tox) His

Ozazm (oz-az-em)* *v.* To Make (Me)

2.48 . . . and *make me* a strong seething . . .

Pronunciation notes:

(**Dee—Ozazm*) Likely three syllables.

Also:

Ozazma (oz-az-ma) To Make (Us)

Note:

Also see *Oln* (made) and *Eol* (made).

Ozazma (oz-az-ma)* *v.* To Make (Us)

30.155 . . . and *make us* partakers of undefiled knowledge.

Pronunciation notes:

(**Dee—Ozazma*) Likely three syllables.

Also:

Ozazm (oz-az-em) To Make (Me)

Note:

Also see *Oln* (made) and *Eol* (made).

Ozien (oh-ZEEN)* *n.* (Mine Own) Hand

3.23 . . . except by *mine own hand.*

Pronunciation notes:

(**Dee—Ozien*) I assume there should be two syllables here. The Early Modern English letter combination *ie* can make a long "e" sound. (It can also make a long "i" sound—but usually in combination with *ght*. So I have settled on the long "e" sound instead.)

(**Dee—ozíen*) See the *48 Claves*. Dee places the accent on the *i*—or the second syllable.

Also:

Azien (az-EEN) — (On Whose) Hands

Zien (zeen) — Hands

Probable shared root:

Ozol (oh-ZOHL) — Hands

Zol (zohd-OL) — Hands

Ozol (oh-ZOHL)* *n.* — Hands**

9.55 . . . and upon *their hands* are marble . . .

Pronunciation notes:

(*Dee—O zol*) Two syllables. The first *O* stands alone. Note how the *z* is not extended to "zohd" in this version of the word. (Compare to *Zol*.) This further supports the theory that the extended *z* is not a grammatical rule, but a lyrical flourish.

(*Dee—ózól*) See the *48 Claves*. Here, Dee placed accent marks over *both* syllables. It is unclear which syllable should take the accent. I have chosen the second syllable based on other versions of this word.

Note:

***Ozol* was translated as "heads" in Key Nine. However, this is apparently a mistake. *Zol* is elsewhere translated as "hands," and this makes much more sense in the English given for the Key.

Also:

Zol (zohd-OL) — Hands

Shared root:

Azien (az-EEN) — (On Whose) Hands

Ozien (oh-ZEEN) — (Mine Own) Hand

Zien (zeen) — Hands

Ozongon (OH-zohn-gon)* *n.* — Manifold Winds

2.31 . . . mightier are your voices than *the manifold winds*.

Pronunciation note:

(**Dee—Ozongon*)

(**Dee—ózôngon*) See *48 Claves*. Apparently three syllables. Dee places an accent on the first syllable. He also places a circumflex over the second *o*—indicating its long sound.

Also:

Zong (zong) Winds

Mals (P)

P (pee) 8

9.8 . . . which have 8 vials of wrath . . .

Pronunciation notes:
A letter standing alone sounds like the English name of that letter.

Note:
This word was not originally given with Key Nine. It was added later when Nalvage transmitted the English for the Key (see *TFR*, p. 191). This seems to have been the case with many of the numbers mentioned in the Keys.

Pa (pah) *prop. n.* Letter *B*

Note:
The name of the Angelical letter for *B*. It is likely that these letter names have translations of their own. (For instance, note the Hebrew alphabet: the letter *B* is named *Beth*, but *Beth* also translates as "house" or "dwelling.") However, such translations for the Angelical letters are never given. (See the *Five Books*, p. 270.)

Compare from *Loagaeth*:
Pa

"Paaox" (PAY-ay-oks) *v.* To Remain

Compounds:
Dspaaox (dee-SPAY-ay-oks) [Ds +" Paaox"] Which Remain

Also:
Paaoxt (PAY-ay-oxt) (Let) Remain

Note:
Compare this word to the name of the Angel *Paax* (an Angel of medicine of the Western Watchtower).

Paaoxt (PAY-ay-okst)* *v.* To Remain

30.133 No place, *let it remain* in one number.

Pronunciation notes:

(**Dee—Pa a oxt*) Three syllables. Both *a*'s appear to make the long vowel sound. The accent on the first syllable is taken from *Dspaaox.*

Also:

"Paaox" (PAY-ay-oks) To Remain

Note:

It is possible that the difference in spelling between "Paaox" and *Paaoxt* is merely a phonetic gloss.

Pacaduasam (pak-ad-yew-as-sam) n/a

Note:

(*Dee—Huseh Huseh Huseh garmal, Peleh Peleh Peleh pacaduasam.*) See the *Five Books*, p. 415. This is part of a prayer recited jointly by the Archangels Michael, Raphael, and Uriel. No translations are suggested.

Possible shared root:

Pacaph (pak-af) n/a

Compare from *Loagaeth*:

Pacad, Pacadaah, Pacadabaah, Pacadura, Pachad, Pachadah, Pachadora, Pachadpha, and maybe *Paxchadma*

Pacaph (pak-af) n/a

Note:

See the *Five Books*, p. 413. Kelley overhears many voices singing a song at some distance, and these are the words Dee recorded: *Pinzu-a lephe ganiurax kelpadman pacaph*. No translations are suggested.

Note:

The similarity between this word and the Hebrew *Pachad* (fear).

Possible shared root:

Pacaduasam (pak-ad-yew-as-sam) n/a

Compare from *Loagaeth*:

Pacad, Pacadaah, Pacadabaah, Pacadura, Pachad, Pachadah, Pachadora, Pachadpha, and maybe *Paxchadma*

Padgze (paj)* *n.* "Justice From Divine Power Without Defect"**

Pronunciation notes:

(***Dee—Pagze/Pag.*) See the *Five Books*, p. 316. I suspect that Dee is indicating that *gze* should combine into a soft "g" (or "dg") sound. Thus, the word is one syllable, suggested by *Pag* in Dee's phonetic note.

From *Loagaeth*:

(**Dee—Justice from Divine Power without defect.*) See the *Five Books*, p. 316.

Paeb (pay-eb)* *n.* Oak

10.8 . . . *an oak* whose branches are 22 nests . . .

Pronunciation notes:

(**Dee—Pa eb*) Two syllables. The *a* appears to take its long sound. The *e* should be short.

(**Dee—*pæb) See the *48 Claves*. Here, Dee uses the "ash" (æ), which can make a short "a" sound or a long "e" sound. However, this conflicts with his two-syllable phonetic note in *TFR*. I have settled on the *TFR* version in this case.

"Page" (pay-jee) *v.* To Rest

Compounds:

Pageip (pay-jee-ip) ["Page" + Ip] Rest Not

Compare from *Loagaeth*:

Pagesgem, Pageh, Pagel, Arpagels, Arpaget, and maybe *Nagel.*

Pageip (pay-jee-ip)* ["Page" + Ip] *comp.* Rest Not

10.50 . . . which *rest not* neither know any long time . . .

Pronunciation notes:

(*Dee—Pa ge ip*) Three syllables. The *a* and *e* likely take long sounds. The *g*—preceding an *e*—should take the soft "j" sound.

(*Dee—pagêip*) See the *48 Claves*. Here, Dee placed a circumflex over the *e* to indicate its long sound.

Paid (pay-id)* *adv.* Always

30.52 . . . may be *always* drunken and vexed . . .

Pronunciation notes:

(*Dee—Pa id*) Dee here indicates two syllables.

Pal (pal)* *prop. n.* Letter *X*

Note:

The name of the Angelical letter for *X*. It is likely that these letter names have translations of their own. (For instance, note the Hebrew alphabet: the digraph *Tz* is named *Tzaddi*, but *Tzaddi* also translates as "fish hook.") However, such translations for the Angelical letters are never given. (See the *Five Books*, p. 270.)

Pronunciation notes:

(*Dee—The p being sounded remissly.*) The Latin word *remissus* means "to relax"—from which we get the English word *remiss* (to neglect or ignore). Therefore, the *P* in Pal must be very relaxed—nearly silent.

Compare from *Loagaeth*:

Pal

Pala (pay-la) *n.* — Two, separated*

From *Loagaeth*:

(**Dee—Pola and Pala signify Two. Pola signifieth two together, and Pala signifieth two separated.*) See *Five Books*, p. 304. *Pola* (two together, or couple) appears in *Loagaeth*, while *Pala* is mentioned only in the marginal note. See also *Viv* (second).

Also:

Olani (oh-el-AY-nii) — Two Times, Twice
Pola (poh-la) — Two-together

"Pam" (pam) *adv.* — Not

Compounds:

Ipam (ip-am) [I + "Pam"] — Is Not
Ipamis (ip-am-is) [I + "Pamis"] — Can Not Be

Note:

The words "Pam" and "Pamis" are very uncertain. In Angelical, the word *I* (is / are) becomes its own antonym in the form of *Ip* (not). However, both *Ipam* and *Ipamis* demand the essential form of the word *I* (for "is" and "be" respectively). That leaves "Pam" and "Pamis" as possible words. Of course, *Ip* could stand as a root here. See also *"Ge"* (not) and *Ag* (none).

Pambt (pamt)* *prep.* — Unto (Me)

18.26 Be thou a window of comfort *unto me*.

Pronunciation notes:

(**Dee—Pambt*) One syllable. I suspect the *a* should take a short sound. The *b* in the letter combination *mb* is likely near-silent—as in the English words *comb* and *bomb*.

Note:

Also see *Tia* (unto) and *Pugo* (as unto).

"Pamis" (pam-is) *v.* Cannot

Compounds:

Ipam (ip-am) [I + "Pam"] Is Not

Ipamis (ip-am-is) [I + "Pamis"] Can Not Be

Note:

See note at "Pam."

Panpir (pan-per)* *v.* To Pour Down (Rain)

3.51 . . . *pouring down* the fires of life and increase . . .

Pronunciation notes:

(*Dee—Panpir*) Likely two syllables.

Paombd (pay-omd)* *n.* Members (Parts, Appendages)

30.75 All *her members*, let them differ . . .

Pronunciation notes:

(*Dee—Pa Ombd*) Dee indicates two syllables. I assume the *mb* represents the same sound as in the English words *comb*, *tomb*, and *bomb*. As for the vowel sounds, the note indicates a long *a* immediately followed by a short *o*—as in the English word *chaos*.

Papnor (pap-nor)* *n.* Remembrance (Memory)

7.43 For *to this remembrance* is given power . . .

Pronunciation notes:

(*Dee—Pap nor*) Two syllables. Both vowels are likely short.

Par (par)* *pron.* (In) Them

9.65 . . . the God of Righteousness rejoiceth *in them*.

Pronunciation notes:
(**Dee—Par*) One syllable.

Parach (pay-RAK)* *adj.* Equal

30.81 . . . no one creature *equal with* another . . .

Pronunciation notes:
(**Dee—Pa rach Ah Ach*) Two syllables. Dee seems to indicate that the final *ch* can take a softer "h" sound or a harder "kh" sound (as in the English word *ache*). I suggest a combination of the two, for a very soft "kh." (Also note the pronunciation of *Paracleda* (wedding), which uses a hard "c" sound.)
I have adopted the accent from *Paracelda*.

Probable shared root:
Paracleda (par-AK-lee-da) Wedding

Note:
Also see *Lel* (same).

Paracleda (par-AK-lee-da)* *n.* Wedding

2.17 . . . I have prepared as cups *for a wedding* . . .

Pronunciation notes:
(**Dee—Paracleda*) Should be four syllables. The *c* should take the hard sound when followed by an *l*—as in the English words *clean* and *climb*.
(**Dee—paráclêda*) See *48 Claves*. The accent is on the second syllable. The *e* has a circumflex, indicating its long sound.

Probable shared root:
Parach (pay-RAK) Equal

Note:
Also see *Pala* (two together, couple).

Paradial (pay-ray-DII-al)* *n.* Living Dwellings

7.13 . . . 28 *living dwellings* . . .

Pronunciation notes:

(**Dee—Pa ra dí al*) Four syllables, with an accent on the third syllable. (**Dee—paradíal*) See the *48 Claves*. The accent is again on the third syllable.

Note:

The word for "house" is given elsewhere as *Salman*. Here in Key Seven, however, this word is used after *Paradiz* (virgins) at 7.3. I assume these "living dwellings" are directly related to the Paradiz in some fashion.

Probable shared root:

Paradiz (pay-ray-DII-zohd) Virgins

Paradiz (pay-ray-DII-zohd)* *n.* Virgins

7.3 The east is a house of *virgins* . . .

Note:

There seems to be some relationship between Paradiz here, and the word *Paradial* (living dwellings) that appears later in the same Key. Paradial is obviously a special case, as the word for "house" is given elsewhere as *Salman*.

Pronunciation notes:

(**Dee—Pa ra di zod*) Four syllables. The *z* stands alone. Also, see *Paradial* (living dwellings) for the accent on the third syllable.

Probable shared root:

Paradial (pay-ray-DII-al) Living Dwellings

Parm (parm)* *v.* To Run

9.47 . . . from their mouths *run* seas of blood.

Pronunciation notes:

(**Dee—Parm*) One syllable.

Also:

Parmgi (parm-jii) (Let) Run

Parmgi (parm-jii)* *v.* (Let) Run

30.58 Her course, *let it run with* the heavens . . .

Pronunciation notes:

(**Dee—Parm gi*) Two syllables. The *g* preceding an *i* likely takes the soft sound.

Also:

Parm (parm) To Run

Pasbs (pas-bes) *n.* Daughters

14.3 . . . *the daughters* of the just . . .

Note:

The transmission of Key Fourteen is missing from Dee's journals. We only have the English for this Key given later (see *TFR*, p. 193). Plus, the word appears in this location in Dee's *48 Claves*.

"Patralx" (PAY-tralks) *n.* Rock

Compounds:

Lpatralx (el-PAY-tralks) [L + "Patralx"] One Rock

Paz (paz) *prop. n.* "The Fourth Aethyr"

30.3 . . . which dwell in *the fourth aethyr* . . .

Note:

This (word 30.3) is the single space in the Key of the Aethyrs, which must be changed for each invocation—replacing word 30.3 with the name of the appropriate Aethyr. No established definitions were given for these names.

Paz contains the three Parts of the Earth *Thotanp*, *Axziarg*, and *Pothnir*.

PD (pee-dee)* 33

4.10 . . . Thunders of Increase numbered *33* which reign . . .

Pronunciation notes:

(**Dee—PD Pe De*) Two syllables, each letter stands alone.

Peleh* (pee-lay) Worker of Wonders(?)

Note:

(**Dee—Huseh Huseh Huseh garmal, Peleh Peleh Peleh pacaduasam.*) See the *Five Books*, p. 415. This is part of a prayer recited jointly by the Archangels Michael, Raphael, and Uriel. No translations are suggested.

Note:

The Divine Name "PELE" appears on Dee's Ring of Solomon. This Name appears in Agrippa's *Three Books* . . . , Book III, chapter 11: (*Pele, signifieth with us, a worker or miracles, or causing wonders.*) In Hebrew, it is spelled *Peh, Lamed, Aleph*. (Also see "Lzirn"—To Work Wonders).

Compare from *Loagaeth*:

Peleh

PERAL (pee-AR-al)* 69636

5.34 . . . lamps *69636* whose numbers are . . .

Pronunciation notes:

(**Dee—Pe ó al*) Dee originally received this word as "Peoal," but it was later corrected to *Peral* (see *TFR*, p. 191). For my pronunciation, I have retained the structure of Dee's phonetic note, but applied it to the corrected word. It should therefore be three syllables, with an accent on the second. The *r* (instead of *o*) stands alone, and takes the accent.

(**Dee—Peóal*) See the *48 Claves*. This note essentially matches that from *TFR*. Dee did not correct the spelling of this word in the *48 Claves*.

Phama (fama) *v.* — I Will Give*

From *Loagaeth*:

(**Dee—Phamah/fama = I will give.*) See the *Five Books*, p. 320.

"Pi" (pii) *pron.* — She

Compounds:

Pii (pii-ii) ["Pi" + I] — She Is

Also:

"Ip" (ip) — Her

Note:

Also see *Tilb* (her).

Piad (pii-AD)* *n.* — (Your) God

3.3 . . . behold, sayeth *your God* . . .

Pronunciation notes:

(**Dee—Pi ad*) Two syllables. Likely a long "i" sound. I have adopted the accent from similar words.

Also:

Geiad (jej-AYD) — Lord and Master
Iad (yad) — God
"Iadoias" (jad-oh-JAS) — Eternal God
Iadpil (ii-AD-pil) — (To) Him
Ioiad (joh-JAD) — Him That Liveth Forever
Mad (mad) — (Your) God
Oiad (oh-ii-AD) — Of God

Probable root:

Ia (yah) — n/a

Piadph (pii-AD-ef)* *n.* The Depths of (My) Jaws

2.12 . . . burning flames have framed within *the depths of my jaws* . . .

Pronunciation notes:

(**Dee—Piadph*) Dee gives us little clue here.

(**Dee—pi-ádph*) See *48 Claves*. Likely three syllables. The *i* takes its long sound. The accent is on the second syllable.

Note:

This reference may be similar to "from the bottom of my heart" or even "deep in my gut." Otherwise, it may indicate "in my throat"—as the reference here in Key Two is to a song.

Piad (your God) does not appear to be intended in this case. It is perhaps a coincidental similarity in spelling.

"Piamol" n/a

Note:

Not an Angelical word. Dee and Kelley experienced problems during the reception of this word—intended for position 1.70 (righteousness). The Angels blamed the difficulty on interference from false spirits. This resulted in the erroneous transmission of "Piatol"—apparently a combination of the word preceding it in the Key (1.69—*Piap*) and the word actually intended here (1.70—*Baltle*). Dee's first attempt to correct the word—made while the false spirits continued to interfere—resulted in "Piamol." The next day, the Angels corrected it to *Baltle* (a form of *Balt*). See *Baltle*.

Piap (pii-ap) *n.* Balance

1.69 . . . *the balance of* righteousness . . .

"Piatol" n/a

Note:

Not an Angelical word. Dee and Kelley experienced problems during the reception of this word—intended for position 1.70 (righteousness).

The Angels blamed the difficulty on interference from false spirits. This resulted in the erroneous transmission of "Piatol"—apparently a combination of the word preceding it in the Key (1.69—*Piap*) and the word actually intended here (1.70—*Baltle*). Dee's first attempt to correct the word—made while the false spirits continued to interfere—resulted in "Piamol." The next day, the Angels corrected it to *Baltle* (a form of *Balt*). See *Baltle*.

Pibliar (pib-lii-AR)* *n.* — Places of Comfort

7.30 . . . strong towers and *places of comfort*.

Pronunciation notes:

(**Dee—Pib li ar*) Three syllables. The first *i* should take a short sound, while the second *i* should take its long sound.

(**Dee—piblîar*) See the *48 Claves*. Dee places a circumflex over the second *i* to indicate the long sound.

I have adopted the accent from *Bliora* (comfort).

Also:

"Bigl" (big-el)	Comforter
"Bliard" (blii-ARD)	Comfort
Blior (blii-OR)	Comfort
Bliora (blii-OH-ra)	Comfort
Bliorax (blii-OH-raks)	To Comfort
Bliorb (blii-ORB)	Comfort
Bliors (blii-ORS)	Comfort
"Bliort" (blii-ORT)	Comfort

Pidiai (pii-dii-ay-ii)* *n.* — Marble

9.57 . . . and upon their heads are *marble* sleeves.

Pronunciation notes:

(**Dee—Pi di a i*) Four syllables. The *a* and final *i* each stand alone.

Pii (pii-ii)* ["Pi" + I] *comp.* She Is

30.111 . . . *she is* the bed of an harlot . . .

Pronunciation notes:

(*Dee—Pi i*) Two syllables. I assume a long *i* in the first syllable. The *i* in the second syllable stands alone, also making a long "i" sound.

Pilah (pee-ii-lah)* *adv.* Moreover

1.47 *Moreover*, you lifted up your voices . . .

Pronunciation notes:

(*Dee—Three syllables. P is distinctly sounded by itself.*)

(*Dee—Pïlah*) See *48 Claves*. There is a dieresis placed over the *i*, to indicate that the vowel stands alone.

Pild (pild)* *adv.* Continually

3.54 . . . upon the earth *continually*.

Pronunciation notes:

(*Dee—Pild*) Seems to be one syllable.

Note:

See also *Cocasb* (time), *Capimali* (successively), *Cacacom* (flourish).

Pilzin (pil-zin)* *n.* Firmaments of Waters

6.6 . . . mighty in the *firmaments of waters* . . .

Pronunciation notes:

(*Dee—Pilzin pilzen*) Likely two syllables.

Shared root:

Zlida (zohd-lida) To Water

Note:

Pilzin is a noun, while *Zlida* is a verb.

Pinzu (pin-zoo)* n/a

Note:

See the *Five Books*, p. 413. Kelley overhears many voices singing a song at some distance, and these are the words Dee recorded: *Pinzu-a lephe ganiurax kelpadman pacaph*. No translations are suggested.

Pronunciation notes:

(**Dee—This "a" was sounded to the end of pinzu as we use in english ballads, as with this word "down" is sounded as "downa, down a down a," etc.*) There is an extra "a" appended to Pinzu in Dee's journal (pin-zoo-ah). His marginal note explains this is merely a melodic flourish in the song, and not part of the word itself:

Pir (per) *n.* Holy (Ones)

1.41 . . . a law to govern the *holy ones* . . .

Note:

Apparently a reference to the celestial bodies/Angels.

Based on the words that seem to share *Pir* as their root, I suspect the *i* in *Pir* is a phonetic gloss.

Possible root for:

Piripsax (per-IP-saks)	The Heavens
Piripsol (per-IP-sol)	Heavens
Piripson (per-IP-son)	(Third?) Heaven
"Pirgah" (pur-jah)	The First Glory
"Pirgi" (pur-jii)	Fires
"Prg" (purj)	Flame
Prge (purj)	Fire
Prgel (pur-jel)	Fire
"Purg" (purj)	Flames

"Pirgah" (pur-jah) *n.* "The First Glory" (lit., Flames)

Compounds:

Ialpirgah (YAL-pur-jah) ["Ialprt" + "Pirgah"] Flames of the First Glory

Also:

"Pirgi" (pur-jii)	Fires
"Prg" (purj)	Flame
Prge (purj)	Fire
Prgel (pur-jel)	Fire
"Purg" (purj)	Flames

Possible root:

Pir (per) Holy Ones

Note:

"Pirgah" is obviously a form of the word *Prge* (fire), and must mean "the First Glory"—that is, the Light of Divinity. (Possibly a reference to the rising Sun.)

Also see *Ialpirt* (light), which seems to indicate light from celestial beings.

Also see *Busd* (glory), which seems to indicate "wondrous."

Also see *Adgmach* (glory), which seems to indicate "adoration, praise."

"Pirgi" (per-jii) *n.* Fires

Compounds:

Malpirgi (mal-per-jii) ["Mal" + "Pirgi"] Fires of Life and Increase

Also:

"Pirgah" (pur-jah)	The First Glory
"Prg" (purj)	Flame
Prge (purj)	Fire
Prgel (pur-jel)	Fire
"Purg" (purj)	Flames

Possible root:

Pir (per) Holy Ones

Note:

See *Prge* (fire).

Piripsax (per-IP-saks)* *n.* Heavens

30.59 . . . let it run with *the heavens* . . .

Pronunciation notes:

(*Dee—Pe rip sax*) Three syllables. Dee shows an *e* at the end of the first syllable, but it should take the short sound, as the letter is actually *i*.

(*Dee—perípsax*) See the *48 Claves*. Here, Dee places an accent over the *i* in the second syllable.

Also:

Piripsol (per-IP-sol) Heavens

Piripson (per-IP-son) (Third?) Heaven

Note:

Also see "Madriax" (Heavens) and *Oadriax* (Heavens).

Possible shared root:

Pir Holy Ones

Piripsol (per-IP-sol)* *n.* Heavens

5.12 . . . the brightness of *the heavens* . . .

30.21 . . . the brightness of *the heavens* . . .

Pronunciation notes:

(*Dee 5.12—Pir ipsol*)

(*Dee 30.21—Pe ríp sol*) Three syllables, accent on the second syllable. Dee's note at 30.21 seems to indicate a long "e" sound in the first syllable—but his note at 5.12 does not show such. I have settled upon the short "e" sound.

(*Dee 5.12—péripsol*) See the *48 Claves*. Here, Dee moved the accent to the first syllable.

(*Dee 30.21—perípsol*) See the *48 Claves*. Here, Dee moved the accent back to the second syllable.

Also:

Piripson (per-IP-son) (Third?) Heaven

Piripsax (per-IP-saks) The Heavens

Note:

Also see "Madriax" (Heavens) and *Oadriax* (lower Heavens).

Possible shared root:

Pir Holy Ones

Piripson (per-IP-son)* *n.* (Third?) Heaven

8.3 . . . first, is as the *third heaven* . . .

Pronunciation notes:

(**Dee—Pi ríp son*) Three syllables, with an accent on the second syllable. The first *i* seems to take a long sound in Dee's phonetic note. However, other versions of this word clearly indicate a short "i" sound instead (which I have shown in my pronunciation as a short "e" sound).

(**Dee—piri̍pson*) See the *48 Claves*. The accent is again shown on the second syllable.

Note:

The word *D* (third) does not appear here. This could be a proper name for the third Heaven.

Also:

Piripsol (per-IP-sol) Heavens

Piripsax (per-IP-saks) The Heavens

Note:

Also see "Madriax" (Heavens) and *Oadriax* (lower Heavens).

Possible shared root:

Pir (per) Holy Ones

Plapli (play-plii)* *n.* Partakers (of)

3.79 . . . *partakers of* the secret wisdom . . .

30.156 . . . make us *partakers of* undefiled knowledge.

Pronunciation notes:

(**Dee 3.79—It is Plapli*)

(**Dee 30.156—Pla pli*) Two syllables, and none of these letters stand alone.

Plosi (ploh-sii)* *idiom* As Many

10.47 . . . 1000 times *as many* . . .

Pronunciation notes:

(**Dee—Plo si*) Two syllables. The *o* and *i* should take their long sounds.

Note:

Also see "Irgil" (how many)

Poamal (poh-mal)* *n.* Palace

1.64 . . . in the midst of *your palace* . . .

Pronunciation notes:

(**Dee—Poamal*) The Early Modern English letter combination *oa* makes a long "o" sound (as in the English words *boat* and *coat*). Therefore, I suspect this word should have two syllables.

Poilp (poylp)* *v.* To Divide

8.45 . . . the crowns of the Temple and the coat of Him . . . are divided.

Pronunciation notes:

(**Dee—Poilp; one syllable*) Dee indicates one syllable for this word. Therefore, the *oi* letter combination should make an "oy" sound—as in the English words *boil* and *boy*.

Also:

Yrpoil (yur-POY-il) Division

Pola (poh-la) *n.* Two together, Couple*

From *Loagaeth*:

(**Dee—Pola and Pala signify Two. Pola signifieth two together, and Pala signifieth to separated.*) See *Five Books*, p. 304. *Pola* (two together, or couple) appears in *Loagaeth*, while *Pala* (two-separated) appears only in the marginal note.

See also *Viv* (second)

Also:

Olani (oh-el-AY-nii) Two Times, Twice

Pala (pay-la) Two, separated

Pop (pop) *prop. n.* "The Nineteenth Aethyr"

30.3 . . . which dwell in the nineteenth aethyr . . .

Note:

This (word 30.3) is the single space in the Key of the Aethyrs, which must be changed for each invocation—replacing word 30.3 with the name of the appropriate Aethyr. No established definitions were given for these names.

Also note this word is a palindrome, spelled the same forward and backward.

Pop contains the three Parts of the Earth *Torzoxi*, *Abriond*, and *Omagrap*.

"Praf" (praf) *v.* To Dwell

Compounds:

Dspraf (dee-es-praf) [Ds + "Praf"] Which Dwell

Pragma (prag-ma) n/a (?)

Note:
See *TFR*, p. 32. Here, the Angel Madimi has just interrupted the session to exorcise several demons from the body of Kelley. (See *Carma*.) These spirits came out of Kelley violently, scratching each other in the face and swarming about Madimi. To her, the spirits spoke in Angelical, "*Gil de pragma kures helech*." Dee asks Madimi what this means, and she replies (in Latin), "We want to live here in our [friends]." (Madimi does not offer definitions for the individual words.)
When Dee asks who these "friends" are supposed to be, the spirits indicate Kelley as their place of habitation. (Probably meaning both Dee and Kelley.) Madimi then banishes these spirits.

Prdzar (purd-zar)* *v.* — To Diminish

30.137 Add and *diminish* until the stars be numbered.

Pronunciation notes:
(**Dee—Prd zar Pur*) Two syllables. The *r* takes the "ur" sound.
(**Dee—prd-zar*) See the *48 Claves*. Dee again indicates two syllables.

Note:
Perhaps there is a relationship between this word and the Name of God *Ardza*, found on the Eastern Watchtower, ruling the Angels of medicine. If so, its attribute may be "to diminish" disease.

"Prg" (purj) *n.* — Flame

Pronunciation notes:
See note at *Prge* (Fire).

Compounds:

Ialprg (YAL-purj) ["Ialprt" + "Prg"]	Burning Flame
Malprg (mal-purj) ["Mal" + "Prg"]	Through-thrusting Fire

Also:

"Pirgah" (pur-jah)	The First Glory
"Pirgi" (pur-jii)	Fires
Prge (purj)	Fire

Prgel (pur-jel) Fire
"Purg" (purj) Flames

Possible root:

Pir (per) Holy Ones

Note:

Both this word and *Vep* (flame) are nouns. For a verb form, see *Ialpon* (to burn). For an adjective form, see *Ialpor* (flaming). See also *Ialpirt* (light), which seems to indicate light from celestial beings.

Prge (purj)* *n.* Fire

1.32 . . . with *the fire of* gathering . . .

Pronunciation notes:

(**Dee—as purge*) The *e* in Prge is likely a phonetic gloss, giving the *g* its soft sound. See the following words for more of Dee's phonetic glosses upon "Prg."

Also:

"Pirgah" (pur-jah) The First Glory
"Pirgi" (pur-jii) Fires
"Prg" (purj) Flame
Prgel (pur-jel) Fire
"Purg" (purj) Flames

Possible root:

Pir (per) Holy Ones

Note:

See note at "Prg."

Prgel (pur-jel) *n.* Fire

9.3 A mighty guard of *fire* . . .

Pronunciation notes:

(**Dee—Pur gel*) Two syllables. The *r* takes the extended "ur" sound. The *g* should be soft before the letter *e*. The *e* in this word is likely a phonetic gloss. See note at *Prge* (fire).

Also:

"Pirgah" (pur-jah) — The First Glory
"Pirgi" (pur-jii) — Fires
"Prg" (purj) — Flame
Prge (purj) — Fire
"Purg" (purj) — Flames

Possible root:

Pir (per) — Holy Ones

Note:

See note at "Prg."

Priaz (prii-AYZ)* *pron.* or *adj.* — Those

30.122 . . . govern *those* that govern . . .

Pronunciation notes:

(**Dee—Priáz*) Likely two syllables, with the accent on the second syllable. I assume the *i* takes a long sound, because it is followed by an *a* (as in the English *dial*). I have given the *a* its long sound based on the pronunciation of *Priazi* (those).
(**Dee—priáz*) See the *48 Claves*. Here, Dee again places the accent upon the second syllable.

Also:

Priazi (prii-AY-zii) — Those

Priazi (prii-AY-zii)* *pron.* or *adj.* — Those

30.128 Bring forth with *those* that increase . . .

Pronunciation notes:

(*Dee—Pri á zi*) Three syllables. The *a* stands alone in the second syllable and takes the accent.

Also:

Priaz (prii-AYZ) Those

Pugo (pug-oh)* *prep.* As unto

3.78 . . . unto us *as unto* partakers of the secret wisdom . . .

Pronunciation notes:

(*Dee—It is Pugo*) Likely two syllables, and I suggest a short *u* and a long final *o*.

Note:

Also see *Tia* (unto) and *Pambt* (unto).

"Puin" (pew-in) *n.* (Sharp) Sickles

Compounds:

Tapuin (TAY-pew-in) [Ta + "Puin"] As (Sharp) Sickles

"Puran" (pew-ran) *v.* To See

Compounds:

Odipuran (ohd-II-pew-ran) [Od + Ip + "Puran"] And Shall Not See

"Purg" (purj) *n.* Flames

Compounds:

Ialpurg (YAL-purj) ["Ialprt" + "Purg"] Burning Flames

Malpurg (mal-purj) ["Mal" + "Purg"] Fiery Darts (Arrows)

Also:

"Pirgah" (pur-jah) The First Glory

"Pirgi" (pur-jii)	Fires
"Prg" (purj)	Flame
Prge (purj)	Fire
Prgel (pur-jel)	Fire

Possible root:

Pir (per)	Holy Ones

Note:

See note at "Prg."

Ger (Q)

Q (kwah)* *conj.* Or

30.71 . . . no creature upon *or* within her . . .

Pronunciation notes:
(**Dee—Q*) One syllable. Likely takes the "kwah" sound.

Compounds:
Qmospleh [Q + "Mospleh"] Or the Horns
Qta [Q + Ta] Or as

Qaa (kwah-AY-ay)* *n.* Creation (or "Garments")

1.21 . . . measureth *your garments* . . .
(RFP) . . . open the mysteries of *your creation* . . .
30.153 Open the mysteries of *your creation*.

Pronunciation notes:
(**Dee 1.21—QAA three syllables*)
(**Dee 1.RFP—Call it QAA. Three syllables with accent on the last A*)
(**Dee 30.153—Q á a*) These notes tell us that each letter should stand by itself, making a word of three syllables. In one case (1.RFP), the accent is placed on the third syllable. Yet, elsewhere, it is placed on the second. I have opted for the second syllable accent, as we can also see in *Qaan* (creation).
(**Dee 1.21—Qa-a*) See *48 Claves*. Here, Dee indicates a word of two syllables instead.
(**Dee 11.RFP—Qaá*) See *48 Claves*. Dee indicates the accent on the third syllable.
(**Dee 12, 30.RFP—Qáa*) See *48 Claves*. Here, Dee indicates the accent on the second syllable.
(**Dee 13, 14, 15, 16, 17, 18.RFP—Qäa*) See *48 Claves*. Dee places a dieresis over the first *a*, giving it a long sound.

Note:

The first Key is the only place where *Qaa* is translated as "garments." I get the impression that this rogue definition of *Qaa* is meant to indicate "created forms" instead of clothing. It has been common to Western mysticism (Platonism, Neoplatonism, Gnosticism) to refer to the physical body (the created form) as a "garment" worn by the soul. (See Layton's *The Gnostic Scriptures*, p. 38, "Repentance and Elevation of Wisdom," where the word *garment* is used to refer to the body.)

Note that the common word for "garment" (or clothing) in Angelical is given as *Oboleh*, and related to the word *Obloch* (garland)—indicating a dressing.

Note also that *Zimz* (vestures) is *not* a reference to clothing.

Compounds?:

Qaal (kwah-AY-el) (Qaa + L) — Creator
Qadah (kwah-AY-dah) [Qaa + Iaida?] — Creator

Also:

Qaan (kwah-AY-an) — Creation
Qaaon (kwah-AY-ay-on) — Creation
Qaas (kwah-AY-as) — Creation

Qaal (kwah-AY-el)* [Qaa + L] *comp.* — Creator

4.41 . . . in the name of *the Creator* . . .

Pronunciation notes:

(**Dee—Qa al*) Appears to be two syllables. However, also see the *48 Claves*:

(**Dee—Q-á-al*) See the *48 Claves*. Here Dee shows the proper three syllables, with an accent on the second syllable. The *Q* and the first *a* each stand alone.

Note:

The word *Qaa* is translated as "Creation." Combining this with *L* implies "the First Creator."

Also:

Qadah (kwah-AY-dah) [Qaa + Iaida?] — Creator

Qaan (kwah-AY-an)* *n.* Creation

3.81 . . . secret wisdom of *your creation* . . .

Pronunciation notes:

(**Dee—It is q á an*) Three syllables, with the accent on the second syllable.

(**Dee—Qáan*) See the 48 *Claves*. The accent is again on the second syllable.

Also:

Qaa (kwah-AY-ay) Creation (or Garments)
Qaaon (kwah-AY-ay-on) Creation
Qaas (kwah-AY-as) Creation

Qaaon (kwah-AY-ay-on)* *n.* Creation

6.43 . . . your God *in your creation* . . .

Pronunciation notes:

(**Dee—Q a a on*) Four syllables. The *Q* and both *a*'s stand alone.

(**Dee—Q-a-a-on*) See the 48 *Claves*. This note matches that from *TFR*. I have adopted the accent from other versions of this word.

Also:

Qaa (kwah-AY-ay) Creation (or Garments)
Qaan (kwah-AY-an) Creation
Qaas (kwah-AY-as) Creation

Qaas (kwah-AY-as)* *n.* Creation

5.46 . . . obey *your creation* . . .

Pronunciation notes:

(**Dee—Q á as*) Three syllables, with an accent on the second syllable. The first *a* stands alone.

(**Dee—Q-á-as*) See the 48 *Claves*. This note matches that from *TFR*.

Also:

Qaa (kwah-AY-ay) — Creation (or Garments)
Qaan (kwah-AY-an) — Creation
Qaaon (kwah-AY-ay-on) — Creation

Qadah (kwah-AY-dah)* [Qaa + Iaida?] *comp.* — Creator

7.38 . . . sing praises unto *the creator.*

Note:

The word *Qaa* is translated as "Creation." Combining this with *Iaida* may imply the *Highest Creator.*

Pronunciation notes:

(**Dee—Q á dah*) Three syllables, with an accent on the second syllable. Both the Q and the *a* stand alone.
(**Dee—q-a-dah*) See the *48 Claves*. This note is essentially the same as that in *TFR*—without the accent mark.

Also:

Qaal (kwah-AY-el) — Creator

"Qanis" (kway-nis) *n.* — Olives

Compounds:

Taqanis (tay-kway-nis) [Ta + "Qanis"] — As Olives

Probable shared root:

Ooanoan (oh-oh-AY-noh-an) — (In Their?) Eyes
Ooaona (oh-ona) — Eyes
Oanio (oh-nii-oh) — Moment

Note:

The similar spelling suggests these three words are connected. This might make sense for *Ooaona* (eyes): the word *Taqanis* (as olives) in Key Five appears to refer to the stars. In biblical literature, the word "eyes" is often used to indicate "stars." (Such as in the visions of St. John and Ezekiel—who both saw celestial Angels with wings "full of eyes.")

If this is the case, then the shared root here may indicate "small units," which would explain its use to indicate a "moment" (*Oanio*).
Also see *Adroch* (olive mount).

Qcocasb (kwah-KOH-kasb)* *n.* — Contents of Time

5.41 . . . the first, ends, and *contents of time* . . .

Pronunciation notes:
(*Dee—Q có casb*) Three syllables, with an accent on the second syllable. The *o* is likely long, as Dee shows it at the end of the second syllable.
(*Dee—Q-có-casb*) See the *48 Claves*. This note matches that from *TFR*.

Also:

Acocasb (ay-KOH-kasb)	Time
"Cacocasb" (kay-KOH-kasb)	Another While
Cocasb (KOH-kasb)	Time
Cocasg (KOH-kazh)	Times

Note:
Q translates in Angelical as "or," which would not fit the phrase here. Therefore, *Qcocasb* is not likely a compound of *Q* + *Cocasb*.

Possible shared root:

Cacacom (kay-SAY-som)	Flourish
Cacrg (KAY-kurg)	Until
Casasam (kay-SAY-sam)	Abiding
Capimali (kay-pii-MAY-lii)	Successively
"Capimao" (kay-pii-MAY-oh)	While
Capimaon (kap-ii-MAY-on)	Number of Time
Capmiali (kap-mii-AY-lii)	Successively

Note:
Also see *Pild* (continually)

Qmospleh (kwah-mos-play)* [Q + "Mospleh"] *comp.* — Or the Horns

3.16 . . . as sharp sickles: *or the horns of* death . . .

Pronunciation notes:

(**Dee—Q Mos Pleh as two words*) Dee's statement indicates that *Qmospleh* is "as two words"—that is, a compound word. The *Q* stands alone.

(**Dee—Q mos-pleh*) See the *48 Claves*. This note matches the note in *TFR*.

"Qrasahi" (kra-sa-hii) *n.* Pleasure

Compounds:

Norqrasahi (nor-kra-sa-hii) ["Nor" + "Qrasahi"] Sons of Pleasure

Qta (kwah-tay)* [Q + Ta] *comp.* Or as

2.18 . . . *or as* the flowers . . .

Pronunciation notes:

(**Dee—Quu Ta*) Two syllables. The *uu* in Early Modern English is a "w" sound—indicating that the *Q* should sound like "kwah."

(**Dee—Q-ta*) See *48 Claves*. Indicates two syllables.

Qting (kwah-tinj)* *n.* or *adj.?* Rotten

30.131 . . . and destroy *the rotten*.

Pronunciation notes:

(**Dee—Q ting dg*) Two syllables. The final *g* takes a soft "dg" (or "j") sound.

Note:

The word *rotten* is usually an adjective. However, it is used in Key Thirty as a noun ("the rotten").

QUAR (kwar) 1636

14.16 . . . which have under you *1636*.

Note:

The transmission of Key Fourteen is missing from Dee's journals. We only have the English for this Key given later (see *TFR*, p. 193). Plus, the word appears in this location in Dee's *48 Claves*.

"Quasb" (kwazb) *v.* — To Destroy

Compounds:

Odquasb (ohd-kwazb) [Od + "Quasb"] — And Destroy

Note:

I suspect the *u* is a phonetic gloss.

Shared root:

Grosb (grozb) — Bitter Sting

Quiin (kwii-in)* *conj.* — Wherein

3.18 . . . *wherein* the creatures of the earth are . . .
7.7 . . . *wherein* the Lord hath opened his mouth . . .

Pronunciation notes:

(**Dee 3.18; 7.7—Qui in*) Two syllables. In Early Modern English, the double *i* makes a long "i" sound. The *n* essentially stands alone.

(**Dee 3.18—Qui-i-n*) See the *48 Claves*. Here, Dee shows three syllables. The second *i* and the *n* each stand alone.

(**Dee 7.7—qui-in*) See the *48 Claves*. This note essentially matches Dee's note in *TFR*. I have settled upon this two-syllable version of the word.

Note:

I assume the *u* in this word is a phonetic gloss.

Qurlst (kurlst)* *n.* — Handmaid

30.62 . . . as *a handmaid* let her serve them.

Pronunciation notes:

(**Dee—Qurlst Kurlst*) Likely just one syllable. The *Q* appears to make a hard "k" sound, while the *u* combines with the *r* to make an "ur" sound. I suspect the *u* is a phonetic gloss.

"Qzmoz" n/a

Note:

This is not likely an Angelical word at all. Dee originally wrote this word as "Qzmoz," but his phonetic note only indicated *Moz*. He also recorded the word as "MOZ" in his *48 Claves*. This same word (*Moz*) appears on the *Corpus Omnium* Table. There, Nalvage says that it can sound like "moz" or use the extended *z* for "mozod." Perhaps "Qzmoz" was a botched attempt to record the sound of the extended "mozod."

See *Moz* (joy, rejoice).

Don (R)

Raas (ray-as)* *n.* East

7.1 *The east* is a house of virgins . . .

Pronunciation notes:
(*Dee—Ra as*) Two syllables. In Early Modern English, a double vowel indicated a long sound—which Dee seems to indicate in the first syllable.

Also:
Raasy (ray-ay-see) East

Raasy (ray-ay-see)* *n.* East

11.9 . . . 5 thunders which flew into *the east* . . .

Pronunciation notes:
(*Dee—Ra a sy*) Three syllables. Both *a*'s take their long sound—and tend to blend into one sound when the word is spoken fluently. (In Early Modern English, a double *a* would simply indicate a long "a" sound.) The final *y* should make the sound of a long *e*—as in the English words *lazy* and *messy*.
(*Dee—raâsy*) See the 48 *Claves*. Here, Dee placed a circumflex over the second *a* to indicate its long sound.

Also:
Raas (ray-as) East

Raclir (ray-kler)* *n.* or *v.* Weeping

10.16 . . . lamentation and *weeping* laid up for the earth . . .

Pronunciation notes:
(*Dee—Ra clir*) Two syllables. The *a* likely takes its long sound. The *c* appears to take its hard ("k") sound, as it combines with the *l*—as in the English words *clean* and *climb*.

Note:

Also compare with the name of the Angel *Rocle*, one of the Sons of the Sons of Light. If there is a connection, then *Rocle*'s name has the etymology of "to weep."

Remiges (rem-ii-jes) n/a

Note:
See the *Five Books*, p. 258. Here, Raphael offers a long prayer, the very end of which is, "How great and innumerable are your [God's] gifts? *O remiges varpax. Kyrie eleyson.*"
No translation is offered for this phrase, although I wonder if it is perhaps the Angelical for the Greek *Kyrie eleyson* (Lord have mercy), often used in Catholic prayer.

Restil (rest-el)* *v.* To Praise (Him?)

4.45 . . . *that you may praise him* amongst the sons of men.

Pronunciation notes:
(**Dee—Rest el*) Two syllables.
(**Dee—rest-el*) See the *48 Claves*. This note matches the note in in *TFR*.

Note:
See also *Oecrimi* (sing praises) and *Faaip* (voices).

Rii (rii-ii) *prop. n.* "The Twenty-Ninth Aethyr"

30.3 . . . which dwell in *the twenty-ninth aethyr* . . .

Note:
This (word 30.3) is the single space in the Key of the Aethyrs, which must be changed for each invocation—replacing word 30.3 with the name of the appropriate Aethyr. No established definitions were given for these names.

Rii contains the three Parts of the Earth *Vastrim*, *Odraxti*, and *Gomziam*.

Rior (rii-or)* *n.* Widow

8.20 . . . like unto the harvest of *a widow*.

Pronunciation notes:

(**Dee—Rior*) Dee gives us little clue here. I assume two syllables, with a long "i" sound.

Ripir (rii-PER)* *n.* No Place

30.132 . . . *No place*, let it remain in one number.

Pronunciation notes:

(**Dee—Ri pír*) Two syllables, with the accent on the second syllable. I suggest a long *i* at the end of the first syllable.

(**Dee—Ripír*) See the *48 Claves*. Dee again placed an accent over the *i* in the second syllable.

Note:

This word is a palindrome, spelled the same forward and backward.

Possible root:

Ip — Not

Rit (rit)* *n.* Mercy

7.34 O you servants of *mercy* . . .

Pronunciation notes:

(**Dee—Rit*) One syllable, with a short vowel.

Compounds:

Othilrit (oh-THIL-rit) (Othil + Rit) — Seats of Mercy

Rlodnr (rel-oh-din-ur) *n.* Alchemical Furnace / Athanor(?)

From the *Alchemical Cipher*:

See *TFR*, pp. 387–89. The Angel Levanael gives translations for all the *Alchemical Cipher* words except this one. However, from the deciphered message itself on p. 387, it would appear that *Rlodnr* is either an Alchemical Furnace (called an *Athanor*) or some process associated with the alchemical application of heat.

Ror (ror)* *n.* Sun

1.12 . . . *the sun* is as a sword . . .

Pronunciation notes:

(**Dee—Ror*) One syllable

Note:

This word is a palindrome, spelled the same forward and backward.

Roxtan (roks-tan) *n.* (Rectified?) Wine

From the *Alchemical Cipher*:

See TFR, pp. 387–89. The Angel Levanael says of this word, "*Roxtan*, is pure and simple wine in herself. *Lulo* is her mother." This could mean wine straight from the bottle. However, as this is an alchemical process, I suspect that "pure and simple wine in herself" could indicate rectified wine. (Rectification removes excess water and other impurities from the wine.)

Compare from *Loagaeth*:

Rox

Rudna (rud-na) n/a

Note:

See *TFR*, p. 3. The Angel *Murifri* here speaks a prayer in Angelical, and Kelley can only overhear a few of the words: *Oh Gahire Rudna gephna oh Gahire.* It is unclear whether this represents a single Angelical phrase, or if they are disconnected words recorded by Dee as Kelley overheard them here and there in the prayer. No translations are suggested.

Fam (S)

S (es) *n.* or *adj.* — Fourth

Compounds:

Sdiu (es-DII-vee) [S + Div] — Fourth Angle

Also:

"Es" (es) — Fourth

Note:

This is the word for "fourth," but not the numeral 4. The word is used here (the fourth angle) as an adjective.

Saanir (say-AY-ner)* *n.* — Parts

30.5 . . . mighty in *the parts* of the earth . . .
30.45 . . . let her be governed by *her parts* . . .

Pronunciation notes:

(*Dee 30.5, 45—Sa á nir*) Three syllables, accent on the second. The *a* stands alone in the second syllable.
(*Dee 30.5, 45—saánir*) See the *48 Claves*. Dee again placed an accent over the second syllable.

"Saba" (SAY-bay) *adj.* — Whose

Pronunciation note:

I have adopted the accent from *Asobam* (whom).

Compounds:

Sabaooaona (say-bay-oh-oh-AY-oh-na) ["Saba" + Ooaona] — Whose Eyes

Also:

Asobam (ay-SOH-bam) — (On) Whom
Sobam (SOH-bam) — Whom
Sobca (SOB-kay) — Whose

“Sobha” (sob-ha) Whose
Soba (soh-ba) Whose
“Sobo” (SOH-boh) Whose
Sobra (SOB-ray) Whose
“Sola” (SOH-lay) Whose

Sabaooaona (say-bay-oh-oh-AY-oh-na) [“Saba” + Ooaona] *comp.*
Whose Eyes

30.18 . . . *whose eyes* are the brightness . . .

Pronunciation notes:
(**Dee—Sa ba o o áo na*) This may be a word of seven syllables—though it can sound more like six syllables when spoken fluently. (The two long “o” sounds run together.) The *ao* should make two sounds, as in the English word *chaos*. The accent is on the fifth syllable. The *a*'s in the first two syllables are long.
(**Dee—sabaooáôna*) See the *48 Claves*. Here, Dee again placed the accent over the *a* in the fifth syllable. He also placed a circumflex over the following *o* to indicate its long sound (thereby confirming that it should stand alone).

Sach (sak) *prop. n.* The Establishers/Supporters

From *Corpus Omnium*:
Associated with the post-Crucifixion portion of the Table, translated in Latin as *Confirmantes* (Those Who Establish).

Sagacor (say-GAY-kor)* *n.* “In One Number”

30.134 . . . no place, let it remain *in one number*.

Pronunciation notes:
(**Dee—Sa gá cor Kor*) Three syllables, with the accent on the second. It appears that Dee intended long *a*'s in the first two syllables. The *g*

should take its hard sound when preceding an *a*. Finally, Dee indicates that the *c* takes the hard "k" sound.
(**Dee—sagácor*) See the *48 Claves*. Here, Dee again placed an accent upon the second syllable.

Note:
The phrase "in one number" seems to indicate something like "constant" or "consistent."

Shared root:

Cormf (kormf)	Number
Cormfa (korm-FA)	Numbers
Cormp (kormf)	Numbered
Cormpo (korm-FOH)	Hath (Yet) Numbered
Cormpt (kormft)	Numbered

Salbrox (sal-broks)* *n.* Live (i.e., Burning) Sulfur

10.30 . . . scorpions and *live sulphur* mingled with poison.

Pronunciation notes:
(**Dee—Sal brox*) Two syllables. Both vowels are short.

Note:
Also see *Dlasod* (sulfur). Where *Salbrox* is the kind of sulfur one would find on a match, *Dlasod* refers to alchemical sulfur.

Sald (sald)* *n.* Wonder

2.6 . . . your voicings of *wonder* . . .

Pronunciation notes:
(**Dee—Sald*) One syllable.

Note:
Also see "Lzirn" (wonders) and *Busd* (Glory).

Salman (SAYL-man)* *n.* — House

11.20 . . . *the house* of death . . .
**16.3 . . . *the house* of justice . . .

Pronunciation notes:
(*Dee—Sal man*) Two syllables. Both *a*'s appear to take their short sounds. However, see *Isalman* (is a house) and *Oisalman* (this house), which indicate a long sound for the first *a*. Finally, I have adopted the accent from *Isalman*.

Note:
**The transmission of the first twelve words of Key Sixteen is missing from Dee's journals. We only have the English given for it on *TFR*, p. 194. However, they do appear in Dee's *48 Claves*.

Compounds:
Isalman (ii-SAYL-man) [I + Salman] — Is a House
Oisalman (oh-ii-SAYL-man) ["Oi" + Salman] — This House

Samhampors (sam-HAM-pors)* — n/a

Pronunciation note:
(*Dee—samhámpors*) See the *Five Books*, p. 302. Dee placed an accent over the second *a*.

From *Loagaeth*:
See the *Five Books*, p. 302. Note the similarity between this word and the Hebrew Name of God *Shem haMephoresh* (Name of Extension). See the note at *Semhaham*.

Possible shared root:
Sem (sem) — n/a
Semhaham (SEM-hah-ham) — n/a

Samvelg (sam-velj)* *n.* — The Righteous

6.14 . . . and a garland to *the righteous*.

Pronunciation notes:

(**Dee—Samvelg*) I assume this should be two syllables. Dee does not indicate a hard or soft sound for the final *g*. I have settled upon a soft sound.

Note:

See also *Baltoh*, *Baltle*, and *Baeouib* (all translated as "righteousness").

Sapah (SAY-fah)* *prop. n.* Mighty Sounds (i.e., Thunders)

5.1 *The Mighty Sounds* have entered . . .

Pronunciation notes:

(**Dee—Sá pah*) Two syllables, with an accent on the first. Dee's phonetic note seems to indicate a hard "p" sound for the second syllable. However, see *TFR*, p. 200, where the Angel Illemese suggests "Saphah" as a pronunciation.

(**Dee—Sapáh*) See the *48 Claves*. In this case, Dee placed the accent on the second syllable.

Note:

The Mighty Sounds mentioned here, and the Thunders mentioned elsewhere in the Keys, are groups of Angels. See *Const* (thunders), *Avavago* (Thunders), and *Coraxo* (Thunders). The so-called *Sapah* (Mighty Sounds) are mentioned only in the fifth Key, which appears to relate to the Southern Quarter of the Universe.

Compare from *Loagaeth*:

Sapoh, Sappoh, Sepah, Sephah

Sdiv (es-DII-vee)* [S + Div] *comp.* Fourth Angle

6.2 The spirits of *the fourth angle* . . .

Pronunciation notes:

(**Dee—S dí u es dí u*) Three syllables, with an accent on the second syllable. The the initial *S* and the final *u*/*v* stand alone.

(**Dee—s díu*) See the *48 Claves*. The accent is again shown on the second syllable.

Sem (sem) *n.?* In This Place*

From *Loagaeth*:
(**Dee—In this place.*) See the *Five Books*, p. 308.

Note:
Perhaps this word is similar to the English word *here*—although *Sem* seems to have a much more formal tone. See also *Emna* (here).

Possible shared root:
Samhampors (sam-HAM-pors) n/a
Semhaham (SEM-hah-ham) n/a

Compare from *Loagaeth*:
Zem

Semhaham (SEM-hah-ham) n/a*

Pronunciation note:
(**Dee—sémhaham*) See the *Five Books*, p. 310. Dee indicates an accent over the *e*.

From *Loagaeth*:
(**Dee—This word hath 72 significations.*) See the *Five Books*, p. 310. Note the similiarity between this word and the Hebrew *Shem haMephoresh* (Name of Extension). This is a Qabalistic Name of God composed of seventy-two individual names. Interestingly, the *Shem haMephoresh* seems to have an association with the twenty-four Elders (or Seniors) that appear in the Great Table of the Earth (Watchtowers). See my article "Shem haMephoresh: the Divine Name of Extension."

Possible shared root:
Sem (sem) n/a
Samhampors (sam-HAM-pors) n/a

Ser (ser) *n.* Sorrow

From *Corpus Omnium*:
Found in the Tribulation portion of the Table, in the phrase *Osf Ser Iad* (Discord and Sorrow of God).

Note:
Also see Tibibp (sorrow).

Siaion (sii-AY-ii-on)* *n.* Temple

8.41 . . . the crowns of *the temple* and the coat . . .

Pronunciation notes:
(**Dee—Si a i on*) Four syllables. Both *i*'s and the *a* should take their long sounds.
(**Dee—siáîon*) See the *48 Claves*. Dee added an accent over the *a* (second syllable). He also added a circumflex over the second *i* to indicate its long sound.

Note:
Perhaps there is some relationship between this word, and the name "Sion" (or Zion)—where the Holy Temple stood in Israel.

Siatris (sii-ay-TRIS)* *n.* Scorpions

10.28 . . . the heads of *scorpions* and live sulphur . . .

Pronunciation notes:
(**Dee—Si a trís*) Three syllables, with the accent mark placed in the middle of the third syllable. The first *i* and the *a* should take their long sounds.
(**Dee—siâtris*) See the *48 Claves*. Here, Dee placed a circumflex over the *a* to indicate its long sound.

Sibsi (sib-sii)* *n.* Covenant

30.145 . . . appear before *the covenant of* his mouth . . .

Pronunciation notes:

(**Dee—Sib si*) Two syllables.

Note:

Also see *Aisro / Isro* (promise of), *Surzas* (sworn), and *Znrza* (swore).

"Smnad" (sem-en-ad) *pron.* or *adj.* — Another

Compounds:

Lsmnad (el-sem-en-ad) [L + "Smnad"] — One Another

Probable shared root:

Asymp (ay-simp) — Another

Symp (simp) — Another

Note:

The root here may be "sm" or "sym."

Soba (SOH-bay) *adj.* — Whose

1.29 . . . *whose* seats I garnished . . .
1.56 . . . *whose* beginning is not . . .
5.35 . . . *whose* numbers are as the first . . .
7.23 . . . *whose* kingdoms and continuance . . .
10.9 . . . *whose* branches are 22 nests . . .
11.28 . . . *whose* number is 31 . . .
12.19 . . . *whose* name amongst you is wrath . . .
17.3 . . . *whose* wings are thorns . . .

Pronunciation notes:

(**Dee 5.35; 10.9; 11.28; 12.19—So ba*)

(**Dee 7.23;m 17.3—Soba*) Two syllables. The *o* should take its long sound.

I have adopted the accent from *Asobam* (whom).

Compounds:

Sobaiad (soh-BAY-ad) [Soba + Iad] — Whose God

Sabaooaona (say-bay-oh-oh-AY-oh-na) ["Saba" + Ooaona]

Whose Eyes

Also:

Asobam (ay-SOH-bam)	(On) Whom
"Saba" (SAY-bay)	Whose
Sobam (SOH-bam)	Whom
Sobca (SOB-kay)	Whose
"Sobha" (SOB-hay)	Whose
"Sobo" (SOH-boh)	Whose
Sobra (SOB-ray)	Whose
"Sola" (SOH-lay)	Whose

Note:

Overall, the root of these words seems to be "Sob." However, *Soba* itself seems rather important in most cases.

See also *Casarm* (whom).

Compare from *Loagaeth*:

Sebas, *Sebo*, *Sebra*, *Zeba*

Sobaiad (soh-BAY-ad)* [Soba + Iad] *comp.* Whose God

17.14 . . . *whose God* is wrath in anger . . .

Pronunciation notes:

(**Dee—So bai ad*) Three syllables. The *o* takes its long sound. Dee also indicates that the *ai* (or "ay") combine to form a long "a" sound—as in the English words *day* and *play*.

(**Dee—sobaíad*) See the *48 Claves*. Here, Dee placed an accent over the *i* in the second syllable.

Sobam (SOH-bam)* *pron.* Whom

2.9 . . . *whom* the burning flames . . .

4.16 . . . *whom* none hath yet numbered . . .

6.7 . . . *whom* the First hath planted . . .

Pronunciation notes:

(**Dee 2.9—S o bam*)

(**Dee 4.16—So bam*)

(**Dee6.7—Sobam*) It would appear that Dee heard three syllables in Key Two—so that the *S* took the sound of "es." However, in later instances, the word had only two syllables. The three-syllable version of the word is likely a poetic or lyrical gloss, rather than a rule of pronunciation. I have adopted the accent from *Asobam* (whom).

Also:

Asobam (ay-SOH-bam) (On) Whom
"Saba" (SAY-bay) Whose
Soba (SOH-bay) Whose
Sobca (SOB-kay) Whose
"Sobha" (SOB-hay) Whose
"Sobo" (SOH-boh) Whose
Sobra (SOB-ray) Whose
"Sola" (SOH-lay) Whose

Also see:

Casarm (whom).

Sobca (SOB-kay)* *adj.* Whose

9.13 . . . *whose* wings are of wormwood . . .
9.37 . . . cursed are they *whose* iniquities . . .

Pronunciation notes:

(**Dee 9.13, 37—Sob ca ka*) Two syllables. The *c* takes a hard "k" sound. I have adopted the accent from *Asobam* (whom).

Also:

Asobam (ay-SOH-bam) (On) Whom
"Saba" (SAY-bay) Whose
Soba (SOH-bay) Whose
Sobam (SOH-bam) Whom
"Sobha" (SOB-hay) Whose
"Sobo" (SOH-boh) Whose

Sobra (SOB-ray) — Whose
"Sola" (SOH-lay) — Whose

Also see:

Casarm (whom).

"Sobha" (SOB-hay) *adj.* — Whose

Pronunciation note:

I have adopted the accent from *Asobam* (whom).

Compounds:

Sobhaath (sob-HAY-ath) ["Sobha" + "Aath"] — Whose Works

Also:

Asobam (ay-SOH-bam) — (On) Whom
"Saba" (SAY-bay) — Whose
Soba (SOH-bay) — Whose
Sobam (SOH-bam) — Whom
Sobca (SOB-kay) — Whose
"Sobo" (SOH-boh) — Whose
Sobra (SOB-ray) — Whose
"Sola" (SOH-lay) — Whose

Also see:

Casarm (whom)

Sobhaath (sob-HAY-ath)* ["Sobha" + "Aath"] *comp.* — Whose Works

6.38 . . . *whose works* shall be a song of honour . . .

Pronunciation notes:

(*Dee—Sob há ath*) Three syllables, with an accent on the second syllable. In Early Modern English, a double vowel indicated a long vowel—which Dee likely intends for the second syllable. Then a quick short *a* is sounded at the beginning of the third syllable.

(*Dee—sob-há-ath*) See the *48 Claves*. This note matches that from *TFR*.

Note:

See *Soba* (whose).

"Sobo" (SOH-boh) *adj.* Whose

Pronunciation note:

I have adopted the accent from *Asobam* (whom).

Compounds:

Sobolzar (soh-BOL-zar) ["Sobo" + "Lzar"] Whose Courses

Also:

Asobam (ay-SOH-bam) (On) Whom
"Saba" (SAY-bay) Whose
Soba (SOH-bay) Whose
Sobam (SOH-bam) Whom
Sobca (SOB-kay) Whose
"Sobha" (SOB-hay) Whose
Sobra (SOB-ray) Whose
"Sola" (SOH-lay) Whose

Also see:

Casarm (whom).

Soboln (soh-bohln)* *n.* West

9.22 . . . settled their feet *in the west* . . .

Pronunciation notes:

(**Dee—So boln*) Two syllables, with a long *o* in the first syllable.

(**Dee—sobôln*) See the *48 Claves*. Here, Dee placed a circumflex over the second *o* to indicate that it, also, takes its long sound.

Note:

The similar spelling of *Soboln* (west) and *Sobolzar* (whose courses) appears to be coincidental. Unless the "courses" (Sobolzar) mentioned in Key Six are westward moving.

Sobolzar (soh-BOL-zar)* ["Sobo" + "Lzar"] *comp.* Whose Courses

6.21 . . . *whose courses* visit with comfort . . .

Pronunciation notes:

(*Dee—Sobol zar*) Should be three syllables.

(*Dee—sobólzar*) See the *48 Claves*. The accent is placed on the second syllable.

Note:

See note at *Soboln* (west).

Sobra (SOB-ray)* *adj.* Whose

1.10 . . . *in whose* hands the sun is as a sword . . .

Pronunciation notes:

(*Dee—Sobra*) Two syllables. The *o* appears short in this case. I have adopted the accent from *Asobam* (whom).

Also:

Asobam (ay-SOH-bam)	(On) Whom
"Saba" (SAY-bay)	Whose
Soba (SOH-bay)	Whose
Sobam (SOH-bam)	Whom
Sobca (SOB-kay)	Whose
"Sobha" (SOB-hay)	Whose
"Sobo" (SOH-boh)	Whose
"Sola" (SOH-lay)	Whose

Note:

Overall, the root of these words seems to be "sob." However, *Soba* itself seems rather important in most cases.

See also *Casarm* (whom).

Compare from *Loagaeth*:

Sebas, *Sebo*, *Sebra*, *Zeba*

"Sola" (SOH-lay) *adj.* Whose

Pronunciation note:

I have adopted the accent from *Asobam* (whom).

Compounds:

Solamian (soh-LAY-mii-an) ["Sola" + "Mian"] Whose Continuance

Also:

Asobam (ay-SOH-bam) (On) Whom

"Saba" (SAY-bay) Whose

Soba (SOH-bay) Whose

Sobam (SOH-bam) Whom

Sobca (SOB-kay) Whose

"Sobha" (SOB-hay) Whose

"Sobo" (SOH-boh) Whose

Sobra (SOB-ray) Whose

Also see:

Casarm (whom).

Solamian (soh-LAY-mii-an)* ["Sola" + "Mian"] *comp.* Whose Continuance

8.14 . . . *whose long continuance* shall be . . .

Note:

The word *long* is not indicated by the Angelical.

Pronunciation notes:

(**Dee—So lá mi an*) Four syllables. The accent is placed on the second syllable. I assume the *o*, the first *a*, and the *i* are all given their long sounds—as they fall at the ends of their syllables.

Note:

The similarity between this word and the name of the solar Angel *Salamian*. He is found in the *Heptameron*—associated with that grimoire's "Call of Sunday." This Angel also appeared to Dee and Kelley in the *Five Books*, pp. 81–82. There, Salamian claims to "rule in the heavens, and bear sway upon Earth . . . My name is Salamian, Mighty in the Sonne, worker of worldly actions . . . " Salamian also tells Dee that he is under the direction of Michael—who is the Archangel of the Sun.

Solpeth (sol-peth)* *v.* Harken (unto)/Listen to

6.32 Wherefore, *harken unto* my voice.

Pronunciation notes:

(*Dee—Sol peth*)

(*Dee—sol-peth*) See the *48 Claves*. These notes indicate two syllables. Both vowels appear to take their short sounds.

Note:

See also *Toatar* (harken).

Sonf (sonv)* *v.* To Reign

1.2 I *reign* over you, saith the God of Justice . . .

Pronunciation notes:

(*Dee—sonf*) Dee indicates a single syllable here. The *nf* tends to sound like "nv" when this word is spoken fluently.

Compounds:

Dsonf (dee-sonv) [Ds + Sonf] That Reign

Note:

Also see Bogpa (to reign).

Sor (sor) *n.* Action (especially that taken by a king)

From *Corpus Omnium*:

Found in the post-Crucifixion portion of the Table, in the phrase *Gru Sor Iad* (Cause of the Actions of God).

Surzas (sur-zas)* *v.* To Swear (Promise)

30.148 . . . which *he hath sworn* unto us . . .

Pronunciation notes:

(**Dee—Sur zas*) Two syllables. Based on the two forms of *Surzas / Znrza*, I suspect the *u* in this case is a phonetic gloss.

Also:

Znrza (snur-za) Swore

Note:

Also see *Aisro / Isro* (promise of) and *Sibsi* (covenant).

Symp (simp)* *pron.* or *adj.* Another

30.66 One season, let it confound *another* . . .

Pronunciation notes:

(**Dee—Symp*) One syllable.

Also:

Asymp (ay-simp) Another

Shared root:

"Smnad" (sem-en-ad) Another

Note:

The root here may be "sm" or "sym."

Gisg (T)

"T" (tee) *pron.* It

Compounds:

Ti (tii) ["T" + I] It Is

Ta (tay)* *prep.* or *conj.* As

1.14 . . . sun is *as* a sword . . .
1.17 . . . moon *as* a through-thrusting fire . . .
1.26 . . . *as* the palms of my hands . . .
1.68 . . . *as* the balance of righteousness . . .
2.15 . . . *as* cups for a wedding . . .
8.54 . . . of such *as* are prepared . . .
9.31 . . . *as* the rich man doth his treasure . . .
11.26 . . . *as* they are whose number is . . .
30.61 . . . *as* a handmaid let her serve them . . .

Pronunciation notes:

(**Dee 1.14, 17, 26, 68—TA)*

(**Dee 2.15; 8.54; 9.31; 11.26; 30.61—Ta*) *Ta* is likely just one syllable. It is uncertain if the *a* should take a long or short sound. However, various compounds that begin with *Ta* indicate the long "a" sound.

Note:

For the most part, *Ta* (as) seems to be used as a preposition—often synonymous with the word *like*: i.e., "the sun is as a sword" = "the sun is like a sword." A prepositional *as* can also mean "in the role of," as we see in the phrase . . . *who reigneth amongst you as the balance of righteousness and truth. Ta* can also be a pronoun, when used in phrases like "Appear to our comfort . . . and such as are prepared." (In this case, *such as* is the same as "those who.")

Compounds:

Chista (kiis-tay) [Chis + Ta] Are as
Chistad (kiis-tad) [Chis + Ta + D] Are as (the) Third
Corsta (kors-tay) [Cors + Ta] Such as

Ita (ii-tay) [I + Ta] Is as
Qta (kwah-tay) [Q + Ta] Or as
Tablior (TAY-blii-or) [Ta + Blior] As (Continual) Comforters
Tage (tayj) [Ta + "Ge"] As (Is) Not
Talo (tay-el-oh) [Ta + "Lo"] As the First
Talolcis (tay-LOL-sis) [Ta + "Lolcis"] As Bucklers
Taqanis (tay-kway-nis) [Ta + "Qanis"] As Olives
Tapuin (tay-pew-in) [Ta + "Puin"] As Sharp Sickles
Taviv (tay-viv) [Ta + Viv] As the Second

Also:
"Ca" (kay) As

Further:
"Ta" (tay) *conj.* And(?)

Compounds:
Taviv (tay-viv) ["Ta" + Viv] And(?) the Second

Tabaan (or Tabaam) (tay-BAY-an)* *n.* Governor

15.2 O thou, *the governor of* . . .

Note:
The transmission of Key Fifteen is missing from Dee's journals. We have only the English for the Key given on *TFR*, p. 193. However, this word is given later by Illemese, on *TFR*, p. 200.
It also appears in Dee's *48 Claves*—where it is spelled with an *n* instead of an *m* (*Tabaan*).
I have adopted the accent from *Tabaori* (to govern).

Pronunciation notes:
(**Dee—tabâan*) See the *48 Claves*. Dee gives us little clue here. He only placed a circumflex over the second *a* to indicate its long sound. The first *a* is possibly long as well, based on other versions of this word. This likely makes a word of three syllables. (I have settled upon the *Tabaan* version of this word in my pronunciation, because the *n* appears in other versions of this word.)

Also:

Anetab (ay-NEE-tayb) — (In) Government
Gnetaab (nee-TAY-ab) — (Your) Governments
Netaab (nee-TAY-ab) — Governments
Netaaib (nee-TAY-ay-ib) — Government
Tabaord (tay-BAY-ord) — (Let) Be Governed
Tabaori (tay-BAY-oh-rii) — To Govern
"Tabas" (tay-BAS) — To Govern

Further:

Cab (kab) — Rod/Scepter
Caba (ka-BA) — To Govern

Tabaord (tay-BAY-ord)* *v.* — (Be) Governed

30.44 . . . *let her be governed by* her parts . . .

Note:

The word *her* is implied in the Angelical here only by context.

Pronunciation notes:

(**Dee—Ta ba ord*) Three syllables. The *a* preceding an *o* should take the long sound (as in the English word *chaos*). I have adopted the accent from *Tabaori* (to govern).

Also:

Anetab (ay-NEE-tayb) — (In) Government
Gnetaab (nee-TAY-ab) — (Your) Governments
Netaab (nee-TAY-ab) — Governments
Netaaib (nee-TAY-ay-ib) — Government
Tabaam (tay-BAY-an) — Governor
Tabaori (tay-BAY-oh-rii) — To Govern
"Tabas" (tay-BAS) — To Govern

Further:

Cab (kab) — Rod/Scepter
Caba (ka-BA) — To Govern

Tabaori (tay-BAY-oh-rii)* *v.* — To Govern

30.121 . . . *govern* those that govern . . .

Pronunciation notes:

(**Dee—Tabá o ri*) Four syllables, with an accent on the second syllable. The first *a* should take a long sound, as seen in other versions of this word. The second *a* takes the long sound when preceding an *o* (as in the English word *chaos*). Dee shows that the *o* stands alone—taking its long sound.

(**Dee—Tabáôri*) See the *48 Claves*. Here, Dee again placed the accent on the second syllable. He also placed a circumflex over the *o* to indicate its long sound.

Also:

Anetab (ay-NEE-tayb) — (In) Government
Gnetaab (nee-TAY-ab) — (Your) Governments
Netaab (nee-TAY-ab) — Governments
Netaaib (nee-TAY-ay-ib) — Government
Tabaam (tay-BAY-an) — Governor
Tabaord (tay-BAY-ord) — (Let) Be Governed
"Tabas" (tay-BAS) — To Govern

Further:

Cab (kab) — Rod/Scepter
Caba (ka-BA) — To Govern

"Tabas" (tay-BAS) *v.* — To Govern

Pronunciation note:

I have adopted the accent from *Tabaori* (to govern).

Compounds:

Artabas (ar-tay-bas) [Ar + "Tabas"] — That Govern

Also:

Anetab (ay-NEE-tayb) — (In) Government
Gnetaab (nee-TAY-ab) — (Your) Governments
Netaab (nee-TAY-ab) — Governments

Netaaib (nee-TAY-ay-ib) — Government
Tabaam (tay-BAY-an) — Governor
Tabaord (tay-BAY-ord) — (Let) Be Governed
Tabaori (tay-BAY-oh-rii) — To Govern

Further:

Cab (kab) — Rod/Scepter
Caba (ka-BA) — To Govern

Note:

Compare to the name of the Part of the Earth (and its Angelic Governor) *Tabitom*. Perhaps this shares the "tab" root, and is perhaps even a compound with the word *Om* as well. Thus the name would mean "Governor of knowledge" or "wise Governor."

Tabges (tab-jes)* *n.* — Caves

30.98 . . . let them become *caves* for the beasts . . .

Pronunciation notes:

(**Dee—Tab ges*) Two syllables. The *g* followed by an *e* is likely soft.

Tablior (TAY-blii-or)* [Ta + Blior] *comp.* — As Comforters

5.13 . . . as continual* comforters unto whom I have fastened . . .

Note:

(*The word *continual* is not represented in the Angelical.)

Pronunciation notes:

(**Dee—Tá blior*) Likely three syllables, with an accent on the first. See pronunciation notes for *Blior* (comfort) for the long "i" sound.

"Tad" (tad) [Ta + D] *comp.* — As the Third

Compounds:

Chistad (kiis-tad)* [Chis + Ta + D] — Are as the Third

Tage (tayj)* [Ta + "Ge"] *comp.* As (Is) Not

2.36 . . . such *as is not* but in the mind . . .

Pronunciation note:

(**Dee—Tage*) Appears to be one syllable. The final *e* would be silent, and it would make the *a* long. Rhymes with the English words *cage* and *rage*.

Tal (tzall)* *prop. n.* Letter *M**

Note:

The name of the Angelical letter for *M*. It is likely that these letter names have translations of their own. (For instance, note the Hebrew alphabet: the letter *M* is named *Mem*, but *Mem* also translates as "water.") However, such translations for the Angelical letters are never given. (See the *Five Books*, p. 270.)

Pronunciation notes:

(**Dee—In sound stall or xtall*) I suspect that Dee's "xt" is similar to the "tz" sound (as in Hebrew *Tzedek*)—which is somewhere between a "t" sound and a "z" sound ("tzuh").

Compare from *Loagaeth*:

Tal

Talho (tal-ho)* *n.* Cups

2.16 . . . I have prepared as *cups* for a wedding . . .

Pronunciation notes:

(**Dee—Talho*)

Talo (tay-el-oh)* [Ta + "Lo"] *comp.* As the First

4.30 . . . are *as the first* 456 . . .

Pronunciation notes:

(**Dee—Ta l o*) Three syllables. The *l* and *o* stand alone.

Talolcis (tay-LOL-sis)* [Ta + "Lolcis"] *comp.* As Bucklers

8.16 . . . shall be *as bucklers* to the stooping dragons . . .

Pronunciation notes:

(**Dee—Ta lol cis or sis*) Three syllables. Dee indicates that the *c* should take a soft ("s") sound.

(**Dee—ta lól-cis*) See the *48 Claves*. Here, Dee places an accent on the second syllable.

Tan (tan) *prop. n.* "The Seventeenth Aethyr"

30.3 . . . which dwell in *the seventeenth aethyr* . . .

Note:

This (word 30.3) is the single space in the Key of the Aethyrs, which must be changed for each invocation—replacing word 30.3 with the name of the appropriate Aethyr. No established definitions were given for these names.

Tan contains the three Parts of the Earth *Sigmorf*, *Avdropt*, and *Tocarzi*.

Tapuin (TAY-pew-in)* [Ta + "Puin"] *comp.* As (Sharp) Sickles

3.15 . . . the rest are *as sharp sickles* . . .

Pronunciation notes:

(**Dee—Ta pu in*) Three syllables. Dee originally spelled *Tapuin* with a *v* instead of a *u*. However, he indicates the "u" sound in his phonetic note.

(**Dee—tá pû-im*) See *48 Claves*. Note the accent on the first syllable. Dee added a circumflex over the *u* to indicate its long sound. Also note that Dee seems to have mistakenly spelled this word with a final *m* instead of an *n*.

Taqanis (tay-kway-nis)* [Ta + "Qanis"] *comp.* As Olives

5.6 . . . *as olives* in the olive mount . . .

Pronunciation notes:
(**Dee—Ta qu a nis*) This appears to be four syllables. I believe Dee's *qu* makes the same sound as *q* standing alone—"kwah." However, the *qu a* (or "kwah-ay") tends to blend into one sound when this word is spoken fluently.
(**Dee—ta qa-a-nis*) See the *48 Claves*. This note matches that from *TFR*.

Tastax (tas-taks)* *v.* Going Before (To Precede)

17.12 . . . lamps living *going before* thee.

Pronunciation notes:
(**Dee—Tas tax*) Two syllables. Both *a*'s take their short sounds.

Note:
This is likely an instance of the *-ax* suffix, indicating action.

Also compare this word with the name of the Part of the Earth (and its Angelic Governor) *Tastoxo*. This could even be a compound (Tastax + Tox) for "Going Before Him" or "He Who Precedes."

Tatan (tay-tan)* *n.* Wormwood

9.16 . . . whose wings are of wormwood . . .

Pronunciation notes:
(**Dee—Ta tan*) Two syllables. The first *a* is likely a long vowel.

Note:
Wormwood is a biblical reference to poison. In the Book of Revelation, a star named Wormwood falls to the Earth, and thereby poisons a third of the world's water supply.
See also *Faboan* (poison).

Compare from *Loagaeth*:
Tantas, Tantat

Taviv (tay-viv)* [Ta + Viv] *comp.* As the Second

6.28 . . . and continuance *as the second* and third . . .

Pronunciation notes:
(**Dee—Ta viv*) Dee indicates two syllables here.

Further:
Taviv (tay-viv)* ["Ta" + Viv] *comp.* And(?) Second

5.28 . . . brothers of the first *and second* . . .

Note:
Here is the only case where Ta (as) is strangely translated as "and." Could this be a mistake on the part of Dee or Kelley? Perhaps this word should be *Odviv*.
Also see *Taviv* (as the second).

Pronunciation notes:
(**Dee—Ta ui u*) Looks like three syllables, but it is most likely only two. Dee originally wrote this word with *u*'s instead of *v*'s—however, it is unlikely that he intended "u" sounds in this case. Instead, see word 6.28 (*Taviv*), which indicates the "v" sounds.

TAXS (taks-is)* *7336*

17.10 . . . and hast *7336* lamps living going before thee.

Pronunciation notes:
(**Dee—Taxs*) Probably two syllables, as in the English *taxes*. Also, see the following note:

Note:
(**Dee—Faxes or Faxis to be sounded. I find in the Call Taxs. I find also in some words T and F are indifferently used.*) See *TFR*, p. 194. This is an interesting

observation on Dee's part. Because the use of *T* or *F* is indifferent here, I have chosen to stick with the "T" sound in my pronunciation.

Teloah (TEE-loh-ah)* *n.* Death

8.27 . . . shall not see *death* until this house fall . . .

Pronunciation notes:

(**Dee—té lo ah*) Three syllables, with an accent on the first syllable. The *e* and the *o* should each take their long sounds.

(**Dee—téloâh*) See the *48 Claves*. Dee again shows the accent on the first syllable. The *âh* should indicate a short "o" sound (as in the words *father* and *fall*).

Also:

Teloch (tee-LOCH) Death

Teloch (tee-LOCH)* *n.* Death

3.17 . . . the horns of *death* . . .

11.21 . . . gathered them together in the house of *death* . . .

Pronunciation notes:

(**Dee 3.17—Teloch as och in hotch pot*)

(**Dee 11.21—Te loch hotch*) Two syllables, and the *ch* sounds as it does in the English words *church* and *chime*. However, also see *Telocvovim*, which suggests the *ch* may take the "ch" sound *or* the "kh" sound (as in the English word *ache*).

(**Dee—telóch*) See the *48 Claves*. Here, Dee placed an accent upon the second syllable.

Compounds:

Telocvovim (tee-LOCH-voh-vee-im) [Teloch + "Vovim"] Death Dragon

Also:

Teloah (TEE-loh-ah) Death

Telocvovim (tee-LOCH-voh-vee-im)* [Teloch + "Vovim"] *comp., prop. n.* Death Dragon

30.115 . . . the dwelling place of *him that is fallen* . . .

Pronunciation notes:

(**Dee—Te lóc vo v im lotch, or loch*) Likely five syllables, with an accent on the second. The *c* at the end of the second syllable is actually a "ch" digraph (as in *church*). Finally, the *v* in the fourth syllable stands alone.

Note:

"Death Dragon" is the literal translation of *Telocvovim*, which itself is likely a proper noun for Satan—"Him That Is Fallen."

Also see *Githgulcag* (likely a name for Lucifer) and *Choronzon* (Satan, the Devil).

Tex (teks) *prop. n.* "The Thirtieth Aethyr"

30.3 . . . which dwell in *the thirtieth aethyr* . . .

Note:

This (word 30.3) is the single space in the Key of the Aethyrs, which must be changed for each invocation—replacing word 30.3 with the name of the appropriate Aethyr. No established definitions were given for these names.

Tex contains the four Parts of the Earth *Taoagla*, *Gemnimb*, *Advorpt*, and *Doxinal*.

Thil (thil) *n.* Seats

1.30 . . . whose *seats* I garnished . . .

*14.9 . . . upon 24 *seats* vexing all creatures . . .

Note:

*The transmission of Key Fourteen is missing from Dee's journals. We only have the English for this Key given later (see *TFR*, p. 193). Plus, the word appears in this location in Dee's *48 Claves*.

Also:

Othil (oh-thil) — Seats of
Thild (thild) — Seats
"Thiln" (thiln) — Seats

Thild (thild)* *n.* — Seats

5.31 . . . *their own seats* which are garnished . . .

Note:

The word *own* does not seem to be indicated in the Angelical.

Pronunciation notes:

(**Dee—Thild, one Syllable*)

Also:

Othil (oh-thil) — Seats of
Thil (thil) — Seats
"Thiln" (thiln) — Seats

"Thiln" (thiln) *n.* — Seats

Compounds:

Thilnos (thil-nos) ["Thiln" + Os] — 12 Seats of

Thilnos (thil-nos)* ["Thiln" + Os] *comp.* — 12 Seats (of)

3.33 . . . placed you in *seats 12 of* government . . .

Pronunciation notes:

(**Dee—Thilnos*) Likely two syllables.

Ti (tii)* ["T" + I] *comp.* — It Is

11.25 . . . *it is* as they are whose . . .

Pronunciation notes:

(*Dee—Ti*) One syllable. The *i* is likely a long vowel.

Tia (tii-a)* *prep.* Unto (Us)

30.149 . . . he hath sworn *unto us* in his justice.

Pronunciation notes:

(*Dee—Tia*) Likely two syllables. I suggest a long *i*—because it is followed by an *a* (as in the English word *dial*).

Note:

Also see *Pambt* (unto) and *Pugo* (as unto).

Tianta (tii-AN-ta)* *n.* Bed

30.112 . . . she is *the bed of* an harlot . . .

Pronunciation notes:

(*Dee—Ti án ta*) Likely three syllables, with an accent in the middle of the second syllable. In the first syllable, I suggest a long *i*—because it is followed by an *a* (as in *dial*).

Tibibp (tib-ib-ip)* *n.* Sorrow

12.8 . . . the lanterns of *sorrow* . . .

Pronunciation notes:

(*Dee—Tibibp*) Dee gives us little clue for this word. I assume it should be three syllables. I would have assumed the final *p* stands alone, though Dee does not indicate such. Therefore, I have simply combined the *b* and *p* into the sound of "bip."

Note:

Also see *Ser* (sorrow).

Tilb (tilb)* *adj. or pron.* Her

30.28 . . . *her* unspeakable variety . . .

Pronunciation notes:

(**Dee—Tilb*) One syllable.

Also:

Tiobl (tii-AHB-el) (Within) Her

Compounds:

Busdirtilb (buz-der-tilb) [Busdir + Tilb] Glory (of) Her
Elzaptilb (el-ZAP-tilb) ["Elzap" + Tilb] Her Course
Omptilb (omp-tilb) ["Omp" + Tilb] Her Understanding

Note:

Also see "Ip" (her) and "Pi" (she).

Tiobl (tii-AHB-el)* *pron.* (Within) Her

30.49 . . . let there be division *in her* . . .
30.72 . . . no creature upon or *within her* . . .

Pronunciation notes:

(**Dee 30.49—Ti óbil*)
(**Dee 30.72—Ti ob l*) Three syllables, with an accent on the second syllable. The *o* is not shown standing by itself, thus I assume it has a short sound. The second phonetic note (word 30.72) indicates the *l* stands alone.
(**Dee 30.49, 72—tióbl*) See the *48 Claves*. Here, Dee again placed an accent on the second syllable.

Also:

Tilb (tilb) Her

Note:

Also see "Pi" (she).

Tliob (tlii-ob)* *v.* To Separate (Classify?) Creatures

16.17 . . . that understand and *separate creatures*.

Pronunciation notes:

(**Dee—Tli ob*) Dee indicates two syllables—forcing the *Tl* to combine grudgingly into one sound. The *i* likely takes its long sound.

Note:

"To separate creatures" as into differing classifications. The entire phrase "that understand and separate creatures" appears to indicate intelligence or logical thought.

Toatar (toh-AY-tar)* *v.* Harken (To Listen)

17.19 Gird up thy loins and *harken.*

Pronunciation notes:

(**Dee—To a tar*) Three syllables. The *o* takes its long sound. The first *a* seems to stand alone.

(**Dee—toátar*) See the *48 Claves*. Here, Dee placed an accent over the *a* in the second syllable.

Note:

See also *Solpeth* (harken unto).

Also compare to the name of the Angel *Autotar*, an Elder of the Eastern Watchtower. Perhaps his name means "He Who Listens."

Tofglo (TOF-gloh)* *n.* All (Things)

30.35 . . . to dispose *all things* according to . . .

Pronunciation notes:

(**Dee—Tóf glo*) Two syllables, with the accent on the first syllable.

(**Dee—tófglo*) See the *48 Claves*. This note is essentially the same as that in *TFR*.

Note:

Also see *Ton* (all).

Toh (toh)* *v.* To Triumph

1.55 . . . him that liveth *and triumpheth* . . .

Pronunciation notes:

(**Dee—tóh*) See *48 Claves*. Note the accent mark over the *o*. (The previous word in the Key—*Hom*—is just one syllable without an accent. Thus, both words are likely to be taken together, with the accent on *Toh*.)

Possible compounds:

Baltoh (bal-toh) [Balt + Toh] — Righteousness
Iadbaloth (ii-ad-BAL-toh) [Iad + Balt + Toh] — God of Righteousness

Also:

"Toha" — Triumph?

"Toha" (toh-ha) *n.* — (My) Triumph?

Compounds:

Baltoha (bal-toh-ha) [Balt + "Toha"] — (My?) Righteousness

Note:

The *-a* could be an affix added to the word *Toh* (triumph).

Also:

Toh (toh) — Triumph

Tohcoth (toh-koth) *n.* — "Nature Spirits"*

From *Loagaeth*:

(**Dee—This name comprehendeth the number of all the fairies—who are devils next to the state of man.*) See the *Five Books*, p. 315. In other words, *Tohcoth* indicates earthbound nature spirits. (Also see *Gah*, which likely means "pure spirits.")

Also see:

Tolham (tol-HAYM) — All Creatures
Tolhami (tol-HAY-mii) — (Upon) All Creatures
Toltorg (tol-TORJ) — Creatures
Toltorgi (tol-TOR-jii) — With (Her) Creatures
"Toltorn" (tol-TORN) — Creature

Tolham (tol-HAYM) *n.* All Creatures

14.11 . . . vexing *all creatures* of the earth with age . . .

Pronunciation notes:

I have adopted the accent from *Tolhami.*

Note:

The transmission of Key Fourteen is missing from Dee's journals. We only have the English for this Key given later (see *TFR*, p. 193). Plus, the word appears in this location in Dee's *48 Claves*.

Here, the Angelical word *Caosgo* (of the earth) follows *Tolham*. See *Toltorg*.

Also:

Tolhami (tol-HAY-mii) (Upon) All Creatures
Toltorg (tol-TORJ) Creatures
Toltorgi (tol-TOR-jii) With (Her) Creatures
"Toltorn" (tol-TORN) Creature

Compare from *Loagaeth*:

Tohcoth

Tolhami (tol-HAY-mii)* *n.* (Upon) All Creatures

7.22 . . . such as work wonders *on all creatures*.

Pronunciation notes:

(**Dee—Tol há mi*) Three syllables, with an accent on the second syllable. The *a* and the final *i* likely take their long sounds.
(**Dee—tol-hâ-mi*) See the *48 Claves*. Note the circumflex over the *a*—indicating its long sound.

Also:

Tolham (tol-HAYM) All Creatures
Toltorg (tol-TORJ) Creatures
Toltorgi (tol-TOR-jii) With (Her) Creatures
"Toltorn" (tol-TORN) Creature

Compare from *Loagaeth*:
Tohcoth

Toltorg (tol-TORJ)* *n.* — Creatures

3.19 . . . wherein *the creatures of the earth* are . . .

Pronunciation notes:
(**Dee—Toltorg org as in george*) Likely two syllables, with a soft *g* at the end. I have adopted the accent from other versions of this word.

Note:
The Angelical for "of the earth" (*Caosgo*) does not appear here. See *Tolham*.

Also:
Tolham (tol-HAYM) — All Creatures
Tolhami (tol-HAY-mii) — (Upon) All Creatures
Toltorgi (tol-TOR-jii) — With (Her) Creatures
"Toltorn" (tol-TORN) — Creature

Compare from *Loagaeth*: *Tohcoth*

Toltorgi (tol-TOR-jii)* *n.* — (With) Creatures

5.23 . . . to water the earth *with her creatures* . . .

Pronunciation notes:
(**Dee—Toltórgi*) Likely three syllables, with an accent on the second syllable. The *g* preceding an *i* should take the soft ("j") sound.
(**Dee—toltórgi*) See the *48 Claves*. This note matches that from *TFR*.

Also:
Tolham (tol-HAYM) — All Creatures
Tolhami (tol-HAY-mii) — (Upon) All Creatures
Toltorg (tol-TORJ) — Creatures
"Toltorn" (tol-TORN) — Creature

Compare from *Loagaeth*:

Tohcoth

"Toltorn" (tol-TORN) *n.* Creature

Pronunciation note:

I have adopted the accent from other versions of this word.

Compounds:

Agtoltorn (ay-jee-tol-torn) [Ag + "Toltorn"] No Creature

Agltoltorn (ag-el-tol-torn) [Ag + L + "Toltorn"] No One Creature

Also:

Tolham (tol-HAYM) All Creatures

Tolhami (tol-HAY-mii) (Upon) All Creatures

Toltorg (tol-TORJ) Creatures

Toltorgi (tol-TOR-jii) With Creatures

Ton (ton)* *adj.* All

30.74 *All* her members, let them differ . . .

Pronunciation notes:

(**Dee—Ton*) One syllable.

Note:

Also see *Tofglo* (all things).

Also see Vomsarg, which is "All" (or Every One) used as a pronoun.

Tonug (too-nuj)* *v.* To Deface

30.95 . . . the work of man and his pomp, *let them be defaced.*

Pronunciation notes:

(**Dee—To nug g dg*) Two syllables. The final *g* takes the soft "j" sound.

Tooat (toh-OH-at)* *v.* To Furnish

30.31 . . . her unspeakable variety, *furnishing* you with . . .

Pronunciation notes:

(*Dee—To ó at*) Three syllables, with an accent on the second syllable. The *o* stands alone in the second syllable.

(*Dee—toóat*) See the *48 Claves*. Dee again placed the accent over the *o* in the second syllable.

Tor (tor) *prop. n.* "The Twenty-Third Aethyr" (To Rise?)

30.3 . . . which dwell in *the twenty-third aethyr* . . .

Note:

This (word 30.3) is the single space in the Key of the Aethyrs, which must be changed for each invocation—replacing word 30.3 with the name of the appropriate Aethyr. No established definitions were given for these names.

Tor contains the three Parts of the Earth *Ronoomb*, *Onizimp*, and *Zaxanin*.

Possible shared root:

Torgu (tor-GOO) Arise
Torzu (tor-ZOOL) Arise
Torzul (tor-ZOOL) Shall Rise
Torzulp (tor-ZOOLP) To Rise

Torb (torb) *n.* One Hundred

10.41 . . . roar *with a hundred* mighty earthquakes . . .

Note:

This word was not originally given with Key Ten. It was added later when Nalvage transmitted the English for the Key (see *TFR*, p. 192). This seems to have been the case with many of the numbers mentioned in the Keys.

This would appear to be the word for "one hundred" and not the numeral 100.

Compounds:

Matorb (may-torb) [Matb + Torb] Long (period of time)

Torgu (tor-GOO)* *v.* Arise

4.32 *Arise*, you sons of pleasure . . .

Pronunciation notes:

(*Dee—Torgu*) Likely two syllables. I assume the *g* should have a hard sound in front of a *u*, as in the English words *gulp* and *gun*. The final *u* itself likely has a long sound.

(*Dee—Torgú*) See the *48 Claves*. Note the accent on the last syllable.

Also:

Torzu (tor-ZOO) Arise
Torzul (tor-ZOOL) Shall Rise
Torzulp (tor-ZOOLP) To Rise

Possible shared root:

Tor (tor) "The Twenty-Third Aethyr"

Torzu (tor-ZOO)* *v.* Arise

2.40 *Arise* sayeth the First.
30.117 O you heavens, *arise* . . .
30.141 *Arise*, move, and appear . . .

Pronunciation notes:

(*Dee 2.40—Torzú*) Dee places an accent on the final syllable.

(*Dee 30.117, 141—Tor zu*) Two syllables.

Also:

Torgu (tor-GOO) Arise
Torzul (tor-ZOOL) Shall Rise
Torzulp (tor-ZOOLP) To Rise

Possible shared root:

Tor (tor) "The Twenty-Third Aethyr"

Note:

Compare to the name of the Part of the Earth (and its Angelic Governor) *Torzoxi*. It would appear that this name is a compound (Torzu + Tox), or "He Who Rises."

Torzul (tor-ZOOL)* *v.* (Shall) Arise

3.27 . . . which sleep and *shall rise*.

Pronunciation notes:

(*Dee—TORZUL*) Dee gives us little clue here. See pronunciation note for *Torzu* (arise). I have adopted the accent from other versions of this word.

Also:

Torgu (tor-GOO) Arise
Torzu (tor-ZOO) Arise
Torzulp (tor-ZOOLP) To Rise

Possible shared root:

Tor (tor) "The Twenty-Third Aethyr"

Torzulp (tor-ZOOLP)* *v.* To Rise

30.40 . . . and *rose up* in the beginning . . .

Pronunciation notes:

(*Dee—Tor zulp*) Two syllables. Based on the other versions of this word, I assume the *u* should have a long vowel sound.
I have adopted the accent from other versions of this word.

Also:

Torgu (tor-GOO) Arise
Torzu (tor-ZOO) Arise
Torzul (tor-ZOOL) Shall Rise

Possible shared root:

Tor (tor) — "The Twenty-Third Aethyr"

Tox (toks) *pron.* or *adj.* — His/Him

14.21 . . . the promise of *him* which is called . . .

Note:

The transmission of Key Fourteen is missing from Dee's journals. We only have the English for this Key given later (see *TFR*, p. 193). Plus, the word appears in this location in Dee's *48 Claves*.

Compounds:

Lonshitox (lon-shii-toks) [Lonshi + Tox] — His Power

Avavox (ay-vay-voks) ["Avav" + Tox] — His Pomp

Oxiayal (oks-AY-al) [Tox? + Iaial] — The Mighty Seat

Possible shared root:

Oxex (oks-eks) — To Vomit

Oxo (oks-oh) — "The Fifteenth Aethyr"

Note:

The root of these words may be "ox."

Tranan (tray-nan)* *n.* — Marrow

9.18 . . . and of *the marrow of* salt . . .

Pronunciation notes:

(**Dee—Tra nan*) Two syllables. The first *a* is likely a long vowel.

Trian (TRII-an)* *v.* — Shall Be

6.39 . . . whose works *shall be* a song of honour . . .

8.15 . . . whose long continuance *shall be* as bucklers . . .

Pronunciation notes:

(**Dee 6.39—Trian*)

(**Dee 8.15—Tri an*) Two syllables. The *i* is likely a long vowel, followed by a short *a*.

(*Dee 6.39—trían*) See the *48 Claves*. The accent is placed on the first syllable.

Note:
Also see *Chiso* (shall be).

Trint (trint) *v.* To Sit

14.6 . . . which *sit* upon 24 seats . . .

Note:
The transmission of Key Fourteen is missing from Dee's journals. We only have the English for this Key given later (see *TFR*, p. 193). Plus, the word appears in this location in Dee's *48 Claves*.

Trof (trof)* *n.* or *v.?* A Building

2.34 . . . you are become *a building* such as . . .

Pronunciation note:
(*Dee—Trof*) Likely one syllable, as "Tr" makes a natural sound in English (as in *trial*, *try*, and *trouble*).

Note:
Also see *Orscatbl* (buildings). I suspect that *Trof* can also stand as the verb "to build."

Turbs (turbs)* *n.* (In) Beauty

2.20 . . . as the flowers *in their beauty* . . .

Pronunciation notes:
(*Dee—Turbs*) Likely one syllable.

Also:
Urbs (yurbs) Beautified

Van (U/V)

Vaa (vay) *prop. n.* n/a

Pronunciation note:

The double *a* In Early Modern English should indicate a long vowel sound.

Note:

See *TFR*, pp. 228–29. The names of most of the Angels encountered by Dee and Kelley can be found in other parts of the Angelic system—such as the *Heptarchia* or Great Table (Watchtower) systems. However, Vaa is one of the few entirely unique Angels that appeared to the two men. It was very late in the Angelic journals, after all of the essential Angelic magick had been transmitted. One day, Kelley saw three little creatures running around the floor of the room. It turned out that they were Angels from the Great Table (Watchtowers)—but their names were *not* derived according to the instructions Ave had previously given to Dee.

Note:

Vaa says of himself: "I am the last of the first, of the fourth.* And I have power to gather up the blessings of God, and to set them (if they be disdained) in a better soil." Dee notes, in Latin: "Transplanter of Gifts." And, a little further down the page: "*Vaa*—It is my duty to transplant the gifts of God."

The three Angels, apparently jointly, say, "For even as the father, son and holy spirit are one, but of themselves and being dilated, is full of power, and many. So are we one particularly in power,** but separated. Notwithstanding, spiritually of, and amongst, others, and dilated in the will of God, and into the branches of his determinations. But, particularly living, and jointly praising God."

Note:

*Dee notes the Angels are numbering the Watchtowers in an odd fashion. So that in this case, he points out, the numbering should follow: First = eastern, Second = western, Third = southern, and Fourth = the northern Watchtower. Vaa is found as the last three letters on the first line of the Northern Watchtower Tablet.

(***On the next page Dee notes: The three names make one name of 7 letters—Gazavaa.*) Further, I note that all three of these names begin with capital letters on the Great Table (Watchtowers). Also, each one of them terminates once it hits the Great Cross, Black Cross, or the end of the Watchtower. We may have discovered an entirely new Angelic system in the Watchtowers.

(See *Ga* and *Za*. Also see *Galvah*, *Mapsama*, *Murifri*, and *Nalvage*.)

Vabzir (vab-zer)* *n.* The Eagle

11.11 . . . and *the Eagle* spake and cried . . .

Pronunciation notes:

(**Dee—Vab zir*) Two syllables. Both vowels appear to take their short sounds.

Note:

This is a direct reference to one of the four Beasts of the Apocalypse. See Revelation, chapters 4ff.

Van (van) *prop. n.* Letter *U/V*

Note:

See the *Five Books*, p. 270. The name of the Angelical letter for *U/V*. It is likely that these letter names have translations of their own. (For instance, note the Hebrew alphabet: the letter *U/V* is named *Vav*, but *Vav* also translates as "nail" or "stake.") However, such translations for the Angelical letters are never given.

Compare from *Loagaeth*:

Van

"Vaoan" (vay-oh-AN)* *n.* Truth

1.72 . . . the balance of righteousness and *truth*.

Pronunciation notes:

(**Dee, recording the words of Nalvage—It is Vooan. It may be sounded Vaoan. Vooan is spoken with them that fall, but Vaoan with them that are, and are glorified. The devils have lost the dignity of their sounds.*) There are two acceptable spellings for this word (see *Vooan*). When working with earthbound or infernal spirits, the word should start with *Vo* (*Vooan*)—sounding akin to "voo-an." However, when working with Angels, the word should start with *Va* ("Vaoan")—sounding akin to "vay-oh-an."

(**Dee—vaoan*) See the *48 Claves*. Here, Dee uses the "Vaoan" spelling of the word, even though the *Vooan* spelling was given in *TFR*. (See *Odvooan* for the accented syllable.)

Note:

Also see *TFR*, p. 80. Here, the Angel Nalvage says of *Vooan*: "The word is, by interpretation, *Ignus vera mater*. The vain Philosophers do think it doth beget bodies. But, in truth, it conceiveth and bringeth forth." It seems that Nalvage accuses the "vain Philosophers" of regarding Vooan (Truth) as a male force (begetting bodies), but that Truth is in fact a feminine force (conceiving and bringing forth)—probably associating Truth with Gnostic images of the Goddess Wisdom (Sophia). The Latin that Nalvage uses to interpret the word—*Ignus vera mater*—seems to mean the "Fiery Truth of the Mother/Source."

Also:

Vooan (voo-AN) Truth

Varpax (var-paks) n/a

Note:

See the *Five Books*, p. 258. Here, Raphael offers a long prayer, the very end of which is, "How great and innumerable are your [God's] gifts? *O remiges varpax. Kyrie eleyson.*"

No translation is offered for this phrase, though I wonder if it is perhaps the Angelical for the Latin *Kyrie eleyson* (Lord have mercy), often used in Catholic prayer.

Note that *Varpax* may have the *-ax* suffix, indicating action.

Vasedg (vay-sej) *prop. n.* — n/a

Note:

See the *Five Books*, p. 160. (*A voice: "Come, O Vasedg."*) Kelley is having a vision of the Seven Biblical Days of Creation at this point—where the Seven Ensigns of Creation are revealed. The call to Vasedg is answered by "a woman" who emerges from the darkness—except for her head—and presents a magickal tablet that produces "many things creeping out of it." She is then, temporarily, eclipsed by another woman who creates the Sun, Moon, and stars. When this other woman leaves, Vasedg steps fully into the light—revealing herself as an old crone. She retrieves clay from her tablet and creates birds with it. Finally, she says, "They are multiplied for your use" and exits the vision.

Note:

Compare this name to the name *Vasg*, an Angel of medicine of the Northern Watchtower.

"Vau" (vah) *v.* — To Work

Compounds:

Vaulzirn (VOL-zern) ["Vau" + "Lzirn"] — Work Wonders

Also:

Vaun (von) — To Work

Vaulzirn (VOL-zern)* ["Vau" + "Lzirn"] *comp.* — Work Wonders

7.21 . . . such as *work wonders* on all creatures.

Pronunciation notes:

(**Dee—Vául zirn*) Two syllables, with an accent on the first syllable. In Early Modern English, the *au* letter combination produces a short "o" sound (as in the English words *auburn* and *autumn*).

Vaun (von)* *v.* To Work

3.49 . . . *you might work* my power . . .

Pronunciation notes:

(**Dee—Vaun*) One syllable. In Early Modern English, the *au* letter combination produces a short "o" sound (as in the English words *auburn* and *autumn*).

Also:

"Vau" (vah) To Work

Ucim (yew-sim)* *v.* Frown Not (To Smile)

9.61 Happy is he upon whom they *frown not*.

Pronunciation notes:

(**Dee—U cim*) Two syllables. The *U* stands alone. The *c* should take its soft "s" sound when preceding an *i* (as in the English words *circus* and *circle*.)

Also:

Ulcinin (yewl-sii-nin) Happy (Is He)

Udl* (yew-del) *n.* The Rest

Alternate spelling:

(**Dee 3.13—Vndl It may be VdL or VndL"*) This is an alternate spelling for *Undl* (the rest).

Also:

Undl (und-el) The Rest

Veh (vay) *prop. n.* Letter *C/Ch/K*

Note:
The name of the Angelical letter for *C/K*. It is likely that these letter names have translations of their own. (For instance, note the Hebrew alphabet: the letter *C/K* is named *Kaph*, but *Kaph* also translates as "fist" or "cupped hand.") However, such translations for the Angelical letters are never given. (See the *Five Books*, p. 270.)

Vep (vep)* *n.* Flame

1.62 . . . which shineth as *a flame* . . .

Pronunciation notes:
(**Dee—It is called Vep*) I assume the *e* in this word is a phonetic gloss. See the word *Vp* in *Loagaeth*.

Note:
Both *Vep* and *Prge* (fire) are nouns. For a verb form, see *Ialpon* (to burn). For an adjective, see *Ialpor* (flaming).

Compare from *Loagaeth*:
Vp

Ugear (yew-JEE-ar)* *n.* Strength (of Men)

7.15 . . . in whom *the strength of men* rejoiceth . . .

Pronunciation notes:
(**Dee—V gé ar*) Three syllables. The accent is on the second syllable. Dee originally wrote this word with an initial *V*—however, it should take the "u" sound, as it precedes a consonant. The *g* is likely soft, as it precedes an *e* (as in the English words *gentle* and *gender*). Also, the *e* in the second syllable appears to take a long sound (likely due to the *ea* letter combination—as in the English words *eat* and *seat*).
(**Dee—vgéar*) See the *48 Claves*. The accent is again shown on the second syllable.

Also:

Ugeg (yew-JEJ) Become Strong

Ugegi (yew-JEE-jii) Waxeth Strong

Note:

Also see *Umadea* (strong towers), *Umplif* (strength), and *Vohim* (mighty). Note how all these words for "strength" begin with *U*/*V*. But, also see *Micaolz* (mighty).

Ugeg (yew-JEJ)* *v.* Become Strong

8.10 . . . the Elders are *become strong* . . .

Pronunciation notes:

(**Dee—V geg*) Two syllables. Dee originally wrote this word with an initial *V*—however, it should take the "u" sound, as it precedes a consonant. The accent on the second syllable is found in the pronunciation notes at *Ugear* (strength of men). The first *g* should be soft, as it precedes an *e*. The final *g* is indicated as soft in Dee's phonetic notes for *Odugeg* (and wax strong).

Compounds:

Odugeg (ohd-yew-JEJ) [Od + Ugeg] And Wax Strong

Also:

Ugear (yew-JEE-ar) Strength (of Men)

Ugegi (yew-JEE-jii) Waxeth Strong

Note:

See note at *Ugear*.

Ugegi (yew-JEE-jii)* *v.* To Wax (Become) Strong

7.48 . . . our strength *waxeth strong* in our comforter.

Pronunciation notes:

(**Dee—V Ge gi*) Three syllables. Dee originally wrote this word with an initial *V*—however, it should take the "u" sound, as it precedes a consonant. The accent falls upon the second syllable, which Dee capitalized

(see pronunciation notes for *Ugear*). The *e* is likely long. The second *g* should take the soft "j" sound, as it precedes an *i* (as in the English words *giant* and *gyrate*).
(**Dee—vgêgi*) See the *48 Claves*. Note the circumflex over the *e* to indicate its long sound.

Also:

Ugear (yew-JEE-ar) — Strength (of Men)
Ugeg (yew-JEJ) — Become Strong

Note:

See note at *Ugear*.

Viiv (vii-iv)* *n.* — Second

2.7 . . . O you *the second of* the first . . .

Note:

The words *O you* are not indicated in the Angelical.
Also, this is the word for "second," but not the numeral 2.

Pronunciation notes:

(**Dee—Vi iv*) Two syllables—although, when spoken fluently, they tend to blend together. In Early Modern English, a double *i* indicated a long "i" sound. (I suspect the second *i* in *Viiv* is just a phonetic gloss.)
(**Dee—vi-iv*) See *48 Claves*. This note matches the one from *TFR*.

Also:

Viv (vii-iv) — Second

Virq (vir-kwah)* *n.* — Nests

10.13 . . . are 22 *nests of* lamentation . . .

Pronunciation notes:

(**Dee—Vir q quu*) Two syllables. The *q* stands alone, and Dee indicates that it should sound like "kwah." (The *uu* is the same in Early Modern English as our modern *w*—so Dee's note indicates "quu" or "qw" as the sound of the second syllable.)

Viv (viv) *n.* Second

Compounds:

Taviv (tay-viv) [Ta + Viv] As the Second
Taviv (tay-viv) ["Ta" + Viv] And(?) Second
Vivialprt (viv-ii-AL-purt) [Viv + "Ialprt"] Second Flame
Vivdiv (viv-DII-vee) [Viv + Div] Second Angle

Also:

Viiv (vii-iv) Second

Note:

This is the word for "second," but not the numeral 2.

Compare this word to the name of the Part of the Earth (and its Angelic Governor) *Vivipos.*

Vivdiv (viv-DII-vee)* [Viv + Div] *comp.* Second Angle

4.12 . . . which reign in *the second angle* . . .

Pronunciation notes:

(**Dee—Vi v di v*) Seems to be four syllables. The second and third *v*'s appear to stand alone.

(**Dee—viv-di-v*) See the *48 Claves*. Here, Dee indicates three syllables instead.

I have adopted the accent from *Sdiu* (fourth angle).

Vivialprt (viv-ii-AL-purt)* [Viv + "Ialprt"] *comp.* Second Flame

**16.2 O thou *Second Flame* . . .

Note:

**The transmission of the first twelve words of Key Sixteen is missing from Dee's journals. We only have the English given for it on *TFR*, p. 194. However, Illemese gives his phonetic note for this word later, on *TFR*, p. 200. It also appears in Dee's *48 Claves*.

Pronunciation notes:

(**Illemese—vivi a purt*) See *TFR*, p. 200. Four syllables. The *r* takes the "ur" sound. Although Illemese dropps the sound of the *l*, I have retained it in my pronunciation. Also see pronunciation notes for *Ialprg* (burning flames).

(**Dee—viuiâlprt*) See the *48 Claves*. Here, Dee placed an accent over the second *i*—which should be the second syllable. He also placed a circumflex over the *a* to indicate a long vowel. However, all other versions of "Ialprt," *Ialprg*, etc., indicate a short *a* in the same place. (I have settled upon the short *a* sound in my pronunciation.)

I have adopted the accent from similar words.

Ul (yewl)* *n.* End

1.58 . . . nor *end* cannot be . . .

Pronunciation notes:

(**Dee—Call it UL, with such sound to U as we pronounce yew, whereof bows are made.*) It is hard to tell if Dee intended one or two syllables for this word. I have settled upon a single syllable.

Also:

Uls (yewls) Ends

Probable root:

L (el) First

Note:

The two instances of *end* are interesting. *L* by itself indicates *the first* or *beginning*, while its usage here is antonymic. See also *I* (is/are), which transmutes into its antonym by the addition of the letter *p*: *Ip* (not)

Ulcinin (yewl-SII-nin)* *adj.* Happy

9.59 *Happy is he* upon whom they frown not.

Pronunciation notes:

(**Dee—Ul ci nin*) Three syllables. Dee originally wrote this word with an initial *V*—but he clearly shows the "u" sound in his phonetic note.

(The *U*/*V* precedes a consonant, so it should take the "u" sound.) The *c* should take its soft "s" sound when preceding an *i*. The first *i* should be long, while the second *i* is short.
(**Dee—vlcínin*) See the *48 Claves*. Here, Dee placed an accent over the *i* in the second syllable.

Also:

Ucim (yew-sim) — Frown Not (Smile)

Uls (yewls)* *n.* — Ends

5.39 . . . first, *ends*, and contents of time . . .

Pronunciation notes:

(**Dee—Uls*) One syllable. Dee originally wrote this word as "Vls"—but his note clearly shows the "u" sound. See the pronunciation note at *Ul* (end) for more info.

Also:

Ul (yewl) — End

Probable root:

L (el) — First

Note:

See note at *Ul*.

Umadea (yew-MAY-dee-a)* *n.* — Strong Towers

7.28 . . . *strong towers* and places of comfort . . .

Pronunciation notes:

(**Dee—V má de a*) Dee originally wrote this word as "Vmadea." However, in Early Modern English, a *v* followed by a consonant would have to take the "u" sound. (This is further supported by the related word *Umplif*.) *Umadea* appears to be four syllables, with an accent on the second syllable. The *V*/*U* stands alone. The *e* should likely take the long sound, as the *ea* letter combination does result in a long *e* (as in the

English words *reading* and *seat*). I suspect the final *a* (though it is written by itself) makes a short sound.
(**Dee—vmádêa*) See the *48 Claves*. The accent is still on the second syllable. The *e* has a circumflex over it to indicate the long sound.

Probable shared root:
Umplif (um-plif) Strength

Note:
Also see *Ugeg* (become strong), *Vohim* (mighty). Note how all these words for "strength" begin with a *U/V*. But, also see *Micaolz* (mighty).

Uml (um-el)* *v.* To Add

30.135 *Add* and diminish until the stars . . .

Pronunciation notes:
(**Dee—Vm l*) Two syllables. The *l* stands alone. Dee originally spelled this word with a *V*—but the pronunciation note indicates that it should combine with the *m* in a single syllable. If so, then it could make the sound of "vem" or it could simply take the sound of "um" instead. Since Dee offers no clue, I have opted for the "u" sound instead of "v."

Umplif (um-plif)* *n.* Strength

7.47 . . . and our strength *waxeth strong* . . .

Pronunciation notes:
(**Dee—Umplif*) Dee originally wrote this word as *Vmplif*. However, his phonetic note clearly indicates the "u" sound. Likely two syllables, with short vowel sounds.

Probable shared root:
Umadea (yew-MAY-dee-a) Strong Towers

Note:
Also see *Givi* (stronger), *Umadea* (strong towers), *Ugeg* (become strong), and *Vohim* (mighty). Note how all these words for "strength" begin with *U/V*.

Un (und)* *prop. n.* — Letter *A*

Note:
See the *Five Books*, p. 270. The name of the Angelical letter for *A*. It is likely that these letter names have translations of their own. (For instance, note the Hebrew alphabet: the letter *a* is named *Aleph*, but *Aleph* also translates as "ox/bull.") However, such translations for the Angelical letters are never given.

Pronunciation notes:
(**Dee—The sound seemed und.*) Likely just one syllable. The *u* in Dee's phonetic note could indicate a "yew" sound (as in *ubiquitous*) or an "uh" sound (as in *under*). I am unsure which is intended, but I have chosen to go with the "uh" sound.

Compare from *Loagaeth*:
Un

Unal (yew-NAL)* *pron.* — These

9.27 *These* gather up the moss of the earth . . .

Pronunciation notes:
(**Dee—V nal*) Two syllables. Dee wrote this word with a "V"—though the letter should take a "u" sound because it precedes a consonant.
(**Dee—Unál*) See the *48 Claves*. Here, Dee placed an accent over the second syllable. He also confirms the "u" sound for the initial letter.

Note:
The word *these* can be an adjective (as in "these books"). However, it is used in the Keys as a pronoun, being used in place of the subject noun.

Compounds:
Unalchis (yew-nal-kiis) [Unal + Chis] — These Are

Unalah (un-al-ah)* *n.* Skirts

3.56 . . . you are become *the skirts of* justice and truth.

Pronunciation notes:

(**Dee—Unalah*) Likely three syllables. Dee did not write the *U* standing alone, which seems to indicate that it combines with the *n* (making a short "u" sound).

Note:

Also see *Miinoag* (corners/boundaries).

Unalchis (yew-nal-kiis)* [Unal + Chis] *comp.* These Are

10.33 . . . *these be* the Thunders . . .

Pronunciation notes:

(**Dee—U nal ckis*) Three syllables. The initial *U* stands alone. The *ch* in the final syllable takes a hard "ck" sound. (See *Chis* for further pronunciation notes.)

(**Dee—Vnâl-chis*) See the *48 Claves*. Here, Dee placed a circumflex over the *a* to indicate a long vowel sound. The initial *V* takes the "u" sound.

Note:

See note at *Unal.*

Unchi (un-kii)* *v.* To Confound

30.100 *Confound* her understanding . . .

Pronunciation notes:

(**Dee—Un chi Ki*) Two syllables. The *ch* in the second syllable takes the harder "kh" sound—as in the English word *ache.*

Also:

Oucho (oh-yew-choh) (Let) Confound

Urch (yurk) The Confusers

Note:

It would appear that "uch" serves as a common root between these words.

Undl (und-el)* *n.* The Rest

3.13 . . . *the rest* are as sharp sickles . . .

Pronunciation notes:

(**Dee—Vnd L*) Two syllables. Dee originally wrote this word with an initial *V*. The *V* likely takes the sound of "u"—because it precedes a consonant. The *l* stands alone.
(**Dee—und-l*) See *48 Claves*. Here, Dee confirms the initial "u" sound as well as the stand-alone *l*.

Also:

Udl (yew-del) The Rest

Unig (yew-nig)* *v.* To Require

9.73 . . . the time is such as *requireth* comfort.

Pronunciation notes:

(**Dee—V nig*) Two syllables. Dee wrote this word with an initial *V*. However, because it precedes a consonant, it more likely takes the "u" sound.

Uniglag (yew-nii-glag)* *v.* To Descend

3.75 . . . move, *descend*, and apply yourselves . . .

Pronunciation notes:

(**Dee—Uniglag*) I assume three syllables here, with a hard *g* in the second and third syllables.
(**Dee—vnîglag*) See the *48 Claves*. Dee placed a circumflex over the *i* to indicate the long sound.

I have adopted the long "u" sound from the similarly spelled *Unig* (to require).

"Vnph" (unv) *n.* Anger

Pronunciation note:

Following the *n*, the *ph* likely has a soft "v" sound. (See the pronunciation notes for *Sonf.*)

Compounds:

Ivonpovnph (ii-VON-foh-unv) [I + "Vonpo" + "Vnph"] Is Wrath in Anger

"Vonpovnph" (VON-foh-unv) ["Vonpo" + "Vnph"] Wrath in Anger

Also:

Vonph (vonv) Wrath

Vonpho (von-foh) (Of) Wrath

"Vonpo" (von-foh) Wrath

Possible shared root:

Vohim (VOH-im) Mighty

"Vonin" (voh-NIN) Dragon

Vonph (vonv)

Wrath

"Vovim" (voh-VIM) Dragon

Vovina (voh-VII-na) Dragon

Vohim (VOH-im)* *adj.* Mighty

10.42 . . . with a hundred *mighty* earthquakes . . .

Pronunciation notes:

(*Dee—Vóh-im) Two syllables, with an accent on the first syllable.

(*Dee—vóhim) See the *48 Claves*. Here, Dee again indicates the accent on the first syllable.

Possible shared root:

"Vnph" (unv) Anger

"Vonin" (voh-NIN)	Dragon
Vonph (vonv)	Wrath
Vonpho (von-foh)	(Of) Wrath
"Vonpo" (von-foh)	Wrath
"Vovim" (voh-VIM)	Dragon
Vovina (voh-VII-na)	Dragon

Note:
Also see *Umadea* (strong towers), *Umplif* (strength), *Ugeg* (become strong). Note how all these words for "strength" begin with *U*/V. But, also see *Micaolz* (mighty).

Compare from *Loagaeth*:
Voh, Voha

Vomzarg (vom-sarj)* *pron.* — Every One/All

3.36 . . . giving unto *every one of you* power . . .

Pronunciation notes:
(**Dee—Vomsarg, arg as in barge*) Likely two syllables, with a soft *g* at the end.

Note:
The word *all* can be an adjective ("all books") or a pronoun ("justice for all"). The word *every* is simply an adjective—but the word *Vomzarg* translates as "every one," which is synonymous with *all* used as a pronoun.

See also *Ton*, which is "all" used as an adjective.

"Vonin" (voh-NIN) *n.* — Dragons

Pronunciation note:
I have adopted the accent from *Vovina* (dragon).

Compounds:

Abaivonin (ay-bay-II-voh-nin) ["Abai" + "Vonin"]	Stooping Dragons

Note:

Stooping here means "diving," as an eagle stooping for its prey.

Also:

"Vovim" (voh-VIM)	Dragon
Vovina (voh-VII-na)	Dragon

Possible shared root:

Vohim (VOH-im)	Mighty
"Vnph" (unv)	Anger
Vonph (vonv)	Wrath
Vonpho (von-foh)	(Of) Wrath
"Vonpo" (von-foh)	Wrath

Vonph (vonv)* *n.* Wrath

13.7 . . . to stir up *wrath of* sin . . .

Pronunciation notes:

(*Dee—Vonph*) One syllable. I assume the *nph* is similar to the *nf* we see in words like *Sonf* (reign). I have indicated this in my pronunciation with "nv." The *v* indicates a sound somewhere between a hard *f* and a very soft *v*.

Compounds:

Ivonph (ii-VONV) [I + Vonph]	Is Wrath

Also:

"Vnph" (unv)	Anger
Vonpho (von-foh)	(Of) Wrath
"Vonpo" (von-foh)	Wrath

Possible shared root:

Vohim (VOH-im)	Mighty
"Vonin" (voh-NIN)	Dragon
"Vovim" (voh-VIM)	Dragon
Vovina (voh-VII-na)	Dragon

Vonpho (von-foh)* *n.* (Of) Wrath

1.9 . . . the firmaments *of wrath* . . .

9.9 . . . vials eight *of wrath* . . .

Pronunciation notes:

(**Dee 1.9—Vonpho*)

(**Dee 9.9—Von pho*) Two syllables.

Also:

Vonph (vonv) Wrath

"Vnph" (unv) Anger

"Vonpo" (von-foh) Wrath

Possible shared root:

Vohim (VOH-im) Mighty

"Vonin" (voh-NIN) Dragon

"Vovim" (voh-VIM) Dragon

Vovina (voh-VII-na) Dragon

"Vonpo" (von-foh) *n.* Wrath

Compounds:

Ivonpovnph (ii-VON-foh-unv) [I + "Vonpo" + "Vnph"] Is Wrath in Anger

"Vonpovnph" (VON-foh-unv) ["Vonpo" + "Vnph"] Wrath in Anger

Also:

"Vnph" (unv) Anger

Vonph (vonv) Wrath

Vonpho (von-foh) (Of) Wrath

Possible shared root:

Vohim (VOH-im) Mighty

"Vonin" (voh-NIN) Dragon

"Vovim" (voh-VIM) Dragon

Vovina (voh-VII-na) Dragon

"Vonpovnph" (VON-foh-unv) ["Vonpo" + "Vnph"] *comp.* Wrath in Anger

Compounds:

Ivonpovnph (ii-VON-foh-unv) [I + "Vonpo" + "Vnph"] Is Wrath In Anger

Vooan (voo-AN)* *n.* Truth**

1.72 . . . the balance of righteousness and *truth.*

Pronunciation notes:

(**Dee, recording the words of Nalvage—It is Vooan. It may be sounded Vaoan. Vooan is spoken with them that fall, but Vaoan with them that are, and are glorified. The devils have lost the dignity of their sounds.*) Thus, there are two acceptable spellings for *Vooan.* When working with earthbound or infernal spirits, the word should start with *Vo* (*Vooan*)—sounding akin to "voo-an." However, when working with Angels, the word should start with *Va* ("Vaoan")—sounding akin to "vay-oh-an."

(**Dee—vaoan*) See the *48 Claves.* Here, Dee uses the "Vaoan" spelling of the word, even though *Vooan* was given in *TFR.* (See *Odvooan* for the accented syllable.)

Note:

(***Dee recording the words of Nalvage—The word is, by interpretation, Ignus vera mater. The vain Philosophers do think it doth beget bodies. But, in truth, it concieveth and bringeth forth."*) See *TFR*, p. 80. It seems that Nalvage accuses the "vain Philosophers" of regarding Vooan (Truth) as a male force (begetting bodies), but that Truth is in fact a feminine force (conceiving and bringing forth)—probably associating Truth with Gnostic images of Wisdom (Sophia). The Latin that Nalvage uses to interpret the word—*Ignus vera mater*—seems to mean the "Fiery Truth of the Mother/Source."

Compounds:

Odvooan (ohd-voo-AN) [Od + Vooan] And Truth

Also:

"Vaoan" (vay-oh-AN) Truth

Vors (vorz)* *prep.* Over

3.39 . . . power successively *over* 456 . . .

Pronunciation notes:

(**Dee—VORS*) One syllable. See the pronunciation note for *Vorsg*.

Also:

Vorsg (vorzh) Over (You)

Note:

Also see the *Five Books*, p. 311. Here, several spirits appear and demand of Dee and Kelley, "Vors Mabberan?" Dee records (*Vors Mabberan = how now: what hast thou to do with us?*) Given the known definition of *Vors* (over—especially in a hierarchy), I assume this phrase is a challenge as if to say, "What authority do you have over us?" Dee responds by reciting a prayer that sends these spirits fleeing.

Compare from *Loagaeth*:

Vor, Vors, Vorza, Vorzad, Vorzed

Vorsg (vorzh)* *prep.* Over (You)

1.3 . . . I reign *over you*, sayeth the God of Justice . . .

Pronunciation notes:

(**Dee—Vorsg*) It is unclear if Dee intends this word to be one syllable or not. The *g* may stand alone, or it could combine with the *s* to make a kind of "zhuh" digraph. I have chosen the latter, and have presented it as "zh" in my pronunciation.

Also:

Vors (vorz) Over

Compare from *Loagaeth*:

Vor, Vors, Vorza, Vorzad, Vorzed

"Vovim" (voh-VIM) *n.* — Dragon

Pronunciation note:

I have adopted the accent from *Vovina* (dragon).

Compounds:

Telocvovim (tee-LOCH-voh-vee-im) [Teloch + "Vovim"] Death Dragon

Also:

"Vonin" (voh-NIN) — Dragons
Vovina (voh-VII-na) — Dragon

Possible shared root:

Vohim (VOH-im) — Mighty
"Vnph" (unv) — Anger
Vonph (vonv) — Wrath
Vonpho (von-foh) — (Of) Wrath
"Vonpo" (von-foh) — Wrath

Vovina (voh-VII-na)* *n.* — Dragon

8.32 . . . until this house fall and *the dragon* sink . . .

Pronunciation notes:

(*Dee—Vo uí na*) Three syllables, with an accent on the second syllable. The *o* and the *i* should take their long sounds. Dee originally wrote this word with a *U* in the second syllable. However, the *U*/V should take the "v" sound when preceding a vowel. (Further supporting this, see the pronunciation notes for *Taviv*, as well as other versions of *Vovina*.)

(*Dee—Vouína*) See the *48 Claves*. Dee again indicates the accent on the second syllable.

Also:

"Vonin" (voh-NIN) — Dragon
"Vovim" (voh-VIM) — Dragon

Possible shared root:

Vohim (VOH-im) — Mighty
"Vnph" (unv) — Anger

Vonph (vonv) Wrath
Vonpho (von-foh) (Of) Wrath
"Vonpo" (von-foh) Wrath

Upaah (yew-pay-ah)* *n.* Wings

2.2 Can *the wings* of the winds understand . . .
9.14 . . . whose *wings* are of wormwood . . .
17.4 . . . whose *wings* are thorns to stir up vexation . . .

Pronunciation notes:

(**Dee 2.2; 9.14; 17.4—V pa ah*) Three syllables. Dee originally wrote this word with an initial *V*. However, it should take the "u" sound because it precedes a consonant. The second syllable probably has a long *a*.
(**Dee 2.2—v-pa-âh*) See *48 Claves*. Three syllables. Note the circumflex over the second *a*. This is not the only case where "âh" seems to indicate the short "o" sound (as in the English words *father* and *fall*).
(**Dee 9.14; 17.4—vpâah*) See *48 Claves*. Here, Dee places the circumflex on the first *a* instead.

Also:

Upaahi (yew-pay-hii) Wings

Upaahi (yew-pay-hii)* *n.* Wings

15.5 . . . under whose *wings* are 6739 . . .

Note:

The transmission of Key Fifteen is missing from Dee's journals. We only have the English for this Key given later (see *TFR*, p. 193). Plus, the word appears in this location in Dee's *48 Claves*.

Pronunciation notes:

(**Dee—vpaáhi*) See the *48 Claves*. Likely three syllables. Dee originally wrote this word with an initial *V*. However, it should take the "u" sound because it precedes a consonant. He placed an accent over the second *a*, which is possibly the second syllable. In Early Modern English, a double *a* should indicate the long "a" sound.

Also:
Upaah (yew-pay-ah) Wings

Ur (owr)* *prop. n.* Letter *L*

Note:
The name of the Angelical letter for *L*. It is likely that these letter names have translations of their own. (For instance, note the Hebrew alphabet: the letter *L* is named *Lamed*, but *Lamed* also translates as "ox-goad.") However, such translations for the Angelical letters are never given. (See the *Five Books*, p. 270.)

Pronunciation notes:
(**Dee—In sound our or ourh.*) I would assume this word rhymes with the English word *hour*.

Compare from *Loagaeth*:
Vr

Uran (yew-RAN)* *n.* Elders

8.8 . . . in whom *the Elders* are become strong . . .

Note:
This is apparently a direct reference to the twenty-four Elders of the Apocalypse (see Revelation, chapter 4).

Pronunciation notes:
(**Dee—V rán*) Two syllables, with the accent on the second syllable. Dee shows a *V* at the beginning of this word—however, in Early Modern English, a *U*/*V* before a consonant should take the vowel ("u") sound.
(**Dee—Vrán*) See the *48 Claves*. Again the accent is placed on the second syllable.

Compare from *Loagaeth*:
Uran

Urbs (yurbs) *v.* To Beautify

1.35 . . . which *beautified* your garments . . .

Also:

Turbs (turbs) In Beauty

Urch (yurk) *prop. n.* The Confusers

From *Corpus Omnium*:

Associated with the Tribulation portion of the Table, translated in Latin as *Confundantes* (The Confusers)—which has a connotation of "to dissolve back to chaos."

Also:

Oucho (oh-yew-choh) (Let) Confound

Unchi (un-kii) Confound

Note:

It would appear that "uch" is the shared root between these words.

Compare from *Loagaeth*:

Urchan

Urelp (yer-elp)* *n.* (A Strong) Seething

2.49 . . . and make me *a strong seething* . . .

Pronunciation note:

(**Dee—Vrelp*) This seems to be two syllables, which means the initial *V* likely takes its soft "u" sound.

Note:

There have been suggestions that this word should be translated as "seething," indicating that the speaker of the Key is asking to be granted visions. I find this unlikely. The speaker of the Key is attempting to "stir up" the Angels, and the English might thus better read " . . . and make (for) me a strong seething."

Also note that *seething* would normally be an adjective (as in "he displayed a seething anger"). However, in Key Two, it is used as a noun.

Uta (yew-tay) *prop. n.* "The Fourteenth Aethyr"

30.3 . . . which dwell in *the fourteenth aethyr* . . .

Note:
This (word 30.3) is the single space in the Key of the Aethyrs, which must be changed for each invocation—replacing word 30.3 with the name of the appropriate Aethyr. No established definitions were given for these names.

Uta contains the three Parts of the Earth *Tedoond*, *Vivipos*, and *Ooanamb*.

Uti (yew-tii) *prop. n.* "The Twenty-Fifth Aethyr"

30.3 . . . which dwell in *the twenty-fifth aethyr* . . .

Note:
This (word 30.3) is the single space in the Key of the Aethyrs, which must be changed for each invocation—replacing word 30.3 with the name of the appropriate Aethyr. No established definitions were given for these names.

Uti contains the three Parts of the Earth *Mirzind*, *Obvaors*, and *Ranglam*.

UX (yewks)* 42

13.4 . . . which have *42* eyes to stir up . . .

Pronunciation notes:
(*Dee—Ux*) Likely just one syllable. It is unclear if the *U* should be long or short. I have settled upon the long sound.

Note:

This word was not originally given with Key Thirteen. It was added later when Nalvage transmitted the English for the Key (see *TFR*, p. 193). This seems to have been the case with many of the numbers mentioned in the Keys.

Pal (X)

There are no Angelical words (to date) that begin with the letter *Pal* (X). Usually, a word beginning with an *X* will take a "z" sound (as in the English words *xylophone* and *xenophobe*). Therefore, I assume that any such word in Angelical would begin with a *Ceph* (Z) instead.

Ceph (Z)

Za (zay)* *prop. n.* n/a

Pronunciation note:

(**Dee: Zaa*) Dee spells the Angel *Za*'s name with two *a*'s in a marginal notation (see the note below), which may indicate the long "a" sound.

Note:

See *TFR*, pp. 228–29. The names of most of the Angels encountered by Dee and Kelley can be found in other parts of the Angelic system, such as the *Heptarchia* or Great Table (Watchtower) systems. However, Za is one of the few entirely unique Angels that appeared to the two men. It was very late in the Angelic journals, after all of the essential Angelic magick had been transmitted. One day, Kelley saw three little creatures running around the floor of the room. It turned out that they were Angels from the Great Table (Watchtowers), but their names were *not* derived according to the instructions Ave had previously given to Dee.

Za says of himself: "I am the second of the third,* which dwell in the spirit, and power of God in earth.** I have power to scourge them that resist the power, will and commandment of God. And I am one of those that stand, and is perpetual." Dee notes, in Latin: "*Zaa*—Scourger of resistance to the power, will and commandment of God."

The three Angels, apparently jointly, say, "For even as the father, son, and holy spirit are one, but of themselves and being dilated, is full of power, and many. So are we one particularly in power,*** but separated. Notwithstanding, spiritually of, and amongst, others, and dilated in the will of God, and into the branches of his determinations. But, particularly living, and jointly praising God."

Note:

*Dee notes the Angels are numbering the Watchtowers in an odd fashion. So that in this case, he points out, the numbering should follow: First = eastern, Second = western, Third = southern, and Fourth = the northern Watchtower. Za is found as the last two letters in the upper-left subquadrant of the Southern Watchtower Tablet.

**In Dee's diagram of the Holy City (see Geoffrey James' *Enochian Magick of Dr. John Dee*, p. 103), the Southern Gates are associated with the zodiacal triplicity of Earth.

(*** *On the next page Dee notes: The three names make one name of 7 letters-Gazavaa.*) I note that all three of these names begin with capital letters on the Great Table (Watchtowers). Also, each one of them terminates once it hits the Great Cross, Black Cross, or the end of the Watchtower. We may have discovered an entirely new Angelic system in the Watchtowers.

(See *Ga* and *Vaa*. Also *Galvah*, *Mapsama*, *Murifri*, and *Nalvage*.)

Zaa (zay) *prop. n.* "The Twenty-Seventh Aethyr"

30.3 . . . which dwell in *the twenty-seventh aethyr* . . .

Note:

This (word 30.3) is the single space in the Key of the Aethyrs, which must be changed for each invocation—replacing word 30.3 with the name of the appropriate Aethyr. No established definitions were given for these names.

Zaa contains the three Parts of the Earth *Saziami*, *Mathula*, and *Orpanib*.

Zacam (ZAY-kam) *v.* To Move

6.36 . . . I have talked of you and *I move you* . . .

Pronunciation notes:

(**Dee—Za cam*) Two syllables. I would suggest the *a* takes a long sound, as it falls as the end of its syllable.

(**Dee—zácam*) See the *48 Claves*. The accent is placed on the first syllable.

Note:

Remember that both *I* and *you* are generally implied in Angelical. Neither of these pronouns is indicated in the word itself.

Also:

Zacar (ZAY-kayr *or* ZOHD-ay-kayr) Move

Zacar (ZAY-kayr *or* ZOHD-ay-kayr)* *v.* Move

1.73 . . . *move*, therefore . . .
2.42 . . . *move*, therefore . . .
3.74 . . . *move*, descend . . .
4.42 . . . *move*, and show yourselves . . .
7.35 . . . *move*, appear . . .
12.23 . . . *move*, I say . . .
(RFP) . . . *move*, and show yourselves . . .
30.142 . . . *move* and appear . . .

Pronunciation notes:

(**Dee 1.73—Call it Zacar. E must come after R: but without number, and so it is Zacare*) Nalvage was still giving numbers with each letter of the words at this point. However, the letter *e* was not drawn from the Tables of *Loagaeth*, so it is "without number." Instead, it was only appended to the word in Dee's phonetic note to indicate that the preceding *a* should be long. It is purely a phonetic gloss.

(**Dee 2.42; 4.42; 30.142—Zacar*)

(**Dee 7.35—Za car*) This note suggests two syllables.

(**Dee 3.74—Zod a car*) Here, Dee indicates that the Z should stand alone, making the "zohd" sound (producing three syllables instead of two). Since this is not indicated in other instances of the word, I suspect the extended Z is a poetic or lyrical gloss, rather than a rule of pronunciation. Finally, note that words 7.35 abd 3.74 each indicate a long *a* in the first syllable.

(**Dee 1.73; 11.RFP—ZACARe*) See the *48 Claves*. In these places, Dee placed a lowercase *e* at the end of the word—supporting the note in *TFR*, word 1.73.

Finally, I have adopted the accent from the word *Zacam* (to move).

Note:

Could there be a relationship between this word and the name of *Acar*, an Angel of fire in the Northern Watchtower?

Also:

Zacam (ZAY-kam) To Move

Zamran (zam-ran)* *v.* To Appear

1.76 ...move, therefore, and *show yourselves*...

2.45 ...move, therefore, and *show yourselves*...

(RFP) ...move, therefore, and *show yourselves*...**

7.36 ...move, *appear*, sing praises...

8.47 ...*appear* to the terror of the earth...

11.35 ...move, therefore, and *show yourselves*...

12.26 ...move, I say, and *show yourselves*...

Pronunciation notes:

(**Dee 1.76—Call it Zamran*)

(**Dee 2.45—Zamran*)

(**Dee 7.36; 8.47—Zam ran*) Two syllables

Note:

**The wording of the RFP does change slightly in some of the Keys. See either the Angelical Keys cross-reference (chapter 2) or the Angelical Psalter (in volume I).

Compounds:

Odzamran (ohd-zam-ran) [Od + Zamran] And Appear

Zax (zaks) *prop. n.* "The Tenth Aethyr"

30.3 . . . which dwell in *the tenth aethyr* . . .

Note:

This (word 30.3) is the single space in the Key of the Aethyrs, which must be changed for each invocation—replacing word 30.3 with the name of the appropriate Aethyr. No established definitions were given for these names.

Zax contains the three Parts of the Earth *Lexarph*, *Comanan*, and *Tabitom*.

Zchis (zohd-kiis)* *v.* (They) Are

5.25 . . . *they are* the brothers . . .
9.39 . . . whose iniquities *they are* . . .
11.27 . . . as *they are* whose number is 31 . . .

Pronunciation notes:
(**Dee 5.25; 11.27—Zod chis*)
(**Dee 9.39—Zod Chis kis*) Two syllables. The *ch* makes the harder "k" (or "kh") sound. See the pronunciation notes for *Chis* (are) for the long "i" sound.
(**Dee 5.25; 11.27—z-chis*) See the *48 Claves*. Notes two syllables, with the Z standing alone.

Also:

Chis (kiis)	Are
Chiis (kiis)	Are (They)
"Chisda" (KIIS-da)	Are There
Chiso (kiis-oh)	Shall Be
"Gchis" (jee-kiis)	Are
"Ichis" (jjay-kiis)	Are

Zed (zed) n/a

Note:
See *TFR*, pp. 34-35. This session is recorded entirely in Latin. Here we find this Angelical phrase spoken by "a Voice": "*Garil zed masch, ich na gel galaht gemp gal noch Cabanladan.*" No translation or context is offered.

Zen (zen) *prop. n.* "The Eighteenth Aethyr"

30.3 . . . which dwell in *the eighteenth aethyr* . . .

Note:
This (word 30.3) is the single space in the Key of the Aethyrs, which must be changed for each invocation—replacing word 30.3 with the name of the appropriate Aethyr. No established definitions were given for these names.

Zen contains the three Parts of the Earth *Nabaomi*, *Zafasai*, and *Yalpamb*.

Zid (zid) *prop. n.* "The Eighth Aethyr"

30.3 . . . which dwell in *the eighth aethyr* . . .

Note:
This (word 30.3) is the single space in the Key of the Aethyrs, which must be changed for each invocation—replacing word 30.3 with the name of the appropriate Aethyr. No established definitions were given for these names.

Zid contains the three Parts of the Earth *Zamfres*, *Todnaon*, and *Pristac*.

Zien (zeen)* *n.* Hands

1.28 . . . the palms of *my hands* . . .

Pronunciation notes:
(**Dee—Zien*) I assume there should be one syllable here. The Early Modern English letter combination *ie* makes a long "e" sound—as in the English words *grieve* and *believe*.

Also:

Azien (az-EEN) (On Whose) Hands
Ozien (oh-ZEEN) (Mine Own) Hand

Probable shared root:

Ozol (oh-ZOHL) — Hands

Zol (zohd-OL) — Hands

Zildar (zil-dar)* *v.* — Fly into

11.8 . . . Thunders which *flew into* the east . . .

Pronunciation notes:

(*Dee—Zil dar*) Two syllables. Both vowels appear to take their short sounds.

Possible shared root:

Zylna (zil-na) — "Within"

"Zilodarp" (ZII-loh-darp) — Stretch Forth / Conquest

Note:

Compare this word to the name of the Part of the Earth (and its Angelic Governor), *Zildron*. Thus, there is an etymology of "to fly" in his name.

"Zilodarp" (ZII-loh-darp) *n.* — Stretch Forth / Conquest

Compounds:

Madzilodarp (mad-ZII-loh-darp) [Mad + "Zilodarp"] — God of Conquest

Note:

I have simplified "stretch forth and conquer" into the obvious: "conquest." However, based upon the words that might share a root with this word, I suggest that "stretch forth" is the base of "Zilodarp."

Possible shared root:

Zildar (zil-dar) — Fly into

Zylna (zil-na) — "Within"

Zim (zim) *prop. n.* "The Thirteenth Aethyr" (Entrance or Territory?)

30.3 . . . which dwell in *the thirteenth aethyr* . . .

Note:
This (word 30.3) is the single space in the Key of the Aethyrs, which must be changed for each invocation—replacing word 30.3 with the name of the appropriate Aethyr. No established definitions were given for these names.

Zim contains the three Parts of the Earth *Gecaond*, *Laparin*, and *Docepax*.

Possible shared root:

Zimii (ZII-mii)	To Enter
Zimz (zimz)	Vestures (Territories)

Zimii (ZII-mii)* *v.* To Enter

5.2 The Mighty Sounds *have entered into* the third angle . . .

Pronunciation notes:
(**Dee—Zi mii*) Two syllables. The first *i* is likely a long sound. The double *i*'s in the second syllable would form a long "i" sound in Early Modern English.
(**Dee—zímii*) See the *48 Claves*. Note the accent on the first syllable.

Possible shared root:

Zim (zim)	"The Thirteenth Aethyr"
Zimz (zimz)	Vestures (Territories)

Zimz (zimz)* *n.* Vestures (Territories)

1.23 . . . in the midst of *my vestures* . . .

Pronunciation notes:
(**Dee—Zimz*) Probably one syllable.

Note:

The word *vestures* would not have indicated clothing to Dee and Kelley. Instead, it would have indicated property or territories— especially those given by a king. (It is the root of our modern words *investiture* and *investment*.)

Note that the word *garment* in Angelical is given as *Oboleh*, and related to the word *Obloch* (garland)— indicating a wrapping. Also see *Qaa* (creation).

Possible shared root:

Zim (zim) "The Thirteenth Aethyr"

Zimii (ZII-mii) To Enter

Zip (zip) *prop. n.* "The Ninth Aethyr"

30.3 . . . which dwell in *the ninth aethyr* . . .

Note:

This (word 30.3) is the single space in the Key of the Aethyrs, which must be changed for each invocation—replacing word 30.3 with the name of the appropriate Aethyr. No established definitions were given for these names.

Zip contains the three Parts of the Earth *Oddiorg*, *Cralpir*, and *Doanzin*.

Zir (zer)* *v.* Am, Were, Was

2.51 ...*I am* of him...

3.4 ...*I am* a circle...

Pronunciation note:

(**Dee 2.51; 3.4—Zir*) One syllable.

Note:

As is most often the case in Angelical, the pronoun (*I*) is simply implied.

Compounds:

Zirenaiad (zii-er-NAY-ad) [Zir + Enay + Iad]

I Am The Lord (Your) God

Also:

Zirdo (zer-DOH) Am

Zirom (zer-OM) Were

Zirop (zii-ROP) Was

Compare from *Corpus Omnium*:

Found in the pre-Deluge portion of the Table, in the phrase *Zir Moz Iad* (I am the Joy of God).

Note:

Zir appears to be a form of the verb *to be*. Compare to *I* (is/are).

Also compare with the name of the Part of the Earth (and its Angelic Governor) *Zirzird*. It could be that this name is similar to the biblical Name of God "I Am That I Am." (Also, the Mother of Angels, *Galvah*, once introduced herself as "I Am.")

Zirdo (zer-DOH)* *v.* Am

(RFP) . . . *I am* the servant . . .

Pronunciation notes:

(**Dee 1.83—Call it Zirdo*) I have adopted the accent from *Zirop* (was).

Also:

Zir (zer) Am

Zirom (zer-OM) Were

Zirop (zii-ROP) Was

Zirenaiad (zii-er-NAY-ad)* [Zir + Enay + Iad] *comp.*

I Am the Lord (Your) God

4.37 . . . For, *I am the Lord your God* . . .

Pronunciation notes:

(**Dee—Zire nai ad*) Four syllables. In the first syllable, the final *e* gives the *i* its long sound. ("Zire" likely rhymes with the English words *fire* and *desire*.) In the second syllable, the Early Modern English letter combination *ai* (or "ay") makes the long "a" sound—as in the English words *dais* and *day*.

(**Dee—Zirendiad*) See the *48 Claves*. Note the accent on the third syllable.

Note:

The *e* and *a* in "enay" are phonetic glosses. See *Enay* (Lord).

Zirom (zer-OM)* *v.* Were

11.4 . . . *they were* five thunders . . .

Pronunciation notes:

(**Dee—Zir om*) Two syllables. Both vowels seem to take their short sounds. I have adopted the accent from *Zirop* (was).

Also:

Zir (zer)	Am
Zirdo (zer-DOH)	Am
Zirop (zii-ROP)	Was

Zirop (zii-ROP)* *v.* Was

10.77 . . . is, *was*, and shall be great . . .

Pronunciation notes:

(**Dee—Zi róp*) Two syllables. The accent mark is on the second syllable. The *i* should be long, while the *o* is likely short.

(**Dee—ziróp*) See the *48 Claves*. Again shows an accent over the second syllable.

Also:

Zir (zer)	Am
Zirdo (zer-DOH)	Am
Zirom (zer-OM)	Were

Zixlay (ziks-lay)* *v.* To Stir Up

17.7 . . . thorns *to stir up* vexation . . .

Pronunciation notes:

(**Dee—Zix lay*) Two syllables. The *i* is short, but the *ay* combine to form a long "a" sound.

Note:

Also see *Lring* (to stir up).

Zizop (zis-op)* *n.* Vessels

5.20 . . . gave them *vessles* to water the earth . . .

Pronunciation notes:

(**Dee—Zisop*) Appears to be three syllables. Note the second *z* takes on more of an "s" sound in pronunciation.

Also:

Izizop (iz-is-op) (Your?) Vessels

Note:

Compare this word to the name *Sisp* (or *Siosp*), an Angel of Water in the Northern Watchtower. I find it interesting that the name of an Angel of Water is similar to the *Zizop* (vessels) that are used in Key Five "to water the earth."

Also compare the names *Ziza*, *Izaz*, *Zazi*, and *Aziz*, the four Angels of Secrets from the Northern Watchtower.

Zlida (zohd-lid-a)* *v.* To Water

5.21 . . . vessels *to water* the earth . . .

Pronunciation notes:

(**Dee—Zod-lida. It is a Word and a letter. Zod lida. Z lida*) There was some confusion at this point in the session, so Dee ended up writing three

distinct phonetic notes for this word. All of them indicate the same thing: the initial Z stands alone (. . . *and a letter*)—probably because it is followed by a consonant.
(**Dee—z-lida*) See the *48 Claves*. This note matches that in *TFR*.

Shared root:
Pilzin (pil-zin) Waters

Note:
Zlida is a verb, while *Pilzin* is a noun.

Zna (snay) *adj.* Motion (Action)

From *Corpus Omnium*:
Found in the post-Deluge portion of the Table, in the phrase *Zna Bab Iad* (Moving Dominion of God).

Pronunciation notes:
Dee may have intended *Zn* to make a unified sound akin to "sn" (as in *snake, snap*, etc.). See the pronunciation given for *Znurza* (swore).

Znrza (snur-za)* *v.* To Swear

1.49 . . . you lifted up your voices *and swore* obedience.

Pronunciation notes:
(**Dee—as Znursa*) It is difficult to be certain, but it would appear Dee intended for the *Zn* to make a sound akin to "sn" (as in *snake, snap*, etc.). Then, the *r* takes the "ur" sound when surrounded by consonants with which it can't combine (in this case, *n* and *Z*).

Also:
Surzas (sur-zas) Sworn

Note:
Also see *Aisro*/*Isro* (promise of) and *Sibsi* (covenant).

Zol (zohd-OL)* *n.* Hands

1.11 . . . in whose *hands* the sun is as a sword . . .

Pronunciation notes:

(**Dee—Zol . . . zod, as ol*) Indicates that the Z should possess its extended "zohd" sound. This extension is likely a poetic or lyrical gloss, rather than a grammatical rule. (Note that other versions of the word do not have the extended "zohd" sound.)

(**Dee—z-ol*) See *48 Claves*. Two syllables, with the Z standing alone.

I have chosen to place the accent on the second syllable for two reasons. First, both *Asien* (hands) and *Ozien* (hand) are accented on the second syllable. Second, the extended "zohd" sound is likely a lyrical gloss, and not an inherent part of the word itself.

Also:

Ozol (oh-ZOHL) Hands

Probable shared root:

Azien (az-EEN) (On Whose) Hands

Ozien (oh-ZEEN) (Mine Own) Hand

Zien (zeen) Hands

Zom (zom) *prop. n.* "The Third Aethyr" (To Encompass?)

30.3 . . . which dwell in *the third aethyr* . . .

Note:

This (word 30.3) is the single space in the Key of the Aethyrs, which must be changed for each invocation—replacing word 30.3 with the name of the appropriate Aethyr. No established definitions were given for these names.

Zom contains the three Parts of the Earth *Samapha*, *Virooli*, and *Andispi*.

Possible shared root:

Zomdux (zom-dooks) Amidst (i.e., "encompassed by")

Zomdux (zom-dooks) *prep.* Amidst (i.e.,"encompassed by")

1.63 . . . shineth as a flame *in the midst of* your palace.

Possible shared root:

Zom (zom) "The Third Aethyr"

Note:

Also see *Nothoa* (Amidst).

Zonac (zoh-nak)* *v.* Appareled (with)

7.18 . . . and *they are appareled with* ornaments . . .

Pronunciation notes:

(**Dee—Zo nac*) Two syllables. The *o* is likely long, while the *A* should take a short sound. I assume the *c* at the end of a word would take its hard sound.

Zong (zong)* *n.* Winds

2.3 Can the wings of *the winds* understand . . .

Pronunciation notes:

(**Dee—Zong*)

Also:

Ozongon (oh-zong-on) Manifold Winds

Zonrensg (zon-renj) *v.* To Deliver

1.43 . . . *delivered you* a rod . . .

Zorge (zorj)* *v.* Be Friendly unto Me

(RFP) *Be friendly unto me.*

Pronunciation notes:
(**Dee 1.RFP—Call it Zorge [Of one syllable]*) The final *e* indicates a soft "g" sound. It probably rhymes with *George* and *gorge*.

Zumvi (zum-vii)* *n.* Seas

9.48 . . . from their mouths run *seas of* blood.

Pronunciation notes:
(**Dee—Zum vi*) Two syllables. The *u* should take its short sound. The final *i* should take a long sound.

Zuraah (zur-AY-ah) *n.?* Prayer?*

Note:
(**Dee—Laua Zuraah = Use humility in prayers to God, that is fervently pray. It signifieth, Pray Unto God.*) See the *Five Books*, p. 324. Between lines 46 and 47 of Table One of *Loagaeth*, some kind of stormy interference erupted in the shewstone. A voice then said the phrase "*Laua Zuráah.*" The two men then prayed as instructed, and the interference cleared. It would appear that *Zuraah* indicates prayer to the Highest God.

Pronunciation notes:
The first *a* of *Zuraah* is accented in Dee's journal. The double *a* should result in a long "a" sound.

Possibly also:
Zurah (zur-AH) n/a
Zure (zur-AY) n/a
Zuresch (zur-ESK) n/a

Compare from *Loagaeth*:
Zurad, Zuram, Zurath, Zureheffa, Zurehoh, Zureoch, Zuresch, and *Zureth*

Zurah (zur-AH) n/a

Pronunciation note:
I have adopted the accent from *Zuraah*.

Note:

See *TFR*, p. 22. Here, the guardian Angel of Lord Lasky of Poland says a prayer on Lasky's behalf, which ends with, "Grant this *Camascheth galsuagath garnastel zurah logaah luseroth.*" (Note the word *Zurah.*) No translation is offered.

Possibly also:

Zuraah (zur-AY-ah) Prayer?
Zure (zur-AY) n/a
Zuresch (zur-ESK) n/a

Compare from *Loagaeth*:

Zurad, Zuram, Zurath, Zureheffa, Zurehoh, Zureoch, Zuresch, and *Zureth*

Zure (zur-AY) n/a

Pronunciation note:

I have adopted the accent from *Zuraah.*

Note:

See the *Five Books*, p. 276. Here, Kelley is once again convinced the Angels are evil devils sent to lead humans astray. The Archangel Raphael holds his hands to Heaven (in what appears to be exasperation) and exclaims, "*Camikas Zure*!" No translation is suggested.

Possibly also:

Zuraah (zur-AY-ah) Prayer?
Zurah (zur-AH) n/a
Zuresch (zur-ESK) n/a

Compare from *Loagaeth*:

Zurad, Zuram, Zurath, Zureheffa, Zurehoh, Zureoch, Zuresch, and *Zureth*

Zuresch (zur-ESK) n/a

Pronunciation note:

I have adopted the accent from *Zuraah.*

From *Loagaeth*:

See the *Five Books*, pp. 288 and 291. This is one of the thousands of untranslated words from the Tables of *Loagaeth*. I have included it here merely because I have discussed it more than once in the text of this study. It is the first word of *Loagaeth* itself (Table One, side A, Word 1), and Raphael made a point that it was to be of seven letters.

Possibly also:

Zuraah (zur-AY-ah) — Prayer?
Zurah (zur-AH) — n/a
Zure (zur-AY) — n/a

Compare from *Loagaeth*:

Zurad, *Zuram*, *Zurath*, *Zureheffa*, *Zurehoh*, *Zureoch*, *Zuresch*, and *Zureth*

Zylna (zil-na)* *prep.* — Within (Itself)

30.56 . . . may be always drunken and vexed *in itself.*

Pronunciation notes:

(**Dee—Zyl na*) Two syllables. Remember the *y* could also be written as an *i*—so the word could also appear as *Zilna*.

Possible shared root:

Zildar (zil-dar) — Fly into
"Zilodarp" (ZII-loh-darp) — Stretch Forth/Conquest

An English to Angelical Dictionary

If you are using this Lexicon to create new prayers and invocations (or to convert existing texts into Angelical), then you are likely to begin here. Simply look up the English word you wish to translate, and you will find the Angelical word, all of its alternate versions, and reference pointers to similar, related, or synonymous words. Decide which version best fits your intent, and then look up the word in the Lexicon itself to see how it is properly used—and much more.

This dictionary is expanded. Because of the fluid definitions associated with Angelical words, I was able to use a thesaurus to to generate a larger pool of interrelated words and concepts. This makes it more likely that you will find the word you are looking for, or at least something closely related.

Tips on Translating English into Angelical

Based on my overall study of the language, I would like to offer some basic tips on translating English texts into Angelical. First of all, write out the text as it exists in English. Then follow these steps:

- Mark out articles (*a*, *an*, and *the*). Articles do not exist at all in Angelical. The word *of* is also unnecessary most of the time, although there does exist an Angelical word for it (*De*), so it can be used if you feel it is unavoidable.
- Mark out most adjectives. You can check the English to Angelical to see if your adjective—or something similar—exists. If it does not, you can drop the adjective, and consider it implied in the Angelical. As an example, if you want to translate the words *a bitter sting*, you would only need to look up the word *sting*. There is no Angelical word for *bitter*, but that adjective is implicit in the Angelical word *Grosb* (bitter sting). The same word might translate as "horrible sting," "painful sting," "poisonous sting," and so forth.
- Also remember that Angelical compounds are often formed between nouns and the possessive adjectives (*his*, *her*, *their*), demonstrative and relative pronouns (*which* / *that*, *this*, *those*), conjunctions (*and*, *or*, *but*), and the forms of *to be* (*is*, *are*, *were*) that indicate them. Therefore, try

linking these words together in the English text, and see if they form natural compounds in Angelical.

- You can take most noun phrases and verb phrases and reduce them to their basic concepts. For instance, consider the sentence *He was running swiftly*. The verbal phrase *was running swiftly* might be represented sufficiently by the Angelical for "to run." Thus *He was running swiftly* could be represented with the single Angelical word *Parm*. Or, another example: *The great sea of the western region* would become just three words: *Drilpa zumvi soboln* ("great sea west"). (Especially look at column 4 of the Angelical cross-reference, to see how simple Angelical translates into elaborate English.)
- If you've written something for which there is no (current) Angelical translation, try re-wording your text. Endeavor to say the same thing in a different way, and see if the Angelical exists for such alternate wording. (A thesaurus can be a big help in this process.) At the same time, you can browse through this English-to-Angelical section for alternate words that might fit your intent.

These are just a few simple suggestions that will allow you to convert English text into a format easily translatable into Angelical. I also strongly suggest that you study the "Angelical Linguistics" chapter, in order to get a better feel for how Angelical grammar works. With these tools at your disposal, you should have little trouble writing and translating Angelical texts.

1
See First, One

2
See Second

3
See Third

4
See Fourth

5
O

6
See Six

8
P

9
See Nine

12
OS

12 Kingdoms
Oslondoh

12 Seats
Thilnos

19
AF

22
OP

24
OL

26
OX

28
OB, NI

31
"GA"

33
PD

42
UX

100
See Hundred

456
CLA

1000
See Thousand

1636
QUAR

3663
MIAN

5678
DAOX

6332
ERAN

6739
DARG

7336
TAXS

7699
ACAM

8763
EMOD

9639
MAPM

9996
CIAL

69636
PERAL

A (Un)

Abide
Casasam (Abiding)
See also Continue, Dwell, Remain

Able
See Can

Abound
See Flourish

Accomplish
See Execute

According
Marb (According to)

Achieve
See Execute

Action
Sor (Action, especially that taken by a king)
Zna (Motion, Action)
See also Move, Motion, Rest Not, Stir

Add
Uml (To Add)
See also Increase

Administer
See Apply

Admiration
Grsam (Admiration)
See also Adoration, Glory, Praise

Adoration
Adgmach (Glory, Adoration, Praise)
See also Glory, Praise, Admiration

Adornment
See Garnish

Advance
"Ar" (To Advance Upon)

Aeon
See Age

Affix
See Bind, Fasten, Truss Together

Afflict/Affliction
See Torment

Age
Homil (Ages)
Homin (Age)
See also While, Period, Season, Time

Agony
See Torment

Ahead
See Before

All
Tofglo (All Things)
Ton (All)
See also Every One

"All Powerful"
Iaidon (the All Powerful God)
See also God, Lord

Always
Paid (Always)

Am
Zir (I Am)
Zirdo (I Am)
See also Are, Is, Was, Were

Amidst
Nothoa (Amidst)
Zomdux (Amidst/Encompassed by)
See also Among, Center

Among
Aai (Amongst You)
Aaf (Amongst)
Aaiom (Amongst Us)
Aao (Amongst)
Eai (Amongst)
Oai (Amongst)
See also Amidst, Center

Amplify
See Magnify

And
Ds (And?)
Od (And)
Ot (And)

And Another While
Odcacocasb

And Appear
Odzamran

And Are
Odchis

And Continuance
Odmiam

And Destroy
Odquasb

And the Dwelling Place
Odfaorgt

And Fourth
Odes

And Has
Odbrint

And Liveth
Odapila

And Powers
Odlonshin

And the Praise
Odecrin

And the Second
Taviv(?)

And Shall Not See
Odipuran

And Truth
Odvooan

And Wax Strong
Odugeg

Angels/Angelic Orders
(It is unclear if these are Angelic Orders or simply different Angelical words for *Angel*.)
Avavago (Thunders of Increase)
Const (Thunders)
Coraxo (Thunders of Judgment and Wrath)
Ialpurg (Burning Flames)
Lang (Those Who Serve)
Luas (Those Who Praise, or The Triumphant)
Pir (Holy Ones)
Sach (The Establishers/Supporters)
Sapah (Mighty Sounds)
Urch (The Confusers)
See also Divine Names, Spirits. (Also see Star, a common biblical term for an Angel.)

Anger
"Vnph" (Anger)
See also Fury, Wrath

Angle
Div

Animal
See Beast, Creature

Another
Asymp (Another)
"Smnad" (Another)
Symp (Another)

Any
Droln (Any)

Apparel
Zonac (Appareled with, Cloathed)
See also Garment, Garland

Appear
Zamran (To Appear)
See also Arise

Appendage
See Member

Apply
Imuamar (To Apply unto)

Are
Chiis (Are)
Chis (Are)
"Gchis" (Are)
Geh (Are/Art)
I (Is, Are)
"Ichis" (Are)
Zchis (They Are)
See also Is, May Be, Shall Be, Was, Were

Are as
Chista

Are as the Third
Chistad

Are Become
Inoas

Are Measured
Chisholq

Are Mighty
Chismicaolz

Are Not
Gchisge (Are Not)
Ichisge (Are Not)

Are There
"Chisda"

Arise/Rise
Torgu (Arise)
Torzu (Arise)
Torzul (Shall Rise)
Torzulp (To Rise)
See also Lift Up, Appear

Ark
Erm (Ark)
See also Harbor

Arrogance
See Pomp

Arrow
"Mal" (Thrust, Arrow, Increase)

Art
See Are

As
"Ca" (As?)
Ta (As)

As Bucklers
Talolcis

As Comforters
Tablior

As the First
Talo

As Many
Plosi (As Many)
See also Many

As is Not
Tage

As Olives
Taqanis

As the Second
Taviv

As Sickles
Tapuin

As the Third
"Tad"

Assortment
See Variety

Asylum
See Ark, Harbor

***Athanor* (Alchemical Furnace)**
Rlodnr (Alchemical Furnace or Heat)

Attach
See Bind, Fasten, Truss Together

Attend
See Apply, Appear

Attire
See Apparel, Garment, Garland

Attractive
See Beauty

Authority
See Dominion

"Avoidance of Earthly Things"
See "Earth-Fleer"

B (Pa)

Balance
Piap (Balance)

Bane
See Torment

Barb
See Thorn

Barrier
See Buckler

Be
See Am, Are, Become, Is, Let There Be, Not, Shall Be, Was, Were

Bear
See Bring Forth

Bear Witness
O (Come and Bear Witness)
Oh (Come and Bear Witness?)

Beast
Levithmong (Beasts of the Field)
See also Creature

Beauty
Turbs (Beauty)
Urbs (Beautified)

Because
Bagle (For, Wherefore, Because)
Baglen (Because)
See also For, Therefore, Wherefore

Become
Inoas (Are/Have Become)
Noaln (May Be)
Noan (To Become)
Noar (Has Become)
Noas (Have Become)
Noasmi (Let Become)

Become Strong
Ugeg (Become Strong)
Ugegi (Become/Grow Strong)
See also Strong

Bed
Tianta (Bed)

Before
Aspt (Before, In Front)
See also Precede

Be Friendly unto Me
Zorge (Be Friendly unto Me)

Beginning
Acroodzi (Beginning)
Amgedpha (I Will Begin Anew)
Croodzi (Beginning of Things)
Iaod (Beginning)
Iaodaf (In the Beginning)
Nostoah (It Was in the Beginning)

Begotten
Iusmach (Begotten)

Behold
Micma (Behold)
See also Look, See

Be It Made with Power
Chramsa
See also Let There Be

Beneath
Oroch (Under)
Orocha (Beneath)
See also Under

Between
See Amidst, Among

Bind
Alar (To Settle, To Place)
Allar (To Bind Up)
See also Set, Settle, Place, Plant

Blood
Cnila (Blood)

Boil
See Seethe

Bolt
See Arrow

Born
See Begotten

Boundaries
See Corners

Branch
Lilonon (Branches)

Breath
Gigipah (Living Breath)

Brightness
Luciftian (Ornaments of Brightness)
Luciftias (Brightness)
See also Light, Shine

Bring Down
Drix (To Bring Down)
See also Cast Down

Bring Forth
Yolcam (To Bring Forth/Bear)
Yolci (To Bring Forth)

Brother
Esiasch (Brothers)

Buckler
"Lolcis" (Bucklers)

Building
Orscatbl (Buildings)
Trof (Building)
See also House, Dwelling

Bulwark
See Buckler

Burn
Ialpon (To Burn)
Ialpor (Flaming)
See also Fire, Flame, Shine

Burning Flame
Ialprg (Burning Flame)
Ialpurg (Burning Flames)

But
Crip (But)
"Crp" (But)
Oq (But/Except)
See also Except

But One
Crpl

C (Veh)

Call
"Ium" (Is Called)
Iumd (Is Called)

Can
Adgt (Can)

Cannot
"Pamis" (Cannot)
Ipamis (Cannot Be)
See also No/None, Not

Carry Out
See Execute

Cast Down
Adrpan (Cast Down)
See also Bring Down

Cause
Gru (To Cause, Bring about, Result)

Cave/Cavern
Tabges (Caves)

Celebrate
See Rejoice

Center
Ovoars (Center)
See also Amidst

Chamber
Ooge (Chamber)

Characteristic
See Quality

Christ in Hell
Iurehoh (What Christ Did in Hell)

Churn
See Mingle, Seethe

Circle
Comselh (Circle)

Classify
See Separate Creatures

Clothed
See Apparel, Garment, Garland

Coat
Mabza (Coat)

Come
Carma (Come Out)
Niis (Come Here)
Niisa (Come Away)
Niiso (Come Away)

Come and Bear Witness
O (Come and Bear Witness)
Oh (Come and Bear Witness?)

Comfort
"Bigl" (Comforter?)
Bigliad (In Our Comforter)
"Bliard" (Comfort)
Blior (Comfort)
Bliora (Comfort)
Bliorax (To Comfort)
Bliorb (Comfort)
Bliors (Comfort)
"Bliort" (Comfort)
Pibliar (Places of Comfort)

Command
See Dominion, Government

Conceit
See Pomp

Conclude
Iaial (To Conclude, Judge)
See also Judgment

Conflict
See Differ, Discord

Confound
Oucho (Confound)
Unchi (To Confound)
Urch (The Confusers)
See also Confuse

Confuse
Urch (The Confusers)
See also Confound

Connect
See Fasten, Truss Together

Conquer
See Stretch Forth / Conquest

Conquest
See Stretch Forth / Conquest

Consistent/Constant?
See "In One Number," Always

Container
See Cup, Vessel, Vial

Continue
Miam (Continuance)
"Mian" (Continuance)
Pild (Continually)
See also Successive, Abide, Remain

Corner
Miinoag (Corners—Boundaries)
See also Skirt

Corrupt
See Rotten

Count
See Number (especially "Numbered")

Countenance
See Face

Couple
Pola (Two, together / Couple)
See also Together, Two, Wedding

Course
"Elzap" (Course)
"Lzar" (Courses)

Covenant
Sibsi (Covenant)
See also Promise, Swear

Cover
Ethamz (To Cover)

Creation
Qaa (Creation / Garments)
Qaan (Creation)
Qaaon (Creation)
Qaas (Creation)
See also Creator

Creator
Qaal (Creator)
Qadah (Creator)
See also Creation

Creature
Tolham (All Creatures)
Tolhami (Upon All Creatures)
Toltorg (Creatures)
Toltorgi (With Creatures)
"Toltorn" (Creature)
See also Beast

Crown
Momao (Crowns)
"Momar" (To Crown)

Cry
Bahal (Cry Loudly)
See also Weep

Cup
Talho (Cups)
See also Vessel, Vial

Curse
Amma (Cursed)
See also Wicked

D (Gal)

Damn/Damned
See Curse

Dark
Ors (Darkness)

Dart
See Arrow, Fiery Arrow/Dart

Daughter
Pasbs (Daughters)

Dawning
See Beginning

Day
Basgim (Day)
See also Midday

Death
Teloah (Death)
Teloch (Death)

Death Dragon
Telocvovim (Death Dragon, "Him That Is Fallen")
See also Devil, Lucifer, Satan

Decorate
See Garnish

Deep
See Sea

Deface
Tonug (To Deface)
See also Destroy

Defense
See Buckler

Deliver
Zonrensg (To Deliver)
Obelison (Pleasant Deliverer, the Angel Befafes)
Obelisong (Pleasant Deliverers)
See also Bring Forth

Demand
See Require

Depths of My Jaws
Piadph (Depths of My Jaws)

Descend
Uniglag (To Descend)
See also Fall, Sink, Stoop

Destroy
"Quasb" (To Destroy)
See also Deface

Devil, The
Coronzom
Githgulcag
Telocvovim (Death Dragon, "Him That Is Fallen")
See also Satan, Lucifer

Devoid
See Empty

Diamond
Achildao (Diamond)

Differ
Dilzmo (To Differ)

Diminish
Prdzar (To Diminish)

Discord
Osf (Discord)

Dispose
Lrasd (To Dispose, To Place)

Dive
See Sink, Stoop, Fall

Diversity
See Variety

Divide
Poilp (Divided)
Yrpoil (Division)
See also Separate

Divine Names
Baeovib (Righteousness)
El (The First)
Enay (Lord)
Gahoachma (I Am That I Am)
Galsagen (Divine Power Creating the Angel of the Sun)
Galvah (The End/*Omega*)
Geiad (Lord and Master)
Gohed (One Everlasting, All Things Descending Upon One)
Iad (God)
"Iadoias" (Eternal God)
Iadpil (Unto Him)
Iaida (The Highest)
Iaidon (The All Powerful)
Ia-isg (Everlasting One and Indivisible God)
Idoigo (Him Who Sits upon the Holy Throne)
Ioiad (Him That Liveth Forever)
L (The First, One)
NA (The Trinity, Lord)
See also Angelic Orders

"Divine Power Creating the Angel of the Sun"
Galsagen

Divine Throne, The
See Mighty Seat

Division
See Divide

Do/Does (Doth)
Gnay (Doth)

Dominance
See Dominion

Dominion
Bab (Dominion)
See also Government, Kingdom

Doth
See Do/Does

Dragon
"Vonin" (Dragons)
"Vovim" (Dragon)
Vovina (Dragon)

Dress
See Apparel, Garment, Garland

Dross
See Moss

Drunk
Orsba (Drunken)

Dry
Orscor (Dryness)

Dwell/Dwelling
Faonts (To Dwell within)
"Faorgt" (Dwelling Place)
Fargt (Dwelling Places)
"Praf" (To Dwell)
See also Living Dwellings, Building, House

E (Graph)

Eagle
Vabzir (Eagle)

Earth
Caosg (Earth)
Caosga (Earth)
Caosgi (Earth)
Caosgin (Earth)
Caosgo (Of the Earth)
Caosgon (Unto the Earth)

"Earth-Fleer"
Nalvage (Earth-Fleer, or Avoidance of Earthly Things)

Earthquakes
Gizyax (Earthquakes)

East
Raas (East)
Rassy (East)

Elder
Uran (Elders)

Empty
Affa (Empty)

End
Ul (End)
Uls (Ends)
See also Omega

Endure
See Abide

Enigma
See Mystery

Enjoyment
See Pleasure, Joy

Enlarge
See Magnify

Enter
Zimii (To Enter)

Eon
See Age

Equal
Parach (Equal)
See also Same

Era
See Age

Essence
See Marrow

Establish
Sach (The Establishers)

Eternal God
"Iadoias" (Eternal God)
See also Everlasting, Him That Liveth Forever, God, Lord

Even
Nomig (Even as)

Everlasting
Ia-isg (Everlasting One and Indivisible God)
Gohed (One Everlasting...)
See also God, Eternal God, Him That Liveth Forever, Lord

Every One
Vomzarg (Every One / All)
See also All

Everything
See All

Exalted
See Great

Except
Oq (But/Except)
M (Except)
See also But

Excite
See Stir

Execute
Fisis (To Execute, Carry Out)

Eye
Ooanoan (Eyes)
Ooaona (Eyes)

F (Or)

Face
Adoian (Face)

Faith
Congamphlgh (Faith / Holy Ghost)
Gono (Faith / Trust / Loyalty)

Fall
Dobix (To Fall)
Loncho (To Fall)
See also Descend, Sink, Stoop

Fashion
See Frame

Fasten
Amipzi (To Fasten)
See also Truss Together

Fate
See Providence

Fear God
Hoxmarch (To Fear God)
See also Those That Fear God

Feet
Lasdi (Feet)
Lusd (Feet)
Lusda (Feet)
Lusdan (Feet)

"Fervency"
Laua (Fervency / Humility—an attitude in prayer?)

Fiery Arrow / Dart
Malprg (Through-thrusting Fire, Fiery Arrow)
Malpurg (Fiery Arrows)
See also Fires of Life and Increase

Fire
"Pirgi" (Fires)
Prge (Fire, Flame, Flames)
Prgel (Fire)
See also Burn, Flame, Light

Fires of Life and Increase
Malpirgi
See also Fiery Arrow, Through-thrusting Fire

Firmament
Calz (Firmaments)
See also Heaven, Firmaments of Waters

Firmaments of Waters
Pilzin (Firmaments of Waters)
See also Firmament, Heaven, Water

First
El (The First, God)
"Elo" (The First)
Ili (The First)
L (One, The First, God)
La (The First)
Lu (From One)

First Flame
Lialprt

First Glory
"Pirgah" (The First Glory)
See also Flame, Fire

Flame
Ialpirt (Light, Flame)
Ialpor (Flaming)
"Ialprt" (Light, Flame)
"Prg" (Fire, Flame, Flames)
Prge (Fire, Flame, Flames)
"Purg" (Fire, Flame, Flames)

Vep (Flame)
See also Burn, Fire, Light

Flames of the First Glory
Ialpirgah

Flourish
Cacacom (To Flourish)

Flower
Lorslq (Flowers)

Fly Into
Zildar (Fly into)
See also Within

Foot
See Feet

For
Bagle (For, Wherefore, Because)
Lap (For)
See also Therefore, Wherefore, Because

Forget
Bams (To Forget)

Form
See Frame

Fourth
"Es" (Fourth)
S (Fourth)

Fourth Angle
Sdiv

Frame
Izazaz (To Frame, To Form)

Friendly
See Be Friendly unto Me

Front
Aspt (Before, In Front)
See also Face

Frown Not
Ucim (Frown Not)
See also Happy

"Furious and Perpetual Fire Enclosed for the Punishment of Them That Are Banished From the Glory"
See Hellfire

Furnace
See Athanor (Alchemical Furnace)

Furnish
Tooat (To Furnish)
See also Provide

Fury
Bagie (Fury)
Baltim (Fury, or Extreme Justice)
See also Anger, Wrath

G (Ged)

Garb
See Apparel, Garment, Garland

Garland
Obloc (Garland)
See also Garment

Garment
Oboleh (Garments)
Qaa (Garments / Creation)
See also Apparel, Garland

Garnish
Gnonp (To Garnish)

Gather
Aldi (To Gather)
Aldon (Gird Up, Gather Together)
See also Gird, Harvest

Gird
Aldi (To Gather)
Aldon (Gird Up, Gather Together)
See also Gather, Bind

Girdle
Atraah (Girdles)

Give
Dluga (To Give)
"Dlugam" (Given)
Dlugar (To Give)
Phama (I Will Give)

Glory, Glorious
Adgmach (Glory, Adoration, Praise)
Busd (Glory, Glorious)
Busdir (Glory, Glorious)
"Pirgah" (Glory)
See also Admiration, Adoration, Praise, Magnify, Wonder

Glory of Her
Busdirtilb

Go Before
See Precede

God
Geiad (Lord and Master)
Iad (God)
"Iadoias" (Eternal God)
Iadpil (To Him)
Iaida (The Highest)
Iaidon (All Powerful)
Ia-isg (Everlasting One and Indivisible God)
Idoigo (Him Who Sits upon the Holy Throne)
Ioiad (Him That Liveth Forever)
Mad (A God, Your God)
Oiad (Of God)
Piad (Your God)
See also First, God of Righteousness, Lord, Worker of Wonders

God Eternally Crowned
Iadoiasmomar (God Is, Was, and Shall Be Crowned)

God Is, Was, and Shall Be Crowned
See God Eternally Crowned

God of Righteousness
Iadbaltoh
See also God, Lord

God of Stretch Forth and Conquer
Madzilodarp (God of Conquest)

Gold
Audcal (Alchemical Gold, Alchemical Mercury)

Govern/Government/Governor
Anetab (In Government)
Caba (To Govern)
Gnataab (Your Governments)
Netaab (Governments)
Netaaib (Government)
Tabaam (Governor)
Tabaord (Be Governed)
Tabaori (To Govern)
"Tabas" (To Govern)
See also Steward, Dominion, Reign

Great
Drilpa (Great)
Drilpi (Greater Than)

Great Name
Monasci (Great Name)

Groan
Holdo (To Groan)

Grow
See Flourish

Grow Strong
Ugeg (Become Strong)
Ugegi (Become/Grow Strong)
See also Strong

Guard
Bransg (A Guard)

H (Na)

Half
Obza (Half)

Hand
Azien (Hands)
Ozien (My Own Hand)
Ozol (Hands)
Zien (Hands)
Zol (Hands)

Handmaid
Qurlst (Handmaid)
See also Minister, Servant

Happy
Ulcinin (Happy)
See also Frown Not

Harbor
Blans (To Harbor)
See also Ark

Harlot
Ababalond (Harlot)

Harmony
See Balance

Harvest
"Giar" (Harvest)
See also Gather

Has
See Have / Has

Have/Has
"Brin" (Have)
"Brint" (Has)
Brints (To Have)

Haven
See Ark, Harbor

He
See Him, His

"He That Speaks"
Mapsama

Head
Dazis (Heads)

Hear
See Listen

Hearken
See Listen

Heart
Monons (Heart)

Heaven
"Madriax" (Heavens)
Madriiax (Heavens)
Oadriax (Lower Heavens)
Piripsax (Heavens)
Piripsol (Heavens)
Piripson (Third? Heaven)
See also Firmament

Hellfire
Donasdogamatastos (The Furious and Perpetual Fire Enclosed for the Punishment of Them That Are Banished From the Glory)

Her
"Ip" (Her)
Tilb (Her)
Tiobl (Within Her)
See also She

Her Course
Elzaptilb (Her Course)

Her Understanding
Omptilb

Here
Emna (Here)
Sem (In This Place)

Highest
Iaida (The Highest)
See also God, Lord

Him
Iadpil (Unto Him—God)
Tox (His, Him)
See also His

"Him That Is Fallen"
Telocvovim (Death Dragon, "Him That Is Fallen")
See also Devil, Lucifer, Satan

"Him That Liveth Forever"
Ioiad (Him That Liveth Forever)
See also Eternal God, God, Lord

"Him Who Sits upon the Holy Throne"
Idoigo (Him Who Sits upon the Holy Throne)
See also God, Lord

His
Tox (His, Him)
See also Him

His Pomp
Avavox

His Power
Lonshitox

Hollow
See Empty

Holy
Pir (Holy Ones)
See also Angels

"Holy Ghost"
Congamphlgh (Faith/Holy Ghost)

Honor
Iaiadix (Honor)

Horn
"Mospleh" (Horns)

House
Salman (House)
See also Building, Dwelling

How Many
"Irgil" (How Many)
See also Many

How Many Are There
Irgilchisda

How Now
Mabberan (How Now?)

Humility
Laua (Fervency/Humility—an attitude in prayer?)

Hundred
Torb (One Hundred)

Hyacinth Pillars
See Pillar

I (Gon)

I
Ol (I)

"I Am That I Am"
Gahoachma

I Am the Lord (Your) God
Zirenaiad

"I Desire Thee, O God"
Arphe

In Front
See Before

"In One Number"
Sagacor (In One Number)

"In This Place"
Sem
See also Here

Increase
"Coazior" (To Increase)
"Mal" (Thrust, Arrow, Increase)
See also Add

Ineffable
See Unspeakable

Iniquity
Madrid (Iniquity)
See also Sin

Intent
Fafen (Intent, Train)

Is
I (Is, Are)
See also Am, Are, Is Not, May Be, Shall Be, Let There Be, Was, Were

Is 31
Iga

Is As
Ita

Is Given
Idlugam

Is a House
Isalman

Is Not
Ipam (Is Not)
Ipamis (Cannot Be)
See also No/None, Not

Is One
Il

Is Such As
Icorsca

Is Wrath
Ivonph
See also Is Wrath in Anger

Is Wrath in Anger
Ivonpovnph
See also Is Wrath

It
"T" (It)

It Is
Ti

J (Ged)

Join
See Fasten, Truss Together

Joy
Moz (Joy, Joy of God)
See also Pleasure

Judgment
Balzizras (Judgment)
See also Conclude

Just/Justice
Balit (The Just)
Balt (Justice)
Baltan (Justice)
Baltim (Extreme Justice, or Fury)
Padgze (Justice From Divine Power Without Defect)

K (Veh)

Kindness
See Mercy

Kingdom
Adohi (Kingdom)
Londoh (Kingdom)
See also Dominion

Know
See Knowledge, Understand

Knowledge
Iadnah (Knowledge)
Iadnamad (Pure Knowledge)
See also Understand

L (Ur)

Laborer
See Workmen

Laid Up
Maasi (Laid up, Stored)

Lamentation
Eophan (Lamentation)
See also Sorrow, Woe

Lamp, Lantern
Hubaio (Lanterns)
Hubar (Lamps)
Hubaro (Living Lamps)
See also Lantern

Law
See Legislate

Lead
See Before

Legislate
Ohorela (To Legislate)

Let
"Ix" (Let)

Let Her Be Known
Ixomaxip

Let There Be
Christeos (Let There Be)
See also Are, Shall Be

Lift Up
Goholor (Lift Up)
See also Arise

Light
Ialpirt (Light, Flame)
"Ialprt" (Light, Flame)
See also Brightness, Flame, Shine

Like
"Azia" (Like unto)
Aziazor (Likeness of)

Like unto the Harvest
Aziagiar

Limb
See Branch, Member

Limitless
Maoffas (Measureless)

Listen
Solpeth (Hearken, To Listen)
Toatar (Hearken, To Listen)

Live
"Apila" (To Live)
Hom (To Live)

Living Breath
Gigipah (Living Breath)

Living Dwellings
Paradial (Living Dwellings)
See also Dwell/Dwelling

Loathsome
See Rotten

Loins
"Dax" (Loins)

Long
See Age, Period, Time, While

Look
Dorpha (To Look about)
Dorphal (Looking with Gladness Upon)
See also Behold, See

Lord
Enay (Lord)
Geiad (Lord and Master)
NA (Lord, the Trinity)
See also God

Lower Heavens
Oadriax (Lower Heavens)
See also Heaven

Loyalty
See Faith

Lucifer
Coronzom
Githgulcag
Telocvovim (Death Dragon, "Him That Is Fallen")
See also Devil, Satan

M (Tal)

Made/Make
Eol (Made)
Eolis (Making)
Oln (Made of)
Ozazm (To Make)
Ozazma (To Make)

Made a Law
See Legislate

Made Mankind
Olcordziz

Magnify
Ovof (To Magnify)
See also Adoration, Glory, Praise

Make
See Made/Make

Man
"Olap" (Men)
Ollog (Men)
"Ollor" (Man)
Olora (Of Man)
See also Mankind, Work of Man

Mankind
Cordziz (Mankind)
See also Man

Mansion
See Palace

Many
"Irgil" (How Many)
Plosi (As Many)

Marble
Pidiai (Marble)

Marrow
Tranan (Marrow)

Master
Geiad (Lord and Master)
See also Lord

May Be
Noaln (May Be)
See also Are, Become, Let There Be, Shall Be

Measure
Holq (To Measure)
Maoffas (Measureless)

Member
Paombd (Members, Parts, Appendages)
See also Part

Memory
See Remember

Men
See Man, Mankind

Mercury
Audcal (Alchemical Gold, Alchemical Mercury)

Mercy
Iehusoz (God's? Mercies)
Rit (Mercy)

Midday
"Bazem" (Midday)
Bazemlo (Midday the First)
See also Day

Middle
See Amidst, Center

Midst
See Amidst

Mighty
Canse (Mighty)
Cruscanse (More Mighty)
Micalp (Mightier)
Micalzo (Mighty, Power)
Micaoli (Mighty)
Micaolz (Mighty)
Omicaolz (Be Mighty)
Vohim (Mighty)
See also Strong, Power

Mighty Seat
Oziayal (Mighty Seat—Throne of God)
See also "Him Who Sits upon the Holy Throne"

Millstone
Aviny (Millstones)

Mind
Manin (In the Mind)

Mingle
Cinxir (To Mingle)

Minister
Cnoquodi (Ministers)
See also Handmaid, Servant

Misery
See Torment

Mix
See Mingle

Moment
Oanio (Moment)

Moon
Graa (Moon)

More
"Crus" (More, Greater?)

More Mighty
Cruscanse

Moreover
Pilah (Moreover)

Moss
Mom (Moss, Dross?)

"Mother of Vinegar"
See Tartar

Motion
Zna (Motion, Action)
See also Action, Move, Rest Not, Stir

Mount of Olives
See Olive Mount

Mourning
See Sorrow, Lamentation

Mouth
Butmon (Mouth)
Butmona (Mouth)
Butmoni (Mouths)

Move
Zacam (To Move)
Zacar (Move)
See Action, Motion, Rest Not, Stir

Mystery
Cicle (Mysteries)
Cicles (Mysteries)
See also Secret

N (Drux)

Name
Dooain (Name)
Dooaip (In the Name)
Dooiap (In the Name)
Monasci (Great Name)
Omaoas (Names)

Need
See Require

Neither
Larag (Neither/Nor)
See also No/None, Not

Nest
Virq (Nests)

Night
Dosig (Night)

Nine
Em (Nine)

No/None
Ag (No, None)
See also Not, Neither

No Creature
Agtoltorn

Noise
Nidali (Noises)

None
See No, Neither

Noon
See Midday

No One
"Agl"

No One Creature
Agltoltorn

No Place
Ripir (No Place)

"Nor"
See Neither

North
Lucal (North)

Not
"Ge" (Not)
Ip (Not)
Ipam (Is Not)
Ipamis (Can Not Be)
"Pam" (Not)
"Pamis" (Cannot)
See also Cannot, Neither, No/None

Number
Capimaon (Number of Time)
Cormf (Number)
Cormfa (Numbers)
Cormp (Numbered)
Cormpo (Hath Yet Numbered)
Cormpt (Numbered)
Sagacor ("In One Number"—Consistent/Constant?)
See also Successive

O (Med)

Oak
Paeb (Oak)

Obedience
Adna (Obedience)
See also Obey

Obey
Darbs (Obey)
See also Obedience

Ocean
See Sea

Of
De (Of)

Olive
"Qanis" (Olives)

Olive Mount
Adroch (Olive Mount)

***Omega* (The End)**
Galvah (The End—*prop. n.*)
See also End

One
L (One, The First—God)
Lu (From One)
See also First

One Another
Lsmnad

"One Everlasting, All Things Descending Upon One"
Gohed
See also One, Lord, God

One Rock
Lpatralx

One Season
Lnibm

One While
Lcapimao

Only
See But

Open
Odo (To Open)

Or
Q (Or)

Or as
Qta

Organize
See Dispose

Or the Horns
Qmospleh

Over
Vors (Over)
Vorsg (Over You)

P (Mals)

Pair
See Couple

Palace
Poamal

Palm
Nobloh (Palms of the Hands)

Part
Saanir (Parts)
See also Member

Partake
Plapli (Partakers)

Peace
"Etharzi" (Peace)

Perform
See Execute

Period
Matorb (Long, period of time)
See also Age, Time, While

Persecute
See Torment

Persist
See Abide

Philosopher's Stone
Darr (The Philosopher's Stone)

Pillar
Nazarth (Pillars of Gladness)
Nazavabh (Hyacinth Pillars)
See also Strong Towers

Place
Aala (To Place)
Oali (To Place)
See also Bind, Dispose, Set, Settle, Sit, Plant

Places of Comfort
Pibliar (Places of Comfort)

Plant
Harg (To Plant)
See also Bind, Place, Set, Settle, Sit

Pleasant Deliverer
Obelisong (Pleasant Deliverers)
Obelison (Pleasant Deliverer, the Angel *Befafes*)

Pleasure
"Qrasahi" (Pleasure)
See also Joy

Plummet
See Fall, Sink, Stoop

Poison
Faboan (Poison)
See also Wormwood

Pomp
"Avav" (Pomp)

Pour
Panpir (To Pour Down)

Power
Gmicalzo (In Power)
Iaidon (The All Powerful—God)
Lansh (Exalted Power)
Lonsa (Power)
Lonshi (Power)
"Lonshin" (Powers)

Micalzo (Power, Mighty)
Nanaeel (My Power)
See also Mighty, Strong

Power of Understanding
Gmicalzoma

Praise
Adgmach (Glory, Adoration, Praise)
"Ecrin" (Praise)
Luas (Those Who Praise or The Triumphant)
Oecrimi (To Sing Praises)
Restil (To Praise Him?)
See also Admiration, Adoration, Glory, Magnify

Pray/Prayer
Zuraah (Prayer?)

Precede
Tastax (Going Before, To Precede)
See also Before

Prepare
Abramig (To Prepare)
Abramg (To Prepare)
See also Provide

Pretty
See Beauty

Pride
See Pomp

Produce
See Bring Forth

Promise
Aisro (To Promise)
Isr (Promise?, A Son of the Sons of Light)
Isro (Promise of)
See also Covenant, Swear

Prosper
See Flourish

Prostitute
See Harlot

Provide
Abraassa (To Provide)
See also Prepare, Furnish

Providence
Yarry (Providence)

Psalm
See Song

Pure (Undefiled)
Mad (Your God, "Pure/Undefiled")

Pure Knowledge
Iadnamad

Put
See Place

Q (Ger)

Quality
Aspian (Qualities, Characteristics)

R (Don)

Rage
See Fury, Wrath

Rain
See Pour

Raise
See Lift Up, Arise

Read
Hardeh (To Read?)

"Reasonable Creature"
See Man, Mankind

Receive
Ednas (Receivers)

Recollection
See Remember

Refuge
See Ark, Harbor

Regret
See Repent

Reign
Bogpa (To Reign)
Sonf (To Reign)
See also Govern

Rejoice
Chirlan (To Rejoice)

Remain
"Paaox" (To Remain)
Paaoxt (Let Remain)
See also Abide, Continue

Remainder
See Rest

Remember
Papnor (Remembrance, Memory)

Repent
Moooah (To Repent)

Require
Unig (To Require)

Rest
"Page" (To Rest)
Udl (The Rest)
Undl (The Rest)
See also Sleep

Rest Not
Pageip
See also Action, Move

Rich
"Las" (Rich)

Rich Man
Lasollor

Righteous
Baeovib (Righteousness)
Baltle (Righteousness)
Baltoh (Righteousness)
Baltoha (My Righteousness)
Samvelg (The Righteous)

Rise
See Arise

Roar
Yor (To Roar)

Rock

"Patralx" (Rock)

See also Stone

Rod

Cab (Rod/Scepter)

Room

See Chamber

Rotten

Qting (Rotten)

Rule

See Govern, Reign

Run

Parm (To Run)

Parmgi (Let Run)

S (Fam)

Safeguard
See Buckler

Salt
Balye (Salt)

Same
Lel (Same)
See also Equal

Sanctuary
See Ark, Harbor

Satan
Coronzom
Githgulcag
Telocvovim (Death Dragon, "Him That Is Fallen")
See also Devil, Lucifer

Say
Gohia (We Say)
Goho (To Say)
Gohol (To Say)
Gohon (Have Spoken)
Gohulim (It Is Said)
Gohus (I Say)
See also Speak, Talk

Sayeth the First
Gohel

Sayeth the Lord
Gohoiad

Scepter
See Rod

Scorpion
Siatris (Scorpions)

Scourge
See Torment

Scythe
See Sickle

Sea
Zumvi (Seas)

Seal
Emetgis (Seal)

Season
"Nibm" (Season)
See also Period, Age

Seat
Othil (Seats)
Thil (Seats)
Thild (Seats)
"Thiln" (Seats)
See also Mighty Seat

Seats of Mercy
Othilrit
See also Mighty Seat

Second (2nd)
Viiv (Second)
Viv (Second)
See also Two

Second (unit of time)
See Moment

Second Angle
Vivdiv

Second Flame
Vivialprt

Secret
Ananael (Secret Wisdom)

Laiad (Secrets of Truth)
See also Mystery

Secrets of Truth
Laiad (Secrets of Truth)

Secret Wisdom
Ananael (Secret Wisdom)

See
"Puran" (To See)
See also Behold, Look

Seethe
Vrelp (Strong Seething)

Senior
See Elder

Separate
Pala (Two, separated)
See also Two, Divide, Separate Creatures

Separate Creatures
Tliob (To Separate Creatures, Classify?)
See also Separate

Servant
Cnoqod (Servants)
Cnoquol (Servants)
Lang (Those Who Serve)
Noco (Servant)
See also Handmaid, Minister, Serve

Serve
Aboapri (To Serve)
Booapis (To Serve)
See also Servant

Set
Othil (To Set/Seat)
See also Bind, Place, Plant, Settle, Sit

Settle
Alar (To Settle, To Place)
Allar (To Bind Up)
See also Set, Sit, Bind, Place, Plant

Shall Be
Chiso (Shall Be)
Trian (Shall Be)
See also Are, Let There Be, May Be

Shall Not See
"Ipuran"

She
"Pi" (She)
See also Her

Sheath
See Sleeve

She Is
Pii

Shelter
See Harbor, Ark

Shine
Loholo (To Shine)
See also Burn, Brightness

Show Yourself
See Appear

Sibling
See Brother

Sickle
"Puin" (Sickles)

Signify
Alca (To Signify?)

Sin
Doalim (Sin)
See also Iniquity

Sing Praises
Oecrimi (To Sing Praises)
See also Praise

Sink
Carbaf (Sink)
See also Fall, Descend, Stoop

Sit
Trint (To Sit)
See also Place, Set, Settle

Six
Norz (Six)

Skirt
Unalah (Skirts)
See also Corner

Sleep
Brgda (To Sleep)
See also Rest

Sleeve
Collal (Sleeves/Sheaths)

"Slimy Things Made of Dust"
Apachana (The Slimy Things Made of Dust)

Smile
See Frown Not
See also Happy

Sol
See Sun

Son
"Nor" (Son)
"Norm" (Son/Sons)
Noromi (Sons)

Song
Faaip (Voicings, as in Songs or Psalms)
Luiahe (Song of Honor)

Sons of Men
Normolap

Sons of Pleasure
Norquasahi

Sorrow
Ser (Sorrow)
Tibibp (Sorrow)
See also Lamentation, Woe

South
Babage (South)
Babagen (South)

Speak
Brita (To Speak of, Talk About)
Camliax (Spake, Spoke)
See also "He That Speaks," Talk, Say

Speech from God
Loagaeth (Speech from God—the Holy Book)

Spirit
Gah (Spirits—Angels?)
Tohcoth (Nature Spirits)

Staff
See Rod

Stand
Biab (To Stand)

Star
Aoiveae (Stars)

Start
See Beginning

Steward
Balzarg (Stewards)
See also Governor

Sting
Grosb (Bitter Sting)

Stir
Lring (To Stir Up)
Zixlay (To Stir Up)
See also Action, Mingle, Motion, Move, Rest Not, Seethe

Stone
Orri (Barren Stone)
See also Rock, Philosopher's Stone

Stoop
"Abai" (Stoop)
See also Fall, Descend, Sink

Stooping Dragons
Abaivonin

Store
See Laid up

Stranger
Gosaa (Stranger)

Strength
Umplif (Strength)
Ugear (Strength of Men)
See also Strong

Stretch Forth/Conquest
"Zilodarp" (Stretch Forth/Conquest)

Strong
Givi (Stronger)
Ugear (Strength of Men)
Ugeg (Become Strong)
Ugegi (Become/Grow Strong)
Umadea (Strong Towers)
Umplif (Strength)
See also Mighty, Power, Strength

Strong Towers
Umadea (Strong Towers)
See also Pillar

Subtract
See Diminish

Successive
Capimali (Successively)
Capmiali (Successively)
See also Number

Such
Cors (Such)
Corsi (Such)

Such As
Corsta

Sulfur
Dlasod (Alchemical Sulfur)
Salbrox (Live Sulfur)

Sun
Ror (Sun)

Surge
Molvi (Surges)

Surround
See Circle

Surrounded
See Amidst, Among

Swear
Surzas (To Swear)
Znrza (Swore)
See also Covenant, Promise

Sword
Napeai (Swords)
Napta (Two-edged Swords)
Nazpsad (Sword)

T (Gisg)

Talk
Brita (To Speak of, Talk about)
See also Speak, Say

Tartar
Lulo (Tartar, Mother of Vinegar)

Temple
Siaion (Temple)

Territories
See Vestures

Terror
Ciaofi (Terror)

That
Ar (That)
Ds (Which/That)
See also Which, These, Those

That Govern
Artabas

That Increase
Arcoazior

That Understand
Dsom

Thee
See You

Them
Par (Them)

There
"Da" (There)
Geta (There)

Therefore
"Ca" (Therefore)
Darsar (Wherefore, Therefore)
See also For, Because, Wherefore

These
Unal (These)
See also This, Those

These Are
Unalchis

They
See Them

Third
D (Third)

Third Angle
Duiv

Third Flame
Dialprt

This
"Oi" (This)
See also That, These, Those

This House
Oisalman

Thorn
Nanba (Thorns)

Those
Priaz (Those)
Priazi (Those)
See also That, This, These

Those That Fear God
Amzes ("Those That Fear God"?)
See also Fear God

Thou
See You, Yourself

Thought
Angelard (Thoughts)

Thousand
Matb (One Thousand)

Throne (of God)
See Mighty Seat

Through-thrusting Fire
See Fiery Arrow

Thrust
"Mal" (Thrust, Arrow, Increase)

Thunder
Avavago (Thunders of Increase)
Const (Thunders)
Coraxo (Thunders)
Sapah (Mighty Sounds)

Thy
Aqlo (Thy)
"Yl" (Thy)
See also You, Yourself

Time
Acocasb (Time)
Capimaon (Number of Time)
Cocasb (Time)
Cocasg (Times)
Qcocasb (Contents of Time)
See also Age, Period, Season, While

To
See Unto

Together
Pola (Two, together/Couple)
See also Couple, Two, Wedding

Torment
Mir (Torment)
See also Vex

Torture
See Torment

Tower
See Strong Towers, Pillar

Train
Fafen (Train, Intent)

Treasure
Limlal (Treasure)

Trinity
NA (Lord, Trinity)

Triumph
Luas (Those Who Praise or The Triumphant)
Toh (To Triumph)
"Toha" (Triumph)

Troop
See Guard

"True Measure of the Will of God in Judgment, Which is by Wisdom"
Miketh

True Worshiper
Hoath (True Worshiper)

Truss Together
Commah (To Truss Together/Join)
See also Fasten, Bind

Trust

See Faith

Truth

"Vaoan" (Truth—Higher)

Vooan (Truth—Lower)

Twice

See Two

Two

Pala (Two-separated)

Pola (Two-together, Couple)

Olani (Two Times, Twice)

See also Second

U (Van)

Undefiled
See Pure

Under
Oroch (Under)
Orocha (Beneath)
See also Beneath

Understand
Om (To Understand/Know)
"Oma" (Of Understanding)
Omax (To Know)
"Omp" (Understanding)
See also Knowledge

Unspeakable
Adphaht (Unspeakable)

Until
Cacrg (Until)

Unto
Pambt (Unto Me)
Pugo (As unto)
Tia (Unto Us)

Upon
Mirc (Upon)

V (Van)

Vacant
See Empty

Van
"Ar" (To Van, i.e., to Advance Upon)

Van the Earth
Arcaosgi (To Van the Earth)

Vanity
See Pomp

Variety
Damploz (Variety)

Vessel
Izizop (Your Vessels)
Zizop (Vessels)
See also Cup, Vial

Vestment
See Apparel, Garment, Garland

Vesture
Zimz (Vestures, Territories)
See also Garment

Vex
Dodpal (To Vex)
Dodrmni (Vexed)
Dods (To Vex)
Dodsih (Vexation)
See also Torment

Vial
Efafafe (Vials)
Ofafafe (Vials)
See also Cup, Vessel

Victory
See Triumph

Vinegar, Mother of
See Tartar

Virgin
Paradiz (Virgins)

Visage
See Face

Visit
Ef (Visit)
F (Visit)

Visit in Peace
Fetharzi

Visit the Earth
Fcaosga

Visit with Comfort
Fbliard

Voice
Bia (Voices)
Bial (Voice)
Bien (My Voice)
Bahal (Cry with a Loud Voice)
Faaip (Voicings—as in Songs or Psalms)
Farzem (Uplifted Voices)

Void
See Empty

Vomit
Oxex (To Vomit)

W

Walk
"Insi" (To Walk)

Want
See Require

Was
Zirop (Was)
See also Am, Are, Is, Were

Water
Pilzin (Waters)
Zlida (To Water)

Wax Strong
Ugeg (Become Strong)
Ugegi (Become/Grow Strong)
See also Strong

Wealthy
See Rich

Weave
"Oado" (To Weave)

Wedding
Paracleda (Wedding)
See also Couple, Together

Weed Out
Fifalz (Weed Out)

Weep
Raclir (Weeping)

Were
Zirom (They Were)
See also Am, Are, Is, Was

West
Soboln (West)

Wherefore
Bagle (For, Wherefore, Because)
Darsar (Wherefore, Therefore)
See also For, Because, Therefore

Wherein
Quiin (Wherein)

Which
Ds (Which/That)
Dst (Which Also)
See also That, This

Which Are
Dschis

Which Dwell
Dspraf

Which Have
Dsbrin

Which Is
Dsi

Which Is Called
Dsium

Which Prepared
Dsabramg

Which Reign
Dsonf

Which Remain
Dspaaox

Which Walkest
Dsinsi

Which Weave
Dsoado

While
"Cacocasb" (Another While)
"Capimao" (While)
See also Age, Period, Season, Time

Whom/Whose
Asobam (On Whom)
Casarm (Whom)
Casarma (Whom)
Casarman (Whom/Under Whose)
Casarmg (In Whom)
Casarmi (Under Whom)
"Saba" (Whose)
Soba (Whose)
Sobam (Whom)
Sobca (Whose)
"Sobha" (Whose)
"Sobo" (Whose)
Sobra (Whose)
"Sola" (Whose)

Whore
See Harlot

Whose Continuance
Solamian

Whose Courses
Sobolzar

Whose Eyes
Sabaooaona

Whose God
Sobaiad

Whose Works
Sobhaath

Why
See Wherefore

"Why Didst Thou So?"
Gascampho

Wicked
Babalon (Wicked)
See also Curse

Widow
Rior (Widow)

Will
See Your Will Be Done

Wind
Ozongon (Manifold Winds)
Zong (Winds)

Window
"Como" (Window)

Window of Comfort
Comobliort

Wine
Roxtan (Rectified Wine)

Wing
Upaah (Wings)
Upaahi (Wings)

Winnow
See Van

Wisdom
See Secret Wisdom, Knowledge, Understand

"With Humility We Call Thee, with Adoration of the Trinity"
Argedco

Within
Zylna (Within Itself)

Woe
Ohio (Woe)
See also Sorrow, Lamentation

Wonder
Sald (Wonder)
"Lzirn" (Wonders)
See also Glory

Work
"Aath" (Works)
"Vau" (To Work)
Vaun (To Work)

Work of Man
Conisbra (The Work of Man)
See also Man, Mankind

Workmen
Canal (Workmen)

Work Wonders
Vaulzirn

Worker of Wonders
PELE (Worker of Wonders)
Peleh (Worker of Wonders?)
See also God

World
See Earth

Wormwood
Tatan (Wormwood)
See also Poison

Worship
See True Worshiper

Worthy
Naghezes (To Be Worthy?)

Wrath
Vonph (Wrath)
Vonpho (Of Wrath)
"Vonpo" (Wrath)
See also Anger, Fury

Wrath in Anger
"Vonpovnph"

X (Pal)

There are no Angelical words in Dee's records that translate into English words beginning with the letter *X*.

Y (Gon)

Yea
See Yes

Yell
See Cry

Yes
Noib (Yea, Yes)

You (pl.)
Nonca (You)
Noncf (You)
Nonci (You)
Noncp (You)
See also You (sing.), Yourself

You (sing.)
Bolp (Be Thou)
Yls (Thou)
Ylsi (Thee)
See also You (pl.), Yourself, Thy

Your
See Thy

Your Loins
Daxil

Yourself
Amiran (Yourselves)
See also You (sing.)

Your Will Be Done
Gemeganza

Z (Ceph)

There are no Angelical words in Dee's records that translate into English words beginning with the letter *Z*.

Bibliography

Adler, Aufsteigender. *Soyga/Agyos: Tractatus Astrologico Magicus Aldaraia sive Soyga Vocor, Flight of the Condor—Contemporary Shamanism* (2001) (Online at http://www.kondor.de/enoch/soyga/Soyga_starte.htm.)

Agrippa, Henry C. (edited by Stephen Skinner and trans. by Robert Turner). *The Fourth Book of Occult Philosophy*. Berwick, ME: Ibis Press, 2004.

———. (edited by Donald Tyson and trans. by James Freake). *Three Books of Occult Philosophy*. St. Paul, MN: Llewellyn, 1992.

Allan, Jim, ed. *An Introduction to Elvish*. Hayes, UK: Bran's Head Books, 1978.

Ashe, Steven. *Qabalah of 50 Gates*. Glastonbury, UK: Glastonbury Books, 2006.

Bible, The. King James Version. (See *BibleGateway.com*, http://www.biblegateway.com.)

Bouwsma, William J. *Concordia Mundi: The Career and Thought of Guillaume Postel, 1510–1581*. Cambridge, MA: Harvard University Press, 1957.

Budge, E. A. Wallis, trans. *The Egyptian Book of the Dead: The Papyrus of Ani in the British Museum*. New York: Dover, 1967.

Charles, R. H., ed., and W. R. Morfill, trans. *The Book of the Secrets of Enoch*. Escondido, CA: Book Tree, 1999. First published in 1896. (This is *2 Enoch*, "The Slavonic Book of Enoch.")

Charlesworth, James H., ed. *The Old Testament Pseudepigrapha, vol. 1*. Garden City, NY: Doubleday, 1983. (Includes *1 Enoch*, "The Ethiopic Book of Enoch"; *2 Enoch*, "The Slavonic Book of Enoch"; and *3 Enoch*, "The Hebrew Book of Enoch.")

Clulee, Nicholas H. *John Dee's Natural Philosophy: Between Science and Religion*. London: Routledge, 1988.

Dalley, Stephanie. *Myths from Mesopotamia : Creation, the Flood, Gilgamesh, and Others*. Oxford: Oxford University Press, 1998.

Dan, Joseph. *The Ancient Jewish Mysticism*. Tel Aviv, Israel: MOD Books, 1993.

Davidson, Gustav. *A Dictionary of Angels, Including the Fallen Angels*. Reissue edition. New York: Free Press, 1994.

Dee, John. *A True and Faithful Relation of What Passed For Many Years Between Dr. John Dee [. . .] and Some Spirits*. New York: Magickal Childe, 1992. First published in 1659. Other editions also available. A PDF version is available at *The Magickal Review*, http://www.themagickalreview.org/enochian/tfr.php (accessed March 1, 2010).

Dee, John. (Peterson, Joseph H., ed.). *John Dee's Five Books of Mystery: Original Sourcebook of Enochian Magic*. Boston: Weiser, 2003.

———. *Mysteriorum Libri Quinti: or, Five Books of Mystical Exercises of Dr. John Dee*. Magnum Dyfed, UK: Opus Hermetic Sourceworks, 1985.

Eliade, Mircea. *Shamanism: Archaic Techniques of Ecstasy*. Princeton, NJ: Princeton University Press, 2004.

"Enochian-l" (e-mail list). http://www.gnostica.net/mailman/listinfo/enochian-l.

Ginzberg, Louis. *Legends of the Bible*. New York: Simon and Schuster, 1956.

Godwin, Malcolm. *Angels: An Endangered Species*. New York: Simon and Schuster, 1990.

Harkness, Deborah E. *John Dee's Conversations with Angels: Cabala, Alchemy, and the End of Nature*. Cambridge: Cambridge University Press, 1999.

———. *The Scientific Reformation: John Dee and the Restitution of Nature*. (Unpublished PhD thesis, University of California, Davis, 1994.)

Heidrick, Bill. "The Star Sponge and the Fifty Gates, Two Passages to Attainment." *Thelema Lodge Calendar*, 5 / 90 e.vol. "From the Out Basket" (copyright 1975 and 1990). Online at http://www.digital-brilliance.com/kab/50gates.txt (accessed March 1, 2010).

Heinlein, Robert. *Stranger in a Strange Land*. New York: Putnam, 1961.

James, Geoffrey. *The Angel Summoner*. St. Paul, MN: Llewellyn, 1998.

———. *The Enochian Magick of Dr. John Dee*. St. Paul, MN: Llewellyn, 1994.

Kaplan, Aryeh. *Sepher Yetzirah: The Book of Creation*. York Beach, ME: Weiser, 1997.

Kircher, Athanasius. *Oedipus Aegyptiacus*. Online at http://www.billheidrick.com/Orpd/AKir/AKOeAeII.htm (accessed March 1, 2010).

Krakovsky, Levi Isaac. *Kabbalah: The Light of Redemption*. Brooklyn, NY: Kabbalah Foundation, 1950.

Laurence, Richard, trans. *The Book of Enoch the Prophet*. Bensenville, IL: Lushena Books, 2001. First published in 1883. Also online at http://www.livius.org/ei-er/enoch/enoch.htm.

Laycock, Donald. *The Complete Enochian Dictionary: A Dictionary of the Angelic Language as Revealed to Dr. John Dee and Edward Kelley*. Revised edition. York Beach, ME: Red Wheel/Weiser, 2001.

Layton, Bentley, trans. *The Gnostic Scriptures*. New York: Doubelday, 1995.

Leitch, Aaron. "The Angelic Alphabet." Found online at http://kheph777.tripod.com/art_angelical_alphabet.pdf.

———. "Gnosticism: Sethian to Valentinian." *Diamond Fire* magazine, Winter 2003. (Also online at http://kheph777.tripod.com/)

———. "Introduction to the Hebrew Alphabet." *Diamond Fire* magazine, Summer 2004. Also online at http://kheph777.tripod.com/.

———. *John Dee's Journals Abridged: The Angelic Language, Loagaeth, the Parts of the Earth and the Great Table of the Earth.* (working title) Unpublished manuscript, 2004.

———. *Secrets of the Magickal Grimoires: The Classical Texts of Magick Deciphered.* St. Paul, MN: Llewellyn, 2005.

———. "Shem haMephoresh: Divine Name of Extension." *Diamond Fire* magazine, Fall 2003. Also online at http://kheph777.tripod.com/.

———, (moderator). *The Solomonic Yahoo Group.* http://groups.yahoo.com/group/solomonic.

Liber Loagaeth. Online at http://www.geocities.com/peripsol/Enoch/5LiberLoagaeth.htm.

Magickal Review, The. http://www.themagickalreview.org/

———., ed. *Enochian Manuscripts Online.* Digital scans of the British Library microfilms: MSS. Sloane 3188, 3189, 3191, and Cotton Appendix MS. XLVI Parts I and II. (Online at http://themagickalreview.org/enochian/)

Mastros, Sara Leanne. "The Fifty Gates of Understanding." Online at http://www.ugcs.caltech.edu/~abszero/mine.html.

Mathers, S. L. MacGregor, ed. and trans. *The Key of Solomon the King.* Mineola, NY: Dover, 2009.

McLean, Adam, ed. *A Treatise on Angel Magic.* San Francisco: Weiser, 2006.

Odeberg, Hugo, trans. and ed. *3 Enoch; or the Hebrew Book of Enoch.* New York: Ktav Publishing, 1973.

Orwell, George. *Nineteen Eighty-Four.* New York: Harcourt, Brace, 1949.

Peterson, Joseph H., ed. *John Dee's Five Books of Mystery.* York Beach, ME: Weiser, 2003.

———. *Liber Loagaeth or Liber Mysteriorum, Sextus et Sanctus*, 1997. Online at http://www.esotericarchives.com/dee/sl3189.htm (accessed October 22, 2009). The full text of *Loagaeth* can be purchased on CD from this webpage.

———. *Twilit Grotto: Archives of Western Esoterica*. Online at http://www.esotericarchives.com (accessed October 22, 2009).

Radiant, Callisto, ed. *Enochian Linguistics*. Online at http://www.madimi.com/enochlng.htm (accessed October 22, 2009).

Reeds, Jim. "Breakthrough in Renaissance Cryptography: A Book Review." *Cryptologia* magazine, January 1999. Available online at http://findarticles.com/p/articles/mi_qa3926/is_199901/ai_n8848725/ (accessed October 22, 2009).

———. "John Dee and the Magic Tables in the Book of Soyga." In Clucas, Stephen, ed. *John Dee: Interdisciplinary Studies in English Renaissance Thought*. Dordrecht, The Netherlands: Springer, 2006. Also available online at http://www.dtc.umn.edu/~reedsj/soyga (accessed October 22, 2009).

———. "Solved: The Ciphers in Book III of Trithemius's Steganographia," *Cryptologia* magazine, October 1998. Available online at http://www.dtc.umn.edu/~reedsj/steg.html (accessed October 22, 2009).

Reuchlin, Johann. *On the Art of the Kabbalah: De Arte Cabalistica*. Trans. by Martin Goodman and Sarah Goodman. Lincoln, NE: University of Nebraska Press, 1993.

Rogers, William E., and Diana Ervin. *The History of English Phonemes*. Online at http://alpha.furman.edu/~wrogers/phonemes/ (Greenville, SC: Furman University, 2000). See particularly the section entitled "Early Modern English: 1500–1800 C.E.," online at http://alpha.furman.edu/~wrogers/phonemes/phone/eme (accessed October 22, 2009).

Rowe, Benjamin. "A Note on Fifteenth Century Syntax and Interpretation." Originally posted to the "Enochian-l" e-mail list. Also available online at http://www.madimi.com/syntint.htm (accessed March 1, 2010).

Sandars, N. K., trans. *The Epic of Gilgamesh: An English Version with an Introduction*. London: Penguin, 1972.

Scholem, Gershom (trans. by Ralph Manheim). *On the Kabbalah and Its Symbolism*. (Original German title: *Zur Kabbala und ihrer Symbolik*.) New York: Schocken, 1996.

Scrolls From the Dead Sea. Library of Congress exhibition (2002). Online at http://www.loc.gov/exhibits/scrolls/toc.html (accessed October 29, 2009).

Shaffer, Patricia. *DeesPronunciationNotes.RTF*. Online at http://kheph777.tripod.com/DeesPronNotes.doc (accessed March 1, 2010).

Sichos in English.org. *Chasidic Discourses*. Online at http://www.sichosinenglish.org/cgi-bin/calendar?holiday=pesach10441 (accessed March 1, 2010).

Simpson, D. P. *Cassell's Latin Dictionary: Latin-English, English-Latin*. London: Cassell, 1977.

Skinner, Stephen, and David Rankine. *The Practical Angel Magic of Dr. John Dee's Enochian Tables*. Singapore: Golden Hoard Press, 2005.

A Specimen of the Tables or Book of Enoch. Online at http://www.geocities.com/peripsol/Enoch/5SampleTable.html.

Szönyi, György E. *John Dee's Occultism: Magical Exaltation Through Powerful Signs*. Albany, NY: State University of New York Press, 2004.

Tolkien, J. R. R. *The Hobbit*. Boston: Houghton Mifflin, 1997. First published in 1937.

———. *The Lord of the Rings*. Boston: Houghton Mifflin, 1993. First published in 1955.

Typo.cz and DesignIQ.cz. *Diacritics: All You Need to Design a Font with Correct Accents*. Online at http://diacritics.typo.cz/index.php (accessed October 22, 2009).

Tyson, Donald. *Enochian Magic for Beginners: The Original System of Angel Magic*. St. Paul, MN: Llewellyn, 2002. First published in 1997.

———. *The Power of the Word: The Secret Code of Creation*. St. Paul, MN: Llewellyn, 2004.

———. *Tetragrammaton: The Secret to Evoking Angelic Powers and the Key to the Apocalypse*. St. Paul, MN: Llewellyn, 2002.

Vinci, Leo. *GMICALZOMA!: An Enochian Dictionary*. London: Regency Press, 1976.

Warnock, Christopher. *Renaissance Astrology*. Online at http://www.renaissanceastrology.com/ (accessed October 22, 2009).

Westcott, W. Wynn, trans. (Edited by Darcy Kuntz.) *Sepher Yetzirah: The Book of Formation and the Thirty-Two Paths of Wisdom with Hebrew Text*. Sequim, WA: Holmes, 1996.

Wheelock, Frederic M. *Wheelock's Latin, Sixth Edition Revised*. New York: HarperResource, 2005.

Whitaker, William. *Words, Latin to English* (a Latin-to-English dictionary). Online at http://lysy2.archives.nd.edu/cgi-bin/words.exe (accessed October 22, 2009).

Whitby, Christopher. *John Dee's Actions with Spirits: 22 December 1581 to 23 May 1583*. New York: Garland, 1988.

Wilson, Robert Anton. *Prometheus Rising* (reprint edition). Phoenix, AZ: New Falcon, 1992.

Yahsanet Studies. *The Fifty Gates of Understanding* (in *A Study of the Book of Revelation*). Online at http://www.yashanet.com/studies/revstudy/fifty-gates.htm (accessed March 1, 2010).

Yates, Frances A. *The Rosicrucian Enlightenment*. London: Routledge, 2001.

Zalewski, Pat. *Golden Dawn Enochian Magic*. St. Paul, MN: Llewellyn, 1990.

———. *The Kabbalah of the Golden Dawn*. St. Paul, MN: Llewellyn, 1993.

Original Manuscripts

The following manuscripts are included for reference. All of these manuscripts can be found, under the manuscript numbers given here, at the British Museum in London:

Cotton Appendix 46, parts 1–2 (Published as *A True and Faithful Relation . . .*, Casaubon.)

"Sloane MS 3188" (Published as *John Dee's Five Books of Mystery*, Peterson.)

"Sloane MS 3189" (Kelley's handwritten copy of the *Book of Loagaeth*. See Peterson and *The Magickal Review*.)

"Sloane MS 3190" (A copy of *A True and Faithful Relation . . .*, unpublished.)

"Sloane MS 3191" (Dee's grimoire. Published as *The Enochian Magick of Dr. John Dee*, James.)

Further Reading

These texts also come highly recommended in the study of general Enochiana and the occult world of Dr. John Dee and Sir Edward Kelley:

Chase, Steven, trans. *Angelic Spirituality: Medieval Perspectives on the Ways of Angels*. New York: Paulist Press, 2002.

Clucas, Stephen, ed. *John Dee: Interdisciplinary Studies in English Renaissance Thought*. Dordrecht, The Netherlands: Springer, 2006. (Includes Jim Reeds' "John Dee and the Magic Tables in the Book of Soyga.")

Eco, Umberto. *The Search for the Perfect Language*. Oxford, UK: Blackwell, 1997.

Farmer, S. A. *Syncretism in the West: Pico's 900 Theses (1486): The Evolution of Traditional Religious and Philosophical Systems*. Tempe, AZ: MRTS, 1998.

French, Peter J. *John Dee: The World of an Elizabethan Magus*. London: Routledge, 1987.

Karr, Don. *Notes on Editions of Sepher Yetzirah in English* (1991, 2007). Online at http://www.digital-brilliance.com/kab/karr/syie.pdf.

Pseudo-Dionysius, the Areopagite. (Translated by Colm Luibheid.) *Pseudo-Dionysius: The Complete Works*. New York: Paulist Press, 1987.

VanderKam, James C. *Enoch: A Man for All Generations*. Columbia, SC: University of South Carolina Press, 1995.

Woolley, Benjamin. *The Queen's Conjurer: The Science and Magic of Dr. John Dee, Adviser to Queen Elizabeth I*. New York: Henry Holt, 2001.

To Write to the Author

If you wish to contact the author or would like more information about this book, please write to the author in care of Llewellyn Worldwide and we will forward your request. Both the author and publisher appreciate hearing from you and learning of your enjoyment of this book and how it has helped you. Llewellyn Worldwide cannot guarantee that every letter written to the author can be answered, but all will be forwarded. Please write to:

Aaron Leitch
℅ Llewellyn Worldwide
2143 Wooddale Drive
Woodbury, MN 55125-2989, U.S.A.

Please enclose a self-addressed stamped envelope for reply, or $1.00 to cover costs. If outside the U.S.A., enclose an international postal reply coupon.

Many of Llewellyn's authors have websites with additional information and resources. For more information, please visit our website at http://www.llewellyn.com.